ERASMUS: His Theology of the Sacraments

RESEARCH IN THEOLOGY
EDITED BY DIETRICH RITSCHL

ERASMUS
HIS THEOLOGY OF THE SACRAMENTS

John B. Payne

Acknowledgment is made to quote from the following:

The Colloquies of Erasmus, by Craig R. Thompson (Chicago: The University of Chicago Press, 1965). © 1965 University of Chicago Press. Used by permission.

The Enchiridion of Erasmus, translated by Raymond Himelick. Copyright © 1963 by Indiana University Press. Reprinted by permission.

Inquisitio de fide, by C. R. Thompson. Used by permission of Yale University Press.

Opus Epistolarum Des Erasmi Roterdami, edited by P. S. Allen, H. M. Allen, and H. W. Gerrod. Used by permission of the Clarendon Press, Oxford.

The Praise of Folly, by Desiderius Erasmus, translated from the Latin with an essay and commentary by Hoyt Hopewell Hudson. Copyright 1941, © 1969 by Princeton University Press. Used by permission.

Standard Book Number: 8042-0553-X

Library of Congress Catalog Card Number: 70-82938

© M. E. Bratcher 1970

Printed in the United States of America

CONTENTS

ACKNOWLEDGMENTS

———◆—◆◆▶—◆———

This study, originally submitted in 1966 as a doctoral dissertation at Harvard University, is now offered in its revised published form as a contribution to the fifth centenary celebration of Erasmus' birth, which has helped to stir a veritable Erasmus renaissance.

I wish to express my gratitude to my dissertation committee, Professors Heiko A. Oberman, George H. Williams, and Herbert W. Richardson, for their helpful suggestions to improve the manuscript for publication. I am especially indebted to Professor Oberman, who is now at the University of Tübingen, for his counsel, careful reading, and criticism of the dissertation at each stage of the process. In addition, I am grateful to Professor Roland H. Bainton for his keen interest in the publication of this work and for his useful comments on the original manuscript, to Dietrich Ritschl and his committee for their constructive criticisms, and to Mrs. William M. Breazeale, reference librarian at Randolph-Macon Woman's College, for her assistance in securing for me books on interlibrary loan. Finally, I give special thanks to my wife, Nancy, without whose patience and help in the preparation of the manuscript this book might not have seen the light of day.

JOHN B. PAYNE

Peoria, Illinois
May 3, 1970

ERASMUS: His Theology of the Sacraments

I

ERASMUS AS THEOLOGIAN

———————◆·◄◆►·◆———————

Some readers of this book may be startled at the outset by its title. Did Erasmus have a theology of the sacraments? Did Erasmus have a theology of anything? Was he not rather a philologian, a man of letters, a humanist, strictly speaking, and a moralist, but not at all a theologian? This view has been held by many, if not most, scholars up to the present.[1] Before launching into an examination of Erasmus' theology of the sacraments, therefore, it seems useful and necessary first to discuss him as a theologian. In this introductory chapter we undertake a general examination of what might be called the more formal elements of his theology. In the following chapters we deal more particularly with the material content which significantly shapes his doctrine of the sacraments.

Erasmus was no speculative or systematic theologian. He did not possess a metaphysical mind. In fact, he had an aversion to speculation and precise definitions. However, statements that he was not in any sense a theologian, that he had no doctrine, that he had little or no understanding of theology seem to be quite exaggerated assertions.

Even prior to his encounter with Colet in 1499 Erasmus had devoted his life to the study of theology.[2] He dedicated himself especially to the sources of theology, first of all to the Scriptures but also to the ancient Church Fathers. With remarkable toil he translated, edited, and exegeted the whole of the New Testament and translated and edited many of the Church Fathers. During his student days in Paris he was forced to apply himself also to the scholastics. As the letter to Thomas Grey reveals,[3] Erasmus had little taste for their debates, which appeared to him to deal with useless questions, but he probably did absorb something of their theology; how much it is difficult to know. Later, however, as he engaged in debates with Roman Catholic and Protestant opponents, he undoubtedly renewed and deepened his knowledge of recent theology. Christian Dolfen has demonstrated Erasmus' knowledge of many of the scholastic authors and their disputes.[4]

The writings of Erasmus show a considerable knowledge of the theological tradition, ancient and modern, on such questions as the Trinity, Christology, original sin, grace and free will, Church and sacraments. He wrote a long exposition of the Apostles' Creed, which appears also in abbreviated form in a dialogue and in a poem.[5]

It is true that little of his theological writing has as its aim a systematic presentation of Christian doctrines, such as that given in the *Symbolum;* indeed, it consists mainly of exegesis and devotional treatises. Yet, as Alfons Auer points out, only an arbitrary judgment limits the theological field to speculative or dogmatic theology. Exegesis and *Erbauungstheologie* are also part of the theological enterprise.[6]

I. The General Character of Erasmus' Theology

Emphasis on Piety and Antispeculation

Erasmus emphasizes that the aim of theology is practical, not speculative. It has to do with the transformation of life rather than the display of knowledge.[7] He likes to quote I Timothy 1:5 concerning the end of theological knowledge: ". . . the goal of our rule is charity proceeding from a pure heart, a good conscience, and a sincere faith . . ."[8]

Indeed, the relation between theology and piety is so close for Erasmus that it is difficult to draw any clear distinction. In a familiar passage from the famous *Paraclesis* (1516) he says:

This kind of philosophy is more truly located in the affections than in syllogisms; it consists more of life than of disputation, rather of inspiration than of erudition, more of transformation than of logic. Only a few can be learned, but no one is prevented from becoming a Christian, no one is prevented from becoming devout, and, I shall boldly add, no one is prevented from becoming a theologian.[9]

Erasmus applies to theology the statement of James concerning the wisdom from above: "For true theological wisdom is first modest, then gentle, pacific, pliant, full of mercy and good fruit, devoid of harsh judgment or insincerity."[10] It cannot be denied that by making such statements as these Erasmus leaves himself open to the charge of completely equating theology with piety or piety with theology. What he really means is clear from his response to the attack of Latomus.[11] He suggests here that the theologian must be existentially involved in his studies. What he reads and speaks he must love also. Not only the mind but also the heart must be present. His studies must bear practical fruit, or they are worthless.

The practical direction of Erasmus' theology, the spurning of speculation for the beneficial effect of theology upon the pious life, can be noted more clearly and concretely by illustrating his attitude toward certain key theological doctrines. About the Trinity he says that we ought not to investigate this mystery but piously worship and adore it and express in our lives the concord of the Three Persons.[12] Concerning the procession of the Holy Spirit, whether from the Father *through* the Son or from the Father *and* the Son, Erasmus says one will not be condemned if he cannot answer this question. But one will not escape destruction if he does not attend to the fruits of the Spirit: charity, joy, peace, patience, etc.[13] Erasmus urged also not a cognitive but an inward, affective appropriation of Christ.[14] Likewise, concerning sin and grace he asks the question of what use it is to dispute how sin may be understood, whether as a mere privation or a stain inherent in the soul. Let the theologian rather lead people to hate sin and shrink from it. Similarly he rejects scholastic speculation concerning the nature of grace and presses for a practical understanding.[15] And finally, he satirizes empty disputes concerning the nature of a sacrament "when their use is necessary to all for salvation."[16]

Therefore, there can be little question that Erasmus was not so much interested in a theoretical or dogmatic interpretation of Christian doctrines as in their practical application in the lives of believers. Much theological discussion appeared to him as idle, curious speculation, which he constantly attacked.

As the preceding discussion indicates, the first factor determining his negative attitude toward speculation was his moralism, which, however, was shaped by a genuine piety. He liked to quote the Socratic adage *Quae supra nos, nihil ad nos.*[17] He noted that Socrates called philosophy away from the contemplation of nature to a study of morality. And in a like manner he wished to call the theology of his day away from useless speculations to life.[18]

A second determinant of his critical outlook on theological speculation was a reverence before the divine mystery. Erasmus had a deep sense of the ultimate inscrutability of the divine, "a consciousness of the indefiniteness of the ground of all things."[19] God's nature lies beyond us. To probe it by human reason is impious curiosity, dangerous audacity, even madness. Whoever searches after God's majesty is oppressed by his glory. The eye of faith is simple, reverently beholding God in the way in which he wishes to be known, not curiously seeking out those things he wishes to hide from us.[20]

Combined with this reverence *coram mysterio tremendo* is a skepticism concerning the capacity of human intelligence to comprehend the ultimate truth or move beyond probability in any kind of knowledge. As Mestwerdt has pointed out, Erasmus had expressly declared as early as the *Antibarbari* that he favored the modesty of the ancient Academy with respect to knowledge.[21]

From this standpoint his aversion to metaphysics can be understood. The essence of natural things cannot be fully comprehended, let alone the essence of the divine. Moreover, he

continues, metaphysicians disagree concerning their first principles.[22] Manifestly, therefore, they do not possess the certain
knowledge that they pretend to have. Erasmus mocks their pre-
tended knowledge in the *Laus stultitiae* (1509):

> For to prove that they have good intelligence of nothing, that
> is a sufficient argument; they can never explain why they dis-
> agree with each other on every subject. Thus knowing nothing
> in general, they profess to know all things in particular; though
> they are ignorant even of themselves, and on occasion do not
> see the ditch or the stone lying across their path, because many
> of them are blear-eyed or absent-minded; yet they proclaim
> that they perceive ideas, universals, forms without matter, pri-
> mary substances, quiddities, and ecceities—things so tenuous,
> I fear, that Lynceus himself could not see them.[23]

Erasmus believed that the reason for so much curious
speculation in theology was the intrusion of philosophy, especially that of Aristotle. He complained that the authority of
Aristotle had come to be almost more revered than that of
Christ. Theologians had tried to cement together the doctrine
of Christ and the principles of Aristotle—that is, to mix fire with
water. To Erasmus it was evident that the doctrine of Christ and
the wisdom of the philosophers, especially of Aristotle, had
nothing in common.[24] They were to be sharply distinguished.
Therefore, for philosophy to make its way into theology could
only mean the corruption of the latter. These statements, however, require qualification. When Erasmus talks of the adultera-
tion of theology by philosophy, it seems clear that he has in
mind metaphysics and logic, not ethics, since he frequently
points to an affinity of the *philosophia Christi* with the ethics of
some of the ancient philosophers—namely, Socrates, Plato,
Cicero, Seneca, and Plutarch.[25]

Another reason for Erasmus' opposition to speculation is
his sense of the simplicity of truth and faith. In his reply to the
censures of the Paris faculty of theology he defines simplicity in
opposition to curious subtleties.[26] Erasmus believed that truth
is simple[27] and capable of being grasped by faith alone. There
is no need for many complex human arguments. One does not

have to be a philosopher or a theologian gifted with the powers
of dialectic in order to be able to understand the teachings of
Christ. Christ's most simple doctrine is open to all, even to
peasants.[28]

Faith and Reason

The contrasts drawn in the preceding section between theology and philosophy and between the simplicity of truth and
faith and the complexity of human argumentation lead to a
discussion of the relation of faith and reason in Erasmus'
thought. In the first place, Erasmus makes a sharp distinction
between the two. Reason has no certain knowledge, whether
derived from the senses or from the intuition of first principles.
The senses often deceive us; for example, the sun seems two
feet wide although in reality it is larger than the whole earth.
Likewise, the knowledge deduced from the perception of causes
or principles of things is uncertain, because the professors of
philosophy sometimes hesitate concerning these principles.
Also, the knowledge issuing from reason is complex, and is
attained slowly and circuitously with the greatest difficulty.
Faith, on the other hand, has certain knowledge, and proceeds
directly and easily to its highest object.[29]

If reason in its own sphere works unsteadily, even less has
it the possibility of comprehending what lies entirely outside its
range of operation: the mysteries of the nature of God, the
Trinity, creation, incarnation, resurrection, and the presence of
Christ in the Eucharist. Not only is reason unable to grasp these
realities, but to it they seem impossible. Therefore, the adjec-
tive "Almighty" is added in the Apostles' Creed to the description of God so that we may know that what seems impossible
to human reason is possible with God.[30]

Only faith is able to grasp matters of ultimate mystery. Reason is here not only helpless but superfluous. As Erasmus says
concerning the Trinity in the preface to his edition of Hilary,

> If I believe what has been handed down, that the three are of
> one substance, what need is there for laborious disputation? If
> I do not believe, no human arguments will persuade me.[31]

Moreover, reason may not only be of no positive assistance to faith, but actually constitute a threat. By piling up questions and by anxious, curious, subtle inquiry, reason may cause faith to totter.[32] Erasmus says that he has known of some who were made to vacillate by Scotus' arguments concerning the Eucharist.

However, in spite of the fact that faith does not need reason and in spite of the danger posed to faith by reason, Erasmus does not entirely forbid its use to the believer. A sober inquiry is permitted after the establishment of a firm foundation of faith.[33] Erasmus would no doubt consider as an example of this kind of inquiry the one he conducts in his exposition of the Apostles' Creed—modest, cautious, simple, yet showing considerable understanding of what were to him the chief articles of the faith. In a number of places he states that a "pious curiosity"[34] is permitted, one with a keen awareness of the limits of theological investigation and with more interest in the relation of theology to life than in subtle speculation.

It is the *speculative* use of reason which Erasmus resists and which he believes is dangerous to faith. Certainly, he does not intend to do away with reason altogether, for he makes use of it in his critical, philological, and historical study of Scripture and of the writings of the Fathers. He also uses reason in overturning the speculations of his theological opponents by pointing to the inconsistencies and contradictions in their arguments and among the authorities upon whom they rest their cases.

Like Abelard and the *via moderna,* Erasmus opposes speculative reason with critical reason in order to make room for faith. Like the nominalists, Erasmus is skeptical concerning the capacity of human reason to comprehend and demonstrate ultimate reality. Skepticism here does not mean an agnosticism or an uncertainty about religious truths but rather a doubt concerning the possibility of human reason fully to grasp and explicate these truths.[35] Anyone, therefore, who speaks of Erasmus as a skeptic without qualification misunderstands him.[36] The major difference between Erasmus and the nominalists at this

point is that his critical tool was not so much logic as philology
and historical criticism.

Simplicity

Closely associated with Erasmus' view of the simplicity of
faith and truth is his desire for a simple theology consisting of
only a few articles of faith.[37] In the midst of the doctrinal conflict
between Reformers and Roman Catholics in 1523, he urged in
a new preface to the *Ratio verae theologiae* dedicated to Albert of
Brandenburg that the definition of the articles which all must
believe be limited to very few and that the others be either
prohibited to inquiry or left to each individual's judgment.[38] He
maintained this wish to the end of his life. In a letter to Paul III
only a year and a half before his death he wrote:

> Let the definition of dogmas be reserved for a synod. I do not
> think it is necessary that the synod pronounce concerning all
> kinds of dogmas, but only concerning those upon which the
> Christian doctrine hinges.[39]

To embrace theology in a few chief articles conforms to the
doctrine and desire of Christ, thinks Erasmus. Christ's very
simple doctrine was explained in a few clear words: "Love the
Lord your God with your whole heart and your neighbor as
yourself."[40] He wished the yoke of his doctrine to be easy and
light, not burdened by a multitude of human opinions.[41]

A simple theology also conforms to the practice of the Apostles and the ancient Church Fathers, who spoke sparingly of
divine things. They were compelled by the heretics to speak
more openly and fully than they would have preferred. Because
of the impious temerity of the Cerinthians and Ebionites, John
the Evangelist was constrained to assert more openly the divine
nature of Christ. Likewise, the audacity of the Arians forced the
orthodox Fathers to define the person of Christ more elabo-
rately than they would have favored. In the preface to Hilary,
Erasmus describes how theology evolved from a state of simplicity to one of increasing complexity:

Once faith was more in life than in the profession of articles. Soon necessity urged that articles be prescribed, but they were few and of Apostolic sobriety. Next the wickedness of heretics compelled a more exact examination of the divine volumes . . . At length faith was contained in writings rather than in hearts, and soon there were as many faiths as there were men. Articles increased, but sincerity decreased: contention grew violent, while charity grew cold.[42]

In order to educate the laity in the essentials of the Christian faith, Erasmus suggested that a summary of Christian faith and doctrine be set forth yearly with "lucid brevity" and "learned simplicity."[43]

Two major motives of simplicity in theology are (1) evangelistic—to draw as many as possible to Christ and the Christian life, and (2) ecumenical—to produce peace and unity within the Church.

II. Erasmus' Conception of the Bases of Theology—Authority of Scripture and Tradition

Scripture

The theology which has more to do with piety than with speculation, which rests more on faith than on reason, which is simple, not complex, is biblical theology. Erasmus constantly urged theologians to return to the sources, to the solid foundations of our faith. Here is his line of argument from the *Paraclesis* and the *Ratio.* We do not question the labor required for learning the precepts of the sophists, the commentaries on Aristotle, the conclusions of Scotus. Why should we begrudge the effort necessary for learning the sacred books?[44] It is strange that we spend so much time and effort in the study of human opinions, which disagree among themselves, and so little in the contemplation of the divine writings, when from these "clearest fountains" we draw much more fruit with far less difficulty. Christ, the aim and center of theology, is nowhere more truly and more clearly represented than in the gospel letters.[45] As he states elsewhere, the limits of theological investigation are prescribed by Scripture.[46] It makes for a simple theology compressed in a few articles if not everything is defined but ". . . merely those things which have been evidently expressed in the sacred letters or without which the plan of our salvation may not be clear."[47] Scripture possesses an irrefutable and unshakable divine authority since it contains the very words of God.[48]

The principal argument for the divine authority of canonical Scripture is the seal of the Holy Spirit confirming by secret inspiration in our minds that all these books were written by God. Erasmus, however, acknowledges several secondary reasons for the certainty of the divine character of Scripture. These include the marvelous signs by which they were published, the wonderful agreement of the records among themselves, the fact that what is presented in figures and prophecies in the Old Testament is accomplished and fulfilled in the New Testament, the agreement of all times and nations as to the excellence of this philosophy, the power of this philosophy which prevailed against all the onslaughts of the devil without worldly assistance, and its agreement with natural reason.[49]

For Erasmus the humanist probably the most important of the secondary arguments for the authority of Scripture is its agreement with natural reason or natural law. This argument receives special emphasis in the lists both of the *Symbolum* and of *Ecclesiastae* by being placed first in the former and last in the latter. On the one hand, the gospel or the philosophy of Christ, which is the center of Scripture, fulfills, perfects, or restores nature;[50] on the other hand, the teachings of nature confirm the doctrine of Christ and the Apostles.[51] In the *Hyperaspistae I* (1526) Erasmus insists that the light of nature confirms Scripture on free will.[52] In the *Christiani matrimonii institutio* of the same year he asserts that natural reason confirms the injunction of Paul with regard to the reciprocity of conjugal rights.[53]

Although Erasmus recognized all canonical Scripture as authoritative, yet he discerned a "canon within the canon," certain books more authoritative than others. It is clear that for him the New Testament is far superior to the Old Testament. But also within each of the Testaments he notes the preeminence of certain books over others. In the Old Testament he places Isaiah over Judith and Esther, and in the New Testament, Matthew over Revelation as well as the epistles to the Romans and Corinthians over the epistle to the Hebrews. Erasmus thought so little of Revelation that it was the only New Testament book upon which he did not write a paraphrase. The center of gravity lies in the Gospels, where the *philosophia Christi* is to be found in all its purity and simplicity.[54.]

The Apostles' Creed

Alongside Scripture as a second primary basis of faith and theology is the Apostles' Creed, which is essentially a summary of the articles of faith contained in Scripture.[55] On the basis of his reading of Valla's philological, historical criticism of the Creed and of his own critical study, Erasmus doubted that the Creed was written by the Apostles, although it reflects the gravity, majesty, brevity, and spirit of the Apostles. He thought, as did Valla, that the Creed originated at the Council of Nicea. In spite of its late origin, however, its authority is equal to that of the canonical Scriptures.[56]

Theologians are to pay special attention to the Apostles' Creed, not only because of its authoritative character, but also because it contains the sum and substance of the catholic faith.[57] The importance of the Creed to Erasmus is shown by the three compositions he wrote concerning it. In the *Inquisitio de fide* (1524), the significance of which Thompson has clearly demonstrated,[58] Erasmus as the interlocutor Aulus examines Barbatius, who is Luther or a Lutheran, on the matter of the Creed. The result of this examination is that Barbatius is pronounced orthodox because of his agreement with the articles of the Apostles' Creed.[59] The contention of Erasmus seems to be, as Thompson rightly points out, that on essential doctrines as tested by the Apostles' Creed there is no disagreement between Luther and the Roman Church.

Tradition

Doctores Ecclesiae

Although for Erasmus theology was to be based primarily on Scripture and the Apostles' Creed, it was to be based secondarily on the work of the *doctores,* the interpreters of Scripture. In the *Hyperaspistae I* (1526) Erasmus says to Luther that, although he attributes the first authority to Scripture, he does not spurn the doctors to whom the Catholic Church has allotted so much authority for so many centuries.[60]

Scripture alone does not suffice as the rule of faith in spite of its irrefutable authority because it contains ambiguities and obscurities.[61] Especially against Luther, who held to the clear and plain sense of Scripture, did Erasmus maintain this point of view. In the *De libero arbitrio* (1524) he asks concerning the evident basis of Luther's doctrine of free will in Scripture: "If Scripture is so clear, why were so many excellent men blind on this point for so many centuries?"[62] In the *Hyperaspistae I* (1526) he points to the disagreements of the Reformers among themselves as to the sense of Scripture. Carlstadt, Zwingli, Oecolampadius, and Capito all disagree with Luther and among themselves.[63] Because of the ambiguity of some passages of Scripture, Erasmus thus affirmed the necessity of confirmation not only by natural reason but also by the consensus of the interpreters of Scripture or of the whole Church, especially if it is a universal and perpetual consensus—a definition of tradition not at all dissimilar to Vincent of Lerins, as "that which is believed everywhere, always, by everyone . . ."[64]

The Church Fathers

It is clear that the doctors who ranked first in Erasmus' estimation were the early Church Fathers, the ancients rather than the moderns, those who stood nearest to the sources. But not all the ancients were on a par. The Greeks excelled the Latins. Among the Greeks Origen ranked first, and after him Basil, Nazianzus, Athanasius, Cyril, and Chrysostom. Among the Latins it was Erasmus' beloved Jerome[65] who stood out over

Ambrose, Hilary, and Augustine, in that order.[66] In our exposition of Erasmus' theology of the sacraments we shall pay special attention to traces of Origen's thought, since he was Erasmus' favorite among the Fathers.

There were several reasons for Erasmus' preference for the ancients over the moderns. First, as a humanist he had a love of antiquity. For him what was ancient was bound to be better than what was recent. Those who stood nearest to the crystalline sources were certain to have expounded them more purely than those separated by many centuries. Second, the early Church Fathers, especially Origen and Jerome, provided for Erasmus the ideal union of classicism and Christianity: a pure, elegant, classical style and knowledge of antiquity with a clear understanding of the Bible and the pious life. They combined classical erudition with piety to form a *docta pietas*. Also, their theology was practical, not speculative, situated more in life than in dogmas. Then, too, they evinced great reverence for the divine mystery. They were circumspect in their language, which was based almost entirely on Scripture. Finally, they insisted on both a knowledge of the sacred languages and a spiritual, allegorical exegesis. For all these reasons Erasmus felt himself in spiritual communion with the Fathers.

The Scholastics

Although Erasmus much preferred the old doctors of the Church, he did not totally spurn the new ones, the scholastics. There is no doubt that he was sharply critical of the newer theologians. As more than one writer has pointed out, Erasmus' criticism was directed not only against their barbarous Latin and ignorance of the good letters but also against the very boldness of their efforts to comprehend the divine reality.[67] The principal grounds for his opposition to scholasticism have already been given: his skepticism concerning the possibility of rational penetration of the divine mystery, his shrinking from dogmatic assertions and systematic formulations on the basis of this skepticism, his conviction that theology has more to do with life than with speculation, his belief that truth is simple and can be grasped merely by faith without the need of complex argumentation, and his opinion that the scholastics had neglected the "sources" of the faith in which this simplicity is to be found.[68]

However, though Erasmus is certainly critical of much of scholastic theology, he states in several places that he intends its reform, not its destruction. He maintains that he does not want to overthrow scholastic theology but to correct it and render it purer and more learned by providing theologians with a knowledge of the sacred languages and of good letters, by recalling them to a knowledge of the *fontes* and of the old doctors of the Church, by calling them away from superfluous debate and ostentation to more sober studies.[69] In the *Ratio verae theologiae* (1520), he declares that he does not totally condemn scholastic debates, since truth often arises from a clash of minds, but he asks for measure and discrimination.[70]

Erasmus did not make round denunciations of scholasticism without a penetrating and basic study of the scholastics themselves. A close reading, especially of the polemical works, indicates that he possessed considerable knowledge of various scholastic authors.[71] We shall have occasion in the course of our exposition to point out references in Erasmus' works to such scholastics as Peter Lombard, Thomas Aquinas, Duns Scotus, Durandus, Jean Gerson, and Gabriel Biel.[72]

Two of these, Thomas and Gerson, deserve special consideration because they are mentioned with some frequency in Erasmus' works. For Thomas, Erasmus had high praise. He admired his diligence, his erudition, and his saintly life.[73] He reproached him for having brought so much philosophy into theology.[74] The *Annotationes in Novum Testamentum* reveal a knowledge especially of Thomas' exegetical writings. Dolfen notes at least forty references to the Dominican doctor in the *Annotationes.*[75] By my count, however, there are at least sixty-seven. It is not clear how much of the theological opus of Aquinas Erasmus knew. Dolfen is correct that "only seldom does he cite a theological work, and only now and then with exact reference."[76] We shall notice later that Erasmus refers to Thomas' opinions regarding the problem of grace and free will and the Eucharist.

However celebrated a writer Thomas is, one is nevertheless permitted to disagree with him. And Erasmus frequently does part with him both in exegetical critical matters in the *Annotationes* and on several important theological issues, including the sacraments.[77]

More notable is the prominence of Gerson in Erasmus' writings. In a letter to Beda, 15 June 1525, Erasmus remarks: "As a youth I read some little works of Gerson, and they did not at all displease me."[78] In view of the comparative frequency of references to Gerson and his opinions in the Erasmian corpus, we can view this admission as an understatement. In my studies of the *Opera* I have counted some twenty-seven references to Gerson.[79] Most of these are actual citations of Gerson's views. Of special interest to us will be statements which elicit Gerson's support on the sacraments of confession and baptism. Important for the theme of this chapter is a long citation from two of Gerson's works concerning the degeneration of the study of theology. From the *De quatuor domibus* and from the *In lectionibus super Marcum* he cites passages which condemn theological ostentation and sophistical argumentation and urge that theology be characterized rather by a concern for faith and the moral life.[80] As Dolfen observes, R. Seeberg had already pointed to the importance of Gerson for Erasmus.[81] My studies only confirm this suggestion of Seeberg and the research of Dolfen. Only future research can fully determine how much the practical theology of Erasmus owes not only to the *Devotio Moderna* and to the humanism of such men as Lorenzo Valla and John Colet but also to the school of Jean Gerson.[82]

That Erasmus had a considerable knowledge of the scholastic tradition is evident not only from his specific references to various scholastic authors but also from his presentation of some of the scholastic debates which to him seem not germane to the Christian life. In the long note on I Timothy 1:6 he gives a number of these debates concerned with the essence and power of God, the nature of the Trinity and of Christ, and the power of the Pope.[83] Dolfen discusses how Erasmus' listing accurately reflects many of the scholastic disputes. After a close study of the question, Dolfen does not believe that Erasmus borrowed these examples from the various *Summa*'s; they seem rather to originate from the leading schoolmen themselves.[84] Especially in his soteriology and sacramental theology Erasmus shows considerable knowledge of the scholastic tradition, and in both he stands more in line with the late medieval nominalist than with the Thomist or the Scotist traditions.[85]

In spite of his respect for the theological tradition, both patristic and scholastic, Erasmus stressed the human, and therefore fallible and relative, character of the opinions of the *doctores ecclesiae*. Scripture alone is free from error; all the Fathers, even the most illustrious, err. Their views often conflict with one another, and are changing. They are all relative, given for a time. They should therefore be read with discrimination. The temporal circumstances of their interpretations should be weighed. Later times may demand a somewhat different judgment. For example, on the question of divorce, Erasmus is aware that he stands against the whole theological tradition in urging that this remedy be considered for the many ill-begotten marriages of his time, but suggests that certain things the Fathers have said can be changed or at least adapted to another period. "But it is possible that the Spirit of Christ did not disclose everything at once to his Church."[86]

Therefore, Erasmus' position relative to the tradition of the *doctores* is both positive and negative. Because the Spirit of Christ only gradually reveals some things to the Church, to reject out of hand the later interpretation of the Fathers would be to reject the revelation of Christ. However, because these later interpreters are fallible and historically conditioned, their opinions must be viewed critically on the basis of the purest teaching of Christ in Scripture. As Mestwerdt has put it, here there is both a "relatives *Recht*" and a "*relatives* Recht."[87]

The authority of the doctors is great when many concur in their interpretation of Scripture and when that consensus is perpetual, but when there is conflict, one is free to follow whoever seems to be the more correct.[88]

On the one hand, Erasmus recognized a unity between Scripture and the interpretation of the early Fathers. In contrast to the later doctors, for the most part they simply laid forth the contents of Scripture. They hesitated to affirm anything not expressed in Scripture.

On the other hand, by stressing the divergences even among the Fathers he pointed to a split between Scripture and tradition. This distinction is further underlined by Erasmus' acknowledgment that some doctrines were received by the Church with a universal consensus as handed down by the ancients even though not contained in Scripture; e.g., the perpetual virginity of Mary and the invocation of the saints.[89] What therefore seems most decisive is not whether the doctrines were contained in Scripture but whether they were held by a universal and perpetual consensus of the Fathers and of the Church. Erasmus preferred a tradition which was wholly grounded in Scripture, but he recognized and accepted a tradition which allowed for extrascriptural truths.[90]

General Councils

Superior to the authority of the *doctores* and inferior only to the authority of Scripture for Erasmus was the authority of general councils. In the *Symbolum* (1533) he sets forth as the first mark of the Church ". . . the authority of the ancient synods, especially what has been confirmed by a perpetual consensus of so many ages and so many nations."[91] In the colloquy Ἰχθυοφαγία (1526) the fishmonger states: "But what proceeds from the authority of a universal council is a heavenly oracle and carries weight equal to that of the Gospels, or surely almost equal."[92] In a treatise written in the same year against the Zwinglian Jud, Erasmus states that after dogmas expressly contained in Scripture and the Apostles' Creed, he accepts dogmas decreed by universal councils.[93]

Of course, in order for their decrees to be authoritative, the councils must be rightly assembled by the Holy Spirit, con-

ducted, published, and received,[94] that is, approved by a perpetual consensus of the whole Christian people.[95] We note
again the importance for Erasmus of confirmation by the whole
Church of the opinions of the *doctores* and the decisions of
Church councils.

By this definition of true councils Erasmus implied that
some councils were not rightly constituted, received, and approved universally by the Christian people. In the Ἰχθυοφαγία
(1526) the butcher remarks that not all orthodox persons have
approved the recent Councils of Basel (1431-47) and Constance
(1414-17), not to mention the latest Lateran Council (1512-
17).[96] Elsewhere Erasmus indicates that he does not highly regard this Lateran Council.[97]

Erasmus thought that what the Church defined in councils
was not to be regarded as absolutely certain. However, he says
to Luther that even if we grant that a general council may be
corrupt, it is safer and more probable to believe that the truth
and spirit of God were there than in private gatherings.[98] Besides, "if something perhaps had been wrongly established in
a council, it ought to be corrected so that as far as possible it
might be preserved by the authority of [later] councils and the
Roman Pontiff."[99]

He believed that councils should confine their definitions to
the essentials of the faith; i.e., he would undoubtedly prefer that
the councils limit their pronouncements to what was contained
in Scripture. What was so defined was perpetual and inviolable,
but other matters which did not rest on Scripture might be
changed according to the times and circumstances.[100] What was
defined by the Church in councils out of Holy Writ he held with
the greatest assurance, but other dogmas not contained in
Scripture he also received with obedience if they were accepted
by the whole Christian Church—even if he could not understand what was prescribed.[101] Erasmus accepted most willingly
decisions of councils which were grounded in Scripture, but he
accepted—though I think less willingly—even those decisions
which were not so grounded if received by a perpetual and
universal consensus of the Christian people.

However, Erasmus did not hesitate to raise a doubt about certain dogmas recently defined which were not grounded in Scripture. He seems never to have admitted transubstantiation, even though he received the Real Presence in the Eucharist as a clear fact of the tradition. He also questioned the dogma of the immaculate conception promulgated at the Council of Basel.[102]

Of course, in spite of widespread acceptance, neither of these dogmas was unanimously received. There was greater agreement on transubstantiation than on the immaculate conception. Even though transubstantiation had for some time been the view of the vast majority within the Church, nevertheless there were many who raised questions concerning it in the late Middle Ages.[103] In spite of the decree of the Council of Basel, there was strong opposition to the immaculate conception, especially on the part of the Dominicans.

Undoubtedly, both doctrines offended Erasmus' reason and his understanding of Scripture. However, he might reject them also on the basis of his view of tradition: He might have said that we must await a longer and more universal consensus before wholly accepting them.

Therefore, in spite of his aversion to speculation and precise definition Erasmus does not reject all dogmatic definitions, as some critics have declared.[104] Although Erasmus does refuse to accept the arbitrary assertions of theologians as dogma and does oppose the multiplication of dogmas, he does not stand against all dogma.

Many of the theological questions which were dividing Protestants and Roman Catholics at the time of the Reformation he did not consider to be articles of faith: the questions of the power of the papacy, the divine institution of confession, faith versus works, free will, merit, the mass as a sacrifice, indulgences. These questions are not resolved in Scripture, the Creeds, the decisions of universal councils.[105] They remain, therefore, open and debatable issues, not articles of faith.

Erasmus not only distinguished sharply between articles of faith, which are binding, and the opinions of theologians, which one is free to accept or reject, but he also made distinctions among the dogmas, between those which are essential and those which are less essential, between those which are necessary to be known and those which are less necessary.[106] Although he infrequently states which ones he considered to fall in each of these categories, on the basis of our discussion thus far it is clear that for him the essential dogmas are those that are expressly contained in Scripture and the Apostles' Creed; all others are less essential. In an important passage in the *Hyperaspistae I* (1526) he maintains that not all the articles are equal. Some are quite evident, such as that Christ was born of a virgin, that he suffered under Pontius Pilate. Others were approved after long discussion but are not yet unanimously received, such as the perpetual virginity of Mary and the supremacy of the Pope. Others are still being debated, such as the question of Pope versus Council.[107] In another most revealing passage he says to Luther that he does not wish to be considered a skeptic concerning the articles of faith but only concerning contentious dogmas, on which the Church was also a skeptic if one takes into account the long time that elapsed before it defined concerning them. These include the approval of the word *homoousios,* the procession of the Holy Spirit, transubstantiation, the conception of the Virgin Mother, purgatory, no repetition of baptism, baptism of infants, and perhaps also free will:

> . . . I speak concerning these and other questions of this kind, in which, if the Church had defined nothing and I were asked what I think, I would reply that it is not clear to me, but it is known to God. After the Church has defined concerning these things, spurning human arguments, I follow what the Church has decreed and cease to be a skeptic.[108]

These are all questions to which answers are not immediately evident from Scripture and the Apostles' Creed. He would have preferred that the Church had defined nothing with regard to them. He would himself have been inclined to be skeptical about these dogmas if the Church had not defined them.[109] But once the Church has clearly defined them, he accepts them as dogmas.

Thus Erasmus exhibits two important attitudes toward Church dogma. One is negative, the other positive. On the one hand, he is inclined to be skeptical and critical of all dogma not clearly contained in Scripture and the Apostles' Creed. On the other hand, he accepts even dogmas which are not so grounded out of concern for the unity of the Church and out of reverence for its tradition. Erasmus believed in the evolution not only of theological opinions but also, as Renaudet has emphasized, of dogmas[110] on the basis of his conviction that God has not revealed all his truth at once. This belief in the gradual development of Christian dogmas also contained positive and negative elements: (1) the acceptance of dogmas which by degrees had become established in the Church, and (2) the recognition based on his critical, historical understanding that these dogmas were historically conditioned, relative, contingent.

Erasmus' attitude toward dogma illustrates the fundamental contrast running throughout his theology, the contrast between flesh and spirit. Dogma is the inadequate historical embodiment of a fundamentally spiritual reality which cannot be completely expressed in this life and in this history.

The Papacy

As we consider the problem of authority in Erasmus' thought, the next question is that of his attitude toward the papacy. It is clear that the humanist more undermined than enhanced or strengthened the power and authority of the Roman see.[111] By and large he stayed clear of the question of the authority of the Pope versus the authority of councils except to mention that this was as yet an unresolved question.[112] However, a passage from the colloquy Ἰχθυοφαγία of 1526 seems to imply the superiority of Council over Pope.[113] Also, the absence of the phrase "approved by the Pope" in his definitions of dogmas indicates that he hardly considered the authority of the Pope to be at all equal to councils.

Erasmus undercuts the authority of the papacy in various

ways—first, by philological and historical criticism. He eliminates certain key scriptural passages as supports of papal authority. His exegesis of Matthew 16:16-18 is that not Peter
himself but his confession uttered in place of the whole Christian people is the solid rock upon which Christ builds his
Church. The keys of the kingdom are given not to Peter alone
but to the whole Church.[114] In an annotation on II Corinthians
10:8, he asks those who elevate immensely the authority of the
Pope to observe this passage which makes it clear that Paul
received his Apostolic authority not from Peter but directly
from Christ.[115]

Erasmus also insists that John 21:15-19 cannot be used as a
prop for the juridical power of the papacy. His interpretation of
this passage is that here Peter represents the kind of bishop to
whom Christ committed his flock, the one who powerfully loves
Christ, who looks out not for his own gain but for the glory of
Christ, who does not so much *rule* as *feed* the sheep.[116]

The doctrine of the two swords as founded on Luke 22:38
received a jolt from Erasmus' interpretation of this passage.
Both in his annotation and in his paraphrase Erasmus interprets the two swords as referring to a knowlege of the Old and
New Testaments.[117]

Another important passage which was used to bolster papal
authority, I Corinthians 2:15, Erasmus passes over in silence.
As Pineau has pointed out,[118] Erasmus would doubtlessly have
regarded the attempt to found extreme papal authority on this
passage as an example of the forced exegesis which he mentions in the *Laus stultitiae* (1509).[119] On the basis of his theory
of the ultimate authority of the Church as resting in the whole
Church and of the analogy of the Church to the political sphere,
where he expresses a kind of republicanism,[120] we can be sure
that Erasmus would have agreed with the conciliarists that since
the Pope receives his power from the people, he can be judged
by the people and removed by the people if he abuses his power.

Erasmus' critical study of Scripture led him to question the
biblical foundation of papal authority. Likewise, his historical
understanding caused him to see the papacy as a human institu-

tion which emerged gradually. He doubted that the monarchy of the Pope was conspicuous or acknowledged at the time of Jerome.[121] His biblical and historical studies led him to question papal authority as *de iure divino*, as perpetual or handed down by Christ.

Erasmus' keen sense of history not only observed the papacy as an institution which developed gradually but also pointed to the variations among the Popes just as to the differences among the *doctores*. He showed how changing and conflicting were their opinions. The constitutions of earlier Popes had been antiquated by those of later ones as deviating from true piety. There were a number of things in the papal decretals which would now be considered heretical. Therefore, Popes could err and had erred. Their views were human and thus relative, changing, and sometimes corrupt. They could hardly, then, be infallible in matters of faith and morals, as some claimed.[122]

A more subtle, indirect undermining of papal power was his attack not on the Pope himself but on those around him who elevated his power beyond what he claimed or acknowledged out of desire for their own gain.[123]

Another cunning means of placing in doubt the authority of the Holy See was his ironical use of *utinam*:

> Would that he truly have what they attribute to him, that he could not err in matters of piety! Would that he could truly remove souls from the punishment of purgatory![124]

Such optative subjunctives only served to emphasize the split between the wish and the reality. Clearly Erasmus did not think the Pope had such power.

A final most devastating criticism of the Popes which probably did more than any of the foregoing to lower the papacy in the popular mind was his caustic attack on the moral corruption of certain Popes. It was especially in the *Laus stultitiae* (1509) that this assault was effectively expressed. With stinging satire he struck at the Popes, the so-called vicars of Christ, who, instead of imitating the poverty, meekness, and gentleness of Christ and the Apostles, were hungry for riches and power, exercised

the sword, made threats and used "interdictions, excommuni-
cations, re-excommunications, anathematizations, pictured
damnations, and the terrific lightning-bolt of the bull, which by
its mere flicker sinks the souls of men below the floor of
hell."[125] The contrasting images of papal corruption and
Apostolic purity he drew in sharpest relief.

Of course, Erasmus did not want to destroy the papacy, but
only its pretensions and its corruption. He acknowledged the
Pope as the historically evolved supreme ruler of the Church.
For the concord and unity of Christendom it was necessary to
have one highest leader.[126] He wished, however, that the Popes,
as vicars of Christ, would truly represent and imitate Christ by
uniting power with goodness and wisdom. He wished them to
use their power and authority to restore peace and harmony to
Christendom, to battle with spiritual arms against the enemies
of the Church, "simony, pride, evil desire, ambition, anger,
impiety."[127]

Erasmus thus acknowledges the papacy (1) as an outgrowth
of history and (2) as a functional necessity. In the letter to
Slechta he suggests another ground for the papacy which he
places before the pragmatic one. Drawing on tradition which
goes back to Pseudo-Dionysius, Erasmus puts forward the
analogy of the ecclesiastical to the celestial hierarchy.[128] However, as Schätti points out, the emphasis in most of Erasmus'
statements on the subject is decidedly upon the functional
rather than the hierarchical aspects of papal authority.[129]

In sum, for Erasmus the power of the Roman Pontiff is a
moral and rational power, a power which must be blended with
goodness and wisdom to have efficacy.[130] His authority is *de iure
humano,* not *de iure divino.* It is grounded not in the institution
of Christ but in the historical development of the Church, no
doubt under the Spirit of Christ.

His laws ought to reflect as much as possible the laws of
Christ, although Erasmus questions whether the laws of the
Popes can be wholly congruent with those of Christ. In contrast
to those of Christ, the pontifical laws are fallible, relative, and
often corrupt. In authority they clearly fall below Scripture and

the law of nature. When there is a conflict between papal law and the law of Scripture or of nature, Erasmus prefers the latter—for example, in regard to laws governing foods.[131] Also, as we have seen, papal decrees are inferior to those of general councils,[132] and, finally, they are especially inferior to the consensus of the whole Church. Against Luther, Erasmus asserted that he taught confession "not only because the Roman Pontiff commanded it, but much more because the Christian people received it."[133]

The Church as the Universal Christian People

This idea of the Church was what was most decisive for Erasmus. For him the Church did not consist primarily or essentially of the sacerdotal hierarchy culminating in the Pope but rather of the whole Christian people. In two important discussions of adages in 1515, Erasmus criticizes the idea that the Church consists of the priests, bishops, and popes. The Church is rather, he says, the Christian people.[134] Likewise, in the *Inquisitio de fide* (1524) Erasmus, under the pseudonym of Barbatius, says:

> I believe the Holy Church, which is the body of Christ, that is to say, a certain congregation of all men throughout the whole world who agree in the faith of the Gospel, who worship one God the Father, who put their whole confidence in his Son, who are guided by the same Spirit of him; from whose fellowship he is cut off that commits a deadly sin.[135]

The supreme authority of the Church, therefore, is not the decisions of the Roman see but the consensus of all Christian believers. To Willibald Pirckheimer, his humanist friend in Nuremberg, Erasmus twice utters his conception of the authority of the Church as the consensus of the Christian people throughout the whole world and states that this understanding confirms him in his faith in the Eucharistic Real Presence and prevents him from following in the steps of Oecolampadius.[136]

The marks of this consensus, as we have noticed, are first of all the general councils rightly gathered and enacted by the Holy Spirit and secondly the agreement of the doctors. But the decisions of councils and doctors are immediately referred to the consent of the whole Christian people. As the chief prince and doctor of the Church, the Pope has no doubt an important voice in its decisions, but he remains only *primus inter pares.*

We need to say a word in conclusion about the relation between this universal Church, the primary locus of authority, and the Church at Rome, the seat of the papacy. We have already noticed that, though Erasmus sees the authority of the papacy as only *de iure humano* and is critical of papal tyranny and corruption, he acknowledges as a necessary development the ascendancy of one supreme ruler of the Church. Furthermore, it is clear that, though Erasmus surely recognizes a distinction between the universal and the Roman Church, he does not maintain a separation of one from the other. From the beginning of the conflict of Rome with Wittenberg, Erasmus confesses his loyalty both to the Catholic Church and to the Roman Church, and the latter, he thinks, is not opposed to the former. Against Hutten, Erasmus writes:

> First I think that he will confess that the Church is at Rome: for a multitude of evils does not cause it to be less the Church. And I think that it is orthodox, for even if there are many impious, nevertheless the Church appears among the good.[137]

In spite of the evils he sees as present in the curia and the priesthood, Erasmus' love of peace and unity, as well as his sense of tradition, forbid his breaking with the Church at Rome, however critically he may judge it on the basis of a larger conception of the Church. Therefore, he writes to Luther the famous words:

> I have never departed from the Catholic Church. . . . I know that in this Church, which you call Papist, there are many who displease me, but I see such also in your Church. Evils to which you are accustomed are borne more easily. Therefore, I bear with this Church until I see a better one.[138]

On the basis of this passage Renaudet put forward his category of the "third Church" to describe Erasmus' ecclesiology, a term which would suggest that Erasmus' thought was more radical than it really was, that he looked forward to a church embodying the Erasmian ideas of reform which would be neither Roman nor Lutheran. The French scholar, however, qualified his term by stating:

> . . . Third Church, or rather the Roman Church profoundly reformed, rejuvenated, modernized. . . . That Church ought to remain Roman, founded on the rock of Peter, faithful to the memory and the traditions of the martyrs and the saints.[139]

Without doubt Erasmus hoped for the renewal of this Church, but the term "third Church" suggests something more radical, a break with the Roman Church, which does not square well with Erasmus' loyalty to tradition and his sense of history, to which Renaudet correctly points by his qualifying remarks.[140] Renaudet's category of the "third Church" goes hand in hand with an exaggerated notion of Erasmus' so-called modernization and spiritualization of dogma and cult.

Conclusion

This chapter has introduced the more general or formal character of Erasmus' theology which shapes his understanding of the sacraments—his emphasis upon the relation of theology to piety; his stress upon simplicity of faith as opposed to complex argumentation, yet his allowance of a role to reason, especially to philological and historical reason, in the theological enterprise; his skeptical aversion to dogmatic definition, yet his willingness to accept definitions, especially those grounded in Scripture but also those grounded in the universal and perpetual consensus of Christian believers as expressed in Church councils and the agreement of the doctors.

In sum, Erasmus' theology can be characterized as moral theology—stress upon the relation of theology to the moral life —and positive theology—attention to the facts of revelation, whether in Scripture or tradition. Even though he grants to tradition, especially early tradition, a definite validity, he always views it critically on the basis of his understanding of Scripture and, at least whatever is not clearly in line with Scripture, as provisional.

Having sketched the formal principles of Erasmus' theology, we turn now in the next four chapters to a treatment of the material principles which underlie his sacramental views.

II

ANTHROPOLOGY

I. Anthropology and Sacraments

The starting point for Erasmus' sacramental thought, as indeed for his whole theology, is the Platonic conception of the contrast between flesh and spirit, which is grounded in the nature of the world and the nature of man.[1] In two of his earlier writings, the *Enchiridion* (1503) and the *Laus stultitiae* (1509), the parallel between flesh and spirit in man and flesh and spirit in the sacraments is clearly drawn and closely connected. Canon V of the *Enchiridion* states that

> . . . one maintains perfect piety if one seeks always to proceed from the visible things which are either imperfect or neutral to the invisible according to the higher aspect of man.[2]

His discussion of the application of this rule includes the sacraments of baptism, penance, and the Eucharist. Likewise, at the end of the *Laus stultitiae,* having just affirmed that Christians and Platonists agree that the soul is imprisoned by the body and that it is the effort of religious persons to neglect the concerns of the body and seek those things that are invisible, Erasmus asserts: "They say that also in the sacraments and in the very works of religion one discovers body and spirit."[3] An analysis of Erasmus' anthropology is therefore a prerequisite to understanding his sacramental theology.

II. The Platonic Cosmological Basis of His Anthropology

The background for Erasmus' anthropology is the Platonic cosmology of invisible-visible or intelligible-sensible. He supports Canon V of the *Enchiridion* by stating:

> Let us fancy that there are two worlds, the one wholly intelligible, the other visible. The intelligible world, which we may also call angelic, is the one in which God dwells with the blessed minds; the visible world is the heavenly spheres, and what is included in them.[4]

As "a certain third world," man participates in both worlds—visible, according to the body, and invisible, according to the soul.

Unfortunately, Erasmus does not elaborate here or elsewhere upon what precisely he means by the division of the world into these two distinct spheres, nor does he tell us how they are related. He was no speculative thinker, as we have already stressed. His interest was less in cosmology than in anthropology, and the latter was not so much a metaphysical as a practical, ethical understanding of man. However, this primarily practical outlook has a metaphysical and cosmological basis, one which is derived fundamentally from the Platonic tradition. The direct influence of Plato on Erasmus in the *Enchiridion* is evident in several explicit references to Platonic dialogues, especially the *Timaeus,*[5] where this schema of intelligible-visible mainly has its origin, as well as the *Symposium,* the *Phaedo,* and the *Phaedrus.*[6] The indirect influence of Plato on Erasmus comes to him perhaps most prominently through Origen and Augustine[7] among the Church Fathers and, among the contemporary theologians, especially through John Colet,[8] who passed on to Erasmus the revived Platonism of the Florentine Academy.

III. Man—A Dichotomy

According to the above statement concerning man's position within the cosmos as "a third something" who unites both worlds in himself, the invisible through his soul and the visible through his body, man is a being composed of two distinct parts. Other passages in the *Enchiridion* and other writings of Erasmus suggest, however, not just a twofold but a threefold division in man. Indeed, at the beginning of his discussion of the nature of man in the *Enchiridion,* Erasmus seems uncertain whether man is a dichotomy or a trichotomy: "Man is therefore a certain prodigious animal composed of two or three very different parts."[9] Following this statement he discusses the two-fold division of man but later has a section on three aspects: spirit, soul, and flesh.

We shall therefore follow Erasmus' lead in the *Enchiridion* and analyze man first as a dichotomy and then as a trichotomy.

Erasmus' terminology is fluid. He uses various pairs of contrasting words: *anima* and *corpus, spiritus* and *caro, ratio* and *affectus, homo interior* and *homo exterior.* His expressions are derived from both Plato and the New Testament, especially Paul. He does not discern any real difference between Plato and Scripture. We have already noted this passage from the *Laus stultitiae*: "Christians agree with the Platonists that the soul is immersed in and bound to a bodily prison."[10] In the *Enchiridion* he maintains:

> What the Philosophers call reason, that Paul calls now spirit, now the inner man, now the law of the mind. What they name as feeling, he names sometimes flesh, sometimes body, sometimes the outer man, sometimes the law of our members.[11]

Just below this statement he goes on to say:

> Plato puts two souls in one man. Paul makes two men so glued together in the same man that the one cannot exist without the other, neither in glory nor in hell, but may be so disjoined that the death of one is the life of the other.[12]

Here Erasmus seems to recognize that a major difference between Paul and Plato is that for Paul soul and body are never wholly divided, whereas for Plato the soul eventually departs from the body. However, he does not seem to grasp the inti-

mate psychosomatic unity of Paul, because he reads Paul with
Platonic glasses.

Whatever words are used, Erasmus is attempting to point
out the sharp difference between man's inner, spiritual, and
outer, physical, being. In some passages, especially in the *Enchiridion,* Erasmus emphasizes very strongly the distinction between these aspects of man's nature. They are two "greatly
different parts." Because of his soul man is like something
divine; because of his body, like a dumb brute. He even goes so
far as to say that by virtue of his soul man is capable of divinity
and, if it were not for his body, he would be a "god." The soul
is divine, immortal, invisible; the body, crass, mortal, and visible. In an Augustinian manner Erasmus stresses that, as God
is superior to the soul, the soul is superior to the body. The
body is variously considered as the prison, instrument,[13] or
servant[14] of the soul. In any case, the body is clearly placed in
a subordinate position with respect to the soul. In these
thoughts clearly Erasmus is inspired by Plato, especially by the
Phaedo.

On the other hand, there are passages which, while retaining
the inferior position of the body, regard it more positively and
suggest a closer unity between it and the soul. In the *Convivium
religiosum* (1522), he has Eusebius say: "Our bodies, aren't they
partners of our minds? For I prefer 'partners' to 'instruments'
or 'dwellings' or 'tombs.' "[15] The body provides the physical
basis for the faculties of the soul. In the *Enchiridion* Erasmus
refers to the *Timaeus,* in which Plato points to a bodily base for
the various aspects of the soul. The seat of the immortal soul
—that is, reason—is the brain, the highest part of the body. The
parts of the mortal soul are placed in the body according to
their relative likeness or unlikeness to the brain. The higher
emotions—courage, righteousness, indignation—Plato situated between the neck and the diaphragm. The sensual appetite
he consigned to the liver and bowels.[16] Here Erasmus is intent
on emphasizing the wide difference between the upper and
lower parts of the soul, between reason and the passions. Elsewhere he defends the proposition that all the feelings and pow-

ers of the soul have in the body a comparable organ which is their "seat." Making use of Plato's *Timaeus* and Aristotle's *De anima,* he stresses that even reason not only has its seat in the brain (*Timaeus*) but arrives at understanding by making use of sensations it receives from the body (*De anima*).[17]

A more positive stance toward the body is further underlined when he speaks of the participation of the body in redemption. As the divine spirit indwelling our spirit transforms our spirit unto itself, so our spirit indwelling the body transforms the body unto itself.[18] The purpose of creation is to know, love, and glorify God with body and soul.[19] The end of the incarnation is that the whole man correspond to Christ's purity and so be redeemed.[20] It is especially in the resurrection that the body is renewed so that the whole man will sing praises to the Creator,[21] but it seems clear that Erasmus thinks of this renewal as beginning already in the present life. We may conclude then that, even though Erasmus distinguished sharply between the soul and the body and considered the soul to be superior to the body, he did not negate the body but included it in the redemption of the whole man. The strong biblical strands of Erasmus' thought may be viewed here as tempering his neo-Platonism.

IV. Man—A Trichotomy

As we have noted already, Erasmus sometimes divides man not only in two parts but in three: flesh, spirit, and soul. Here he follows Origen,[22] but he thinks that he is following Paul.[23] He also connects Paul and the philosophers on these three parts of man. What the philosophers call *ratio* or τὸ ἡγεμονικόν, Paul calls *spiritus;* what they call *morbi* or πάθη, he calls *caro.* The third, median part, the natural affections, both the philosophers and Paul call *anima.* He seems to be aware, however, that the concepts of the philosophers and Paul cannot be simply equated, for he states:

> For the Philosophers call the highest part of the soul not
> "spirit" [*spiritum*] but "mind" [*mentem*] or "reason" [*rationem*].
> Paul does not identify reason with spirit, but thinks of spirit as
> reason inspired by grace.[24]

In the *Ecclesiastae* (1535) he recognizes also that when Paul
speaks of flesh he does not always refer to the lowest affections
but may refer to reason itself or even to the whole man insofar
as he lacks the spirit of Christ.[25] In the *Hyperaspistae II* (1527) he
does not mention Paul explicitly, but he notes that in Scripture
caro may signify simply the part of the body which covers the
bones, or by synecdoche may refer to the whole body or even
to humanity.[26] It is difficult to understand, therefore, how Erasmus could think that the philosophers and Paul were saying the
same thing unless he was simply predisposed to believe that
there was more harmony between them than there was in fact.
Here a problem of hermeneutics arises. There seems to have
been a conflict which Erasmus did not really resolve between his
Platonic presuppositions and the findings of his critical, philological exegesis.

V. Ethical Implications of the Threefold Division of Man

Flesh

For Erasmus the moralist the ethical implications of this
threefold division of man are more important than the natural
constitution in itself. Flesh from an ethical point of view is also
variously understood in Scripture, according to Erasmus. In
the first place, it may be simply a morally neutral term; that is,
it may refer to the weakness of man's nature which is inclined
to sin.[27] Or it may refer to sensual passions such as lust or
debauchery, but he is careful to point out that sensuality is not
the only manifestation of sinful flesh. When Paul in Galatians
speaks of the works of the flesh, he includes worship of idols,
enmity, envy, quarreling, murder, etc. Erasmus thinks further
that when Paul uses the word "flesh" he has in mind Jewish
ceremonies upon which men are accustomed to rely and which

they substitute for genuine inner morality.[28] Finally, in the passage mentioned above from *Ecclesiastae,* Erasmus states that for Paul:

> ... "flesh" may be not only the crasser feelings, such as lust or drunkenness, but also the very reason of man, nay the whole man with all his natural powers if he is lacking the spirit of Christ.[29]

The flesh then is that part of man which being weak is especially inclined toward sin and tends to drag the whole man down toward sin. But there is no necessity here. The will freely consents to being pulled toward sin.[30]

Spirit

In direct opposition to the flesh is the spirit. As the flesh pulls us down to what is earthy and animal-like, the spirit lifts us up to what is heavenly and God-like. The spirit is that part of us which most expresses the divine image.

> ... the spirit by which we truly express the likeness of the divine nature in which the supreme Builder, from the archetype of his mind, inscribed that eternal law of righteousness with his finger, that is, with his spirit. By this we are joined firmly with God and made one with him.[31]

Constituted in the image of God, man is capable of the highest goodness. As spirit, man loves those things which he knows are pleasing to God.

Soul

The soul, standing between the spirit and the flesh, is from an ethical point of view neutral. Whether it is good or bad depends upon the direction toward which it turns itself.

> If, renouncing the flesh, it is drawn over to the spiritual part, it becomes likewise spiritual. If it degrades itself to the desires of the flesh, it will degenerate likewise into corporeality.[32]

For Erasmus "soul" refers especially to the natural affections—such as care for one's safety, love of family and friends, veneration of parents—which are held in common with the heathen and even animals. These are neither to be especially commended as good nor reprehended as bad. Their morality depends upon the manner in which one exercises these feelings. If he so loves wife or children that he neglects the precepts of God, he transforms the soul into flesh. If he loves them only in Christ, he changes the soul into spirit. The natural affections then can become either fleshly or spiritual depending on the manner in which they are exercised.

VI. The Nature of Sin

In man's original state these widely disparate natures were united by the Creator in a happy harmony, but this union was broken by sin. Consequently, warfare rages between the flesh and the spirit. Once the mind ruled the body without difficulty, and the body willingly and joyfully submitted, but now the flesh has gained control. The correct order of things has been subverted.[33]

For Erasmus original sin in the sense of an inherited depravity from the first parents is not, properly speaking, any sin, but rather a tendency to sin.[34] In infants there is thus no real sin but only the privation of the original grace, the inclination to sin, and the calamity of the human life. These are called sin because they proceed from the sin of the first parents.[35] Erasmus understands Romans 5:12 as referring not necessarily to original sin in the specific sense of an inherited guilt, but to sin by imitation of the example of Adam. He evidently prefers to reserve the word "sin" for personal or actual sins. The tendency to sin which is derived from the first parents is universal, and freely actualized by all. There is no one who does not imitate the example of Adam.[36]

This proneness to sin, however, varies from person to person. Erasmus confesses in the *Hyperaspistae II* (1527) that in certain well-born and well-educated persons there is little proneness to evil. The tendency to sin is increased by a corrupt education and by custom. In fact, the maximum inclination to sin comes from these, not from nature.[37] For the humanist the importance of education is such that he will even go so far as to say that ". . . almost the whole corruption of morals proceeds from a corrupt education,"[38] and "From false opinions arise all of life's sins."[39]

Human nature, originally created good, is not destroyed but corrupted by the Fall. The light of nature has been obscured, yet a spark remains. Human nature has been made not entirely wicked by the Fall but imperfect or sick. Even after the Fall it has reason, by which it can know God and distinguish right from wrong, and a will, which in some things is inclined to good. There is in man both an inclination to vice and an inclination to virtue.[40]

Sin arises largely out of the weakness of the flesh[41] and ignorance. Sinning through weakness or error is a part of human nature and is therefore a universal condition.[42] It may, however, become an intended, fixed malice. A sin resulting from weakness or error will be easily forgiven, but an obstinate malice will not be forgiven.[43] He even says that a fault proceeding from weakness and error deserves mercy, but malice aforethought deserves to perish.[44] The inconstancy of the eleven early disciples is illustrative of weakness; the betrayal by the twelfth, Judas, of malevolence.[45] In the parable of the prodigal son the younger man represents the Gentiles, who sin by error and ignorance rather than by intended malice.[46] Some of the Jews who crucified Christ sinned through error.[47] Paul, in persecuting the Christians, acted not out of viciousness but ignorance.[48] The sin of the Jews in not recognizing Jesus as the Christ is excused out of ignorance and the weakness of the flesh.[49] But when the truth has been clearly revealed by the power and light of the resurrection, then he deservedly perishes who knowingly and willingly refuses to receive it.[50]

III

HERMENEUTICS*

The flesh-spirit conception which determines Erasmus' anthropology likewise shapes his interpretation of Scripture. In a number of passages in various works he links flesh and spirit, or body and soul, in man with letter and spirit in the Bible.[1] The flesh is identified with the letter or literal sense, or with the history or historical sense; the spirit, with the hidden meaning or mystery or allegory. The one is outward and crass; the other, inward and sublime. Erasmus is fond of the simile of Alcibiades, who in the *Symposium* compared Socrates to the statuettes of Silenus, the attendant of Bacchus. These statuettes appear outwardly grotesque but contain the images of the gods. Likewise, the content of Scripture, at a superficial glance, appears laughable, but upon a more penetrating study is found to be full of divine wisdom.[2]

Erasmus was of course not at all original in his contention that there is letter and spirit in the Bible just as there is flesh and spirit in man. He attaches himself to a tradition which is at least as old as Origen.[3] Actually, Origen distinguished three senses of Scripture—literal, moral, and allegorical—as corresponding to the three aspects of man—body, soul, and spirit.[4] Although Erasmus knows and makes use of Origen's tripartite division of man and also on occasion enumerates these three senses of Scripture, he does not link them, as far as I can judge. His parallels are drawn, rather, between the twofold aspects of man and Scripture.

Likewise, Jerome, another of Erasmus' favorites, emphasized that Scripture consists of letter and spirit, that we must probe behind the letter to the hidden mystery, remove the outer shell in order to eat the kernel.[5] Like Jerome, however, Erasmus increasingly gave himself to the letter of Scripture through his philological and historical studies without entirely losing interest in the allegorical meaning. In this respect both Jerome and Erasmus contrast sharply with Origen, who, though not entirely neglecting the historical sense, places the greater stress on the allegorical.[6] In the *Enchiridion* (1503) Erasmus names Origen as the interpreter who next to St. Paul best discloses the hidden meaning.[7] Later he becomes sharply critical of the wild allegorizing of Origen and demands a closer connection between history and allegory than Origen frequently observes.

I. Letter—Literary and Historical Exegesis

To discover the grammatical-historical meaning of a biblical passage, one must first apply the method of textual criticism. The original words of the author must be recovered as far as possible by the restoration of the text. It was not sufficient to rely on the Vulgate translation of Jerome. That translation itself had suffered considerable textual corruption. Besides, Jerome did not restore all things, nor could he do so. Therefore, Erasmus boldly sought to emend the text of the New Testament himself and provide a fresh translation. The result was the *Novum Testamentum* (1516), the first critical edition of the New Testament and the first Latin translation since that of Jerome.[8]

Having determined as far as possible the actual words of the text, the interpreter then uses the method of literary and historical criticism. In any given passage we should weigh "not only what is said but also by whom, to whom, with what words, at what time, on what occasion, what precedes and what follows."[9] In short, the student of Scripture must pay attention to the literary and historical context of the passage he is attempting to understand.

In order to exercise this method it is necessary for the biblical exegete to possess certain equipment. He follows Augustine in recommending a knowledge of the three sacred languages, Latin, Greek, and Hebrew, and of the "profane" disciplines such as dialectic, arithmetic, music, natural science, history, and especially grammar and rhetoric, which, as a humanist, Erasmus much prefers to dialectic. But the beginner in biblical studies must be careful not to grow old in "profane" studies. For there is the danger that when the tongue and palate have been too much infected by absinthe, whatever one eats and drinks will taste like absinthe.[10]

By textual emendation and by a knowledge of grammar the difficulties, ambiguities, obscurities, and seeming contradictions of Scripture are largely removed, but not entirely. Erasmus suggests a method of handling passages which are still obscure even after the tools of textual criticism and grammar have been applied. First of all, we should follow the example of the Fathers Origen and Augustine and collate other passages of Scripture by which the one at hand might be illuminated. Also, the sense of an obscure passage should correspond to the circle of Christian doctrine, the life of Christ, and natural equity.[11] Here we must underline the importance of Christ and natural law for Erasmus' exegesis. Christ is the center of Scripture. He is the one who permeates all Scripture and through whom all Scripture is to be interpreted.[12] Of course, for Erasmus the Christ who is the center of Scripture is primarily the one who as teacher and example is principally revealed in the Gospels, not, as with Luther, the one who as gracious redeemer is chiefly revealed in the Pauline letters. Whereas Luther virtually equated Christ with the article of justification, Erasmus in large measure, though not entirely, identifies Christ with his teaching and commandments. For Luther, Christ means essentially *Gabe;* for Erasmus, both *Gabe* and *Aufgabe,* but with the stress on the latter. A more extended discussion of Erasmus' Christology forms another chapter.

In considering the agreement of natural law with the teaching of Scripture as one of the most important arguments for the authority of Scripture, we have already hinted at the importance of natural law for Erasmus' hermeneutics. In principle, the doctrine and life of Christ and natural law are in close agreement.[13] Even though he considers the law of Christ to transcend the law of nature, he sees no essential conflict between the two. He says in the note on divorce that if something in the Gospels or the Apostolic letters seems to conflict with natural equity, we ought to notice whether it could be otherwise interpreted. The commandment of Jesus concerning no divorce except on the ground of unchastity Erasmus seeks to interpret in such a way as to conform to his own sense of justice; namely, that there are some marriages which for the good of one or both partners ought to be broken. What Christ has commanded may not be abrogated, but it may be interpreted, restricted, or relaxed for the sake of the salvation of men.[14]

Furthermore, in order to understand the meaning of a passage of Scripture, especially when it is obscure to us, we should look to the Fathers, of whom Erasmus prefers the Greeks to the Latins and the ancients to the scholastics. They are to be consulted for both the grammatical and the spiritual meaning of the passage.

In the *De libero arbitrio* (1524) Erasmus admits that Holy Scripture excels the voices of all mortals but maintains that the controversy is not concerning *Scripture,* but the *sense* of Scripture. To get at the sense of Scripture, one ought to have recourse to the ingenuity and erudition of the ancient Fathers.[15]

However, even though Erasmus often rests his interpretation upon that of the Fathers, he also exercises a certain independence of them. He insists that since they are human they can be mistaken. He criticizes them for exegeses which he regards as forced and distorted, especially where they are endeavoring to refute heretics. On this score he is critical of Ambrose, of Augustine, and even of his favorites, Origen and Jerome, to name only the ones to whom he refers most often.[16]

It would appear that for Erasmus in certain instances the principle of natural equity takes precedence over the orb of Christian doctrine as defined by the Church and the interpretation of the Fathers. At least this would seem to be true in the question of the interpretation of Jesus' and Paul's commands on divorce. Erasmus recognizes that here he stands against the whole exegetical tradition and the defined position of the Church, but he still wishes that this commandment could be interpreted in such a way as to allow divorce in the many ill-begotten marriages of his time. He brings into play a sense both of natural equity and of the relativity of Church dogma; that is, that certain things have been so defined that they can be modified according to changing times and circumstances for the sake of the salvation of men.

However, in spite of the application of the tools of grammar and the use of commentaries of the Fathers, the meaning of some passages of Scripture still remains unknown to us. The sense of Scripture, says Erasmus, is not as clear as Luther thinks. If it is, then why the great variety of interpretations among the Fathers of the Church?[17] Evidently God has not wished that we fully comprehend certain things in Scripture. In the end, in spite of the optimism of his scientific exegesis, Erasmus retains a certain reverence[18] and skepticism vis-à-vis the mystery of the Bible.

II. Spirit—Allegorical and Tropological Exegesis
Allegory

The obscurity of scriptural passages is increased by the fact that many have not only a simple, grammatical sense, but also a hidden, spiritual sense. This deeper meaning may be divided into the allegorical and the tropological, or moral.

Erasmus is aware of the fact that the scholastics distinguished four senses of Scripture: historical or grammatical, tropological, allegorical, and anagogical. However, he notes that the early Fathers acknowledged only two senses, grammatical (or literal or historical) and spiritual, which they variously designated tropology, allegory, and anagogy without making any clear distinction. Erasmus follows the Fathers in being quite inexact in his terminology. He uses the term allegory sometimes to refer to the hidden, spiritual meaning of Scripture, whether in the Old or New Testament, which is generally directed toward Christ, at other times to refer to any figure whatever.[19] He also names as allegory what is more properly tropology.[20] The allegorical sense is set over against both the literal sense (i.e., grammatical or historical sense) and the literalistic sense (i.e., taking figures literally). Like Origen and the other Fathers, Erasmus failed to recognize figures as part of the literal sense.[21]

Either necessity or usefulness dictates the movement from the letter to the spirit or allegory. We are compelled to shift from the letter to allegory whenever the words as understood literally are manifestly absurd or false or whenever they conflict with the doctrine of Christ or morality. The anthropomorphic language concerning the Deity in the Old Testament, the stories of the immoralities of Old Testament personalities, as well as certain commands of Jesus—concerning cutting off the right hand, plucking out the eye, hating father, mother, etc.—because they are manifestly absurd or in conflict with our moral sense, require allegorical interpretation.[22] Here allegory has to do with interpreting figurative expressions in a nonliteral manner and with finding a hidden meaning in stories which are morally offensive.

Allegorical interpretation is not so much necessary as very desirable when the literal sense contains no manifest absurdity but is of little or no use. For example, the stories of Eve and the serpent and of the bronze serpent hanging on the tree may be accepted as literally true, but are of little value unless we interpret them also allegorically or tropologically.[23]

Although in agreement with Augustine, Erasmus thinks that allegories may not be used to prove dogmas of faith;[24] he believes they are useful in confirming certain dogmas. For example, the allegory of the dry bones (Ezekiel 37) has as its primary meaning the regathering and renewal of the dispersed and desperate people of Israel, but it may have as its secondary meaning the resurrection.[25]

Erasmus lists as purposes of allegory: (1) to veil the mysteries from the impious; (2) to exercise the minds of the pious, since they are more avid for what is hidden and acquired with labor than for what comes to them easily; (3) to fix the divine truth in their memory through imagery;[26] (4) to lead them by degrees to perfect knowledge. As the Old Testament through types and enigmas prepared the world for the light of the gospel, so Christ gradually disclosed to his disciples the more sublime mysteries: Not immediately but by parables and wonderful deeds he prepared the minds of his disciples to believe first that he was a good man, then a prophet; to suspect soon that he was more than a prophet; and finally to acknowledge in him a power greater than man. But all these things remained as in a dream, until that fiery Holy Spirit came and awakened the dream and led into all truth.[27] The pedagogical theme is a favorite one for Erasmus. We shall find it reappearing in his understanding of the sacraments. It is closely related to the idea of accommodation which is so prominent in his thought and which is also derived from the Church Fathers, especially Origen.[28] In Holy Scripture God accommodates himself to our weakness and babbles with us as a mother stammers with her infants.[29]

> Holy Scripture has its own language by which it adapts itself to our understanding. For in it we read that God is angry, grieved, indignant, furious, that he threatens and hates, or again that he has mercy, repents, changes his mind. Expressions such as these do not mean changes take place in the nature of God, but are rather modes of speech appropriate for our weakness and stupidity.[30]

Relation Between Historical and Allegorical Exegesis

In the *Enchiridion* (1503) Erasmus placed so much emphasis upon a spiritualistic, allegorical exegesis, upon the words of Jesus in John, "The flesh is of no use at all, it is the spirit which makes alive,"[31] that he neglected the literal or grammatical sense. However, apparently as a result of his increasing preoccupation with philological studies, he gained a new appreciation of the historical sense and, as is already evident in the 1515 preface to the *Novum Instrumentum*, asserted that the lowest

sense is not to be scorned, since it is the foundation upon which
the mystical meaning is built.[32] In his later writings he insists
upon the exact weighing of the historical sense before proceeding to allegory, upon no conflict between the allegory and the
literal sense, upon not rejecting the historical sense except in
case of necessity.[33]

Erasmus does not think all history can be rendered allegorically. "It is sufficient to pull out those matters which more expressly reflect the type of truth."[34] However, he somewhat
vitiates his insistence upon the grammatical sense as the anchor
for correct allegorical exegesis by permitting the exegete to
depart from the actual sense, provided his interpretation is
pious and in agreement with other passages of Scripture. Still,
it is best not to depart from the germane sense.[35] While allowing the interpreter some freedom, Erasmus puts the stress on
prudence, restraint, and simplicity in allegorical exegesis.

In the *Ecclesiastae* (1535) Erasmus is interested in finding a
middle way between literalism and wild allegorization.

> As those verge on Judaism who exclude tropes and allegories
> from the Scriptures and make the law which Paul says is
> spiritual carnal, so those subvert the foundation of Scripture
> who reject the lowest sense when there is no necessity to do
> so.[36]

While in the *Enchiridion* (1503) Erasmus praises without
qualification Origen as the prince of allegorical interpretation,
in the *Ratio* (1519) he continues to set forth the Alexandrian
Father as a model of allegorical exegesis but points out that
Jerome sometimes slapped at him for doing violence to Scripture.[37] In an addition of 1523 to the latter work he qualifies his
earlier approval of the Father's allegorization with a more explicit criticism of his distortions of the historical sense.[38] In the
Ecclesiastae he continues to accuse Origen of having often de-
parted from the letter too freely, but partly excuses him because
of the times in which he lived. In order to commend the books
of the Old Testament to the Greeks, it was necessary for him
to resort to allegory.[39] Those critics are therefore in error who
think that Erasmus in his exegetical method simply returned to

Origenistic spiritualism[40] or even went beyond Origen in his scorn for the flesh of Scripture.[41]

Tropology

Though Erasmus is not always clear, he usually distinguishes two spiritual senses, allegory and tropology, following the Fathers, especially Origen.[42] For Erasmus the moralist the tropological is the most important of the senses. The chief end of exegesis is to be seized and transformed by what you learn. Indeed, the moral sense is so prominent that concern for it causes him to allow an exception to one of his cardinal principles of exegesis, correspondence to the grammatical-historical sense of the passage.

> He departs from the actual sense of Scripture with no danger to his salvation, provided what is received agrees with piety and truth: it is not an insignificant benefit of our study if what we interpret, though it is of no value for the present passage, is of value for the good life, provided it agrees with the remaining passages of Scripture.[43]

The importance of the tropological is further underlined by the weight he gives it in his exegesis of the Psalms. He does not neglect the allegorical, i.e., Christological and ecclesiological, exposition of the Psalms, but the moral interpretation is dominant.[44]

Not only is the tropological sense the most important, but it is the clearest and the easiest to understand. The tropological is more closely connected with the historical sense and is therefore less arbitrary, less dependent on the imagination of the exegete than is the allegorical.[45] At the end of his commentary of Psalm 2, Erasmus states that the treatment of the allegorical or Christological is very difficult, but once the application of the passage to Christ has been determined, it is no great labor to relate it to those who are members of his body.[46] Finally, although not all passages of Scripture can be allegorized, any passage can be accommodated to tropology.[47] Because Scripture contains not only the letter but also allegory and tropology, the exegete must approach it not only with the tools of literary and historical criticism but also with purged emotions, a clean heart, and supreme purity of mind.[48] The attitude of the exegete is an important prerequisite to the understanding of Scripture. It is necessary to be spiritual in order to judge concerning spiritual Scripture.[49] Therefore, from first to last Erasmus holds to the necessity of a "mystical" and ethical as well as a philological understanding of Scripture. The emphasis here is, however, relatively more upon the ethical than upon the "mystical."[50]

As those critics are in error who think Erasmus went beyond Origen in his scorn for the letter of Scripture, so likewise do other critics err who neglect the spiritualistic, allegorical, and moral side of Erasmus' exegesis and emphasize entirely the philological, rational, and historical element.[51] The mature Erasmus (from the preface to the *Novum Instrumentum* [1515] to the *Ecclesiastae* [1535]) seeks to strike a compromise between an overly literal and an overly spiritual interpretation of Scripture. He combines in an uneasy balance the Jeromian philological, historical traditions and the Origenistic Platonizing, spiritualistic traditions of biblical exegesis.

We shall notice later a parallel tension and a parallel change of emphasis on the relation between flesh and spirit within his sacramental thought.

IV

CHRISTOLOGY

I. Flesh and Spirit in Christ

The principle of flesh and spirit operates in Erasmus' Christology just as in his understanding of Scripture. In fact, he makes explicit the connection between incarnation and Scripture. In Christ the humanity hides the divinity, just as in Scripture the historical sense hides a deeper, spiritual meaning. Furthermore, in each case the outward appearance is contemptible, absurd. As Erasmus states it in the 1515 preface to the *Annotationes*:

> He who wonders why that divine spirit wished to hide his riches in these masks [i.e., syllables and letters] may wonder why the eternal wisdom assumed the form of a poor, humble, contemptible, and condemned man.[1]

In the *Sileni Alcibiadis* (1515), he applies the simile of Silenus not only to Scripture but also to Christ. Like Silenus, Christ has the appearance of weakness, poverty, and ignominy, but when seen by those whose eyes have been opened, he is observed to possess power, riches, and glory.[2] In the case of both Scripture and Christ the divine purpose is at work to cause us to look with spiritual eyes beyond the outward to the inward, beyond the physical to the spiritual. The Jews discern only the letter of Scripture as they discerned only the flesh of Christ.[3]

There is undeniably a certain tendency of Erasmus toward a spiritualistic understanding of Christ. His spiritualism is again most apparent in the *Enchiridion* (1503). There he states:

"The physical presence of Christ is useless for salvation," and even, "Assuredly the flesh of Christ was an obstacle."[4] The relative importance of the spiritual over the physical presence of Christ is indicated for Erasmus by the statement of Jesus to his disciples in the fourth Gospel, "Unless I go away, the Comforter will not come. It is best for you that I go,"[5] and by Paul's indifference to a knowledge of Christ in the flesh as manifest in the words, "Even if we have known Christ in the flesh, we know him no longer."[6] A similar emphasis on the value of Christ's withdrawal of his body is evident also in later writings such as the *Paraphrasis in evangelium Ioannis* (1523)[7] and the one at his life's end, the *Ecclesiastae* (1535).[8] In two of his introductory writings to the New Testament he maintained that Christ is present more effectively in the Gospels and Epistles than when he walked among men.[9] The stress on the inward and spiritual as over against the outward and physical is revealed in this statement from one of the annotations: "Christ is not divided; he is not a corporeal object. Christ is wherever there are feelings worthy of Christ."[10]

In spite of this tendency toward spiritualism the historical reality of the incarnation is by no means undercut. As we shall notice, Erasmus was far from being a docetist. The full humanity of Christ is a frequent subject of his writings. Without denying the physical reality of the incarnation, Erasmus means to insist upon the inner appropriation of the spiritual content.

Here the important theme of accommodation once more appears. Like the letter of Scripture and the flesh of the sacraments, the flesh of Christ is primarily an accommodation to our weakness. The bodily appearance of the Lord is the temporary adaptation to our weakness and stupidity, by which he leads us gradually to a stronger, more perfect spiritual faith.[11] Just as we move from love of the body to love of the spirit, so the association with the human nature is an enticement to draw us to a love of the Lord Jesus and from there to a love of the divine power.[12] Christ subjected himself to our bodily infirmity that he might raise us to his heavenly, spiritual sublimity.[13]

II. The Person of Christ

Deity

As we have already observed, Erasmus opposes speculation concerning the nature of Christ. More important is an inner, moral appropriation of Christ's life and work. Nevertheless, his writings reveal a theological understanding of Christ's person. He seems fully to accept the Nicene and Chalcedonian declarations concerning Christ's deity and humanity, but regrets the necessity of these creedal formulations.

However, he made some statements which caused a number of persons to question his orthodoxy concerning the deity of Christ. We recall that he pointed out the reticence of the Apostles and the Fathers to elaborate on the deity of Christ. In a number of passages he says that the word "God" is infrequently applied to Christ in Scripture; more often do we find the word "Lord."[14] Not only did the Apostles at first shrink from openly speaking of Christ as God, but even Jesus himself urged silence about his divine nature to avoid offending certain ones or to reserve such knowledge for its own time.[15] Here Erasmus' idea of a gradual revelation is again apparent: "God wished to become known to the world by degrees."[16]

The suspicions of the orthodox were especially aroused when Erasmus questioned the propriety of interpreting so many biblical passages as proofs of Christ's deity against the Arians. One of the more famous passages used to prove the Trinity and Christ's deity was I John 5:7: "For there are three who bear witness in heaven, Father, Word, and Holy Spirit: and these three are one." Erasmus did not come upon this verse in any Greek manuscript, nor did he find it quoted by any Greek Father or by Augustine.[17] He therefore omitted it in his 1519 edition of the New Testament. Roundly denounced by Lee, he said he would restore the reading if a single Greek manuscript could be discovered to support it.[18] Such a manuscript was brought forth, the Codex Montfortianus of Trinity College, Dublin,[19] and Erasmus restored the verse in his 1522 edition, "lest there be occasion for calumny."[20] But Erasmus continued to insist that, even if the text were authentic, it would not overthrow the Arians because it asserted only that the Father, Word, and Holy Spirit were one, not that they were of the same substance. One need not refer to substance, but merely to "a concord and mutual charity."[21]

Another important but much disputed text was Romans 9:5: ". . . and of their race according to the flesh is the Christ. God who is over all be blessed forever . . ." or "Christ, who is God over all, blessed forever." The Greek permits either reading.[22] It is a question of the punctuation. Erasmus prefers the former because he thinks it is more in keeping with the Pauline usage. Paul is accustomed to apply the word "God" to the Father only. Besides, the first reading is closer to the form of other Pauline doxologies such as II Corinthians 11:36. In any case, because of the uncertainty of the reading, it is not an effective weapon against the Arians. However, both his translation and his paraphrase betray his succumbing to the orthodox point of view.

Likewise, he does not regard Philippians 2:6 as a decisive text against the Arians. In the first place, the Arians did not deny that Christ was God; indeed, they thought that he was a great God blessed above all, but that the Father was in some special manner to be called God. In the second place, the Apostle did not so much intend to speak here about Christ's nature as to afford an example of modesty and humility.[23]

Similarly, Isaiah 7:14 (Matt. 1:23) is not an appropriate text for defeating the Arians. Here is an illustration of an allegory whose interpretation depends on the historical sense. The historical sense of Isaiah 7:14, as pointed out by Jerome, says Erasmus, is that "God with us" refers not to God's *nature* but to his *favor.* Consequently, the allegory which understands Jesus Christ as "God with us" has to do not with Christ's nature as God, but with Christ as a manifestation of God's favor toward men.[24]

In spite of Erasmus' skeptical judgment concerning the number of texts which openly demonstrate Christ's deity, it is nevertheless clear that Erasmus thought there were enough passages from which one could correctly deduce that doctrine.

The statement of the disciple Thomas, "My Lord and my God,"[25] was the one passage in which the evangelist plainly declares that Christ was God. Yet Erasmus thinks that there are other passages where it is clear to "pious minds" that Christ was God.[26] One of these, he says, is surely John 1:1, "the Word was God." Erasmus holds that this passage does not explicitly teach that Christ was God although that is a rightly reasoned judgment on the basis of the text and its context. One has to connect "the Word" with "Christ." Even after establishing from either direct or indirect New Testament evidence that Christ was God, however, one must use a process of reasoning in order to come to the orthodox faith of Christ as one of substance with the Father, for the word ὁμοούσιος is not to be found in the New Testament.[27]

Although Erasmus was often accused of Arianism, it is my judgment that the accusation was unjust. In his reply to the Spanish monks he lists a whole host of passages in his writings where he claims to teach the orthodox view.[28] After reading this list one can hardly maintain that Erasmus was Arian in his Christology. His criticism of favorite proof texts, as well as his occasionally vague and hyperbolic language, left him open to false charges on this score.

His view can more accurately be labeled Origenistic than Arian. There is a definite strand of subordinationism in his Christology.[29] Repeatedly he asserts that the Father is the one absolute *principium,* although he does not wish to exclude the Son from being in some sense also *principium.* In commenting on I Timothy 1:17, Erasmus asks, ". . . why could not the Father alone in some manner be called God, from whom the Son derives his deity?"[30] In the annotation on Colossians 1:15, he holds that the Father alone is called invisible since the Son receives his invisible nature from the Father.[31] Elsewhere he states: ". . . Father of lights, from whom every good proceeds to all, from whom Christ even according to his higher nature has his origin without detriment to his equality . . ."[32] Finally, in his last great work he retains the same sentiment. The Father is the only true God in the sense that he alone is the fount of

Deity.[33] Thus the Son is of the same nature with the Father, but because he receives his being from the Father, he is subordinate or subject to the Father. With Origen Erasmus emphasized the Johannine description of the λόγος as θεός not ὁ θεός.[34]

Humanity

Even more strongly does Erasmus teach the full humanity of Christ. His judgments on this subject remain constant from his earliest to his latest writing. His close study of the New Testament led him consistently to describe Jesus as a fully human being who hungered, thirsted, became weary, suffered mental and physical torment, and died the lowliest of men as a criminal and in one sense a sinner because all the sins of the world were heaped upon him.[35]

Early in his career he entered into debate with two humanist friends on the question of the humanity of Christ, John Colet and Jacques Lefèvre. It is interesting that Erasmus is the only one of these three humanists who does not allow his exegesis to shrink from the implications of the concrete humanity of Jesus.

The dispute with Colet was a friendly affair. It originated in a conversation at Oxford concerning the reasons for Christ's agony in the Garden of Gethsemane. Erasmus held the view that Christ's anguish resulted from his anticipation as a human being of the sufferings that were before him. Colet, on the other hand, accepted the opinion of Jerome that Christ was in torment over the guilt of the Jews. After being urged by Colet to reflect further on this matter, Erasmus set forth his arguments in the form of a letter and sent it to Colet. Erasmus expanded his letter into a treatise for publication, *Disputatiuncula de taedio, pavore, tristitia Iesu, instante supplicio crucis,* etc. (1503). Erasmus reveals his willingness to ascribe genuine weariness and fear of death to Christ in the Garden. These point to his fully human nature and to his love for us. "As he suffered his own death, not ours, for our sake, not his, he dreaded his own death not for himself, but for us."[36] Furthermore, in fearing death, yet overcoming this fear and death, he prepared for us an example of

patience, gentleness, and obedience which we not only admire,
but love and emulate.

The altercation with Lefèvre was much more heated and
bitter. It resulted in the temporary alienation of the two humanists. The issue had to do with the correct translation and interpretation of Hebrews 2:7. Lefèvre had translated the text
minuisti eum paulo minus a Deo, resting his translation and interpretation on the Hebrew text of Psalm 8 and the interpretation
of Jerome. His translation thus elevates Christ's dignity. Erasmus prefers the translation *Fecisti eum paulisper inferiorem angelis.*
With St. Thomas, says Erasmus, he believes the verse refers to
Christ's human nature. However, in contrast with Thomas, who
thought that Christ was inferior to the angels not according to
the soul but only according to the body, Erasmus is willing to
allow the verse to refer to Christ's whole humanity, soul and
body, which was lower than the angels.[37] Erasmus notes that the
Hebrew word *Elohim* is subject to various meanings—God,
Gods, angels, even men worthy of admiration—so that Lefè-
vre's arguments here are not decisive. "$\beta\rho\alpha\chi\acute{v}$ $\tau\iota$" is here best
interpreted as an adverb of duration, not of dignity. The impor-
tance of Erasmus' interpretation as far as we are concerned is
that again he insists upon the full humanity of Christ. Indeed,
he suggests that Christ descended not only below the angels but
below the most abject of men insofar as he took upon himself
more affliction than any man has ever suffered or ever will
suffer. He gladly applies to Christ Psalm 22:6: "But I am a worm,
and no man."[38] He interprets this passage in Hebrews along the
lines of the kenosis of Philippians 2. Erasmus thinks that the
divine humiliation refers not simply to the assumption of human nature, but to the abuses Christ took upon himself, to his
suffering and crucifixion as a sinner and criminal.

However much Erasmus may have stressed Christ's full participation in man's calamities, he did not wish to threaten his
sinlessness. In his note on II Corinthians 5:21 Erasmus wonders why the French humanist is so concerned that someone
might understand the passage as implying that Christ sinned,
for the text plainly states that God made Christ not a sinner but

sin; i.e., "He wished him to suffer punishment just as if he had sinned in every way although he alone had not at all sinned."[39]

Elsewhere, Erasmus expresses the conviction that Christ alone is free of all sin,[40] "the fount of all innocence and light."[41] In one of the apologies Erasmus explains what he means by the phrase "touched by no stain of sin": ". . . I embrace [with these words] whatever in any manner has any affinity with sin, human sluggishness, error, any petty human feeling, ignorance, and an imperfect love of God."[42] We have already observed in Erasmus' anthropology the connection of sin with error and ignorance. It is not surprising that for him Christ must be free of these in order to be sinless. However, that Christ was wholly without ignorance does not square well with Erasmus' understanding of Matthew 24:36 (Mark 13:32). In his comment on this passage in the *Novum Testamentum* (1519), Erasmus notes that the reading "nor the Son" is not present in the Greek manuscript available to him, but that, according to Jerome, it is contained in some Latin codices, and that Origen retains it.[43] Erasmus indicates his suspicion that the phrase was removed in order not to give the Arians an opportunity to confirm their opinion that the Son was inferior to the Father. It is interesting that in spite of his translation which leaves out this phrase, he includes the words "neither did the Son of man know" in his paraphrase.[44] Thus, Erasmus seems to have been fully aware of one instance of Christ's ignorance though he does not reveal it in his reply to Beda.

There he is interested in elevating the perfection of Christ in such a way that it becomes more difficult for any other human being also to be called pure or perfect. The point at issue is the immaculate conception of Mary, which Beda evidently accuses Erasmus of undermining by the phrase "Christ alone touched by no stain of sin." That there was a hidden polemic against Mary in this phrase, the like of which was so frequent in Erasmus' works, seems probable in spite of his disclaimers.[45] The humanist had no liking for the extreme elevation of Mary. He did not think the doctrine of the immaculate conception could be grounded in Scripture and did not believe that the Church had clearly spoken on the subject in spite of the Council of Basel, whose authority he called into doubt.

In the *Ratio verae theologiae* (1519) Erasmus enumerates instances of biblical evidence for Christ's innocence. He points first to Christ's birth and upbringing by righteous parents (Erasmus' interest in Christian nurture is apparent); then to the many witnesses of his innocence: the angels, the Magi, the shepherds, John the Baptist, Martha, the disciples, Pilate, Caiaphas, the centurion, even the betrayer himself. Again Erasmus displays an inclination to tie doctrinal statements down to the concrete facts of biblical revelation.

Erasmus repudiates any discussion of the manner of the union of the human and divine in Christ, but the way in which he affirms that relation is clearly along Antiochian lines. The emphasis is ever upon the distinction of the two natures.[46] "In Jesus there were two very different things, divine majesty, than which nothing is more sublime, and human weakness, than which nothing is more abject."[47] Elsewhere he expresses wonder that in view of the contrast between the two natures, they could be so united as to become one person.[48]

The debate with Lefèvre is instructive on the question of the relation between the two natures. It has to do not simply with a differing exegesis but with a different Christological apprehension. The French humanist accuses Erasmus of breaking asunder the unity of the hypostasis of Christ when he applies Hebrews 2:7 to the human nature alone.[49] Lefèvre wants to understand the passage as referring to the one Christ who as the Lord, Word, and Son of God is equal and even identical with God, but who in the incarnation, without ceasing to be God, assumed a humanity which was crowned with glory and honor so that even as incarnate he was only a little less than God. His emphasis is so much upon the unity and the dignity of the person of Christ that he threatens to undercut his full humanity. He rejects as impious Erasmus' statements concerning Christ as below the meanest of men, as a worm and no man from Psalm 8, and as having no proportionality with divinity.[50]

Erasmus, while affirming the unity of the two natures and

even recognizing the *communicatio idiomatum* on the basis of this unity, places the greater stress on the distinction of the two natures and the genuine humanity of Christ. Erasmus disagrees with Lefèvre's contention that the term "son of man" denotes only the one hypostasis of Christ. He has little trouble in showing that traditionally the term refers to the humanity of Christ. He also takes issue with Lefèvre's understanding of the term "Jesus Christ" as denoting him only as Lord and Son of God. Rather, Erasmus says, the name can be applied to both natures, the human and the divine. Erasmus asks the Frenchman, "If Jesus Christ is only Lord and Son of God, how can he be understood to have been diminished?"[51] Erasmus holds that, as Lord and Son of God, Christ is equal to God, but as Son of Man he is far below God, indeed in one sense the lowliest of men because he took upon himself the ills of all men. Likewise, Erasmus, enlisting the support of the Fathers, argues that it is appropriate to call Christ a creature because of his assumed nature. Again, he asks Lefèvre, How can Christ even be said to be less than God, if he is not a creature? And if Christ can be called a creature, can it be regarded as impious to say that Christ according to the assumed nature has no proportion to divinity?[52] There is little question but that Erasmus had won the debate. Lefèvre didn't bother to make a rejoinder.

The Antiochian ring of Erasmus' Christology is confirmed by other passages in his writings. He likes to set the evidences of the human and divine natures side by side, as in this passage:

> The signs of the human nature are that he is conceived in a female womb; of the divine nature, that he is conceived by the Holy Spirit; of the human nature, that he is born of a pregnant woman at the appointed time; of the divine nature, that he is born without masculine agency. He is shown to be a true man by the fact that he is continually called a son of Adam, that he grows up in the customary manner of his day, that he sleeps, eats, hungers, thirsts, becomes weary from a journey, has human affections . . . On the other hand, the divine appeared in the performing of so many miracles, for he preferred to declare it by deeds rather than by words. Yet by words also he testifies that he is the Son of God sent from heaven, that he both was

in heaven and is in heaven although he walks on earth . . .
Finally, when he arises from the dead, he is carried away to
heaven, then sends the Paraclete, which suddenly renews the
Apostles.[53]

We can thus summarize Erasmus' position on the person of
Christ: Though he clearly asserted Christ's deity, he moved in
the direction of a subordinationism. More emphatically did he
maintain the full humanity of Christ. Indeed, his expressions on
this subject were so strong that he offended even some of his
friends, who felt he detracted from the dignity of Christ.
Though Erasmus held to the indissoluble union of the two
natures and mentioned the possibility of the *communicatio idiomatum* on the basis of this union, he always placed greater
stress on their distinction and gave little or no consideration to
the manner of their unity. Furthermore, even in his parallel
exposition of the two natures, the weight is heavier on the
humanity, which he delights in illustrating with specific, historical detail.[54] But whether of Christ's divinity or his humanity,
Erasmus chooses to speak not abstractly but concretely. In his
close attention to the facts of revelation, as Bouyer suggests,
Erasmus may have made an important contribution to theology.[55]

III. Work of Christ

Christ as Redeemer

Many critics have insisted that for Erasmus the work of
Christ as redeemer is absent or at least very much in the background. His conception of Christ is strictly that of a moralist
and rationalist, they say; Christ is almost exclusively understood as teacher and example.[56] The research of the present
writer has led him to the conclusion that though Erasmus does
place the strongest emphasis upon Christ's work as teacher and
example, he does not neglect Christ's reconciling and redeem-
ing work as much as these critics contend. Erasmus was indeed
a moralist and understood Christ along moralistic lines. However, he was not only a moralist; he was also a Catholic Christian

who knew how to speak about Christ as redeemer.

Erasmus sets forth no elaborate theory of the atonement. He speculates no more on the work than on the person of Christ. He merely states quite briefly the fact of the redemptive act in such passages as these: "God himself put on manhood and reconciled men to God by his death."[57] ". . . he wants to possess alone and entirely that which he has redeemed by his blood."[58] "[Christ] freed mankind from the tyranny of sin and death."[59] "Grace comes through the Son who redeemed us undeserving ones by his death."[60]

Though Erasmus seldom elaborates on the meaning of Christ's atonement, it seems clear that his thought is closer to the classical and Abelardian views than the Anselmian. That there are strains of the classical theme of conflict and victory in Erasmus' writings is not strange in the light of his reading and appreciation of the Greek Fathers, especially Origen.[61] Also, since he conceives of the Christian life primarily as a battle with the enemies of flesh, world, and the devil, it is not surprising that he understands Christ's work in terms of struggle and triumph. He frequently refers to Christ's work as conquering the powers, or freeing us from the tyranny, of sin, flesh, world, death, and Satan. In his paraphrase of the temptation story in Luke he even makes use of the ancient imagery of the bait: "The weakness of the human body is offered as bait, by which the temptor is caught in the net of divine power."[62]

The Abelardian motif is manifest in Erasmus' discussion of the response of love evoked by Christ's person and work. This responding love is elicited not only by Christ's death but by his whole life, by the many beneficent deeds he wrought for us, by his being a man familiar to us.[63] We love more strongly what is known and related to us—that is, according to the proverb, "like joined to like."[64]

Whether classical or Abelardian, the stress is ever upon the manward side of the atonement rather than on the Anselmian Godward side. There is occasional mention of Christ as a sacrifice for our sins or as paying the punishment for our sins,[65] but these thoughts are very much in the background. Because

Erasmus is little aware of the tension between God's love and his wrath, his mercy and his justice, he does not feel the need of Christ as an expiation or satisfaction for our sins.[66]

Consonant with the heavy stress on the love of God as manifested in Christ's life and death is Erasmus' emphasis upon the universality of Christ's saving work. "He is the savior of all, he excludes no one from salvation, he offers the evangelical light to all. Whoever rejects it . . . may impute the blindness to himself; whoever perishes, perishes by his own fault."[67] The theme of universal salvation is understandably a favorite one for the humanist, who wished to include the ancient virtuous pagans in his catalogue of saints.

Christ as Teacher and Example

Though the texts show that Erasmus does not regard Christ exclusively as teacher and example, it must be conceded that the humanist's chief interest is in this aspect of Christ's work. In his exposition of the Apostles' Creed, Erasmus sets forth a twofold purpose of the incarnation:

> Christ came into the world not only to redeem the world but to teach us with perfect authority and to set us on fire by divine arguments with love of the heavenly life.[68]

Erasmus' zeal for the second of these purposes led him sometimes to express himself less circumspectly. Commenting on the first of the Beatitudes in Luke he states:

> Here that heavenly teacher disclosed his secret philosophy, and so that he might communicate it to his own, he descended from heaven to earth.[69]

That Erasmus intended to limit the purpose of the incarnation to the communication and exemplification of the heavenly philosophy is, however, extremely doubtful. To Luther, who accused him of doing so, in an appendix[70] to an edition of the *Novum Testamentum,* Erasmus answered that he was not speaking of the whole Christ when he said that Christ was sent to teach us more fully the will of the Father and to provide us with an absolute example.[71] When Erasmus considers the subject more carefully, he holds together the twofold purpose of the incarnation. Nevertheless, the weight is assuredly on Christ as teacher and example.

Christ as *Doctor*

The importance of Christ as teacher for the humanist is apparent in the *Enchiridion* (1503), where in a moment of unguarded enthusiasm he simply identified Christ with whatever he taught.[72] This famous utterance must not be allowed to stand alone as a description of the meaning of Christ for Erasmus, but it does serve to show his major interest—at least in the *Enchiridion,* if not retained, as I think in large measure it was, throughout his life.

Christ is repeatedly and variously called *coelestis doctor, coelestis philosophiae doctor, optimus doctor,* or *unicus doctor.* By these terms Erasmus wants to stress the unique, supernatural origin of Christ's teaching. He insists on the difference between Christ's doctrine and that of the philosophers. Of course, he also spoke of the similarity between Christ's teaching and that of certain philosophers. When he sharply contrasts the two, he has in mind, as we have observed, principally metaphysics. Christ did not indulge in complicated speculation or sophistical debate, but taught simply and purely the precepts of right living. When, on the other hand, he compares the two more favorably, he has in mind some of the ethical doctrines of the philosophers. Even here, however, the humanist wished to be discriminating. He does not want to include all of their ethical instruction, but only that portion which agrees with the doctrine of Christ.[73]

The uniqueness of Christ for Erasmus further stems from the fact that Christ is the unique author of salvation who alone teaches salutary things. Thus, even in the *Paraclesis* (1516), where Erasmus intends to stress Christ's role as teacher and example, he does not separate it from his role as redeemer. Finally, the uniqueness of this teacher is confirmed by the fact that he alone accomplishes what he teaches.[74]

If "from false opinions all the sins of life arise,"[75] then knowledge is necessary to live righteously, specifically knowledge of Christ's teaching. As Erasmus says in the *Enchiridion,* the most important weapons of Christian warfare are prayer and knowledge, and in the *Paraclesis*: "The first thing is to know what he [Christ] taught; the second to accomplish it."[76]

Because Erasmus stresses Christ's role as teacher, characterizes his teaching as the *philosophia Christi,* and emphasizes the necessity of knowledge of this philosophy for right living, one could gain the impression that Erasmus is a thoroughgoing rationalist. But such is not the case. Not only does Erasmus discuss Christ's work as redeemer, even closely associating the roles of author of salvation and teacher, and point to the unique, supernatural origin of his teaching, but also he suggests that the very content of the *philosophia Christi* is the message of the rebirth[77] and that this doctrine has to do not so much with the mind as with the heart.

Christ as *Exemplum*

Closely associated with the description of Christ as teacher is that of him as example. Indeed, his teaching is authoritative in part because he alone performs what he teaches. There is the closest possible correspondence between his teaching and his life. Christ is the absolute example who provides us with the true pattern or norm of right living.[78] Especially in the *Paraphrases* Erasmus repeatedly points to Christ's actions as designed to provide us with an example. In the story of the temptation Christ conquers the devil to show us that he can be conquered and teaches us the method of doing so.[79] Jesus healed the woman with the flow of blood, "not that he might claim praise for himself before men, but that by this example he might teach all men how powerful is a firm trust."[80] The Lord's leaving Capernaum after performing miracles there shows us by a simple example that we ought to depart after performing good deeds lest we seem to expect a reward.[81] Noting that, according to Mark 2:2, Jesus preached before healing the sick, Erasmus says that Jesus by his example demonstrated what is the more important part of man.[82]

Modesty, humility, patient endurance, simplicity, gentle-

ness, leniency, love, and prudence are the chief traits which
Christ exemplifies and which we are to emulate. Christ shows
his humility and modesty by taking the form of the servant, by
performing miracles not to call attention to himself but for the
salvation of men, by not speaking openly of himself as divine,
by riding into Jerusalem on an ass, by washing the feet of his
disciples, and finally by allowing himself to be crucified between
two thieves. The cross is exemplary also of his absolute long-
suffering or endurance (*tolerantia*). Christ constantly manifests
simplicity, which is for Erasmus always opposed to what is complicated or encumbering, whether related to intellectual speculation or ceremony. He demands only a simple faith, free of
complex ideas, and a love free of burdensome laws.[83] Perhaps,
however, the traits which most stand out in Erasmus' portrait
of Christ are his gentleness, leniency, amiability, mildness; in
short, his love,[84] although he seemed to prefer to describe that
love in the preceding terms. A thought dear to the peace-loving
Erasmus was that Christ conquered not by force but by gentleness. The picture of Christ which here emerges is a rather
sentimental one not at all unlike some nineteenth-century lives
of Jesus.[85]

Closely associated with love and gentleness is another characteristic of Christ—prudence. Out of love and prudence Christ
conducts himself differently toward different men and accommodates himself to their weakness that he might draw them to
himself. Christ accommodated himself to his disciples, speaking to them in parables, tolerating their infirmity until they were
capable of higher things. "So that he might heal sinners, he
walked on friendly terms among them. So that he might draw
the Jews, he was circumcised, purified, and baptized; observed
the Sabbath, was baptized, and fasted."[86]

Christ as *Imperator*

Another most significant appellation given to Christ by
Erasmus was that of *imperator,* or the very similar *dux, princeps,*
or *caput.* This designation of Christ is a favorite one for Erasmus. From the early *Enchiridion militis Christiani* (1503) to the

late *De praeparatione ad mortem* (1534), a recurring theme of his writing is the battle of the Christian soldier under the banner of Christ, his commander. Under this rubric the two major roles of Christ as redeemer and as teacher-example come together. As our commander-redeemer Christ conquered the enemies of devil, flesh, and world for us; he hands them over to us with their power broken, so that with his aid and by our endeavor, we may likewise conquer, or rather he may continue to conquer in us.[87] As our leader he is also our teacher and example inasmuch as he showed us the method of conquering which we are urged to imitate.[88] The weight here is, however, less upon the once-and-for-all event than upon the continuing process. Christ's role as commander has thus less to do with his work in the past as redeemer than with his work in the present as helper and example.[89]

This theme of struggle under the standard of Christ will occupy us again in the next chapter on Erasmus' soteriology and in the later discussion of Erasmus' understanding of baptism, for it is in baptism that we enlist in the service of Christ, our commander.

V

SOTERIOLOGY

To comprehend Erasmus' thought on the sacraments, it is necessary to have some understanding of his doctrine of redemption. His thoughts on baptism, penance, and the Eucharist all presuppose his ideas on grace and free will, justification and sanctification, and the nature of the Christian life in general. His sacramental ideas function within the context of his soteriology as a whole.

I. Law and Gospel

The starting point for an understanding of Erasmus' doctrine of redemption is an awareness of his view on the relation between the law and the gospel. Erasmus distinguishes a threefold law: a law of nature, a law of works, and a law of faith. The law of nature was the law planted in the hearts of men at creation by which it was possible for some of the philosophers to know what was right conduct, so that they could teach many things which were congruent with the philosophy of Christ.[1] This law, however, was gradually obscured by the sins of men.[2]

The law of works identified with the law of Moses refers first of all for Erasmus to ceremonies. He constantly reiterates the view that with the coming of Christ this crasser part of the law has been abrogated, at least according to the letter. Ceremonies are mere shadows, images, types of the light, reality, and truth to come, so that when the light is revealed, the shadows recede. According to the mystical sense, however, they may be viewed as prefiguring Christ so that in substance but not in form they still remain in effect.[3] Understandably, however, his stress is upon the abrogation of these aspects of the law in view of his animus against the multitude of encumbering ecclesiastical rites.

Also abolished with the advent of Christ, at least for the pious, was the law of Moses insofar as it held man's nature in check by threatening punishment. The principle of equity expressed in the judicial commands of the Old Testament is retained, though not necessarily in the form in which it was expressed in the time of the Old Testament, for the form of its expression varies with the times.[4] Even the gospel does not conflict with this principle. We recall that in the important note on divorce Erasmus states that when something in the Gospels or Apostolic letters seems to conflict with natural equity, we ought to try to discover whether it could be otherwise interpreted.

However, the moral precepts of the law which are summarized in the commandment to love God and the neighbor are not removed, but are rendered clearer and more perfect by the gospel.[5]

The familiar contrast between flesh and spirit emerges once more here. Erasmus distinguishes two aspects in the one law: one, physical; the other, spiritual; just as in the one man there are two aspects.[6] Under the physical aspect of the law he includes most often that part dealing with ceremonies, but also sometimes the part which deters man from wrongdoing by threatening punishment. He also suggests that the flesh or letter of the law refers to the written commandment which is observed only externally by rote. The spirit of the law has to do with the inward appropriation of the commandment in love. By the spiritual aspect he also means the commands concerning morals and piety which find their fulfillment in Christ.[7]

When Erasmus has in mind the physical part of the law, he draws the sharpest contrast between law and gospel. They may be contrasted as shadow and light, figure and reality, letter and spirit, visible and invisible, earthly and heavenly, antiquated and new, temporary and eternal, fear of punishment and love of God, and slavery and freedom.[8]

On the other hand, the Mosaic law spiritually interpreted is the same as the law of Christ. The sum and substance of both is perfect love of God and neighbor. The only difference between the law of works and the law of faith or of the gospel is that, while both make the same demands, those of the law of works are made without grace, whereas those of the law of faith are mild because grace is added.[9] The distinction between law and gospel at this point is rather hazy. The gospel appears as both the norm, *norma recte vivendi,*[10] and the demand to fulfill this norm, as well as the gift which makes the norm not only possible but easy to fulfill. From the Lutheran point of view what is absent in Erasmus is a sense of the impossibility of the demand (Erasmus understands the Great Commandment as hyperbole[11]) as well as of the sheer gift quality of the gospel. For Luther the gospel, at least in its primary office, does not come as demand at all but as the gracious message that the law has been fulfilled for us by Jesus Christ.[12]

According to Erasmus the gospel is not only the renewer and perfecter of the old law of Moses, but also the renewer and perfecter of nature. One of the favorite themes of the humanist, which he announced in the introductory writings to the New Testament, is that of the gospel as the restoration of nature, originally created good.

The purposes of the law are several. First, to convict us of our sin and awaken desperation in us so that we cease to rely on ourselves and embrace more readily the remedy of divine grace. Second, to restrain sins by threats of punishment and promises of reward.[13] In this capacity the law acts as bridle and spur. However, the purpose of the law here is not wholly negative but positive insofar as it causes a man to sin more lightly and be better prepared for the gospel.[14] Neither the law of nature nor the law of Moses justifies, but both prepare for justification. The law is then the pedagogue which leads us to Christ. Third, for the pious the law has a positive function in providing guidance and instruction.[15]

Erasmus emphasizes, however, that believers have been released from the law understood as threat, since their free, spontaneous love accomplishes more than the old law by its demanding and warnings of punishment. Love is what is decisive.

> Sincere love prescribes more rightly what ought to be done than any laws, however many they may be. If it [love] be present, what need is there for the precepts of the law: if it be not present, of what use is the observation of the law?[16]

Here there is an antilegalism which can even accept Augustine's injunction to "love God and do as you wish."[17]

Erasmus is not so clear on how this free, spontaneous love arises in believers. The emphasis is not so much, as with Luther, upon the joy of the forgiven life which results from Christ's having fulfilled the law for us and which issues in free, glad love of the neighbor, as upon the love of Christ as gift and example which awakens in us a responding love, but not without our own effort.

II. Grace and Free Will

Grace and Free Will Before 1524

Prior to the treatise of 1524 against Luther, Erasmus had written no orderly presentation of his views on grace and free will. His remarks on the subject were random and cursory. Now free will,[18] now grace,[19] received the greater emphasis. More often he was content to speak of both as necessary without elaborating on how they are related to each other.[20] His interests, as always, were not at all theoretical but practical. He wished to steer a middle course between two evils: a false sense of security which causes one to relax and an arrogance which ascribes salvation to one's own endeavors. The practical attitude that Erasmus commended is to strive with all one's effort for the goal of salvation, while at the same time to claim nothing for oneself but to ascribe all to divine grace.

Treatise on Free Will

My intention is not to consider the whole range of issues involved in the debate between Luther and Erasmus but merely to sketch the position of Erasmus on the relation of grace and free will as recorded in that debate.

The presupposition for understanding the humanist's views on grace and free will expressed in the *Diatribe* is a knowledge of his sentiments on the status of the will after the Fall and before the reception of grace. We have already touched on this question in the discussion of Erasmus' anthropology. The point of view outlined there is consonant with the opinions set forth in the *Diatribe*. According to Erasmus, both free will and reason, the source of the will, were "corrupted," "obscured," "wounded," but not extinguished by the Fall. The sin of the first parents does not produce sin in us but rather an inclination to sin, which does not completely remove free will. As the Church Fathers pointed out, says Erasmus, there remain some seeds of the good in man's nature by which he can partially both know and seek the good.[21] This thought is dear to the humanist who earnestly desires to believe that some of the ancient philosophers possessed a knowledge and love of God and virtue.

This basic presupposition that free will has not been canceled by the Fall and is therefore able to participate in the work of salvation is supported by arguments from Scripture and from reason. First, from Scripture: The commandments of the Bible presuppose that men may will to keep the commandments. Again, Scripture affirms the existence of reward and punishment, but these, since they imply merit and guilt, are possible only if there is free will.[22] Even those passages of Scripture which exalt grace do not remove free will but can be understood to involve the cooperation of free will with grace. Second, from reason: The humanist discloses the repugnance of Luther's views to his reason when he says:

> But my mind is very much disturbed when I hear that there is no human merit; that all human works, even the pious ones, are

> sins; that our will can do no more than the clay in the potter's
> hand; that everything we do or want to do is reduced to absolute
> necessity . . .[23]

Luther's idea of absolute necessity appears to Erasmus' reason
to undermine the personal status of man, his freedom and
moral responsibility. Furthermore, the notion of absolute
necessity detracts from God's goodness and justice.

Grace, for Erasmus, signifies a benefit freely given. But he
distinguishes four kinds of grace, adopting scholastic terminology: natural grace, special or operating grace, justifying
or cooperating grace (*gratia gratum faciens*), and completing
grace. Natural grace refers to the grace of creation, which,
though corrupted by sin, was not blotted out, and by which one
is free to carry on certain actions such as speaking or keeping
silent, standing or sitting, reading sacred books, listening to a
sermon. While, says Erasmus, some think that these actions
have nothing to do with eternal salvation, others hold that by
such good deeds one can stir the mercy of God.

However, there are those who believe that such a thing can
happen only by the special grace of God.[24] Erasmus here makes
no judgment as to which is his opinion, but from what he says
elsewhere in the *Diatribe* it would appear that he holds the view
that redemptive grace, not just natural grace, stands at the
beginning of the process of salvation.[25] Nevertheless, he clearly
wants to retain the idea that the grace of nature is really grace,
though common to all.

A second grace is what Erasmus calls *gratia peculiaris* (what
the scholastics also call the *auxilium speciale*), by which God mer-
cifully provokes the sinner to repentance. Aided by this grace
one can perform morally good works by which he can become
a candidate for that supreme grace which makes one acceptable
to God (*gratia gratum faciens*). It is partly left to our free will both
to apply for this grace and to receive it. Finally, there is the
grace which leads to the final goal of salvation. Augustine calls
it the gift of perseverance, but Erasmus does not use that
term.[26]

Having briefly sketched the arguments of Erasmus for free

will and his understanding of grace in the *Diatribe*, we are in a position to outline his conception of the relation between the two as expressed in this treatise. Erasmus enumerates several possible positions regarding grace and free will. He ranges them on a continuum from Pelagius to Luther. Pelagius taught that once the will was healed and freed by grace, no new grace was needed but free will of its own power could reach eternal salvation. Close to him is the opinion of the Scotists that free will of its own natural power through morally good works can merit *de congruo,* but not *de condigno,* that supreme grace by which we are justified (*gratia gratum faciens*). Then there are those who attribute much to grace without denying free will, who insist that man can will the good only by the special grace of God and that he can begin, progress, and reach the goal only by the perpetual aid of divine grace. Erasmus does not give any names here, but in the *Hyperaspistae I* (1526), he informs us that he had in mind St. Augustine, St. Thomas Aquinas, and their followers.[27] Opposed to those who affirm free will are two positions which in different degrees deny its value: first, that of Carlstadt (though Erasmus does not mention his name here, but in the *Hyperaspistae I*), which he characterizes as follows:

> . . . the will can do nothing other than sin, and grace alone can produce good in us not *through* free will or *with* free will but *in* free will so that the will is like wax in the hands of its molder.[28]

More extreme than this view, Erasmus thinks, is that of Luther (though he does not give his name here either), which, according to the humanist, asserts

> . . . that free will is an empty name, that neither among the angels, nor in Adam, nor in us, whether before or after grace, could or can it accomplish anything, but that God accomplishes both good and evil in us and all things happen of mere necessity.[29]

In this treatise Erasmus seems to take the second of the two mediating positions, that of Augustine and Thomas Aquinas, which, according to him, ascribes the work of salvation largely

to grace but without entirely overthrowing free will.[30] Of the
various opinions on free will and its relation to grace, he holds
this one to be the most probable. This view seems to Erasmus
to avoid the extremes both of overconfidence in human merits
and of excessive reliance on God's grace which removes personal responsibility. As interpreted by Erasmus, this position
grants some role to free will in the continuation or cooperation
of saving action, but divine grace both initiates and concludes
it. Expressed in Aristotelian or Thomistic language, grace is the
primary cause; free will, the secondary cause.

However, the humanist is certainly not always clear and consistent. He occasionally hints at his liking of the Scotist-nominalist conception. He suggests his approval of the *meritum de
congruo* in the following statement:

> It nevertheless does not follow from this [Rom. 5:20] that
> before the reception of sanctifying grace [*gratiam gratum facien-
> tem*] man, aided by divine grace, could not through morally
> good works prepare himself for divine favor.[31]

We conclude therefore that Erasmus either was not yet certain
as to his own position on this question or was trying to be as
conciliatory to Luther as possible; perhaps both. One moment
free will, the next moment grace, has the better of the argument.[32] It is no wonder that Luther was easily able to cut his
discussion into ribbons by showing its inner inconsistency. Although Erasmus' primary inclination here is for a semi-Augustinian position, in the *Hyperaspistae* he will reveal himself actually
to be in closer sympathy with the Scotist-nominalist view.

The *Hyperaspistae*

In this lengthy apology[33] for his treatise on free will written
after Luther's ruthless attack in the *De servo arbitrio,* Erasmus
shifts the grounds of his argument and his own position somewhat. In the *Diatribe* he assumed a common ground of argumentation with Luther, largely on the basis of scriptural testimony.
In the *Hyperaspistae* he makes a far freer use of the tradition, both
patristic and scholastic. We have already noticed the impor-

tance of this treatise for his position on Scripture and tradition. We now merely refer to that discussion in which it was stated that Erasmus thought that the interpretations of the Fathers of the Church and the decisions of councils must be taken into account in order to arrive at a safe understanding of difficult questions, since the sense of Scripture is not always evident. The problem of grace and free will is just this kind of knotty topic concerning which Scripture is not clear. Neither had there been as yet a conciliar decision on this question, although the Church Fathers had devoted a considerable amount of writing to it.

Erasmus thinks that, with the exception of Wyclif, Hus, and possibly Valla, the doctors of the Church, ancient and modern, are of one voice in affirming that some place be given to free will in the work of salvation. He recognizes that the theologians of the Church varied concerning the precise definition of the relation between grace and free will, but says that they all had agreed that free will plays some part in the saving work.[34] He thus seeks to isolate Luther from the tradition.

Erasmus still vacillates between a semi-Augustinian and a Scotist position but, especially toward the end of *Hyperaspistae II,* reveals his inclination for the latter view. The Augustinian view, he believes, holds that the will cannot operate effectively unless grace is present, whether stimulating or operating or cooperating or consummating; but that nevertheless, whether in application or conversion or cooperation, the will does something with the aid of grace. This opinion Erasmus continues to call "probable" in the first book of the *Hyperaspistae* because, although it credits divine grace with the primary work of salvation, it nevertheless allows room for human striving. I prefer to call this position semi-Augustinian or even semi-Pelagian because it gives a greater role to free will than Augustine himself actually granted it.[35]

The Scotist position he again sets forth as one which holds that through morally good works proceeding from the power of nature without special grace, man can merit *de congruo* the efficacious grace of God because God will not allow him to perish who accomplishes what is in him. He does not reach salvation by his own power, but by some divine agreement (*pactum*) becomes capable of grace.[36] Erasmus repeats this opinion throughout both books of the *Hyperaspistae* as one view which the Church has neither accepted nor rejected. He also states that he sets it forth simply as one possible viewpoint of which he neither approves nor disapproves.[37] Toward the end of *Hyperaspistae II* Erasmus finally admits that he is more inclined to approve than to disapprove of this opinion.[38]

Erasmus' frequent references to this position and his use of it in the closing pages of the *Hyperaspistae II* attest to the fact of his inclination to accept it. He is especially concerned to show that a merit of fitness does not conflict with grace:

> But if we understand the *meritum congruum* as a certain human indignity which the goodness of God accepts as proceeding from some quality of our efforts and if we understand the *meritum condignum* as applicable to those deeds accomplished with the aid of grace, the righteousness freely given and the salvation freely given do not conflict with the word "merit."[39]

However, Erasmus is unclear as to what constitutes the *meritum congruum*. In one place he suggests that it is the assent to the grace of preparation,[40] but elsewhere that it is morally good works prior to justification.[41] He states further that it makes little difference whether anyone attributes these works to free will alone or to free will as always inspired and led by God's grace. The former view would be closer to the position of Occam; the latter to that of Scotus.[42]

While Erasmus wavers between a Scotist and Occamist position on justification, his view on predestination is much more nearly Occamist than Scotist. On this subject Duns Scotus retained the Augustinian understanding that the sole cause of election is the divine will. The cause of the reprobation of the wicked, on the other hand, is their sin. According to Scotus, on the basis of his formal distinction, there are four logical moments in the divine decree. (Peter and Judas are respectively the examples of the elect and the reprobate.) (1) God wills that Peter be saved. (2) He wills the means to that end, grace. In these first two instances God wills nothing regarding Judas. He is concerned only with Peter. (3) He permits Peter and Judas alike to belong to the mass of perdition. (4) God foresees that Peter, the elected one, will be withdrawn from the mass of perdition, but that Judas, the non-elected one, will remain there and thus be justly condemned.[43]

In contrast to Scotus, the nominalists Occam and Biel posit a predestination *post praevisa merita.* It is true that *de potentia absoluta* God does not have to grant eternal salvation to the human merits which he foresees. But *de potentia ordinata*[44] he has committed himself to reward with eternal life those who *de condigno* merit it. If one ought to stress the *potentia absoluta,* i.e., the freedom and sovereignty of the Occamistic God, then one must conclude with P. Vignaux that even for Occam God's foreordination precedes his foreknowledge and that, therefore, Occam has protected himself from Pelagianism.[45] On the other hand, if, as is more likely, one ought to emphasize the *potentia ordinata,* that is, the order of creation and redemption as God has actually ordained it, one must conclude with H. A. Oberman that Occam teaches that foreknowledge precedes predestination.[46]

Erasmus' view on this subject, which he expresses more than once in the *Hyperaspistae II,* is in agreement with the view of Occam and Biel that foreknowledge precedes predestination— that God's foreknowledge of our good works is logically prior to his election of us.[47] Therefore, in spite of Erasmus' statement that he is inclined to approve what he calls the opinion of Scotus on grace and free will, his own views cannot *ohne Weiteres* be identified with those of Scotus. Although in the *Hyperaspistae* he appears to share the Scotist position on the *meritum de congruo* (which is also the nominalist position of Occam and Biel),[48] he clearly goes counter to the Scotist understanding of predestination while he much more nearly approximates that of Occam and Biel. However, he does not refer to them nor to any similarly minded late medieval theologian explicitly.

Following Scotus and the nominalists, Erasmus also makes use of the distinction between the *potentia absoluta* and *potentia ordinata* (although he does not use these terms) in his answer to the problem of conflict between the divine sovereign freedom and human freedom which makes merit possible. He acknowledges that God can do with the human will what he wills. He can operate as the potter with the clay if he so chooses. But he has chosen to act otherwise—to grant some role to free will, whether for the perseverance in piety or the imputation of impiety. Erasmus connects this thought with the understanding of the relation between the divine will and the sacraments. Just as God has committed himself to operate through the sacraments although he could do otherwise, so has he committed himself to reward those who make a good use of their free will and thus are deserving, even though there is here no absolute necessity.[49]

Humbertclaude is cautious about identifying Erasmus with the "Scotist" or "modern scholastic opinion" on the *meritum de congruo*: "However, the incessant fluctuations of Erasmus' thought do not permit us to affirm that he resolved exclusively upon the opinion of the 'modern scholastics' or 'Scotists.' "[50] In this view Humbertclaude is largely correct. In the two *Hyperaspistae* Erasmus does reveal a basic uncertainty as to precisely how grace and free will are to be related. His own skepticism and vagueness in dogmatic expression prevent his adopting definitely and exclusively any one theological opinion on an issue upon which there had been no authoritative decision. Yet the Scotist-nominalist position apparently appealed to him because, while it granted a significant place to free will, it allowed for a certain incommensurability between human merit and God's grace.

His continuing uncertainty about the precise manner of stating the relationship between grace and free will, and at the same time his inclination to accept the Scotist-nominalist position, are further corroborated in a letter of March 30, 1527, to Thomas More. The letter was written after the completion of *Hyperaspistae I* and before the beginning of *Hyperaspistae II*.[51]

> If I shall have treated the material with the soul of monks and theologians, who attribute too much to the merits of men on account of the gain returning to them, I shall speak indeed

against my conscience, and knowingly I shall obscure the glory of Christ. But if I shall have so tempered my style that I attribute something to free will, much to grace, I shall offend both sides, as I found by experience in the *Diatribe*. But if I follow Paul and Augustine, there is very little which is left to free will. . . . To me the opinion is not displeasing which thinks that we *ex meris nature viribus* apart from special grace can *de congruo* . . . establish grace, unless Paul is resisted, although not even the scholastics receive this opinion.[52]

Grace and Free Will After *Hyperaspistae II*

After the second *Hyperaspistae* Erasmus does not reconsider at length the question of the relation of grace and free will. His references to the matter are for the most part brief, casual, and ambiguous. In a commentary in 1528 on Psalm 85, Erasmus emphasizes the prevenience of grace to human merit, yet also the necessity of good works—which, however, we do not arrogate to ourselves—and human cooperation with the divine grace.[53] In one passage he seems to suggest that the bestowal of grace is contingent on a kind of *meritum congruum,* though he does not use that term.[54] In fact, I do not find Erasmus using that scholastic expression again after the *Hyperaspistae II.*

The *meritum de congruo* is also implied in some passages in the *Enarratio in psalmum XXXIII* of 1530. Erasmus states that God saves us by his grace, but "he wishes us to strive after that grace by prayers, tears, sighs, and alms."[55] He also suggests that the mind is blind unless illumined by faith, which is a gift of God. But no one receives this gift unless he "approaches," i.e., unless "he places no obstacle to the grace of God, but rather *prepares* himself by prayers and alms."[56] And then, finally, in a similar vein:

> Therefore, if we wish the Lord to be near us, let us *prepare* the domicile of our hearts, that he might perfect his virtue in our humility.[57]

In the *Enarratio psalmi LXXXIII* of 1533, a treatise also concerned with healing the schism in Christendom, Erasmus sets forth an intentionally ambiguous formula on free will:

> Concerning free will, it is more truly a thorny rather than a
> fruitful disputation. If it must be investigated, let it be soberly
> discussed in theological diatribes. Meanwhile among us it is
> sufficient to agree that a man can do nothing of his own power,
> and whatever he can do, he owes wholly to his grace by whose
> office we are whatever we are, that we might acknowledge in all
> things our weakness and glorify the mercy of the Lord.[58]

The phrase "his grace by whose office we are whatever we
are" may refer to the grace of creation or to the grace of redemption or to both; if to the grace of redemption, either to the
gratia specialis or the *gratia gratum faciens*. Undoubtedly, Erasmus
intended a vague formula, both because of his earnest desire
for unity and because of his opinion that more precise language
was really neither possible nor necessary. It makes no difference to Erasmus whether it is on the basis of the *gratia naturalis*
or only of the *gratia specialis* that the *meritum de congruo* is produced by which the *gratia gratum faciens* is obtained *ex divino pacto*.

In the *De praeparatione ad mortem* (1534) Erasmus describes
the battle of the Christian life in which both grace and free will
operate, but in such a way that the reception of the former is
conditional on the right use of the latter. Christ supplies aid, but
to those who struggle. He conquers in us, provided we remain
in him through faith and love. Nothing is so horrible in human
nature that it is not conquered by the aid of Christ, if we commit
ourselves totally to the divine will. The Lord conquers, not that
we might sleep but that we might not despair.[59]

In conclusion, therefore, I find nothing in the writings after
the *Hyperaspistae II* which goes counter to the view there expressed concerning Erasmus' inclination to favor the *meritum de
congruo*. Instead, I find passages which tend to support the thesis that he had adopted this idea, even though the actual term
is absent.[60]

III. Justification and Sanctification

We have already touched on the subject of justification in the
section on grace and free will, especially in connection with the

meritum de congruo. Now we wish to treat the subject more fully as it is set forth in Erasmus' own language, rather than in technical scholastic jargon, and as it is related to sanctification.

On the one hand, Erasmus is concerned with emphasizing that our justification—our acceptance before God—depends on the divine grace, not on our merits.[61] Furthermore, this justification by grace is received through *faith*. Student of Paul that he was, he contrasts faith sharply with works.[62] But Jesus also, thinks Erasmus, attributed salvation to faith rather than works.[63]

Because of such assertions, especially in his paraphrases, Erasmus was accused by his "orthodox" opponents of being Lutheran. In answer to their charges Erasmus argues that whenever he says that Paul or Jesus ascribed salvation to grace or faith, not to works or merits, he excludes merits prior to, but not after, faith and baptism.[64]

However, Erasmus' judgment that justification is owed to God's grace received in faith, not to merit, and that there is no merit prior to faith and baptism does not necessarily exclude a half-merit, the *meritum de congruo* prior to justification, as set forth in the *Hyperaspistae.* He opposes a merit in the full sense because of his awareness of the noncongruence between man's works and God's grace. But even in one of the apologies against Beda, where he stresses grace over merit, he allows room for the *meritum de congruo.*[65]

Further corroboration for the interpretation that Erasmus does not intend to exclude all merit prior to faith and justification is found in the fact that sometimes when he contrasts faith and works, it is only ceremonial works that he has in mind. As part of a long paraphrase (really more of a discourse) on Luke 24:27, Erasmus asks the question, "What does Christ demand of his own but faith alone?"[66] In answer to Beda, who evidently accused him of Lutheranizing, Erasmus points out that by this statement he did not intend to rule out all works, especially those which proceed from faith and love, but only ceremonial works of the law, as the words which immediately follow in the paraphrase indicate.[67]

Faith and Love

But what does Erasmus understand as faith? He can speak in an evangelical manner about it. In many passages, especially in the *Paraphrases* and in the expositions of the Psalms, Erasmus emphasizes that faith is, above all, confidence and trust (*fiduciam*) in the promises and mercy of God—the opposite of confidence in the powers of the self.[68]

Because faith is confidence in the divine promise, it is also hope—hope that God will be faithful to his promises and fulfill them. Erasmus sometimes connects faith as trust with hope. He says that there is little difference between the two, since hope is actually included in faith.[69]

The faith which is confidence and hope is also obedience. Erasmus points out that when Paul speaks of faith as obedience, the Apostle means simple trust in the promises of Christ apart from curious arguments. By faith as obedience, Erasmus has in mind, then, especially, the simplicity of faith vis-à-vis complex reasoning.[70] In addition, the obedience of faith means complete self-surrender to God.

More like Calvin and less like Luther, especially in his late works, Erasmus also calls faith a certain persuasion of all things which are necessary for salvation—namely, those things which Sacred Scriptures narrate and teach.[71] This persuasion, though inspired by the Holy Spirit, is for Erasmus also supported by arguments, in spite of his polemic against speculative reasoning.

Occasionally, Erasmus greatly extols faith. Faith alone will accomplish salvation and will at once abolish whatever sin there is.[72] Without faith it is impossible to please God.[73] It is the source of all evangelical virtue.[74] With Paul, Erasmus can say that whatever is not of faith is sin.[75] Such a great and powerful thing no one bestows on himself; it is rather a gift of God.[76] We shall notice later, however, that these statements require for him some qualification.

Along with these elements which might be considered evangelical, there were also strong catholic strains in his concept of faith. Faith is sometimes for Erasmus primarily an act of the mind. It perfects the intellect as love perfects the will.[77] It enables us to think rightly about God and about the dogmas necessary to our salvation.[78] Faith is then the *fides quae,* assent to correct dogma—to whatever is taught in Scripture, whatever the Church hands down to us out of Scripture, but also whatever the Church with universal consensus holds, even if not contained in Scripture.[79] Especially in his later writings Erasmus seems to adopt a position close to ecclesiastical fideism when he says, sometimes without the above qualification concerning the universal consensus, "The first thing is to believe rightly nor at all to depart from the opinions of the Catholic Church."[80]

Furthermore, in spite of the above remarks about the gift character of faith, it is not an absolutely free gift. There are certain preconditions for receiving it. Faith is given only to the avid and willing; only to those who prepare themselves by prayers and alms; to the undeserving, i.e., those who do not, strictly speaking, merit it; but not to the unworthy,[81] i.e., those who have not produced a *meritum de congruo.* As Erasmus says in the *De libero arbitrio* (1524): ". . . faith itself is a work in which free will to some extent participates by turning to or away from it."[82] Although the term is absent, the *fides acquisita* is clearly present in this thought from the *Hyperaspistae II:*

> But faith, he [Luther] says, is a gift of God; it is not in our power. I acknowledge it, if you are thinking about the faith which justifies through grace; but just as there is a certain knowledge which prepares for the light of faith, so there is a certain human faith which prepares for justifying faith.[83]

That there must be some human preparation for the reception of the gift of justifying faith is entirely in line with our conclusion in the discussion of grace and free will concerning the necessity for Erasmus of the *meritum de congruo.*

Finally, in spite of Erasmus' praise of faith as that which alone pleases God, it is clear that justification for him was not by faith alone, but by faith completed by love. Faith has then both prior and posterior conditions. Just as there must be some preparation of the mind and will for receiving faith, so after faith has been received, there must follow love and good works, which along with faith constitute the basis of acceptance before God. Faith in itself is insufficient; it is the mere beginning of salvation beyond which one must pass in order to be saved.

> To have believed the gospel is the rudiment of salvation; it is completed and perfected by pious actions. Nor is it sufficient to have learned through the gospel that God is the author of salvation through Jesus Christ his Son, unless through this knowledge you grow and bear fruits of Christian charity . . .[84]

In spite of the fact that Erasmus sometimes talks of faith and love as equal and reciprocal necessities in the Christian life,[85] it seems clear that the weight is on love and the new life rather than on faith and forgiveness.[86]

Moreover, for Erasmus justification seems actually to be contingent upon sanctification, i.e., love and good works. "The most excellent way to please God is a gracious good deed toward the neighbor."[87] Erasmus connects the vertical and horizontal dimensions of forgiveness in such a way that the former seems to depend upon the latter.

> If you have forgiven some little fault of your neighbor, God will forgive all your sins. If you have remitted temporary punishment for your brother, God will remit eternal punishment for you.[88]

The conditional character of forgiveness is also to be noticed in this paraphrase of a portion of the Lord's Prayer:

> You will experience the Father toward you in the same manner in which the neighbor experiences you toward him. He does not acknowledge as son him who does not live in harmony with his brother. If you forgive the men who commit crimes against you, your heavenly Father will forgive whatever crimes you commit against him.[89]

Progress in the Christian Life—From Physical to Spiritual

In the light of the fact that forgiveness is conditional, it is not surprising that justification is also a process. We are more and more reconciled to God through good works.[90]

Genuine progress in sanctification is the fundamental feature of the Christian life. The earnest endeavor of Christian
existence is to press ever forward in the growth of Christian
virtue.[91] This progression in piety is modeled after nature; after
Christ's teaching, which is according to nature; and after
Christ's example. Piety has its stages of growth just as does
nature. The Christian life has its infancy, adolescence, youth,
and maturity.[92] In the parable about the seed growing secretly
(Mark 4:26-29), Jesus teaches not only the gradual spread of the
gospel but also the progress of the Christian life, which moves
from the new innocence received in baptism through increase
in piety to full maturity. In his paraphrase of Luke 2:52 Erasmus
suggests that Christ's growth "in wisdom and stature and in
favor with God and man" was intended not only for the salvation of mankind but also for the instruction of our life, that we
should strive to progress from the rudiments of righteousness
to a more nearly perfect state.

Progression in the Christian life from imperfect to perfect
involves the movement from flesh to spirit, as the continuation
of Erasmus' comments on the passage from Luke 2 indicates:

> For Christ increases in us and matures when we proceed from
> the rudiments of faith to the more mysterious wisdom of Scrip-
> ture, when after we have left behind the milk of the flesh, we
> long for the solid food of the spirit, when after we have left
> behind the insipid letter, we long for the mystical sense, when
> after having left behind earthly things, we evolve toward heav-
> enly things.[93]

We thus return to what is perhaps the major theme of Erasmus'
thought, the Platonic-Pauline contrast between flesh and spirit,
the external and the internal, which shapes his understanding
of Scripture, of Christ, and now here of the Christian life.

In the Christian life the movement from flesh to spirit involves in the first place the continual mortification of the carnal
desires and vivification of the inner man by the spirit of Christ.
As we have already noticed, Erasmus follows Paul in including
among the fleshly desires not only the sensual sins of lust and
debauchery, but also enmity, quarreling, jealousy, worship of

idols, etc. In the famous rule five of the *Enchiridion* concerning
the progression from the visible to the invisible, Erasmus has
in mind this aspect of the movement from the flesh to the spirit
when he says:

> Here then lies the way to a pure and spiritual life: to accustom
> ourselves gradually to being alienated from those things which
> are in reality illusory but which sometimes seem to be what they
> are not—gross sensuality, for instance, and worldly glory—and
> which pass away and quickly melt into nothingness; and then to
> be ravished by those things which are truly lasting, immutable,
> and true.[94]

Secondly, and more fundamentally, when Erasmus talks of
the movement from the flesh to the spirit in the Christian life,
he describes the change from an outward, formal religion to an
inward, spiritual piety, the kind of piety which is a matter not
of ceremonies but of the affections.[95] This ever recurrent theme
of Erasmus' religious thought especially applies to his understanding of the sacraments, since by "ceremonies" he meant
not only such outward displays of religion as fasting, choice of
foods, clothing, but also the sacraments and whatever belongs
to the external cult. Because of its prime importance for his
sacramental thought, a more detailed treatment of this subject
is reserved for later chapters. It is sufficient here to state that
Erasmus' view is that the whole external cult is useless unless
it is accompanied by purity of soul and works of love.[96] The
external in religion is not to be condemned as long as it is
subservient and leads to the internal and spiritual.[97] When ceremonies are regarded as signs of piety which admonish us and
remind us of true piety, not as piety in itself, they are useful. But
when ceremonies replace true religion, become multiplied
beyond all measure, are the object of one's confidence, then
they are pernicious.[98]

Their chief value is that they are accommodations to our
weakness. They are especially fitting for those who are in the
infancy of their faith.[99] As we move toward maturity in the
Christian life, we have less need of them.[100] It is, however, not
appropriate for the more mature in piety to despise ceremonies

needed by the weak lest the latter be injured thereby.[101] Moreover, it would seem that, since even the mature never reach true spiritual perfection in this life because they remain encumbered by the physical body, even they stand in partial need of ceremonies to act as supports of their piety.[102]

Militia Christi: Contemplatio et Imitatio

The movement from flesh to spirit in the Christian life is conceived of by Erasmus in terms of a battle.[103] The Christian soldier is engaged in a perpetual warfare between flesh and spirit. Erasmus touches on this theme in the *De contemptu mundi,*[104] more fully expands it in the *Enchiridion,* and continues to set it forth in his later writings. We have already noted it in the consideration of Christ as *imperator,* by whose aid and example we conquer the enemies of flesh, world, and devil.

In this struggle, Erasmus tells us in the *Enchiridion,* we have need of two weapons, knowledge and prayer. By "knowledge" Erasmus means (1) an understanding of ourselves as composed of flesh and spirit along with the awareness of the higher order of spirit toward which we ought always to strive, and (2) an acquaintance with the tools by which the flesh may be overcome —Scripture and certain writings of some of the pagan poets and philosophers. In Scripture it is especially Christ whom we should seek. He becomes for us the principal object of contemplation and imitation. We contemplate him in the struggles of his temptations and in his battle upon the cross. Thus contemplating him with the eyes of faith as our redeemer and example provides strength, solace, and hope, and awakens in us a responding love.[105]

The contemplation of Christ's life of obedience, however much it may be a source of inspiration, is ineffectual unless *contemplatio* leads to *imitatio.*[106] *Imitatio* includes the mortification of the old man, dying to the world, crucifixion of the fleshly desires, before rising with Christ in newness of life. It means the willingness to suffer with him now before reigning with him in glory. As we have already noticed, Christ the commander is not only our example, whose life we contemplate and emulate, but also our redeemer and helper, who has already conquered for us and who continues to supply us with the aid to be victorious, provided we remain in him and exercise our efforts. Thus, prayer, by which we implore his aid, is alongside knowledge an essential weapon of the Christian soldier.

Perfection

The goal of the struggle of flesh against spirit is perfection. Perfection consists, in the first place, of a radical spirituality and inwardness. Erasmus thinks that as nearly as perfection can occur in this life one is deserving of the title "perfect" who loves both the worthy and the unworthy and who humbly ascribes all his virtue to God, not to himself.[107]

Insofar as we have been incorporated into the body of Christ and live under grace, we have been freed not from all sin nor from all inclination to sin, but from the reign of sin.[108] But, refusing to rest securely, we ought to strive steadfastly for a perfect correspondence between the members of Christ's body and the head in whom there is no weakness, error, or vice.[109]

It is not altogether clear what degree of perfection Erasmus thinks is possible in this life. In the *Enchiridion* he says: "But if not *everyone* can attain to the perfect resemblance to our Head, at least we must all struggle in that direction with might and main."[110] Does he mean that *some* can reach Christ's perfection? In the much later work, the *Symbolum* (1533), Erasmus states:

> It is granted to very few men to live without the lighter sins which through carelessness creep on the nature of man. . . . [But] Christians should and can abstain from gross sins with Christ's help.[111]

Does he think that some can and do live without even the lighter sins? Elsewhere he confesses ignorance as to whether perfection is ever complete in this life.[112] Still other passages suggest that he thought that, except for Christ, no true perfection was possible in this life.[113]

But if the weakness of our nature prevents us from attaining that perfect state, Erasmus thinks we should endeavor to come as near to it as possible. He remained optimistic concerning the possibility of a genuine approximation to the goal from his earliest to his latest writing. In the *Enchiridion* he holds:

> If you weigh only your own resources, nothing is harder than to subject the flesh to the spirit; but if you look upon God as your helper, nothing is easier. Only seize with a stout heart upon the principle of the perfect life and press forward in your purpose. Never yet has the human spirit failed to accomplish something it ardently demanded of itself. A large part of the Christian life is to wish wholeheartedly to become a Christian . . .[114]

In a work written only a little over two years before his death he maintains this point of view: "Nothing is so horrible in human nature that it may not be overcome by the aid of Christ, if we commit and submit ourselves wholly to the divine will . . ."[115]

Furthermore, the aim of perfection ought to be present in all Christians. The command to be perfect applies to all disciples of Christ, not just to the monks.[116] In the commandments of Jesus, Erasmus disregards any distinction between the precepts to be observed by ordinary Christians and the counsels to be observed only by the perfect, i.e., the religious. For example, the command not to swear at all pertains to anyone who desires to be perfect.[117]

However, even though the desire for perfection should be felt by all Christians, Erasmus acknowledges in fact degrees of perfection. As we have seen, he thinks that Christians may be divided into classes: (1) the beginners or the weak, (2) those who are progressing, (3) the mature, the strong, or the perfect insofar as perfection is possible in this life. These classes are determined, however, not by anything outward—neither age nor sex nor status nor place nor kind of life—but strictly by the inner condition of the heart.[118]

On this basis he advocates after all a kind of graded morality. Although all of Christ's commands should be obeyed by every Christian, not all Christians can in fact receive every one of his commandments. The command to swear not at all applies therefore especially to the perfect, even though also to those who aim at perfection. Yet swearing, like divorce, must be conceded to the weak. Again we observe the important theme of the necessity for accommodations to human weakness.[119]

Although the perfection of which Erasmus speaks consists in the movement away from the physical to the spiritual, it will in the end quite paradoxically include the body. As the soul is gradually transformed by attention to divine and eternal things, so the body obeying the soul is purged of its crassness and is changed into a body very much like the mind.[120] We have already noticed in connection with Erasmus' anthropology that the humanist is not entirely negative toward the body, but includes it in the redemption of the whole man. This transformation of the body begins to take place in this life, but is completed only in the next. In the resurrection there will be a complete restoration and a perfect correspondence of the whole man with the purity of the Head.[121] The Hebraic-Christian tradition thus qualifies Erasmus' Platonism.

Meditatio Vitae Futurae

Since perfection occurs only in the resurrection, an important aspect of the Christian life is continual meditation upon the future life. Combined with this *meditatio vitae futurae* there is a *contemptus mundi,* just as connected with the vivification by the Spirit there is a mortification of the flesh. Since everything in this world is imperfect—full of suffering, cares, and woes—as well as transitory, it cannot provide genuine joy and peace. Only by contemplation of what is perfect, eternal, and heavenly— God and the future life[122]—can the soul find rest. Thus does Erasmus touch on an important theme of the Middle Ages which goes back at least as far as Augustine.

Because the future life is pictured as the moment not only of supreme perfection but also of supreme happiness, meditation upon it has the purpose of drawing us toward perfection while at the same time undergirding our longing for it by holding out before us the reward of eternal joy.[123] Erasmus teaches therefore a eudaemonism as the complement to his perfectionist ideal. In this drive toward perfection and longing for eternal life there are Platonist and Stoic as well as Christian elements. Also, insofar as already in this life the Christian experiences a foretaste of eternal well-being in the joy and tranquillity of a pure conscience, we may detect not only Stoicism but Epicureanism, which was possibly suggested by Valla.[124]

It has been debated by past scholars whether Erasmus' concept of piety was determined basically by a this-worldly moralism (Troeltsch and Köhler)[125] or by an otherworldly longing for the future life (Schulze).[126] In fact, it is not exclusively one or the other. Rather the matter is more complex. That Erasmus' understanding of redemption and the Christian life was largely that of a moralist cannot be denied. However, his moralism was not simply "this-worldly" but was shaped by the concepts of redemptive grace and eternal life. Finally, although there are undoubtedly Stoic, Platonic, and even Epicurean elements in it, one fails to understand Erasmus' thought unless he recognizes the high degree of Christocentrism present in it. This Christocentrism has to do primarily with Christ as teacher and example, to be sure, but also secondarily, though still significantly, with Christ as redeemer.

IV. Summary of Process of Salvation

The initial dignity of man was not blotted out but was obscured by the Fall. Both the reason and the will have been corrupted, but not radically, by the weakness of the flesh. In the disordered state after the Fall the flesh gained the upper hand. The effort is for the spirit (mind) more and more to regain control of the powers of the self.

The starting point for the process of salvation is the fact that faults arising from ignorance and the weakness of the flesh deserve mercy, but not those issuing from a fixed or intentional malice. The implication is that God would be unjust if he were not to extend his mercy to all who sin out of ignorance and weakness of the flesh, but he justly refuses grace to those who knowingly and willingly sin. We notice the importance of the reason and will already at this point in the process of redemption.

The next step has to do with the preparation of the mind and heart (*meritum de congruo*) for the reception of justifying grace (*gratia gratum faciens*). This grace is received in faith, and the former innocence restored. But such a condition is incomplete unless accompanied by love and righteousness. The gradual growth of sanctification and the struggle of the Christian life are the fundamental features of Erasmus' soteriology. The drive is toward perfection, at which point, as in Wesley, a final justification takes place.

But even in the end there is uncertainty of salvation, for "who knows whether the faith and love which he has are of the kind of gifts which render us acceptable to God and are sufficient for eternal salvation?"[127]

VI

THE SACRAMENTS IN GENERAL

I. Definition of *Sacramentum*

In the *Symbolum* (1533) Erasmus explains that *sacramentum* originally meant an oath of allegiance or obligation which was confirmed by the intervention of a divine power, but that it was adapted to be used for what the Greeks call *mysterium* or *religiosum arcanum*.[1] However, the word in ecclesiastical parlance has come to refer to a sensible sign through which an insensible grace congruent with the sign is infused.[2] In his controversy with Lee and Stunica concerning the foundation of marriage as a sacrament in Ephesians 5:32, Erasmus had already provided other similar traditional definitions of the term. To Lee he writes:

> But that is not immediately and properly to be called a sacrament, because it is a sign of a sacred thing. For they [certain recent theologians] say that that is properly called a sacrament which is a visible form of an invisible grace in such a way that it bears an image thereof, and exists as a cause.[3]

Against Stunica, Erasmus argues that, though there are many signs of sacred things, *sacramentum* in the special sense of the word refers to "a visible sign of a sacred thing, which however, necessarily *velut ex pacto* is accompanied by invisible grace."[4]

The former definition Erasmus simply reproduces from Lombard's *Sentences,* a definition which leaves undecided the exact relation between the visible form and the invisible grace or the sign and the thing signified as well as the nature of the cause present in the sacrament, whether efficient, instrumental, or merely *sine qua non.*

The latter definition and the several others similar to it show that Erasmus had allied himself with the Franciscan tradition, which made a sharp distinction between the sign and the thing signified and which regarded the *causa* existing in the sacrament as merely *sine qua non.*[5] The Franciscans rejected the other, the Dominican, position that the sacraments cause[6] and contain grace so that there is an intrinsic, natural, necessary connection between the sacramental grace and the sacrament. The Franciscan school held rather that God has freely agreed (*ex pacto*) to accompany the use of the sacramental signs with his invisible grace. Divine grace acts therefore not indirectly through the sacraments but directly upon the soul. The fact that sacramental signs accompany the bestowal of grace is due not to natural necessity but to a free decision of God. However, in the light of this decision the operation is necessary (*potentia ordinata,* not *potentia absoluta*).[7]

Erasmus' favorable attitude toward the Franciscan, probably more specifically the Scotist-Occamist, position is further indicated in the *Hyperaspistae II* (1527), where he states that the sacraments would have an uncertain power if it were not for the fact that God had willingly bound himself to bestow such a power with the reception of the sacraments.[8]

It is understandable in view of his own largely symbolic and spiritual conception of the sacraments that Erasmus would prefer the Franciscan to the Dominican definition of a sacrament. If, as is probable, it is the later Franciscan tradition as represented in Scotism and Occamism to which Erasmus here attaches himself, then we have still further corroboration of a connection between him and this stream of thought as over against Thomism.[9]

At the beginning of the *Christiani matrimonii institutio* (1526) Erasmus provides us with his most detailed analysis of what a sacrament is. After calling the sacraments *pignora, monilia,* and *monumenta* which Christ left us of himself till he returns, he states that in marriage, as in the other sacraments, three things

must be borne in mind: *imago, arra,* and *exemplum.* Erasmus says
that he calls the *imago* the congruence of the sign with the
archetype to which the similitude corresponds. For example,
the archetype represented in marriage is especially the union of
God and man in the incarnation but also the union of Christ
with his Church. The *arra*[10] is "the gift of spiritual grace, which
velut ex pacto is infused through the administration of the sacrament."[11] The *exemplum* refers to "what in that similitude is commended to us to be imitated." As we shall have frequent
occasion to notice, Erasmus places the greatest weight on this
third aspect of the sacrament, although he does not leave out
of view the gift of grace which comes through—or better, which
accompanies—the administration of the sacrament.

Such definitions are, however, not characteristic of Erasmus. As we have already observed, this practical theologian is
little interested in definitions. In a passage in the *Ratio verae
theologiae* to which we have already called attention Erasmus
deplores the long disputes and investigation concerning the
nature of the sacrament when its use is necessary for salvation.
Likewise, in the note on I Timothy 1:6, he loathes the many
questions which have grown up around the sacraments of baptism, penance, and the Eucharist, most of which are of little
importance and which can be neither refuted nor tested.[12] What
is primarily significant is the personal appropriation and fulfillment in life of the meaning of the sacraments.

II. Meaning of *Sacramentum* in the New Testament

Erasmus points out in his notes on the word in the *Novum
Testamentum* and his defenses of them in the apologies that not
everywhere in the Vulgate where *sacramentum* is present does it
refer to sacrament in the narrow sense, but in some cases it is
rather simply a translation of the Greek word μυστήριον which
the humanist generally prefers to translate *"mysterium"* or *"arcanum."*

The only translation of this kind which especially disturbed anyone was the one on Ephesians 5:32, because it seemed to undercut marriage as a sacrament. Erasmus wrote even longer notes on this passage in the succeeding editions of the *Novum Testamentum* defending his translation and the note in the first edition. A detailed analysis of Erasmus' comments on this text may be reserved for the later discussion of the sacrament of marriage. It is sufficient to remark here that Erasmus consistently held that marriage as a sacrament in the special and exact sense of the word cannot be grounded in this passage because (1) the word μυστήριον, itself ought to be translated as *mysterium* just as elsewhere in Paul's letters, and (2) "the great mystery" of which Paul speaks has to do not with the union between man and wife but with the marriage between Christ and his Church. Even if marriage is regarded as a sign or sacrament of this sacred reality, it would still be a sacrament only in the larger, not in the narrower, sense of the word.[13] He repeatedly asserts that he does not intend to dispute the sacramental character of marriage but only whether it can be clearly drawn from this passage. If asked then on what basis does he hold to marriage as one of the seven sacraments, if it cannot be gathered from this passage or from any other passage, Erasmus says it is clear to him what he shall reply: ". . . the authority and consensus of the Church move me, yet not alone in this thing, but in many other things also."[14]

We shall discuss in detail later this conflict between Erasmus' critical, philological reason and the authority of the Church in connection not only with marriage but also with other sacraments.

III. Priest and Sacrament

Erasmus is careful to point out in several passages that the power and efficacy of the sacrament comes directly from Christ. The priest is only a minister or dispenser of a foreign benefit. One senses some practical advice to the laity in these words: "He should be honored who, performing his office, administers the sacrament, but he should be adored who renders the sacra-

ment efficacious . . ."[15] Erasmus relays the traditional thought
that the sacraments are effective out of the death of Christ.[16]
Because the power of the sacraments comes from Christ, Erasmus also agrees with the tradition since Augustine that an evil
priest cannot harm the effect of the sacrament.[17] Even though
he carefully distinguishes between the authority of the priest
and the sacrament, he grants to the priest a certain dignity
superior to kings, because as administrator of the sacraments,
he supplies heavenly grace.[18] We shall notice later, however,
that Erasmus regards the dignity of the priesthood to rest more
upon the office of teaching than upon the administration of the
sacraments.

IV. Flesh and Spirit in the Sacraments

The most significant fact about the sacraments for Erasmus
is that they contain both flesh and spirit, both the visible and the
invisible, both the outward and the inward. The disciple of the
Devotio Moderna argued persistently throughout his writings for
a personal, inward appropriation and application of the meaning of the sacraments as over against a merely formal, habitual
use of them. He thought that a bodily participation in the sacrament is of no value unless the mind is present.[19] In other words,
the sacrament is not so much an *opus operatum* as an *opus operantis*.

In some of his writings Erasmus is so critical of an external,
formalistic sacramentalism and states so strongly his preference for a spiritual as over against a physical participation in the
sacraments that he seems to veer toward a complete spiritualism.[20] Some of his orthodox opponents thought that Erasmus
rejected the sacraments altogether when he said in the *Enchiridion* that piety does not consist of visible things.[21] Erasmus
answers by pointing out that, though in that early work he was
critical of a superstitious reliance on ceremonies and sacraments, he did not wish to negate the sacraments as such. They
are of value when what is most important is added—namely, a
spiritual appropriation.[22]

Two passages in the *Convivium religiosum* (1522) which offended the Sorbonne were ones dealing with sacraments and ceremonies. The theological faculty censured Erasmus for saying that the majority of Christians place their whole hope in corporeal ceremonies while neglecting the commandments of God and for speaking against ceremonies in the remark "No wonder those who have puzzled their heads so much over ceremonies all their lives should die thus [i.e., in despair]."[23] Erasmus answers the first charge by asserting that the sacraments of the Church contain both what is material and what is spiritual. The material elements are not life-giving unless the spiritual elements are added. In the colloquy, he said, he had in mind the mass of Christians, who are wholly devoted to externals and neglect those things which make us truly pious.[24] He answers the second charge by rejecting out of hand the claim that he spoke against ceremonies. He says that in this passage he was critical only of those who die trusting in external things and visible sacraments while neglecting what makes for true piety.

Not only his orthodox Roman Catholic opponents but also some of his Protestant admirers saw in a number of Erasmus' comments a contempt for the physical elements of sacramental celebration which they thought brought him in line with the thought of Carlstadt and Zwingli. In response to a pseudonymous work,[25] Erasmus insisted that, contrary to what that author wrote, he had never denied the Real Presence in the Eucharist any more than he had denied the corporeal aspects of the other sacraments. In a long and important passage he writes in a manner very similar to that of his rejoinders to the Spanish monks and the Paris theologians:

> In order that I might call men forth from visible ceremonies to spiritual progress, I show that in all things there is, as it were, a certain flesh and spirit, that is, something visible and invisible: but the invisible, which the majority of mortals neglect, is far more excellent than what is seen, just as in man the soul is more powerful than the body: and this catholic opinion I carry

through all the species of things, the word of God . . . and the
sacraments of the new law, such as baptism, Eucharist, and
unction.[26]

Erasmus emphasizes that even in the *Enchiridion,* Canon V,
where the author of the pseudonymous work saw an exclusively
spiritualistic concept of the sacraments, he had expressly
guarded himself from such a misunderstanding.[27]

Therefore, in spite of what his orthodox detractors and his
Protestant admirers thought, Erasmus steadfastly maintained
that he had never wavered from the position that the sacraments contain both flesh and spirit but that, although the physical is not rejected, the spiritual is preferred. An examination of
the relevant passages on the sacraments as a whole bears out
Erasmus' judgment. Except for a somewhat greater degree of
emphasis on the spirit in the *Enchiridion* (1503) and the *Laus
stultitiae* (1509), Erasmus consistently held this position on flesh
and spirit in the sacraments throughout his life.[28] Only a detailed study of each of the sacraments in particular will fully
confirm this opinion.

V. Order of the Sacraments

Like his friend Colet, Erasmus does not follow the traditional order when he lists the sacraments. In the early catechetical poem, *Christiani hominis institutum* (1514), Erasmus has the
same order as Colet in his *Catechyzon* (c. 1509): orders, marriage, baptism, confirmation, Eucharist, penance, unction.[29]
However, in his later and larger catechetical work, *Symbolum*
(1533), Erasmus changes the order to: marriage, baptism, penance, sacred unction, Eucharist, extreme unction, orders.[30]

No special importance is to be attributed to these varying
orders except that they show a certain freedom shared with
Colet over against the medieval tradition in adopting a chrono-
logical order of the sacraments.

Except for the position of the Eucharist, we shall follow the
earlier order so as to save until last the main weight of our
discussion of Erasmus' views on the sacraments.

VII

ORDERS AND MARRIAGE

––––––––––––

I. Orders

Priesthood of All Believers

We have already briefly mentioned that Erasmus was a champion of lay Christianity. He was interested in emphasizing that by virtue of their faith and baptism all Christians are called to be perfect (not only the monks) and to exercise priestly functions (not only the priests). On the basis of I Peter 2 he urges the priesthood of all believers. Through Christ all believers have access to the throne of God. Likewise, they may exercise the functions of intercession for each other and love and instruction of the neighbor.[1]

Power and Authority of Orders

Nevertheless, Erasmus does not at all intend to undermine the role of holy orders in the Church. In order to insure the dignity, order, and tranquillity of the Church, it is necessary that there be this sacrament, which has been handed down from the ancients. It is neither permissible nor fitting for simply anyone to assume this office.[2]

In the two catechisms Erasmus acknowledges a special power and authority as conferred upon those who receive holy orders by which they are able to perform their functions.[3] Both in the letter to Paul Volz and the *Ratio verae theologiae* Erasmus sees the order of priests, bishops, cardinals, popes, as in the first of three concentric circles around Christ, the *scopus*. The second includes the secular princes; the third, the masses. Although in this idea one perceives a kind of hierarchical arrangement, nevertheless the emphasis is not upon an objective power which flows down from Christ through his successors to the people, but rather upon the responsibility of those who stand closest to Christ so to reflect in their lives the purity and light of Christ that these may be transferred on to the other two circles.[4]

Even though Erasmus does not intend to undercut the legitimate authority of orders, he is critical of what he considers exaggerated pretensions of power among the priests and bishops, as well as popes. Therefore, he says in the *Enchiridion* (1503):

> The rulers of this world exercise power over those they rule, but a Christian does not apply power to his people, but love. He who is greatest of all considers himself servant of all, not master. For this reason I am all the more astonished at the arrogant terms of authority and dominion being applied even to our chief priests and bishops, at our divines'—no less foolishly than pretentiously—not being ashamed to be called "masters" by the common people, even though Christ forbade his followers to permit themselves to be called either "masters" or "lords"; for Christ Jesus, the Head of us all, is both the sole Master and the sole Lord. "Apostle," "pastor," "bishop," are terms of service, not rule; "pope" and "abbot" are words of love, not dominion.[5]

As we shall see, he is especially critical of the tyranny exercised by priests in the hearing of confession and the prescription of satisfaction.

Thus it was probably with some joy that he was able to show not only that the authority of the Pope was *de iure humano,* but also that the priestly words of consecration in the Eucharist and the law of confession were not precisely grounded in Scripture, in which sacraments the power and the jurisdictional authority of the priest were especially exerted.

The power and authority held by priests and bishops is primarily, as for the Pope, a moral power and authority exercised in imitation of Christ.[6]

Such priests as strive to be as were the Apostles, we receive and
obey as Christ himself. But when the priest acts the tyrant,
pursues the business of the stomach, not of Christ, I do not
know whether these words may be appropriately cited, "He who
spurns you, spurns me." I know nevertheless that one ought to
subject himself even to evil ones lest disunion be created, provided that they do not compel impiety.[7]

Functions of the Priesthood

Administration of the Sacraments

One of the functions for which priests have been delegated
authority by virtue of their ordination is the administration of
the sacraments. In the *Ecclesiastae* where Erasmus is concerned
with stressing the preaching and teaching functions of the
priest and bishop, he nevertheless speaks of them as supplying
heavenly grace through the sacraments, and he mentions especially baptism, confirmation, Eucharist, and penance.[8] What he
usually emphasizes when speaking of the relation of priest and
sacrament is, as we have seen, the distinction of the sacramental
from the priestly power. The priest is a minister or dispenser
of a foreign reality. He has no control over it; it belongs to
Christ. In his paraphrase of Mark 7:34, Erasmus says:

> . . . [the priest] does not claim for himself the power of absolv-
> ing, but looks unto heaven, professing and testifying that all
> that is effected by the rites of the sacraments is of divine virtue,
> not of human power.[9]

We shall notice that Erasmus stands in the tradition of those
early scholastics (Abelard and Lombard) and the late medieval
nominalists who stress that the priestly role in absolution is
declarative and intercessory.

Even though an evil priest does not prevent the beneficial
effect of the sacrament, since Christ is able to operate even
through evil dispensers, Erasmus considers it most important
and appropriate that the priests administer the sacraments sin-
cerely and faithfully. He ridicules priests who desecrate the
Eucharist "with a heart unclean and soiled by willful lusts."[10] He
thinks the life of the priest is of no little consequence "in order

that the people might venerate this mystery with dignity."[11] We shall notice likewise that he stresses the importance of the selection of a good priest for confession, since it is the pastoral and intercessory function of the priest in confession which is of the greatest moment to him.

Priest or Bishop as Teacher, Example, and Pastor

Without disregarding the sacramental role of priests and bishops, Erasmus places the greatest weight upon their preaching, teaching, exemplary, and pastoral functions. In the *Ecclesiastae* Erasmus explains that the office of teaching embraces "doctrine, admonition, rebuke, consolation, and refuting those who rail against the evangelical truth." He goes on to explain why he thinks this office is superior to that of administration of the sacraments:

> Even a layman may baptize; the people may pray reciprocally for the priest [especially at the Eucharist]; the administration of the remaining sacraments is not difficult: but to fulfill the office of teaching, it is true, is far more difficult, but likewise it is far more beautiful; certainly its value may be much more widespread. A priest does not always baptize, he does not always anoint or absolve, but the office of teaching is perpetual without which the others are of no use. For of what use is it for adults to be baptized, unless they have learned through catechism what force baptism has, what it is necessary to believe, how to establish life according to the Christian profession? Of what use is it to eat the body and blood of the Lord, unless they have learned how this sacrament was instituted, what it effects in us, and with what faith and purity it should be consumed?[12]

Erasmus connects the office of teaching especially to the work of the bishop. It is the bishop's chief responsibility.[13] Often when Erasmus refers to this role as the bishop's major one, he intends not so much to set it over against that of the administration of the sacraments as over against any secular occupation[14] or use of force, whether in war or in inquisition.[15]

The content of the bishop's teaching is, of course, the most simple doctrine of Christ, the *philosophia Christi*; not Plato, or Aristotle, or scholastic questions.[16] His method in imitation of

Christ is that of love, forbearance, and gentleness.

Since, however, the teaching of the bishop or priest cannot be really effective unless his life corresponds to his teaching, Erasmus stresses also his role as example. The bishop or priest should be free from any suspicion of crime.[17]

Not to be sharply differentiated from his role as teacher and example is his role as pastor, as the above passage describing the office of teaching indicates. On the other hand, Erasmus can embrace teaching and example under the pastoral office, as in this passage: "It is characteristic of a true pastor to feed in a threefold manner with sacred doctrine, with a holy life, with corporeal aid."[18] But it also belongs to the office of pastor to make intercession, to advise, to exhort, and to console. We shall notice that these are the duties which Erasmus emphasizes when he talks about the priest as confessor.

A frequent lament in Erasmus' writings is that there are few such learned and good priests who act as true teachers and pastors to their flocks. Most, he thinks, are filled with ignorance, worldly desires, ideas of gain, ambition, lusts, drunkenness. They act the part of tyrants, not shepherds. They feed themselves, not their sheep. He complains also that the priests are more concerned with ritual than with the good life.

Erasmus deplores the rise of such a great crowd of priests, which he thinks has taken place because of the profit motive and because of the ease with which one can enter this profession. On the other hand, there are very few who are of suitable age, knowledge, or conduct for the office.[19]

To correct these abuses Erasmus proposes a reduction in the number of priests, a greater care on the part of bishops concerning the qualifications of those who are about to be ordained,[20] and the education of priests in the *philosophia Christi* and in the methods of correct preaching and interpretation of Scripture, the chief source of preaching and the Christian life. After having written most of his life principally for the benefit of the layman, Erasmus completed just before his death his great work for Christian preachers, the *Ecclesiastae*.

While proposing the abstention from any secular occupation in order to keep under control those vices which are especially close to ecclesiastical leaders—namely, avarice and ambition—and in order that the attention of priest or bishop might be riveted upon his chief task, Erasmus advises a secular state for priests who are especially troubled by the vice of lust—and that state is marriage. His considerations here are that true celibacy is so rare a condition among the hordes of priests that a chaste marriage is preferable to open adultery,[21] that for a priest to have touched a woman is not so evil as to be polluted by some other crimes,[22] that the regulation concerning celibacy for priests is *de iure humano* and thus can be adapted to changing times and circumstances.[23] He thinks that nothing ought to be more desired than that a priest be free of marriage in order to be able to serve his Lord totally, but that if all the other remedies fail for conquering the rebellion of the flesh, a wife ought to be conceded to the weakness of the flesh so that the priest might compensate for this weakness by living "a life of integrity devoted to piety."[24] In these thoughts Erasmus shows a certain historical and moral contextualism and his understanding of the necessity of accommodation to bodily weakness.

II. Marriage

The State of Marriage

Although it is not clear, in spite of Telle, that Erasmus intended the demise of the celibate state, his words in the main were surely meant to depreciate it by extolling the virtues of marriage. Erasmus appears as a proponent of marriage over against sacerdotal and monastic celibacy.

His first major writing on the subject was the *Encomium matrimonii,* written first probably in 1497 but not published until 1518.[25] In this work, praise of marriage at the expense of celibacy is lavish. He marshals all the powers of rhetorical argument to show the superiority of the marital to the celibate state. Marriage, argues Erasmus, was established by God, sanctioned by nature, consecrated by Christ. Marriage was the first sacra-

ment established in Paradise before the Fall; the other sacraments were instituted as a remedy for sin. Furthermore, thinks
Erasmus, the union of the two natures in Christ as well as the
union of Christ with his Church, as Paul said, commends marriage. The law of nature imbedded in our souls, of which the
Stoics speak, and Roman and Jewish law all are consonant with
marriage but not with celibacy.[26]

> It appears therefore that he who is not touched by the desire
> for marriage does not seem to be a man, but a rock, an enemy
> of nature, a rebel against the divine will . . .[27]

Thus, according to Erasmus, both divine and natural law seem
to sanction marriage, not celibacy.

But when it is objected that Christ after all was not married
and that he was born of a virgin, Erasmus replies that many
things in Christ are to be admired, not imitated, and that Mary
was indeed a virgin, but a married virgin. As to the passage in
Matthew 19 where Christ pronounces those blessed who become eunuchs for the sake of the kingdom of God, Erasmus
thinks these words were especially applicable in that time when
it was expedient for churchmen to be free of all the business of
this world. He notes that Jesus did not command celibacy, although he prohibited divorce. Although even some of the
Apostles appear to have had wives, Erasmus is willing to grant
that they were in the main free from marriage in order to carry
out their Apostolic office. Erasmus says: "Let us concede celibacy to bishops." "Let Apostolic men imitate the Apostles," to
whom "grace was granted that they might bear a more plentiful
progeny for Christ."[28] He is willing to grant this privilege to
priests and monks, who have in this respect succeeded the
Essenes. But, directing himself to William Mountjoy, for whom
this work was intended, Erasmus asks why Mountjoy, a private
secular man far removed from the office of the Apostles, desires
to imitate them in this regard. The basis of his life is different.[29]

Besides, Erasmus thinks, times have changed. Now one may
find less corruption among those who are married. Now "the
most saintly kind of life is a purely and chastely preserved mar-

riage." Thus he recommends, as we have seen, that incontinent priests and even monks be allowed to assume this state.

Celibacy is angelic, divine; marriage, human. Virginity, which once was so widely praised, is now only for the few. Without totally repudiating celibacy or virginity, Erasmus regards this virtue as an exceptional thing.[30] The normal human course is marriage. Finally, he "who has a wife for bearing progeny, not for pleasure"[31] is not far from deserving the praise of virginity. Erasmus thinks in terms of a holy, chaste marriage, which he regards as very close to virginity.[32]

When Erasmus was attacked for overpraising marriage to the detriment of celibacy, he answered that the work was a product of youth, that it was written in a deliberately rhetorical style, and that it argues not whether marriage in general is superior to celibacy but whether for this specific person marriage is preferable.[33] Though these factors, especially the latter two, should be given some weight and should prevent us from determining his whole outlook on this subject on the basis of this one treatise, nevertheless, as Telle has shown, other later writings demonstrate that Erasmus was there speaking his own mind.[34]

Erasmus favors marriage not only because of the necessity of nature but also as a base (along with a renewed appreciation of the meaning of Christian baptism) for a lay as opposed to a sacerdotal and monastic Christianity. Since the aim of Christian perfection can be realized in any condition of life and since true piety is a matter of the heart, not of clothing or foods or outward observances,[35] the religious life can be exercised in a marital state as well as, or perhaps better than, in a monastic state, thinks Erasmus. Marriage for Erasmus, the Christian pedagogue, is then a school for Christian living, in which husband and wife maintain with each other a chaste and holy relationship determined not by perverse pleasure but by a desire for progeny to be educated in the principles of the *philosophia Christi*.[36] Such a state, which is, according to Erasmus, very close to virginity, exhibits what can be called a kind of worldly holiness or, to use Max Weber's term in a different sense, an "intra-mundane asceticism." Thus here Erasmus bridges the gap between the sacred and the profane, between the clergy and the laity, by the recommendation of the marital state to regular and secular clergy and by the incorporation of the ideal of virginity into marriage. Along with the Church and the state, this kind of institution becomes then for Erasmus a major basis for his hope of establishing the universal Christian society.

Marriage as Sacrament

But we are interested in marriage not so much as a state or institution but as a sacrament. We have already noticed that Erasmus placed marriage either first or second in his orders of the sacraments. In view of his high regard for marriage it is probably not without reason that he did so. Besides, we recall that in the *Encomium matrimonii* (1518) he spoke of marriage as the first sacrament, the only one instituted by God before the Fall. He likes to point out that marriage is the *causa sine qua non* of baptism.

> For through marriage we are born into this world: through baptism we are reborn into Christ: it is more excellent indeed to be reborn than to be born, but, nevertheless, unless through marriage we were born, there would not be those who would be reborn by baptism.[37]

For Erasmus, marriage, which represents nature originally created good, is the positive, not simply negative, presupposition for baptism, which represents the *renascentia naturae conditae bene;* just as nature, law, and a *meritum de congruo* on the basis of nature not radically corrupted by evil are the positive presuppositions for receiving justifying grace.

Institution in Scripture and Tradition

However, in spite of his high appreciation of marriage, it is a debatable question whether Erasmus really considered marriage to be a sacrament in the narrower sense of the word. This question arises out of his philological and historical criticism of the New Testament text usually considered as the foundation of this sacrament, Ephesians 5:32, and the debate which issued from this criticism.

We have already suggested in our discussion of Erasmus' understanding of *sacramentum* as used in the New Testament that the humanist undercut the New Testament basis of marriage as a sacrament by his translation of and critical notes on this passage. In 1516 he translates μυστήριον as *mysterium,* not as *sacramentum,* as did the Vulgate. In spite of the attacks made upon it, he maintains this translation in all the succeeding editions of the *Novum Testamentum.*

His short note states merely that marriage as one of the seven sacraments cannot be based on this passage, "not that one ought to doubt about it but that it is not particularly to be gathered from this passage." He thinks that the adversative particle "sufficiently indicates that this great mystery pertains to Christ and the Church, not to husband and wife." Besides, for a man to be joined to a wife is not a great sacrament, since even the heathen are accustomed to such.[38]

In 1519 he greatly expands this note. He qualifies his judgment further by adding, after "not that one ought to doubt about it," these words: "although it is probable that this tradition has come down to us from the Holy Fathers." Although he thus suggests a long extrabiblical tradition behind the orthodox doctrine of marriage as a sacrament, he points to certain of the Fathers as evidently not holding marriage as a sacrament, such as Pseudo-Dionysius, who made no mention of marriage when he expressly dealt with the sacraments; Jerome, who never called marriage a sacrament in all the books that he wrote on the subject; and Augustine, who says nothing about it in his book concerning the goods of marriage.[39] In fact, says Erasmus, Augustine, in his book *De nuptiis ad Valeriam,* in commenting on the Pauline analogy of marriage to the union of Christ with his Church, states that while the latter is a great, the former is the least, *sacramentum.*[40] Erasmus thinks it especially strange, if marriage were considered a sacrament in that time, that Jovinian, the champion of marriage against Jerome, should never refer to it as a sacrament, since that would have helped him clinch his argument. He closes his note by stating that he does not deny that marriage is a sacrament but doubts "whether from this passage it could be demonstrated [*doceri*] that marriage is properly called a sacrament." He emphasizes that the word μυστήριον here means not a sacrament in the later sense of the seven, but *arcanum* or *secretum* as elsewhere in Paul where there can be no question of sacraments.[41]

The only substantive subsequent changes in this note were made in 1522. Erasmus adds "according to the peculiar and exact sense of the word" as a qualification to marriage as one of the seven sacraments which cannot be deduced from this passage. He follows his sentence concerning the long tradition which may lie behind marriage as a sacrament with this qualification: "... even if orthodox scholastics once doubted concerning it [that is, whether marriage was a sacrament in the peculiar and exact sense of the word], indeed were of acknowledged diverse opinion about it."[42] These changes arose out of the debate concerning this translation and these notes, to which we now turn our attention.

The notes were vigorously attacked in turn by Lee, Stunica, Carranza, and the Spanish monks. Since Erasmus' arguments in reply are so similar, we shall discuss them as a whole rather than one by one. Erasmus steadfastly maintains that he does not doubt that marriage is one of the seven sacraments, but simply whether it can be sufficiently deduced from this passage, as he says was already clear from his words in the first edition which were repeated in the second. He states that the most that can be deduced from Ephesians 5:32 is that marriage is a sacrament only in the larger, not in the narrower, sense of the word; that is, as a sign of a sacred thing but not as one which like the others confers grace. He reemphasizes Augustine's statement that, as compared to what is signified—the union between Christ and his Church—the sign, the union between man and wife, is much the less.[43] He says he believes that marriage is a sacrament not because it is here called a mystery but because the Church numbers it among the seven.[44]

To his 1516 and 1519 notes, which pointed to the lack of

scriptural and patristic evidence for marriage as a sacrament in
the later sense of the seven, Erasmus adds the argument that
even some of the scholastics doubted concerning the sacramental character of marriage in the special and exact sense of the
word. He mentions especially Lombard and Durandus. He says
that Lombard was of the opinion that this sacrament does not
confer grace.[45] Durandus, likewise, says Erasmus, questions
whether marriage confers grace and adduces many canonists
who were of this opinion.[46] Erasmus says to Lee, however, that
he embraces the opinion of the most recent theologians that
marriage is a sacrament of the New Law which confers grace,
but he does not think that he who does not accept this opinion
can be regarded as a heretic.[47] Apparently, he is concerned to
allow some freedom of opinion on a question concerning which
there is no clear basis in Scripture or in the early Church Fathers, or even any unanimity among the scholastics, and which
therefore for him needlessly divides Roman Catholics and
Protestants.[48] His position here is admittedly ambiguous because while he seems to acknowledge marriage as a sacrament
in the special sense of the word on the basis of the authority of
the Church, he disputes whether anyone is to be called a heretic
who does not accept this judgment. It is possible that, while he
recognized that there was by then a nearly universal consensus
on this question, to which he would be obedient, he did not
think any binding decision had been made on the subject. In the
reply to Lee he does not mention the decision of the Council
of Florence.[49] When he is apparently reminded of this decree
by Stunica, Erasmus still raises a doubt about whether the
Church has spoken altogether clearly on the question—perhaps
because he did not regard that Council as a genuine ecumenical
council or because he did not think the consensus had been
perpetual and universal enough—but states that, as his writings
testify, he accepts marriage as among those which are properly
called sacraments.[50] On the other hand, in a later reply to
Stunica he confesses that he agreed to the definition of the
Council of Florence even before he knew it had been decreed.[51]

    In spite of the fact that in his debates with his opponents

Erasmus allows his critical reason free play by continuing to question Ephesians 5:32 as a sufficient basis for marriage as a sacrament in the proper sense of the word, by pointing to the lack of evidence for this doctrine among not only the early Church Fathers but also some of the scholastics, by raising a doubt about the force of the decree of Florence, the weight of his statements seems to be that he was willing to accept marriage as a sacrament—though with little pleasure—on the basis of the authority of the Church, for he was aware that on this question there was now a nearly universal consensus. However, he may have felt that this consensus was not old enough to judge anyone a heretic who did not agree with this position.

The evidence for this judgment is, besides the many asseverations in the apologies,[52] the naming of marriage already in his early catechetical poem[53] as one of the seven sacraments conferring grace and the description of the grace of this sacrament in the *Christiani matrimonii institutio* (1526). Undoubtedly, here as elsewhere he prefers a coinherence of Scripture and tradition but accepts nevertheless a tradition which arises out of a universal consensus, even though not grounded in Scripture. Hence one is forced to disagree with Telle, who thinks that Erasmus did not at all accept marriage as a sacrament and was not at all sincere in his avowals of allegiance to the authority of the Church.[54]

The Nature of the Sacrament of Marriage

Before discussing the nature of the sacrament of marriage for Erasmus, it is necessary to treat briefly the medieval tradition on the subject because Erasmus' understanding both of the nature of marriage and consequently also of the sacrament departs from this tradition.

According to canon law and scholastic theology marriage is first of all a contract entered into by mutual consent expressed in the words of the present.[55] Words of the future do not make a marriage, although in the judgment of the Church carnal intercourse following words of the future does make a marriage. The solemnization of this contract, though desirable, was not necessary for the validity of the marriage. The carnal copula does not constitute the marriage, but only completes or consummates it.

The agreement, which is the efficient cause of the contract, is also the efficient cause of the sacrament, although it produced something of a problem how a human agreement could be the cause of a divine sacrament.[56] If the consent is the efficient cause of the sacrament, then the grace which is bestowed in the sacrament issues from this fact, not from the priestly nuptial blessing. Such was at least the opinion of St. Thomas, which became the common one. Bonaventure, on the other hand, held to the necessity of the priestly benediction. This minority view continued to be expressed into the sixteenth century.[57]

The words of the partners constituted the form of the sacrament, according to Albert the Great and Thomas, who did not recognize the problem as did Duns Scotus. Scotus also regarded the words of the present as the sign, but expressly denied that a marriage contracted without words was a sacrament because it would have no sensible sign. He thus split the union of contract and sacrament by this denotation of the form. Toward the end of the Middle Ages, although the Scotist view was still held, the wider opinion held by theologians and canonists was that the existence of the marriage did not depend upon a sensible sign. Any kind of sign would do.

Concerning the matter of the sacrament there was at first no agreement. Some thought of the body which is transferred to the other as the matter. Others thought of the words pronounced by the first of the wedded pair to speak. However, on the analogy of marriage to penance, Albert and Thomas held that the dispositions and acts of the couple were the matter.[58] The final cause was procreation, and education of children.[59] The scholastics enumerated the three goods of marriage after Augustine as faithfulness (*fides*), offspring (*proles*), and indissolubility (*sacramentum*).[60] Indissolubility belongs by nature to marriage as sacrament, which is the image of the indissoluble union of God with man and Christ with his Church.[61] However, only marriages contracted and consummated were strictly indissoluble. For marriages contracted but not consummated, certain impediments were recognized, such as especially vows and orders.[62]

Erasmus breaks with the medieval canonical and theological tradition on marriage by regarding not the contract but the union of souls as the essence of marriage, to which is added secondarily the union of flesh. Near the beginning of the *Christiani matrimonii institutio* he does give in a rather traditional manner the *legitima coniunctio* as the essence and the efficient cause of marriage, but he qualifies that phrase by judging that though the law is the author of marriage, God is the author of the law. God's law as expressed in Genesis 2:24 was that "they will be two in one flesh. On account of this a man will leave his father and mother and will cleave to his wife."[63] A little later he makes his point of view still clearer: "I call marriage not that which is ratified by laws but that which is glued together among those equal in virtue by true affections."[64] Mutuality of love makes the marriage. Where this element is lacking, there is in reality no marriage. In line with his total thought Erasmus is intent upon emphasizing more strongly than the medieval scholastic and canonical tradition the personal and inward element as over against the legal and sacramental. As we shall see, this attitude will affect his thought on divorce.

However, on the basis of this conception of the essence of marriage, Erasmus did not favor free, extralegal marriages. On the contrary, he sharply opposed what he considered to be one of the major evils of his day, clandestine marriages, and proposed some modification in marriage law concerning the all-sufficiency of words of the present for the contracting of marriages, which made this evil possible. He urged that such marriages be declared invalid,[65] or if valid, that divorce be allowed when the union that resulted was not a true union.[66] He recommended for the correction of the evil that the rulers of the Church restore the role of parents in establishing marriages[67] and that marriages be contracted before judges and witnesses by sober, free, solemn words of consent.

While affirming his respect for law and authority, the humanist urges as a basis for his program the idea that laws, like medical remedies, ought to be changed and accommodated for the salvation of men.[68] He complains about the rigor and the complexity of the canonical legislation on marriage and urges some relaxation and moderation of these laws. He is critical of the legislation concerning the impediments, especially of that which elevates the vow of chastity to the detriment of the vow of marriage.[69]

Turning now to Erasmus' understanding of the nature of the sacrament as such, we discover that he applies not the scholastic categories, but rather his own usual terms to describe it: *imago, arra,* and *exemplum.* The image has to do with what is represented or signified by the union of man and wife. Erasmus used his imagination to discover not just one or two but four realities symbolized in marriage: (1) the union of God and man in the incarnation; (2) the union of Christ and his Church; (3) even the collaboration of God and the Virgin Mary in the generation of the human nature of Christ; and (4) the union of Christ and the individual soul. The first of these is according to the allegorical sense, the last according to the tropological sense.[70] Erasmus thus sees in marriage not simply a natural state but one which is a symbol of transcendental reality. For Erasmus marriage is without much question chiefly a sacrament because it is a sign of a sacred thing.

Now arises the question as to what in marriage constitutes the sign or symbol or, to use Erasmus' word, the image of these realities. When talking about the first, the union of God and man in the incarnation, Erasmus mentions the sign as the sensible conjunction of man and wife. He even likens the union between God and man in the incarnation, where the two natures are not confused, to the copula between man and wife, where each of the sexes retains its own nature in the union. However, as is clear a little later and from our discussion of what constitutes the essence of marriage for Erasmus, it is the indivisible conjunction of souls which is the primary sign of this union.[71] In line with his principle of flesh and spirit, though the spirit is preferred, the flesh is not denied.[72] But, as we have seen, in accord with the medieval tradition, Erasmus thinks that the fleshly union itself ought to be chaste, for the purpose of bearing offspring or as a remedy for incontinence.[73]

In connection with the *arra* or *munus* (the gift of spiritual grace), Erasmus recalls once more that the opinions of the theologians have varied. The more ancient ones saw in the sacrament a "sign of most sacred things," but excluded it from the definition of sacrament in the exact sense of the word because they did not think that "a special and sacramental grace was infused." But Erasmus admits that such is now the consensus of the orthodox, and states:

> But the more plausible opinion of the recent doctors has conquered, which hands down that in marriage rightly received, just as in the other sacraments, a special gift of the Spirit is infused, by which we are rendered stronger for perpetual concord, firmer for bearing together the misfortunes of this life, and better prepared for rearing the offspring in piety.

He is thus willing to accept what he still regards as only a more plausible opinion, because he recognizes that it has conquered; but he still does not seem to consider it as a definite dogmatic statement to be received by all, since he also says:

> If anyone should not receive this opinion [that is, that God *velut ex pacto* bestows a special gift as often as the sacramental function is performed], the sacrament nevertheless brings to remembrance that charity and concord and, by recalling, as it were, excites it.[74]

In other words, for those who do not think that a gift of grace is granted, the sacrament may still serve as an *exemplum*. To him it is not of great importance whether one thinks of it as a sacrament only in the larger, or also in the more specific, sense of the term. In the *Symbolum* (1533) Erasmus witnesses once more to his somewhat hesitant acceptance of this opinion and shows that he has allied himself with the minority tradition associated with the name of Bonaventure, which held that the priestly nuptial benediction was essential for the bestowing of grace.[75]

But, says Erasmus, as in the other sacraments, this grace is changed to wrath unless one receives it worthily, unless one corresponds to the high dignity of the office of marriage with dignity of life. The realities of which marriage is the image call for imitation. They represent the example to be followed in order that marriage might be free of divorce, discord, and lewdness, and rich in pious works. Erasmus speaks of the gift as making possible the fulfillment of the demand; but in the end, as elsewhere in his soteriology and sacramental theology, he makes the gift contingent upon the activity of the self.[76]

Divorce

According to the orthodox understanding since Augustine of marriage as sacrament, whether marriage was considered a sacrament only in the larger sense or also in the narrower sense, indissolubility belonged to it by nature. In his ideas on divorce Erasmus charts an independent course.

He first suggests these new ideas in a note on Matthew 19:2 in the 1516 edition of the *Novum Testamentum,* which says that only Christ's commandment on divorce has been strictly retained, whereas the others on not swearing, resisting evil, etc., have been allowed to become antiquated. He wonders, since Moses conceded divorce on account of hardness of hearts, why it could not likewise be conceded to his age which suffered from the same affliction and to which brothels were conceded.

Erasmus greatly elaborates his ideas on this subject in his 1519 note, which is really a dissertation on I Corinthians 7:39.[77] It cannot be our purpose to analyze in detail this treatise, which has already been discussed at some length by Telle, but because of its importance for understanding Erasmus' thought we must set forth its essential ideas.

The starting point for Erasmus' interest in this question was the unfortunate condition of many clandestine marriages. As a moralist he saw this condition as an atrocious evil which required a radical cure. In this extensive note of 1519 he dared to propose earnestly and explicitly divorce as the cure. His arguments, although they are brought forth to meet this specific evil, are, however, far-reaching in their implications for the question of divorce in general and for his understanding of the nature of theology.

Erasmus prefaces his discussion by pointing out that he does not wish to be the author of contentious dogmas, that whatever he advises here he submits to the authority of the Church. On the other hand, he does not think that it is insolent to disagree with some author, however great or old. He moves into the body of his discourse by acknowledging that the tradition is nearly unanimous in opposing divorce, but he thinks that certain things have been received by the authority of the Church in such a way that they could be changed by that same authority. The Scriptures, although they are a most certain rule of life, can be accommodated to public customs.

Even though he admits the general unanimity of the tradition on the subject, he is not willing to concede that the tradition has been in absolute agreement. He thinks that Origen, Tertullian, and Ambrose among the early Church Fathers open the door to the possibility of divorce. Likewise, he notes that the canonists have permitted divorce for marriages contracted but not consummated, a distinction which he thinks is arbitrary, for "either one ought to deny that marriage is marriage, because conjugal intercourse has not confirmed it, or one ought to admit that marriage is rightly divorced."[78] He suggests that in the question of marriage and divorce human matters have become so intermingled with divine that it would not be absurd for yet another human consideration to attenuate the strictness of the divine law—namely, the well-being of so many unhappily married people.[79]

As for this divine law, the commandment of Jesus on divorce, we have already seen that Erasmus suggested:

> But if the matter seems to conflict with natural equity, one should see whether the words might be otherwise interpreted which are read in the Evangelical and Apostolic letters on this subject.[80]

Even though he considers the law of Christ to transcend the law of nature, he does not think there can be any essential conflict between the two. The law of Christ confirms but does not abrogate the law of nature. On this basis he says that Christ did not demand virginity, because it would seem to conflict with nature, although he did pronounce them blessed who can receive it. But Christ adds "for the sake of the kingdom," which Erasmus interprets as meaning the preaching of the gospel, which applies more to those times.[81] As we have seen, he thinks the call to virginity applied especially to Apostolic times.

He reasons similarly here about the commandment on divorce. It was given not to the crowd but to the disciples of Christ, to those who live in the light of the kingdom where there is no need of laws. The saying on divorce is not to be isolated from the other sayings of Christ on not swearing at all, not resisting evil, loving even the enemy. Erasmus asks why we are strict in our understanding of the words on divorce alone and allow the others to be interpreted more loosely and relaxed, to be excused on the grounds that they are counsels for the perfect, not precepts for everyone. Christ wishes that people were of such quality that there would be no need of laws, of divorce, or oath-taking. But if, on account of the weak, who are present in the Church in such great numbers, swearing and repelling force with force are permitted, why not also divorce? If on account of hardness of heart it was once permitted to the Jews, lest worse crimes be perpetrated, why may not the same remedy be granted to Christians who suffer from the same disease?[82]

As for the objection that such a procedure would be going not only against Scripture but also against the laws of the Church, Erasmus answers that the Church has instituted some regulations which it intended to be valid only for a time, as, for example, in the New Testament the Apostolic decree concerning the four prohibitions. Then he proceeds to show that other matters of doctrine and practice have varied and evolved over the centuries, such as the doctrines of transubstantiation and the procession of the Holy Spirit. He says the Church, made up of men, is not without error. It is sufficient that it be without error with regard to the "sum of our faith and religion." The point he wishes to make then is that this question is not one upon which our faith hinges and, in the light of variations on other matters of faith which were of greater consequence in the history of the Church, it could also be changed for the sake of the salvation of men.

He elevates the power of the Pope beyond his usual preference to provide for some modifications of this strict law. He suggests that since some attribute so much authority to the Roman pontiff, could not he in some manner interpret or relax what Jesus commanded? He thinks that since Paul, considerate of human weakness, sometimes relaxed a commandment of the Lord, why could not the Pope do the same?[83]

Thus Erasmus enlists his method of literary and historical exegesis of Scripture[84] and his historical-relativistic understanding of ecclesiastical tradition to support his moral sense, which perceived the necessity of making some accommodation of this law in order to succor the plight of so many ill-formed marriages. He reveals himself not only as a historical, but also as something of an ethical, relativist and contextualist who thinks that love, which is the substance of the law of nature and the law of Scripture, is the only ultimate guide of human behavior—not human, historically conditioned laws. He thinks that love dictates in this matter as in others that some accommodation be made to the weakness of men, lest still worse evils be perpetrated. Although his desire to bring up this whole subject for public discussion was motivated by his concern for the special problem of that day, when marriages could be contracted so easily without the solemnization of public authority, what he had to say on the subject might apply to any marriage, however contracted, when there is no longer a consensus of souls, which for him is the essence of marriage.

As for the objection that marriage as a sacrament is undermined if divorce is permitted, Erasmus first points out again that marriage was not always regarded as one of the seven sacraments, even by so recent a writer as Durandus. He says again here that the ancients following Paul sometimes called marriage a sacrament because they saw in that closest friendship of man and wife an image and type of the union of Christ and the Church. Erasmus agrees that marriage rightly preserved is indeed holy but in itself is not holy, as, for example, the marriage of David with Bathsheba or of Hosea with a prostitute. But he thinks that it is not at all necessary for the type to correspond entirely with what is typified, so that marriage can be called a sacrament in this sense even if there are certain marriages which are not properly congruent with the reality signified.[85]

But, he says, even if we grant that marriage is to be received as a true sacrament, divorce among a few does not necessarily harm the sacrament, for the Church acknowledges that there is a sacrament even when an old man marries an old woman or when a drunken man marries a drunken woman, even though these do not at all correspond to the reality symbolized by marriage. Furthermore, if the sacrament of baptism is not harmed by unclean lives, neither is the sacrament of marriage removed if contaminated by human vices or if in some cases divorce is granted. It is a sufficient congruence of marriage with the mystery symbolized if the intention to remain united is present and if among many marriage remains perpetual. If a type for divorce is desired, the one of Origen can be proposed, that Christ divorced that murderous woman, the Synagogue, and became joined to a bride worthy of him, the Church.[86]

Erasmus thus thinks that in spite of divorce, marriage may be retained as a sacrament, whether one thinks of it as such only in the ancient sense or also in the modern sense. He realizes probably that his thoughts on divorce are less congruent with marriage in the more recent sense of the word, and for that reason he points out that marriage as one of the seven sacraments is of late origin.

VIII

THE EUCHARIST

————————◆·◀◆▶·◆————————

The Eucharist, the supreme sacrament for St. Thomas, was also important for Erasmus, for here is displayed the union with Christ and with one another, with the accent for Erasmus on the latter. It is appropriately placed between the social and the individual sacraments because it is at once a sacrament for the individual and for the whole commmunity, with the emphasis for Erasmus again upon the latter. The Eucharist is also the sacrament in which priests and laity are united. They pray for each other, the first by virtue of delegated office, the second because of brotherly love. It may be related to marriage insofar as the union of Christ with the Church, which is symbolized in marriage, is both symbolized and partially actualized in the Eucharist, and also insofar as in both there is not only a spiritual but a fleshly union, with the stress in each on the spiritual, as one would expect on the basis of Erasmus' preference of spirit over flesh. In fact, that preference is so strong that one might wonder whether Erasmus would at all accept the substantial bodily presence of Christ in the Eucharist. This will be a major subject of discussion in this chapter, in which we shall have to take issue with the principal work that has been done on this topic, the 1955 Erlangen dissertation of Gottfried Krodel.[1] Since his is a rather detailed study, we shall limit our discussion to a summary of its essential features and to a criticism of some of his conclusions.

I. Institution

Words of Consecration

As is the case with other sacraments, Erasmus' application of his critical method to the New Testament texts which are regarded as the foundation of the Eucharist leads him to question some widely held assumptions. Regarding the institution, he disputes the identity of Jesus' words of consecration with those of the priest.

In his annotations on Mark 14 and I Corinthians 11, Erasmus raises a doubt concerning the words with which Jesus consecrated the bread and wine. First in his 1516 note on Mark 14:22 Erasmus points out the erroneous translation of the Greek text ". . . εὐλογήσας ἔκλασεν . . ." by ". . . benedicens fregit . . ." in the Vulgate. The translation ought rather to be "cum benedixissit fregit"—"for he did not at the same time bless and break [the bread]."[2] Erasmus adds further that to bless is not to make the sign of the cross but to give thanks to God.[3]

In the 1519 edition Erasmus is more explicit in an addition to the note on the words concerning the cup. In contrast to what many so often assert, Erasmus says, one may not here read expressly what Jesus' words of consecration were, for the words "This is the cup . . ." were spoken after he had handed it to his disciples and they had all drunk of it.[4] In the next, the 1522 edition, Erasmus qualifies his critical judgment here by suggesting that the passage could be interpreted by the figure πρωθύστερον;[5] that is, the words spoken last may be understood to apply to what stands first. Erasmus does not elaborate on his meaning. In the light of the fact that he makes so little of this device and that he continues to doubt concerning the words of consecration, one should not take too seriously this small effort to stem the tide of criticism.[6]

In his 1516 note on I Corinthians 11:24 Erasmus merely states that the verse ought to be read without the substantive verb 'εστιν, although he does find it in some manuscripts.[7]

Already, therefore, he raises a question concerning the exact form of the words of consecration.

In 1519 he adds to this note a defense from St. Thomas for his doubt concerning the words Jesus used to consecrate the bread. Erasmus reports that Thomas admits that there have been those who have contended that Jesus consecrated the bread with other words before he said, "This is my body." Although he refutes this opinion, Thomas does not call it heretical, even though he does call heretical the view that Christ is not truly in the sacrament, but only as in a sign.[8] He concludes the note first by acknowledging his willingness to accede to the judgment of the Church (although he thinks the expression "This is my body" on the basis of the text itself applies to the bread already consecrated), and then by urging theologians not to assert boldly what cannot be proved out of divine Scriptures.[9]

In 1527 he revises the note somewhat to allay criticism but continues to raise a doubt about the words of consecration. In this note he more directly questions the ground of the priestly form, which was only indirectly the object in view in the previous notes where he wondered concerning Jesus' words. Here he replaces the sentence concerning bold theological statements not grounded in Scripture with these words:

> But unless one acquiesces in the decrees of the Church, it will be very difficult to prove by human reason with what words the priest may consecrate. For even if we grant that Christ consecrated with words of this kind, who without question has initiated this pact with us, how is it possible that we ourselves, reciting different words, consecrate also?[10]

Erasmus points out thus that there is a dichotomy between Scripture and tradition even if one concedes that Christ consecrated with the words "This is my body . . . ," since the words of consecration that the priest uses in the Mass vary somewhat from Jesus' own words.[11] He concludes his 1527 addition with a strong statement on the necessity of subjecting reason to faith in matters of this kind. Erasmus was apparently aware that there

was a conciliar decision concerning the priestly form of consecration,[12] to which, in spite of Scripture and reason, he will be
obedient; but, as we shall see, he will continue to contend that
the Church has not clearly spoken about what were Jesus' words
of consecration.

Erasmus continues to maintain his position on the consecration against friend and foe. First in the *Detectio praestigiarum cuiusdam libelli* . . . (1526), he defends himself against a
Zwinglian Protestant[13] from having impugned the Real Presence in these notes. He continues to hold that his questions in
the notes on Mark 14 and I Corinthians 11 had to do with the
words of consecration, not the Real Presence.[14]

Likewise, in the *Adversus monachos quosdam Hispanos* (1528),
his response to the first heavy barrage from the side of the
champions of orthodoxy, Erasmus, with some elaboration,
maintains his position on this subject. In response to the citation of the note on Mark 14 as against the Eucharist, Erasmus
states that it is not yet clear to him that the Church has distinctly
declared itself on the question of the words used by Christ to
consecrate, even if it is clear that he handed on to us this form
of consecrating. He refers once more to Thomas Aquinas and
also to Gabriel Biel[15] as authors who do not hide the fact that
there have been various theological opinions on the subject,
nor do these writers pronounce him heretical who has some
doubts about it. Finally, they bring out only one authority on the
affirmative, Eusebius Emissenus, "an author of not much favorable renown provided he is the one whose words are reported
in the Decretals. . . ."[16] He offers further as a palliative the figure
$\pi\rho\omega\theta\acute{\upsilon}\sigma\tau\epsilon\rho o\nu$ as a possible method of interpretation, but, passing quickly over this point, goes on to conclude that "Christ
could have consecrated the bread and wine into the body and
blood of Christ without any words."[17]

In his response to the attack on the 1519 note on I Corinthians 11, Erasmus relates his understanding of the words of consecration to his concept of authority. He reminds the monks
that he had prefaced his remarks with a statement of willingness
to subject himself to the authority of the Church on this matter

when the Church has clearly spoken. However, he does not view the various opinions of the theologians or bishops as representing this authority, but only universal synods. He thinks further that even these general councils should be circumspect in what they define, "for there are certain things concerning which it is not necessary to pronounce, others concerning which one is permitted to hesitate."[18] This question is such a one. Though the Church has instructed us on the substance of the body in the Eucharist, it has not so instructed us on the form of the words.[19]

His final statement on this subject is in the response to the Sorbonne's censure of the passage from the preface to the paraphrase of I Corinthians. He repeats that there is not agreement even today on Jesus' words of consecration, nor can it be clearly discovered from Scripture or from the books of the ancients what the Apostolic words of consecration were. As in the response to the Spanish monks, he points to the variations on the words of consecration in the ancient liturgies. He says that he will agree to the idea that the present Roman form of consecration has been handed down from the Apostles (but he would hardly agree that they had been handed down without modification). He maintains, however, that he cannot be reprimanded for wishing that it had been more clearly expressed in Scripture.[20] In these remarks his sense of historical change and his perception of the dichotomy between Scripture and tradition are once more evident.

Eucharist and Fellowship Meal (*Agape*)

Closely connected with the question of the words of consecration is the issue of the relation between the Last Supper, where Jesus consecrated the bread and wine into his body and blood, and the fellowship meal of the early Christian community, in which it is not so clear, says Erasmus, that the Apostles consecrated bread and wine into body and blood. In a note on Acts 2:46 concerning the breaking of bread in the homes of Christians, Erasmus states that "it is uncertain whether here consecrated bread is meant since there is no mention of the cup."[21] In his paraphrase of Acts 2:42 (1524), he calls this act

of communion a symbol of the everlasting covenant and a commemoration of the Lord's passion,[22] phrases which he uses also
in his paraphrase of the accounts of the Lord's Supper.

When Leo Jud wrote that he saw Zwinglian ideas of the
Lord's Supper in these words, Erasmus answered that interpreters are uncertain whether here we have to do with the body
and blood of Christ or with common bread. For neither Jesus
nor the disciples appear always to have consecrated bread into
the body of Christ and wine into his blood when they broke
bread and drank wine. Erasmus points to Jesus' feeding of the
five thousand and the breaking of bread with the two disciples
on the road to Emmaus. Likewise, the Apostles, as reported in
this passage as well as in Acts 2:46, may have eaten only common, not consecrated, bread. (He mentions elsewhere in this
treatise that it is uncertain whether Paul in I Corinthians 11
"speaks properly of the consecrated body and blood of the
Lord."[23]) However, there is nothing wrong with seeing in the
distribution of even common bread a symbol of Christian concord and a commemoration of the Lord's death; so the paraphrase is justified, Erasmus implies, for using these terms
(which will also be applied to the Eucharist in the special sense)
and for omitting any reference to the body and blood of Christ.

Erasmus adds these thoughts to his 1527 note on I Corinthians 11:24. He says that "it is insufficiently clear from the commentaries of the ancients whether Paul here treats of the
sacerdotal consecration of the body and blood of the Lord."[24]
The occasion, Erasmus points out, was a community meal in
which there had already developed a lessening of the early shar-
ing in love, since everyone ate with his own kind, excluding the
poor, so that the poor were not only not fed but humiliated. In
this situation Paul, as Chrysostom and Theophylact explain,

> . . . injects the mention of the Lord's Supper so that by the
> memory of that most sacred feast they might be recalled to that
> seriousness and brotherly fellowship which the Lord exhibited
> by the distribution of his own body among his disciples.[25]

As in the *Detectio* he defends this interpretation by pointing to
the fact that neither Jesus nor the disciples always consecrated

bread into the body of Christ when they broke bread together. He adds in this note, however, a typically wavering comment:

> I do not know whether that bread and cup, which Christians exchanged among themselves with thanksgiving and with the signification of the mutual charity among themselves, they sometimes called the body and cup of the Lord, because they [the bread and cup] were their [body and blood] signs.[26]

In the end, Erasmus says that it would be more pleasing to him if this passage applied to consecration, but he implies that he cannot assert it.

Two letters—one in 1529, the other in 1530—also touch on this question. To Justus Decius went his strongest statement on the subject: ". . . I find no passage in the divine Scriptures whence it is without question evident that the Apostles consecrated the bread and wine into the body and blood of Christ."[27] In a letter to Cuthbert Tunstall his judgment varies somewhat. He declares:

> Nowhere in the canonical letters does one discover a place where the Apostles assuredly consecrated the body of the Lord as it is now consecrated on the altar except in one place, I Corinthians 11; and yet in chapter 10 according to his wording Paul does not seem to talk about consecration.[28]

In view of his 1527 note and the above letter to Decius these remarks can only be regarded as a concession to his staunchly Catholic friend, the Bishop of Durham, who was later himself to write an important treatise in defense of the Roman Catholic doctrine of the Eucharist.[29]

The effect of these doubts concerning the exact connection between the priestly words of consecration and Jesus' own words and concerning the basis for the rite of consecration in the Apostolic practice is to raise a question concerning the New Testament basis or the divine ground of the priestly power of consecration in the Eucharist. Like "this form" or "this law" of confession, *this* form of consecration has a gradual historical development, is therefore *de iure humano,* not *de iure divino,* and is to be accepted primarily on the basis of the authority of the

Church.[30] Also, in spite of his denials, the consequence of his critical discussions was to raise a question about the ground of the doctrine of the Real Presence.

II. Spiritual Meaning

The central feature of Erasmus' teaching on the Eucharist as on the other sacraments is the flesh-spirit concept. As one must move from a merely literal interpretation of Scripture to the hidden spiritual meaning and from a physical to a spiritual understanding of Christ, so one must pass from a merely bodily participation in the Eucharist to an inner appropriation of its spiritual and moral meaning. A merely physical participation is of little or no effect, indeed may be harmful, unless the spirit is added. Erasmus applies John 6:64 to a sacramental eating: "Nay he has even spurned the eating of his flesh and the drinking of his blood unless they are eaten and drunk spiritually. To whom do you think he spoke these words: The flesh is of no use, it is the spirit that gives life."[31] Neither the sacramental elements nor the bodily participation is rejected any more than the letter of Scripture or the humanity of Christ, but the emphasis as always is upon the personal and ethical dimension of sacramental participation, on the *ex opere operantis,* not upon the *ex opere operato.* More important than the use of the physical signs in each of the sacraments is the discernment of the spiritual meaning or reality which these signs symbolize or convey.

Imago—Repraesentatio and *Commemoratio*

As in the other sacraments, so in the Eucharist one can divide the spiritual aspect into the *imago,* the *arra,* and the *exemplum.* The *imago* has to do with what is symbolized or represented in the Eucharist. As Erasmus says many times in his writings, this is first the death or sacrifice of Christ on the cross.[32] However, Erasmus was cool toward the idea of the Mass as a sacrifice for two reasons: (1) because the more important sacrifice is not the objective act on the altar, but the subjective act, the sacrifice of the evil feelings[33] or the sacrifice of praise and thanksgiving which is or ought to be perpetual;[34] and (2) because the deed upon the cross was a unique, unrepeatable event.[35] Therefore, he would prefer to say simply that the sacrifice of Christ is represented in the Mass[36] without adding, like the scholastics, that it is nevertheless a real sacrifice. When the Spanish monks attacked him for saying "It is not a question of articles of faith, but . . . whether the Mass could in some sense be called a sacrifice,"[37] Erasmus replied that he was not against the sacrifice of the Mass, that he considered it indeed a sacrifice but not in the same manner ". . . in which Christ accomplished the true sacrifice on the cross."[38] Considering it a matter of indifference he will even call the Eucharist a sacrifice in some of his later writings,[39] but he will prefer to say that the Mass "renews [*renovare*, undoubtedly in the sense of "renew in mind" or "recall"] that unique sacrifice."[40]

The Eucharistic rite is first of all an objective representation of a mysterious reality, the death of Christ for our sins. However, he moves quickly from the thought of its objective to its subjective representation in our minds and lives,[41] that is, from *repraesentatio* to *commemoratio* and *imitatio*. The representation of the death of Christ in the Eucharist awakens in us the memory of the cross and the immense love of God revealed there. The memorial aspect of the Eucharist is a constant emphasis in Erasmus' writings. Associated with the theme of commemoration is that of contemplation. In memory and faith we contemplate the grace and mystery of this deed.[42] But, as stated earlier, *commemoratio* and *contemplatio* then must lead on to *imitatio*.[43] The commemoration and contemplation of the death of Christ should stir us to mortify the desires of the flesh.[44] The love of God which we commemorate and contemplate in the Eucharist should arouse in us a responsive love to God and to our neighbor.[45] Before considering more fully the normative aspect of the Eucharist, we describe its character as gift for Erasmus.

Arra

According to Erasmus, in the Eucharist as in all the sacraments, besides the *imago* there is the *arra* or *munus*, the gift of spiritual grace which is suggested by the signs and which accompanies their use. This grace is not intrinsically but extrinsically connected with the sacramental signs. Grace does not come through, but parallels, the sacramental action. The action takes place not indirectly through the sacrament but directly upon the soul.

Actually Erasmus conceives the Eucharistic grace as operating not so much sacramentally as psychologically. The sacramental signs represent the supreme evidence (*argumentum*) and pledge (*pignus*) of God's love for us.[46] This concrete pledge keeps alive the memory of Christ's wonderful love upon the cross so that in contemplation and commemoration of that deed our faith is nourished and increased and we are given strength for the battle of the Christian life and consolation for the hour of death.[47] Though the dominant theme is that of Eucharistic grace working through the memory of the crucifixion, Erasmus will talk also more mystically of the present, not simply commemorative, union with the Lord, who is truly exhibited in the Eucharist,[48] so that we are all the more strengthened. Because of the grace received through commemoration and of present union with Christ, the Lord's Supper is a festival of joy and thanksgiving, "whence it is also called Eucharist, because thanksgiving resounds in us."[49]

Exemplum and *Synaxis*

But the *Eucharistia* of the Lord's Supper is limited because Erasmus adds immediately to the gift quality of the Supper the idea of the Supper as demand. In this sacred meal the gracious love of God is represented to us in order that we might respond in love to God and to our neighbor.[50] He moves swiftly from the thought of the Lord's Supper as symbolizing the union of the members of the mystical body of Christ with their Head, to the thought of the Supper as symbolizing and exemplifying the communion of the members with one another,[51] the synaxis conception.[52] The Lord's Supper as the representation of the communion in love of Christians with one another was naturally a favorite theme for the peace- and unity-minded humanist. In one of his treatises on war Erasmus pointed to the incongruity of frequenting the Eucharist, the symbol of friendship and peace, by Christians who were at war.

> Dare any man be so bold as to approach that sacred meal, the symbol of friendship or the banquet of peace, who resolves on war against Christians and prepares to destroy them for whom Christ died, to spill the blood of them for whom Christ shed his blood?[53]

Love and peace with one's neighbor are therefore the preconditions for a worthy and fruitful partaking of the Lord's Supper. Not only love but also a pure conscience is an important presupposition of a worthy eating.[54] As we have seen in our treatment of justification, in the final analysis Erasmus makes the gift contingent on the fulfillment of the demand, as in this passage: ". . . much divine grace would be added to those who purely and worthily would eat."[55]

III. Symbols and Real Presence—Prior to 1525

We have made no attempt to provide a historical analysis of the spiritual meaning of the Eucharist for Erasmus, because, as the references show, his point of view does not vary greatly on this subject.[56] What constitutes for him the most important aspect of the Eucharist, *repraesentatio* and *commemoratio, contemplatio* in faith and *imitatio* in love, remains constant from the *Enchiridion* (1503) to the *De praeparatione ad mortem* (1534). However, when it comes to the question of the Real Presence, we reach an issue upon which there was a shifting emphasis. A more careful historical analysis is therefore required.

Prior to the Eucharistic controversy of the middle 1520's Erasmus, while not denying the Real Presence, stresses the inward appropriation in faith and love of the spiritual meaning of the Lord's Supper. His thought revolves around the themes of *repraesentatio, commemoratio,* and *imitatio.*

Passages which suggest the Real Presence without explicitly declaring it are few, but present. In the early catechetical poem *Christiani hominis institutum* (1514), Erasmus says that Christ is truly and plainly present under the image of bread and wine. In the paraphrase of I Corinthians 11 he speaks alternately about eating the bread and drinking the cup or eating the body and drinking the blood of Christ. A further indication in this paraphrase that Erasmus thinks in terms of some objective reality in the Eucharist is the emphasis upon the mystery, that here we have the representation of an *arcanae rei,* the *res omnium maxime mystica,* which must be treated purely and reverently, and which leads to the destruction of those who eat unworthily.[57]

Finally, in a letter to John Slechta, Erasmus refers to the "pure body and blood of the Lord" which is to be eaten "purely by the pure" as "a most sacred sign and pledge" of Christ's love to us and of our concord among ourselves, but rejects as not conducive to the progress of piety questions concerning the exact mode of his presence in the Eucharist.[58]

These passages, though not many, indicate that Erasmus, however much he might stress in his early writings the subjective aspects of the Eucharistic celebration, could talk also about the Real Presence. His language is typically vague but does not indicate a denial of the objective reality of Christ in the Eucharist. On the other hand, his words on the subject provide us with little illumination on the question of how he conceived of this presence. Does Erasmus think of Christ as bodily or only spiritually present?[59] His sense of reverence before the divine mystery and skepticism concerning theoretical formulations of this mystery naturally led him to prefer to leave questions of this kind untouched. Although in the catechetical poem he spoke of Christ as "truly present,"[60] he does not use the term "substantially" here as he does later after the outbreak of the Eucharistic conflict.

Besides the heavy emphasis on the subjective as compared to the objective aspects of the Eucharist, another factor in assessing Erasmus' early view is his frequent use of the terms *symbolum* and *signum.* In the first place it is clear that though along Franciscan lines *symbolum* and *res* are sharply distinguished, they are not so separated that *symbolum* is an empty term. Erasmus thinks of a "congruence"[61] between sign and

thing signified so that the symbol or sign is "most sacred,"
"mystical," or "mysterious."[62]

What is not clear, however, is what Erasmus intends as the
symbol. He is typically inexact in his application of the terms
"symbol" and "sign." Sometimes it is the meal itself,[63] occasionally even the body and blood of Christ,[64] which is the symbol, but most often Erasmus leaves clouded in obscurity
precisely what he considers the sign to be.[65]

Likewise, Erasmus variously understands what is signified
by the sign—sometimes Christ's death or his love as shown in
his death[66] or the new covenant, sometimes the concord or
friendship among Christians,[67] sometimes both Christ's love
and the fellowship of believers.

Although the use of the terms "symbol" and "sign" in the
designation of the Lord's Supper are frequent, however vague,
their presence does not necessarily imply a purely symbolic,
spiritualistic understanding, that is, that it is only the bread and
wine which are symbols of the body and blood of Christ, as
Erasmus himself correctly insists in the response to Jud.[68]

IV. Background for Erasmus' Later Position on the Eucharistic Presence

Erasmus' later remarks about the Real Presence have as
their background the Eucharistic conflict of the middle 1520's,
into which Erasmus became embroiled willy-nilly, although he
preferred to remain aloof as was his customary but seldom
realizable wish. First Carlstadt, then Zwingli and Oecolampadius, put forward a symbolistic, spiritualistic understanding
of the Eucharist which rejected the corporeal Real Presence.[69]

On December 10, 1524, Erasmus writes to Melanchthon:
"Carlstadt was here, but secretly: he published six books written in German, in which he teaches that in the Eucharist there
is nothing beyond the sign of the body and blood of the
Lord."[70] Actually there seem to have been no less than seven
treatises published for the former associate of Luther during
October and November, 1524, in Basel. In these the spiritualist

reformer rejects for the first time the corporeal presence of Christ in the Eucharist and its sacramental significance, and applies the τοῦτο in the words of institution to Jesus' own body. Köhler points out that in his complete rejection of the objective sacramental character of the Lord's Supper, even as a pledge to confirm faith, Carlstadt goes beyond Zwingli's position at this time.[71]

In a letter to Thomas Lupset, ⟨c. 4 October ⟩1525, Erasmus writes that ". . . Huldrich Zwingli has confirmed with two published books" Carlstadt's persuasion that there is nothing but bread and wine in the Eucharist.[72] Erasmus has in mind probably the *Subsidium sive coronis de eucharistia* (August 17, 1525) and the German paraphrase of this work also in 1525, or perhaps the *Subsidium* and the still earlier *Commentarius de vera et falsa religione* (March 1525), in which Zwingli devoted a lengthy chapter to the Eucharist. In these works Zwingli had moved away from his earlier Erasmian position, which, while rejecting transubstantiation and emphasizing a spiritual eating in faith of the Eucharist as a meal of memorial and fellowship, did not deny the Real Presence,[73] to a purely symbolistic understanding which rejected the Real Presence. This change took place under the influence partly of Carlstadt, but principally of the letter of Cornelius Hoen (written in 1521-22 and edited by Zwingli in 1525),[74] from which Zwingli received the idea that *est* should be interpreted as *significat* in the words of institution. This change is already in evidence in the letter to Matthäus Alber (November 16, 1524), in which for the first time Zwingli understands the supper as a symbolic, commemorative meal in such a manner that he excludes the Real Presence.[75] In the *Commentarius* Zwingli is all the more sure of himself and, beginning with John 6:63 as his scriptural principle, not only affirms that *significat* is the necessary interpretation of *est* but rejects as an absurd question "whether the body of Christ is really, corporeally, or essentially in the sacrament of the Eucharist."[76] He contrasts so sharply a spiritual and a fleshly eating that the former excludes the latter. In his discussion of sacrament he goes so far as to deny the sacrament as a pledge or seal of faith. Faith is a purely spiritual matter which needs no outer confirmation.[77] Now for Zwingli, *sacramentum* has the meaning exclusively of obligation, not gift, recalling the ancient Latin usage of *sacramentum* as *iusiurandum* or *sacramentum militare* or a *pignus* laid on the altar.

Oecolampadius, the leader of the reform movement in Basel, followed Zwingli with a presentation of his views on this subject in his *De genuina verborum Domini 'Hoc est corpus meum' iuxta vetustissimos authores expositione liber* (c. 15 September), 1525, to which Erasmus first refers in a letter to Claudius Cantiuncula, ⟨c. September fin.⟩ 1525, but which he says he has not yet had time to read.[78] In a letter to Michael Boudet, 2 October 1525, he says of this book: "A new doctrine has arisen that there is nothing beyond bread and wine in the Eucharist. That opinion which it would be very difficult to refute has been formulated by John Oecolampadius and so fortified with proofs and arguments that even the elect could be seduced."[79] In several other letters at this time and later, Erasmus makes similar remarks about the Basel Reformer's book. It is the only work of these three men for which Erasmus repeatedly expresses an appreciation. It is of special concern to us in assessing Erasmus' understanding of the authority of the Church as it bears on the Eucharist, for he says more than once later that he could be persuaded by Oecolampadius' arguments if the authority of the Church did not go against them. We therefore save a detailed treatment of Oecolampadius' book and Erasmus' reaction to it until we deal with the topic "Real Presence and the Authority of the Church."

In Basel, Erasmus was caught in the midst of the struggle between the Roman Catholic and Reformed parties. Each party sought to enlist the humanist on its side. Erasmus, though preferring to remain a spectator to the whole affair, did begin writing a book on the subject of the Eucharist apparently even before he was asked by Claudius Cantiuncula to compose a reply to Oecolampadius' treatise. He did not finish it, he tells us later, out of consideration for the public tranquillity.[80]

Though he will not write a book against Oecolampadius, Erasmus does oblige the Town Council of Basel when asked along with Louis Ber, Claudius Cantiuncula, and Boniface Amerbach to give his opinion on Oecolampadius' book. He tells them that in his judgment the book is "learned, clearly and carefully worked out," and he adds, "even pious if anything could be pious which conflicts with the opinion and the consensus of the Church," from which he judges it "dangerous to disagree."[81]

Shortly, Erasmus felt himself compelled to write at greater length concerning the symbolic view of the Eucharist because certain partisans of it were insisting that he really shared their opinion—first Conrad Pellican, then Leo Jud.

To Pellican, associate in theology with Oecolampadius at Basel who had recently been won over to the latter's Eucharistic view, Erasmus wrote a long letter after learning that Pellican was spreading the rumor in Basel that Erasmus agreed with him on the rejection of the Real Presence.[82] The contents of this letter we shall consider more exactly when we take up our systematic analysis. Suffice it to say presently that Erasmus rejects out of hand Pellican's opinion. He admits that among friends he may have spoken freely by way of inquiry but that no one has heard that opinion from his lips, not even in jest. The words of Scripture themselves clearly name the body and blood of Christ, and these, he says, would make him inclined toward the opinion of the Catholic Church even if nothing had been defined. But neither does he spurn the definitions of the Church in councils. The weight in Erasmus' words is rather more upon the side of the tradition of the Church than upon that of Scripture.[83]

Yet another Swiss Reformer sought to enlist Erasmus on his side in the battle over the Eucharist. In April 1526 a little book appeared with the title *Des hochgelerten Erasmi von Roterdam unnd Doctor Martin Luthers maynung vom Nachtmal unnsers herren Ihesu Christi neuwlich aussgangen auff den XVIII tag Aprellens*. It was in the form of a letter from "Ludouicus Leopoldi, pfarrer zu Leberaw, dein lieber bruder" to "Caspar Nagolt bürger zu Nörlingen seinem freund und herzlichen bruder." Erasmus at first suspected that Pellican was the author, but he turned out to be Leo

Jud, an associate of Zwingli at Zurich.[84] In this work Jud tries
to show that Erasmus and Luther at base agree with Zwingli,
Oecolampadius, and Carlstadt on the Eucharist. We are concerned only with what he says about Erasmus, but one is immediately suspicious of a mind which is so blind with prejudice
or lacking in critical ability that it cannot discern any major
difference between Luther and Zwingli. His estimation of the
viewpoint of Erasmus is hardly more accurate. He attributed to
Erasmus a wholly symbolic and spiritualistic conception of the
Eucharist. He says that Erasmus in many places in his writings
calls the Eucharist a symbol, that he even uses the expression
symbolicum panem, that especially in the fifth canon of the *Enchiridion* he uses John 6 to repudiate entirely a fleshly eating and to
assert only a spiritual eating in faith. He goes on to state that
Erasmus names the Eucharist a sacrament only in the sense that
it is a "mysterious sign and symbol of a holy thing, namely
signifying his body given and his blood shed." According to
Jud, Erasmus thinks that "this sacrament is nothing other than
a commemoration of the death of Christ." He asks the humanist
whether he has really changed the opinion which he held as a
youth in the *Enchiridion* and prays that God will give Erasmus
strength to confess what he believes in his heart. Jud recalls to
Erasmus the favorable opinion which the latter had given to the
Council of Basel concerning Oecolampadius' book.[85] He concludes by pointing to certain passages—the annotation on Mark
14, the paraphrases on I Corinthians 10 and 11 and on Matthew
26 and Luke 22—where he alleges that Erasmus calls the bread
and wine symbols.[86] The book gives the impression of being so
hastily composed that Erasmus has little difficulty in showing
that it contains many inaccuracies and misrepresentations.

Erasmus was so disturbed by this little volume that he took
the opportunity to write an immediate, preliminary reply to it
in a letter of May 15, 1526, to the Swiss Confederacy which had
as its major object a response in the negative to an invitation
to attend the conference at Baden, which was to be held May 21
to June 8 of that year and at which Eck debated with Zwingli on
the new ecclesiastical ordinances in Switzerland. Erasmus ac-

cuses the author of either malice or stupidity in so misrepre-
senting his writings and his own inner convictions, which on
this subject have never been different from the consensus of the
Catholic Church.[87]

Soon afterward Erasmus rapidly drafts a more complete
response which is published in June 1526, the *Detectio praestigiarum cuiusdam libelli germanice scripti ficto authoris titulo, cum hac
inscriptione, "Erasmi et Lutheri opiniones de coena Domini."* Review-
ing the passages cited by the *Maynung* one by one, he easily
shows that they do not bear the interpretation ascribed to them
by that book. He demonstrates that though he has indeed used
the word "symbol," he has never applied it directly to the bread,
that he has never held an exclusively symbolistic conception of
the Lord's Supper, that he has not denied the Real Presence in
any passage, but that in some he has almost explicitly stated it.[88]
Furthermore, although in the *Enchiridion* he did indeed stress a
spiritual eating, he did not intend to deny that the true body of
Christ was there. He backs up his point here by noting that even
St. Thomas, the champion of the Real Presence of Christ in the
Eucharist, would agree with what he said in Canon V, that "the
flesh of the sacrament is of no use if spiritual grace is absent."[89]
In short, he says that he has not changed the opinion which he
held as a youth, except that he does admit that "now by various
arguments I could waver to both sides, unless the authority of
the Church confirmed me."[90]

Having now briefly considered the background for Erasmus'
later viewpoint of the Real Presence, we proceed to a systematic
analysis of all the relevant passages.[91]

V. Symbols and Real Presence—1525 and After

Erasmus continues to speak of the Eucharist as a symbol or
pledge or sign. There is no sharp difference with what he has
said formerly except that he emphasizes more strongly that the
body and blood themselves may be considered symbols, a
thought which, however, he had already expressed. In the letter
to Pellican he states that "the flesh which is subject to no

senses" is itself "a pledge of the divine love toward us, a solace of expectation." In not very characteristically Erasmian but more typically Lutheran manner he insists on the literal meaning of the words of institution. He argues that nothing in the biblical text permits the reading, "This is not my body but the sign of my body."[92] He rejects on the basis of Scripture and tradition a symbolic interpretation which would exclude the Real Presence.

In the *Detectio* he demonstrates that he had never said that the bread and wine are symbols of the body and blood of Christ. He interprets the passages in his works where he uses the expression and where it is often unclear what he means by it as saying that the sacramental eating itself is a symbol of our union with Christ and with one another, or of Christ's death and our concord.[93] At the outset of his discussion, however, though denying that he had ever used the expression *panem symbolicum*, as claimed by the author of the *Maynung*, Erasmus asks why it would have been dangerous if he had used this term, for

> . . . are not the consecrated bread and wine symbols of the body and blood of the Lord hidden under them? Finally, are not the body and blood of the Lord, which are disclosed in a certain manner to our senses, symbols of those things which can only be discerned by the eyes of faith?[94]

Erasmus continues therefore to reveal uncertainty as to what is the symbol and what is symbolized, but there is nothing in his words to suggest a purely symbolical understanding of the Supper. In fact, he flatly repudiates the insinuations of Pellican and Jud that he shares the Reformed view. In later passages written to orthodox theologians he takes the high view of symbol, that the body and blood themselves are symbols,[95] but in the end continues to reveal his uncertainty as to what constitutes the symbol, which he implies arises out of the variety of expressions among the Church Fathers.[96]

Erasmus steadfastly refuses to speculate concerning the mode of the Real Presence. In spite of his heavier emphasis upon the Real Presence in his later years, he continues to remain skeptical concerning the doctrine of transubstantiation.

As we shall notice later, though the authority of the Church informs his understanding of the Real Presence, it does not necessitate his acquiescence in this dogma. He thinks it is sufficient "to believe *in genere* what the Church believes."[97] His favorite expression for the miraculous presence of the body and blood in the Eucharist is *ineffabili modo*.[98] Before such a profound mystery our attitude should be one of silence and reverence.[99]

Even though Erasmus is skeptical concerning the "how" of the Presence, he, confirmed by the authority of the Church, maintains, perhaps with some hesitation, the presence of the true and substantial body of Christ in the Eucharist. As over against his earlier writings, one observes the frequency and the emphasis of the statements in this regard, beginning with the letter to Pellican. He intends to separate himself clearly from the viewpoint of the Swiss Protestants.

At this point I disagree strongly with the interpretation of G. Krodel, who holds that Erasmus understood the Real Presence as a mystical or a spiritual, not a corporeal, presence.[100] The texts show that Erasmus holds to the bodily presence of Christ in the Eucharist, although he is uncertain how to express this faith. In the letter to Pellican, he says: "It is flesh, but subject to no senses . . ." In contrast to the Zwinglian view, he continues: "We are commanded to be spiritual, as if the flesh so exhibited impedes the spirit."[101] In the letter to John Lasky of March 8, 1526, in which Erasmus reports an interview between Pellican and himself on the subject of the Eucharist, he writes that when asked about his views on the matter of Presence, Pellican replied that he believed the power of Christ to be present in the Eucharist but not the substance of the body. Erasmus then says he asked Pellican whether he (Erasmus) had ever expressed this opinion and Pellican responded with the truth, namely, that Erasmus had never expressed this view.[102] In a later report of this interview Erasmus more clearly indicates his disagreement with Pellican concerning the substantial bodily presence in the Eucharist.[103] In another letter of March 1526, Erasmus expressed his attitude, though more implicitly than explicitly, toward the substantial bodily presence in the Eucharist.

> Here [in Basel] we are taught by published books that the body and blood of the Lord are not present in the Eucharist substantially. When I was asked my opinion by the magistrate, I replied that I believed nothing else than what the Catholic Church had defined.[104]

Likewise, in the reply to the *Maynung* Erasmus not only denies that he ever held a purely symbolistic understanding of the Eucharist but positively suggests (I hesitate to use the un-Erasmian word "asserts") the substance of the body and blood in the Eucharist. We have already pointed to the passage where, in talking about symbols, Erasmus asks: ". . . are not the body and blood, which are disclosed in a certain manner to our senses, symbols of those things which can only be discerned by the eyes of faith?"—a passage which seems to stand in contradiction to the one quoted above from the letter to Pellican. However, he seems to explain what he means by a statement somewhat later in this work:

> Now although in the synaxis the body is not exposed to the senses, nevertheless there is the reality [*res*] which can be perceived, and yet neither is the presence of this of any use unless those things which are by nature invisible are present.[105]

In two writings of 1530 he makes clearer his understanding of the nature of the Real Presence. In the preface to Alger's treatise on the Eucharist, Erasmus gives his most complete statement on the subject. Though rejecting speculation, remaining cool to transubstantiation, and emphasizing many times the mystery, Erasmus affirms "the true substance of the body and blood of the Lord"[106] on the basis of the words of Jesus and Paul, the "constant authority of synods and so great a consensus of the Christian people," and the "immense power of God to whom nothing is impossible."[107] This body is "of the same substance indeed as the body which hung on the cross, but not of the same quality, undoubtedly already glorified and spiritual."[108] Besides, "it cannot be divided or injured, or suffer abuse, whatever happens to the species."[109]

In a text overlooked by Krodel, also written in 1530, Erasmus explicitly speaks of the corporeal presence as supplementing a spiritual presence:

> It was not enough for him always to be present to his bride through faith and his spirit, just as he had promised, but he prepared a victorious banquet, in which he served his very own body as a living food, added the cup of his blood, whence one may drink as often as he wishes, in order that by this unheard-of method he might be present also *corporeally* in visible sacraments to his sheep.[110] [My italics.]

In other later passages he speaks less explicitly. He writes of the "true body of the Lord," or simply "the body of the Lord," but usually qualifies it with "as the Church hands down" or "as the Church believes."[111]

Finally, in a letter written shortly before his death to Philip Melanchthon, Erasmus shows that he clearly understands the difference between the purely spiritual presence and the corporeal presence of the body of Christ in the Eucharist when he sees through Bucer's camouflage of the differences between himself and the Bishop of Avranches, Robert Ceneau, in the preface to his work written against the bishop.

> Avranches had said that the body of Christ was in the Eucharist, but not corporeally. Hence Bucer gathers that there is the highest agreement between them. You, he says, deny that he is there corporeally; we say that he is there spiritually. But Avranches meant for "not corporeally," "not under the dimensions of a body, not quantitatively," as the scholastics say. He nevertheless thought that the substance of the body was truly present.[112]

On the basis of all the statements which we have cited from Erasmus in his later years, this must have been his position too, one which distinguishes him from a Reformed view holding only to the spiritual presence of Christ in the Eucharist.

Undoubtedly, Erasmus would have continued as earlier to speak vaguely about what he considered a very deep mystery if it had not been for the changed situation occasioned by the rise of the symbolic, spiritualistic view and the attempts of its parti-

sans to force him to share it. The use of such a word as "substance" to define more closely was naturally repugnant to him,
but in the case of necessity he not only could but did use it.

VI. Real Presence and the Authority of the Church

Apart from the texts themselves, which refute the opinion of
Krodel on this subject, one should also consider the view of
Erasmus that he would be inclined to be doubtful about the Real
Presence if the authority of the Church did not confirm him in
his faith. Erasmus would scarcely need the confirmation of the
authority of the Church to assert only a spiritual presence. In
fact, he surely knew that the authority of the Church con-
tradicted such a belief.[113]

We now reach this knotty problem, to which we have alluded
several times, but which has been saved until this point for a
detailed consideration. Erasmus' first utterances on this subject
were occasioned by the publication of Oecolampadius' book on
the Eucharist upon which Erasmus was asked by the council of
Basel to give the opinion already reported. In several other
letters written about the same time, he freely without solicita-
tion offers his view concerning the persuasive quality of the
book, supported as it is by so many arguments.[114] In later
letters to Willibald Pirckheimer, Erasmus expresses himself
even more freely about his favorable attitude toward Oecolampadius' book, but he always qualifies his remarks by an an-
nouncement of his allegiance to the authority of the Church,
defined as a universal consensus.[115]

In view of its importance for assessing Erasmus' later position on this subject, it is advisable to outline here the substance
of Oecolampadius' arguments.

Oecolampadius opens his treatise[116] with an explication of
a sacrament. Μνστήρια (*sacramenta*) are, to begin with, hidden
things which usually only the initiated understand. There are,
however, some mysteries which lie beyond the understanding
of even the initiated. These include the divine generation and
procession, predestination, as well as incarnation and resurrec-

tion. All of these happen in a miraculous manner outside of the order of nature. However, the sacraments of the Church do not belong in this category of mystery. They are intended "for the exercise and confession of faith, in order that through them we either might enroll in a military service, or having enrolled, might testify that we are worthy of our profession."[117] Sacraments in this sense must be comprehensible to the initiated, though they remain hidden to the inexperienced. Already, therefore, Oecolampadius rejects a wholly miraculous mystery such as the Real Presence in the Eucharist.

Turning specifically to the Eucharist, he asserts that "there is in this sacrament no miracle which exceeds our understanding."[118] Only miracles which have the warrant of canonical Scripture are legitimate. He rejects as impossible the belief that the body of Christ is on the altar. If that were so, then there would be "more miracles in one bread than in any of the works of God."[119] It is simply impossible, thinks Oecolampadius, for a human being to be in different places at the same time. Ubiquity is a mark of the Creator, not of the creature. Since Christ's body is creaturely, it must be in one place. A ubiquitous body would be a contradiction, since every body is circumscribed. The reality of such a miracle is further called into question by the thoughts that it remains hidden and deceives the senses, weakens faith, and terrorizes consciences, that a memorial of a miracle which is itself a miracle necessitating another miraculous memorial and so on *ad infinitum* is inconceivable.[120]

Moreover, the bodily presence of Christ contradicts the witness of Scripture and the early Church Fathers. The words of institution, thinks Oecolampadius, are manifestly to be understood as figurative, along the lines of Paul in I Corinthians 10:4, "The rock was Christ." Just as "rock" is here a figure, so "body" in "This is my body" is a figure. If one were to exegete the *est* "as expressing existence (ὑπαρκτικῶς) and substantive without a figure," one would have to hold that "the body of Christ is on the altar, not 'sacramentally,' but truly present just as in heaven." However, if Oecolampadius' exegesis is correct, then there can be no question of transubstantiation or consubstantiation. (This kind of use of figures, thinks Oecolampadius, can be amply documented in Scripture.) As long as the sense is properly grasped, Oecolampadius will allow the *est* to stand. But he also points out that *est* is a mere copula, that in the "Hebrew" language there would have been no verb, since it is characteristic of that language to allow a demonstrative pronoun or adverb to take its place. Had Christ really intended the Real Presence, he would have expressed himself more exactly. Furthermore, the Church Fathers, the Basel Reformer believes, support such an interpretation. He points especially to Tertullian in *Adversus Marcionem*[121] as giving the interpretation of *figura corporis* for the words of institution.

But Oecolampadius rejects not only the possibility but the necessity and the usefulness for faith of the Real Presence. If one maintains that the Real Presence makes possible the true sacrifice of Christ on the altar, one can reply that such a sacrifice renders problematic the unique act on the cross. It also implies that the ancient custom of thanksgiving to God as Creator, Giver, and Sanctifier was not sufficient. Such thanksgiving may be given even apart from the bread, but it is useful that we publicly testify to the love of the Redeemer in this rite instituted by Christ in order that we might give thanks for the benefit of his death, on which account it was called by the ancients a sacrifice of praise or Eucharist. But, asks Oecolampadius, what need is there for his bodily presence in order that we might give thanks? A Christ who is absent bodily, yet present in memory, may awaken gratitude in us as easily as an invisible body.[122] Further, Christ does not need to be bodily present in order to be our guardian and savior. He is much more our guardian as ruling in heaven than as hidden in bread and wine. He is "sufficiently with us, who makes us unconquerable by his grace and power, he is sufficiently with us who has not left us destitute of his spirit." He supports these thoughts by certain dogmatic considerations. To be sure, the flesh of Christ is not separated from the deity and is everywhere worthy of adoration, but the same is not true of the "mystical bread."[123] Christ in his indivisible divine and human natures sits at the right hand of God, to which our hearts and minds are directed, as correctly recognized in the *Sursum Corda* of the liturgy. Christ does not come down from this high place to be present bodily in the Eucharist. The time of the humiliation is past. His bodily presence is to be expected only in that day when he comes in power and glory. Christ removed his body that the Holy Spirit might come and that we might depend not on the flesh but on the Spirit.[124]

Moreover, says Oecolampadius, a bodily eating is not necessary to prepare us in body and soul for the resurrection. It is nonsense to hold that a fleshly eating feeds our souls; it does not perfect them, but weakens them, for "what is of the flesh, is flesh."[125] John 5:54—"Unless you eat of my flesh and drink of my blood . . ."—is an illustration of the fact that not only in the Old but even in the New Testament, the letter kills unless it is spiritually understood—that is, unless it is understood along the lines of John 6:63, "The flesh is of no use, it is the Spirit who gives life." Scripture speaks only of a spiritual eating in faith.

> But, as has been said, faith does not need any external thing when it is genuine. The kingdom of God is within us, and a human being is sanctified, not only in soul but also in body, even without a sacramental eating.[126]

If one asks what use then, alongside this spiritual eating, a sacramental eating can possibly have, Oecolampadius answers that it is of value as a witness to our belonging to the mystical body of Christ and as a means of strengthening faith. Although the divine power occasionally operates effectively in the faithful without sacramental signs, nevertheless "our weakness and the love of the brethren" demand "that certain external tokens of gratitude be not lacking, by which we most truly witness that we shall persevere in Christian warfare."[127] Here the emphasis is on the subjective element, the use of the sacramental signs as a means to external attestation. But notice in the following statement the mention of the signs as an objective means of grace by which faith is strengthened:

> Christ resides bodily in heaven and not in the sacrament, but
> through the sacraments he advises, excites, strengthens, con-
> soles, and does almost all the things which he does through the
> Word, if they are understood.[128]

We need hardly point out that this thought stands in contradiction to the above statement that faith needs no external sign.
Moreover, the body of Christ may be said to be present not
substantially but "mystically . . . with his power and blessing."[129]

But the chief use of the sacrament is as a public attestation
to faith and promotion of the communion of love among members of the body of Christ.

Köhler points out that in spite of the dominantly Zwinglian
orientation of this whole treatise, these latter ideas concerning
the sacrament as a means of grace to strengthen faith, concerning a spiritual presence of Christ in the Eucharist, strike themes
which Zwingli had already left behind.[130] They are more closely
related to Erasmus than to Zwingli. But our purpose is not to
assess the relationship of this treatise to the ideas of Zwingli
nor to trace the influence of Erasmus' understanding on that of
Oecolampadius, but simply to weigh the reasons for Erasmus'
favorable reaction to it.

Because Erasmus' expressions of reaction are brief, we cannot be sure of what he thought in detail about it. His words are
approving, but they need not imply approval of the total work.
On the basis of his total outlook we have to consider the probable reasons for his favorable response. The logic of Oecolampadius' arguments concerning the impossibility of a bodily
presence in the Eucharist, his figurative understanding of the
words of institution, his rejection of the *est* as decisive, since it
is a mere copula, his spiritualistic understanding of John 6:54
and of the presence of Christ after the incarnation, his sense of
the contrast of the Apostolic practice with the later development—all these arguments must have seemed cogent to Erasmus' humanistic reason and scriptural understanding. But
more decisive for Erasmus was not so much the impossibility
(for he could accept on the authority of the Church and the

absolute power of God what seemed against his reason),[131] but
the uselessness of the Real Presence. His most revealing remark on this score was to Pirckheimer:

> The opinion of Oecolampadius would not displease me, except
> that the consensus of the Church goes against it. For I do not
> see what the insensible body effects, nor that it will impart
> usefulness, if it were perceived, provided spiritual grace is
> present in the symbols. And nevertheless I cannot depart from
> the consensus of the Church, nor have I ever departed.[132]

Erasmus' understanding of the Eucharist as primarily commemorative of Christ's death, whereby a true sacrifice on the
altar and the necessity of the Real Presence are called into
question, as symbolic not only of this death but also of the
communion among ourselves, as being characterized mainly by
a spiritual eating, move him in the direction of Oecolampadius'
teaching, even though commemoration and symbol do not exclude for him the Real Presence and even though a spiritual
eating does not necessarily exclude a corporeal eating. Besides,
as the above quotation indicates, it was sufficient to Erasmus
that Christ be present in power and grace without his body. In
a previous chapter we have pointed out the spiritualistic tendency of his Christology. Also, as we have seen, Erasmus does
not at all emphasize a bodily union with Christ in the Eucharist.
The fundamental principle of Erasmus' religious thought, the
preference of the spirit over the flesh, militates against the
necessity and value of the bodily presence. And yet on the basis
of the inner logic of his thought the sacrament of the Eucharist
would be retained, as it was for Oecolampadius, not only as a
symbol of our concord but as a means of strengthening faith
and of consolation because of our weakness.

Nevertheless, Erasmus, as usual, felt that he could not go
against the authority of the Church, defined as a universal consensus. It was abundantly evident to him that on this question
of the Real Presence the whole Church had clearly spoken. He
therefore bows to this authority, as may be demonstrated not
only in the opinions concerning Oecolampadius' book, but also

in other places where Oecolampadius' work is not immediately in view.[133]

Moreover, the authority of the Church was a principle which operated not only extrinsically but also intrinsically in his thought. He not only accepts the Real Presence on this basis but suggests reasons for its usefulness: that the substantial presence of Christ's body is the supreme pledge of his love toward us, that Christ's bodily presence supplements his spiritual reality in the Eucharist. He can emphasize that Scripture as interpreted by the Church also teaches the Real Presence, and even that the words of institution are to be taken literally. These thoughts are not inwardly Erasmian, but show that the authority of the Church shapes his understanding.

We conclude, therefore, that Erasmus, not gladly but actually, accepts the substantial bodily presence in the Eucharist primarily on the basis of the authority of the Church. Although his earlier writings do not so clearly demonstrate it, it is probable that already in these years he held this position, so that he is being mostly honest when he says in the *Detectio praestigiarum* (1526):

> I have not changed the opinion which I held as a young man except that now by various arguments I could waver to both sides, unless the authority of the Church confirmed me.[134]

Submission to the authority of the Church, although it meant acceptance of the Real Presence, did not mean at any time, however, the acceptance of the doctrine of transubstantiation. We may thus notice a dialectical relationship between the authority of the Church and his humanistic reason; the authority of the Church actually informed his understanding, yet his skeptical humanistic reason qualified to some extent the formulations of this authority. It is sufficient "to believe *in genere* what the Church prescribes." The substantial Real Presence, however, on the basis of all the statements we have considered, surely belongs in the category of the *"in genere."*

IX

BAPTISM AND CONFIRMATION

———————◆•◄◆►•◆———————

Having discussed the sacraments which may be regarded as primarily social, we turn now to those which are chiefly for the individual—baptism, confirmation, penance, and extreme unc- tion. In spite of the fact that Erasmus lists marriage before baptism, baptism remains for him the chief sacrament, or at least shares this position with the Eucharist. It is the one sacra- ment that is alone of absolute necessity, the gateway to salva- tion, to the Church, and to the other sacraments. If it is through marriage that we are born into the world, it is through baptism that we are reborn.

I. Institution

Erasmus seems to accept the institution of baptism at the command of Christ as traditionally grounded in Matthew 28:19, Mark 16:16, and John 3:5. He raises no critical questions con- cerning these passages in the annotations to the *Novum Tes- tamentum.* In his paraphrase of Matthew 28:19 the humanist places the emphasis not so much on the institution of the sacra- ment as on the catechetical instruction connected with it.[1] Else- where he states that catechism was once practiced before baptism and this by the institution of the Lord.[2]

In the paraphrase of Mark 16:16 Erasmus underlines the faith which receives the grace of forgiveness of sins but men- tions baptism as the sign of this grace.[3] Likewise, in the para- phrase of John 3:5 he seems to take for granted the institution of baptism and calls attention to the contrast between a spiritual and a carnal birth.[4] In line with his own interests Erasmus stresses here "the Spirit" in the phrase "water and the Spirit."

Though Erasmus appears to assume the institution of baptism at the command of Christ, he does not seem to regard it as grounded in Christ's deed in the sense of his having baptized others. He reports that, according to John, Christ baptized no one, nor is it recorded in any other of the canonical writings that Christ baptized anyone.[5] In the paraphrase of John 4:2 Erasmus reveals another characteristic interest when he points out that the fact that Jesus baptized no one shows that the office of preaching the gospel is more excellent than the office of baptizing.[6] Neither in the *Annotationes* nor in the *Paraphrases* does Erasmus lift up the contradiction between this verse and John 3:22. He has no annotation for the latter passage at all. And in the paraphrase he simply follows the text without elaboration.[7]

On the other hand, he does mention the traditional thought that Jesus by his own baptism consecrated the baptismal waters,[8] so that, in this sense, our baptism can be said to be grounded in his deed.

Erasmus gladly stressed another traditional idea held since Augustine, that because Christ was the author of baptism just as of the other sacraments, the power of the sacrament flowed from him, not from the administrator. The latter is no more than a minister or priest of a foreign gift.[9]

II. A Rhetorical Definition and Description of Baptism

Since Erasmus wrote no treatise concerning baptism, a presentation of his views on this subject must rest on a collection of numerous widely scattered statements. However, fortunately, he provided a rather detailed definition and description of this sacrament in his late and lengthy work for Christian preachers, *Ecclesiastae* (1535). His intention is simply to supply a clear illustration to the reader of all the important elements of a proper rhetorical definition and description.[10] In so doing, however, he reveals conveniently in one place significant aspects of his understanding of baptism which can be duplicated in many other passages of his writings.

Erasmus begins the definition by describing the genus of baptism as its being the first of the seven sacraments of the new law.[11] A narrower definition of the genus would be that it is one of those sacraments which, once it has been conferred in a proper manner, cannot be repeated. Its difference (*differentia*) is the power through faith in Christ of freely washing all sins of whatever kind. That it is not repeatable would seem to be its special characteristic (*proprium*), unless, as more recent theologians think, it is to be regarded as common with certain others which have an indelible character, such as confirmation, extreme unction, and orders. Erasmus says that the occasion for such a point of view was taken from some words of Augustine —whether rightly understood, he does not now dispute.[12] Without denying the indelible character, Erasmus raises a doubt about it. He was decidedly cool toward the "character," and, as far as I can judge, in only one other place does he specifically refer to it.[13] Here, as elsewhere, however, Erasmus had some scholastic company, for both Scotus and Occam were critical of the doctrine of the character and took it over only on the authority of the Church.[14]

Erasmus continues by noting that a definition is constituted by its genus, difference, and special characteristic (*genus, differentia,* and *proprium*), but that one can consider also the *accidents,* which may be variously divided into baptisms of blood, running water, and fire. According to accidents it can also be divided into baptisms of aspersion (such as of those who were about to die, who in jest were once called *"clinici,"* whence they were commonly said to have been sprinkled rather than baptized)[15] and baptisms of infants and of adults.

Baptism may also be understood according to the Aristotelian four causes, thinks Erasmus. The final cause is eternal life. The material cause is the water and word, unless, he says, one prefers to think of these as instruments. The material in

which the power of the sacrament works is the soul of man. The
form is the act of the Holy Spirit. The efficient cause is the Holy
Trinity. The priest or another who baptizes is only the living
instrument or minister. The effect is the innocence freely given
through faith, or the reborn man.[16]

To continue with Erasmus' application of rhetorical terms to
baptism, the beginning (*exordium*) is the perception of the elements of the faith; the increase (*incrementum*), the perception of
the more profound doctrine; the completion (*summa*), the perfection of evengelical piety. Baptism is preceded (*ex anteceden-
tibus*) by repentance of the former life; it is attended (*ex adiunctis
sive continentibus*) by full confidence in the promises of Christ; it
is followed (*ex consequentibus*) by the progress in the innocent life.
We shall notice that baptism as one of the stages in the growth
of the Christian life is a favorite one for the humanist. Likewise,
the insistence on the connection of faith with baptism is prominent not only here, where it has been mentioned three times
regarding the difference, the effect, and the collateral circumstances of baptism, but also elsewhere in his works.

Both generation (*generatio*) and corruption (*corruptio*) may be
observed in the dying of the old man and the rising of the new
man. There is a similitude (*similitudo*) between baptism and the
crossing of the Red Sea: just as the rebels against God perished
in the Red Sea while the Hebrews escaped safely, so in baptism
the sinner is killed while the innocent one emerges alive. A
dissimilitude may be seen in the comparison between baptism
and penance: in contrast to baptism, in which all sins are freely
remitted without confession, even if contrition is not present,
in penance no sins are destroyed without contrition and tears.
The Pauline theme of the mortification of the old man and the
vivification of the new man in connection with baptism is an
otherwise salient feature of Erasmus' understanding of baptism. The association of baptism with penance and the stress on
the act of contrition in penance also occurs elsewhere in Erasmus' writings.

Many other things similar and dissimilar to baptism, says
Erasmus, can be related to it. Circumcision of infants in the old

law is analogous to baptism of infants in the new law. It is a matter of comparison (*comparatio*) whether baptism is more effective for us than circumcision was for the Jews, whether the sacrament of penance can accomplish the same as that of baptism, whether the profession of the monastic life equals or is superior to baptism. The last question is one which especially occupies Erasmus in much of his writing and which he vigorously answers in the negative.

The consequence (*consequentia*) of baptism is that one loves the earthly less and the heavenly more. A contradiction (*repugnantia*) is for one who has enrolled in the army of Christ the captain to serve the world and Satan. The argument could be adduced *a casu sive eventu* that baptism is no mere human matter and was once sought with great zeal by all peoples, and even the loftiest monarchs are not ashamed to be candidates. Erasmus adds still another comparison:

> If a soldier on account of a small sum does the commands of his commander to the extent of the cost of his life, how much more is it necessary for us to obey Christ, our leader, who for a short and light service, promises eternal life in heaven.

A related matter (*coniugatum*) is that "If anyone through baptism becomes a soldier of Christ, it is just to fight with good faith under his standards."[17] The themes of *meditatio vitae futurae* corresponding to a *contemptus mundi* and a military service under Christ the commander we have already noticed as important expressions of Erasmus' understanding of the Christian life which were manifest in his writings as early as the *De contemptu mundi* (c. 1486). Frequently elsewhere he connects these themes with his thoughts on baptism. The mention of baptism as more than a human matter hints at a contrast he likes to draw between the more sacred vow of baptism and that of monasticism.

Passing over the remaining parts of the rhetorical illustration which add nothing material to the understanding of baptism, we come to still further questions which Erasmus says the preacher or teacher ought to raise concerning this sacrament. He ought to inquire, as once was the case, into the method of preparation for baptism, the reverence and rites by which it is necessary for priests to administer the sacrament, and the piety of the catechumens who wish to undertake it. He should ask further about what preserves and augments the grace of baptism as well as, contrariwise, what corrupts it, and thus about ineffective or wicked baptisms. Again, the teacher should know about the various kinds of baptism of the past—heathen baptisms, the washings of the Pharisees, the baptism of John the Baptist, baptisms not properly enacted, the baptisms of heretics, and those of Anabaptists ("by which pest the Church is now being disturbed")—and about the opinion of those who think baptism is not necessary for salvation but only an honorable sign of adoption.

In some of these questions we find hints of genuine concerns of the humanist: concerns for moral and catechetical preparation for baptism, for a reverent and meaningful rite, for the faith and piety of those who undergo it, and for the preservation and augmentation of its grace by the moral life.

Without asserting that the wickedness of priests harms the effect of the sacrament, he reveals his concern as a humanist reformer for the morals of the clergy and their effect, especially upon the young. Undoubtedly, Erasmus prefers one to go to a pious rather than to a wicked priest to receive baptism. Without rejecting infant baptism and the role of sponsors, he suggests doubts concerning that office by questions about the sufficiency of an alien faith for salvation, its historical origin, and the moral turpitude of sponsors.

Lastly and most importantly, Erasmus urges the preacher, as in all matters he treats, to concern himself with what is internal and what is external regarding the sacrament. He will teach that what is hidden is more excellent than what is visible, just as the soul is more excellent than the body.[18] He will point out the superiority of the spirit over the flesh. Here we encounter again this basic theme of Erasmus' religious thought, which can be amply documented beyond this passage in regard to the sacrament of baptism.

III. A Detailed Description of the Nature of Baptism

The Relation of Christian Baptism to
Old Testament Circumcision and the Baptism of John

Having briefly considered this discussion of Erasmus which is found in a work written near the end of his life, we turn now to a more extended analysis of his thoughts on baptism drawn from widely scattered places in the *Opera*. Two questions with which theologians customarily first concern themselves when treating baptism are the relationships of Christian baptism to Old Testament circumcision and to John's baptism.

For Erasmus circumcision normally signifies Jewish piety, ceremonialism, the flesh of the law which has been abrogated by the coming of Christ and by faith in him. It is thus viewed negatively as the sign par excellence of the Judaism detested by Erasmus which consists of a trust in ceremonies. He sharply contrasts Judaism and its confidence in outward observances with Christianity, characterized by faith and love of God or Christ. As circumcision is the mark of the Jew, the sign that he has dedicated himself totally to the law, so baptism is the mark of the Christian,[19] the sign that he has dedicated himself totally to Christ; but in contrast to the Jew, who places his confidence in the actual circumcision of the flesh, the Christian trusts not in the ceremony of baptism as such but in what it signifies.

One can thus apply the familiar contrast of flesh and spirit to both religious ceremonies. There are both a circumcision of the flesh and a circumcision of the spirit or the heart signified by the physical circumcision. The spiritual circumcision involves the removal of earthly cupidity from the soul. This is what Paul means in Colossians 2:11, thinks Erasmus, by the circumcision of Christ.[20] The spiritual reality signified by circumcision has not been abrogated, since it has been taken up into the meaning of Christian baptism. The ceremony itself, given for a time, has been left behind as a shadow of the truth to come.[21] Likewise, baptism has its flesh and its spirit without which the ceremony itself is of no value.

Baptism has then replaced circumcision, and its observance has certain similar features. Like circumcision, which required neither a priest nor a Levite to administer it, baptism may be administered in case of necessity even by laymen.[22] Likewise, both are administered to infants, but baptism with a harder condition—that is, that the baby has to be baptized immediately after being born.[23] We shall notice in connection with the problem of infant baptism that Erasmus did not believe in the necessity of immediate baptism of newborn infants.

According to Erasmus, John the Baptist stands on the border between the law and the gospel. He belongs to the second period in Erasmus' periodization of the economy of salvation, when the shadows of the old law are waning, when the dawn of the light of the gospel is near but not yet come.[24] He is of the old law insofar as he threatened with judgment unless the people repented. He is of the new law insofar as he called not for sacrifices, burnt offerings, or vows, but for baptism and repentance of the former life, and as he announced the approach of the most merciful Messiah who will forgive the sins of all who believe in him. Just as his stern preaching prepared for the evangelical doctrine of grace and mercy, so his baptism was for repentance in preparation for the baptism by which sins are forgiven. His water baptism is not effective for washing away sins, but by a certain image it prepares the immature through repentance for the true baptism, by which the Messiah through his Spirit at once washes away the filth of all who have believed his heavenly doctrine. Erasmus designates the former a carnal baptism, the latter a spiritual baptism.[25]

John's preaching and baptism form an image of the evangelical order of catechism and baptism. Just as John's preaching induced the hatred of the former life, so Christian catechism ought to bring about awareness of one's own turpitude and an acknowledgment of the divine mercy. The first step toward health is to confess one's sickness and then run to the physician. Conscious of one's own sin and desirous of the divine mercy, one is then prepared to receive baptism for the remission of sins.[26] The preaching and baptism of John have then for Erasmus primarily a propaedeutic value within the biblical history of salvation which is analogous to catechism within the psychological process of salvation.

Flesh and Spirit

As with the other sacraments, the fundamental presupposition for understanding Erasmus' conception of baptism is the flesh-spirit contrast. The material elements of this sacrament are especially the water, but also the salt and ointment,[27] and even the words with which baptism is performed. The spiritual aspect of baptism Erasmus understands variously as the "power of purification proceeding from the Holy Spirit,"[28] "invisible grace," faith which receives this grace and which purifies the heart, or the moral renewal of the one baptized.[29]

Erasmus' concern with this distinction as always is to oppose a formalistic sacramentalism. Without denying the external process of baptism, he emphasizes the inner, spiritual event.[30] He abominates a magical understanding of baptism which places its trust in the power of the water. Therefore, he repeatedly connects faith and baptism.[31]

Therefore, also, in a Franciscan manner, he makes a sharp distinction between the sign and the thing signified. "The body is moistened with water, but the mind is anointed with invisible grace."[32] "Baptism is of no value . . . unless God convert the soul by invisible grace."[33] Baptism is simply "a sign of the divinely conferred grace."[34] The baptismal bath and the gift of grace are two parallel operations with only a symbolic, not a natural, intrinsic connection of the one with the other. Grace does not come *through* but *with* the water. The water is not a *causa instrumentalis* but *causa sine qua non.* Nor is it universally and necessarily even this latter kind of cause, for in case of emergency, when lying sick with no minister of baptism present, one can confess his unrighteousness to God and take up the intention to lead a new life. "He is not always present who washes the body, but tears are always present by which you may wash away the filth of the soul." Such a baptism is more effective than at the last moment to be sprinkled with water whether the mind is

cleansed or not.[35] However, the frequent mention of baptism—
often, to be sure, associated with faith as the means of salvation
—indicates that normally he regards this sacrament as the *sine
qua non* of salvation. Yet clearly, the emphasis is more on the
res sacramenti than on the *sacramentum* itself.

The Nature of the *Res Sacramenti*

In connection with the spiritual aspect of baptism we have
already touched on the items of the *res* of the sacrament. These
may be divided into what Erasmus called specifically *arra* and
exemplum, which along with the *congruentia,* he says, ought to be
examined in each of the sacraments.

The *Arra* of Baptism

Erasmus conceives of the beneficial effect of baptism in the
traditional manner, first negatively as the forgiveness of sins,
his favorite expression for which is "innocence."[36] All sin,
whether original or personal, is washed away.[37] Although Erasmus does give utterance to this traditional thought that original
sin is cleansed by baptism, from our study of his anthropology
we learned that in fact he does not think that what is generally
termed "original sin" is technically sin at all. "Sin" is a category
which he prefers to reserve for personal sins. What is called
"original sin" the humanist wants to attribute to an inclination
to sin passed on to all from the first parents. This inclination
to sin is not eradicated but is diminished by baptism.[38]

> For even if baptism has washed away the stain, something of the
> old disease remains in us, both as protection of humility and
> as material or soil of virtue. Remaining are blindness, flesh, and
> infirmity.[39]

But if sin is not totally removed by baptism, it no longer reigns
in him who is truly baptized.[40]

The positive effects of baptism are insertion in Christ's
body[41] and the rebirth.[42] In the latter connection we recall that
Erasmus said that through marriage we are born; through baptism, reborn. The engrafting into Christ's body includes both

entrance into the Church[43] and union with Christ. The union
with Christ has as its consequence that we share in his titles. We
cease to be sons of Satan and become sons of God. Indeed, we
may be rightly called "gods" who are said to be born of God.
Erasmus is, however, careful to point out the distinction between Christ's sonship and ours. His is by nature, ours by
adoption. "He is God eternally begotten out of the substance
of God; we are graciously admitted by him into the association
of immortality."[44]

The union with Christ in baptism has as its further consequence that we are all brothers of Christ, and in him brothers
of each other. The result of a brotherly relationship through
baptism for Erasmus is that Christian lords should concede
freedom to Christian slaves. In a note on Ephesians 6:7 Erasmus says:

> Nay, it seems base among Christians to hear at all the names
> "masters" or "slaves": for since baptism makes all brothers,
> how is it appropriate for a brother to call a brother a slave?[45]

Baptism, then, removes distinctions of station and nationality.
Erasmus emphasizes the Pauline thought that in Christ there is
neither Jew nor Greek nor barbarian nor male nor female nor
freedman nor slave, but all alike are one in him and brothers
with each other.[46] The old carnal distinctions no longer apply
to those who have become spiritual men. Even mariners and
shoemakers are wedded to Christ in baptism. Those who are
lowly in the sight of the world are made equal to kings and
princes by their baptism and union with Christ.[47] Indeed, all
who have been reborn in baptism are priests and kings regardless of their social position.

Further benefits of the union with Christ in baptism are the
inheritance of the heavenly kingdom or eternal life, and the gift
of the Holy Spirit.[48] As far as I can judge, Erasmus seems to
connect this latter gift with baptism, not with a later ceremony
of confirmation, although in one place he does refer to the
bestowal of the Spirit through the Apostolic imposition of
hands to those who were baptized[49] (that is, to Acts 8:17 and

19:6, the major New Testament sources for a disjunction between baptism and the gift of the Spirit which influenced the
rise at a later date of a sacrament of confirmation at which time
the Spirit is granted by the bishop to the person baptized[50]). I
do not think Erasmus carefully considered the question of the
moment of the gift of the Spirit. He does not at all enter into
the Protestant-Catholic debate on confirmation.[51] He seems to
have accepted this sacrament without placing much emphasis
on it.

Baptism as rebirth is frequently discussed along Pauline
lines as death and burial with Christ and resurrection with him
in newness of life. The death with Christ is expressed in terms
of death to the world, vices, the carnal feelings; the resurrection, in terms of a new righteousness. In baptism a metamor-
phosis takes place. One is changed from an old to a new man,
from unrighteousness to righteousness, from a carnal to a
spiritual man.[52]

Erasmus' thoughts and imagery concerning the gifts of baptism thus include the following: innocence, regeneration, union
with Christ, death and resurrection with him, deliverance from
slavery to Satan, sonship, brotherhood with Christ, reception of
the Spirit, inheritance of the heavenly kingdom or eternal life
—all traditional material to be found in the New Testament and
the early Church Fathers. These show that Erasmus is a faithful
representative of the tradition concerning the grace of baptism,
although admittedly his heaviest emphasis is not there, but on
the inner appropriation of these gifts in the exercise of the
moral life.

But before coming to this second, most important aspect of
baptism, we should recall Erasmus' insistence over against his
"orthodox" opponents on the free character of the baptismal
grace. Properly speaking, i.e., *de condigno,* it cannot be merited,
although, as we have already seen, presumably such a thought
does not rule out a half merit, *de congruo,* even when he does not
use these terms. In any case, he stresses that though merits in
the strict sense do not precede faith and baptism, they necessarily follow, else the faith and baptism are in vain.[53]

The *Exemplum* of Baptism

However, the movement is swift from the deed of baptism to its imperative, from the gift (*Gabe*) to the task (*Aufgabe*), from the *munus* to the *exemplum*, as, for example, especially in this paraphrase of Romans 6:3-5:

> And indeed since we have obtained the baptism of Christ, it is not fitting for you to flee what that baptism either effects or designates. For since we are baptized in the name of Christ, we die with him to our former sins, which he took away by his death, and, not only do we die with him, but we are buried with him through the same baptism. Thus, just as he, who although not conquered by sin, nevertheless died for our crimes, was called back to eternal life, not by human powers, but by the power of the Father, so we, having been aroused from the death of vices by him, have died to the former sins and have set in motion the new life, walking in the footsteps of piety and always progressing from virtue to virtue. For, when we were united with the body of Christ through baptism, and in a certain manner transformed into him, whatever we see as having been performed in him, our head, *ought to be expressed or hoped for in us* who are his members.[54] [My italics.]

This is the major stress of Erasmus' view of baptism: the free, personal, inward appropriation and retention of the grace of the sacrament made effective in its moral obligation and application.[55]

The obligation of baptism is expressed in the strong emphasis on the seriousness of the baptismal vow. Erasmus likes to remind his readers of the meaning of this oath: the renunciation of the devil,[56] the world, and the flesh,[57] and the swearing of loyalty to Christ the commander and enlistment in his service.[58] Here, as in Tertullian, the understanding of baptism as a *sacramentum* in the original sense of the Latin word as a military oath of allegiance is especially in view. Closely associated with this meaning of baptism was the idea of an agreement or contract (*foedus*) made with God, a theme which was again especially strong in the legal-minded Tertullian.[59] The person baptized is bound by this agreement. The contract carries with it a debt, an obligation to fulfill the rule of Christ and to reflect the baptismal profession in an ethical life. Because a Christian is bound by this sacrament of baptism, he is not free to sin. "He who does enter into peace with vices violates the agreement struck with God in baptism."[60] Erasmus, like some of the early Fathers, views postbaptismal sin very seriously.

On the basis of this solemn regard for the baptismal vow, Erasmus depreciated the monastic profession. Since there is no more religious or holier vow than this one, since nothing is lacking in the vow if accomplished, a second vow is not necessary.[61] Since he who has been baptized has assumed a divine rule, it is absurd to attribute more to a merely human rule than to this one. Human professions are no more than images of this divine profession. All who forsake it are apostates, not just the monks who forsake the rule of the monastic order. All who have professed Christ have renounced the world, not only the monks. All who have been baptized have dedicated themselves to God, not only the monks. Erasmus suggests satirically that no second dedication is necessary unless one thinks that in baptism half the man was dedicated to God and half to the devil.[62] Because of his baptism one can be a religious person in whatever state, not only in monasticism.[63] Thus Erasmus is a prominent sixteenth-century representative of a lay, vis-à-vis monastic, Christianity which has as its theological basis a renewed appreciation of the meaning of baptism.

The question of the extent of Erasmus' depreciation of monasticism is a complex and debatable one which cannot concern us in detail. Certainly, the humanist's negative judgments on this subject far exceed his positive ones. However, it seems to me that Telle goes too far in his contention that Erasmus' strictures against monasticism hit not simply its evils but were a universal and complete repudiation of the institution as such.[64] In spite of severe censures of monasticism and evil monks, Erasmus always insisted, quite truthfully I think, that he was not altogether opposed to monkdom in itself, that he attacked no individual order, and that he sings the praises of good monks. As Thompson points out, even in the colloquies, where his barbs against ignorant, slothful, immoral monks are many, he speaks favorably of good monks.[65] As this same writer also indicates, in two different letters Erasmus warmly portrayed the lives of two model Franciscans.[66] Finally, in his later years he wrote two letters in praise of the monastic life.[67]

But even the baptismal vow, however sacred, is of no value, thinks Erasmus, unless it is accomplished. We reach now what is surely the most important meaning of baptism for the humanist, its moral application.[68] Neither baptism nor the profession of faith is sufficient for salvation unless reflected in a pious life. In baptism we have received innocence as a gift, but it is partly up to us to persist in and to protect our innocence, and thus render ourselves capable of receiving further gifts. We have indeed been grafted into Christ through baptism, but it remains for us to see that we are not cut off from him by our vices.[69] In the emphasis upon the ethical fruit of baptism Erasmus again follows especially his favorite of the Fathers, Origen.[70]

The moral life as the result of baptism is conceived in terms of the *imitatio Christi*. It is a reflection of Christ's doctrine and life[71] as well as of his death and resurrection. In dying to the self, to the desires of this world, we imitate his death; and in living a life of righteousness and love, we imitate his resurrection.[72] The consequence of baptism is then a continual *mortificatio* and *vivificatio*.

Closely associated with the themes of *imitatio Christi* and *mortificatio* and *vivificatio* with him is the battle of the Christian life under his banner. In baptism we have been enrolled as a soldier of Christ, but it remains for us to fight under the flag of our commander.[73] Again, as for Origen, baptism is the beginning point for life's spiritual struggle.[74]

Likewise, as for Origen, so for Erasmus, baptism as renunciation of the devil and the beginning of continual struggle against his power is the counterpart of the theory of redemption as victory over the devil. The themes of Christ's work as redeemer from the power of the devil, as commander, and as example, and of our work as struggle under his banner in imitation of him come together and are connected with baptism in this passage to which we have already referred:

> In baptism we enroll ourselves under our leader, but we shall do battle under his standards against the forces of Satan. . . . But our chief once broke their [the evil spirits'] power and handed them over to us as conquerable, and he will conquer them again in us, provided we imitate the method of battle by which Christ conquered them.[75]

What Daniélou says of Origen applies also to Erasmus: ". . . baptism confers upon the soul the principle of the spiritual life, but it marks only a first step."[76] Erasmus says:

> Through baptism we are reborn, but it still remains that in much progress of time we gain in greatness and strength, growing by daily exercise of piety into maturity.[77]

Baptism is the first grade of piety, followed by progress and then perfection.[78] Baptism is then the foundation of the Christian life which must be held firm and unperturbed and which is built upon by pious deeds up to the end if we shall reach final felicity. Erasmus insists that it is not safe to rely on one's baptism. It is safest to make as much progress as possible in the course of time.[79] Again, we note the element of uncertainty of salvation. Final justification and salvation are dependent not upon faith and baptism alone but upon moral progress toward perfection following baptism.

Baptism is merely the first step on the road toward perfection, but it is a decisive step. It has set us on this road, from which to wander has severe consequences. Like the early Church Fathers,[80] Erasmus views postbaptismal sin seriously. If he is inclined to excuse prebaptismal sin as often arising out of error and weakness, he characterizes postbaptismal sin as issuing from ingratitude and malice. Those who sin after baptism will be judged more harshly than those who sin out of ignorance before baptism.[81] After baptism the Christian is called upon to lead a new life indeed. There must not be any return to the former wickedness. Christ's death and resurrection once for our sins is a paradigm of our death to sin once and for all in baptism.[82] Of course, as we have already seen, Erasmus does not think that all inclination to sin has been removed by baptism. Hardly anyone may live without the lighter sins, but one ought to be able to live without the gross sins. For washing away the former, prayer, almsgiving, and, principally, the participation in the Eucharist are sufficient.[83] For the latter, if they occur, God has prepared a stronger cure, penance, which will be the subject of detailed analysis in the next chapter.

Baptism and Catechism

Thus far we have attended primarily to Erasmus' thoughts on the meaning of the act of baptism and its consequences in the life of the Christian. However, quite clearly he laid much emphasis also on the necessity of the preparation of the mind and the heart for the reception of baptism, just as Origen did.[84] The close association of faith and baptism would suggest this fact, but he also couples faith with repentance before baptism. The emphasis upon the personal, moral dimension of baptism means for him necessarily the elevation of the practice of catechetical instruction, a subject in which the humanist pedagogue has naturally an intense interest.

We have already pointed out that Erasmus considered that the preaching of John formed an image of evangelical catechism insofar as it induced hatred of the former life. But the stimulus to repentance is only one of the purposes of catechism. It provides knowledge of the rudiments of faith and of the method of right living following baptism.[85] It has then both kerygmatic[86] and morally didactic content. It is thus necessary before baptism (Erasmus stresses the biblical foundation in Matthew 28) so that the latter may be undertaken with the proper disposition, but it is also necessary after baptism so that the baptized person might continue to grow in his faith and in the moral life.[87]

Of course, Erasmus recognizes that the gospel commandment concerning catechism before baptism can apply only to adults. "For what advantage is it for adults to have been baptized," he asks, "unless they have been taught through catechism what power baptism has, what it is necessary to believe, and how to order their lives according to the Christian profession?"[88] However, since infant baptism is now the universal practice—coming down, however, from ancient ecclesiastical authority—he wishes that after baptism children would learn those things "which it is sinful for a Christian not to know."[89]

In an earlier writing, the appendix prefixed to the *Paraphrasis in evangelium Matthaei* (1522),[90] Erasmus had already made a more specific and more startling proposal.[91] He had suggested that yearly during Lent catechetical sermons be preached out of the fountains of the Gospels, the Apostolic letters, and the Apostles' Creed at which baptized youths reaching maturity would be commanded to be present. It should be clarified to them especially what was contained in their profession of baptism. Then they might be examined privately by worthy men in order to determine whether they have comprehended and remembered what the priest had taught. If they are found to have sufficiently understood, then they are to be questioned whether they approve what their sponsors have promised in their name in baptism. If they respond affirmatively, then they are to renew their baptismal vow in festive congregational ceremonies. A measure of sentiment is evidenced when Erasmus remarks about the magnificent spectacle of young people dedicating themselves to Christ, renouncing the world and the devil. Such a ceremony is more moving, he says, than initiations of monks, which usually bring forth tears from the spectators.[92] Presumably, he thinks that it would have its effect on the adults present, reminding them of the meaning of their baptism.

The chief matter here is the personal renewal of the baptismal vow in the light of the catechetical instruction. Two elements are then foremost: (1) the personal appropriation with the mind of the contents of the baptismal confession and the essentials of the Christian faith, and (2) the personal decision, the act of the will, in view of this knowledge, to fulfill the obligation laid upon one by baptism. As Maurer points out, it is, in addition, a matter of the affections insofar as these are awakened by the act in the midst of the assembled congregation. His interest is clearly that through such a ceremony Christians will be established not only in name but in reality, Christians who are conscious of the meaning of their faith and of its obligations.[93] He thus hopes to bring about a renewal of the Church.

Erasmus anticipates the attacks which will be made upon his proposal by acknowledging a twofold difficulty: (1) that the ceremony really signifies a repetition of baptism, and (2) that the youths will not approve what their sponsors did for them. Concerning the first, he explains that this ceremony is best looked upon as a kind of "restoration" (*instauratio*) and "representation" (*representatio*) of the former baptism, much like the daily sprinkling with sacred water. The second problem, he thinks, is solved with greater difficulty. If, after everything has been attempted to prevent their retreating from their first faith, the youths fail to respond affirmatively, then they should not be coerced but simply left to themselves in the hope that they will repent. Their only discipline should consist of exclusion from the Eucharist and the other sacraments but not from the rest of the sacred service, especially not from the sermons. He expresses the optimistic hope that education in the *philosophia Christiana* in which "that pure Christ is depicted . . . not as rough and severe, but as gentle and mild" will bring about their conversion.[94]

Erasmus thus wishes to have a voluntary church without the Anabaptist consequences of a denial of the validity of the first baptism and of a divided Christendom. He is saved from the former by the belief that baptism is indeed valid for youths until they reach maturity but requires in adults supplementation by the inward appropriation in faith and life of the grace of the sacrament.[95] He is saved from the latter in his proposal here only by his optimistic conviction concerning the power of the *philosophia Christiana.*

Erasmus' orthodox opponents hit him hard on both these points.[96] He was accused of desecrating the sacraments of the Church, of creating a new sacrament, of teaching that in a certain manner baptism ought to be repeated. Erasmus categorically denied that he intended to do anything to or with the sacrament of baptism. He insisted repeatedly that his proposal had to do only with reviving the ancient practice of catechism, which once preceded the baptism of adults, and applying it to youths who had already been baptized so that they might have a greater knowledge of the meaning of their baptismal profession and of the faith which they had espoused.[97]

On the second point of difficulty he continued to insist, over against the tactics of the Inquisition, upon the use of pedagogical persuasion rather than force, believing that the mildness of this procedure, more in keeping with the example of Christ, is actually more effective than the severity of the other method. Besides, it insures that people will be genuine Christians rather than, in addition to being heathens, hypocrites.[98]

He replied to the Sorbonne that he did not deny that the Church had power and authority over its baptized infants but doubted whether it was expedient to use this power, for "many things are permitted which are not expedient." Certainly the Church has as much power over her own children as the Synagogue did over hers, he states, but it is not a question of legal right but of the use of this right. Through the gospel the severity of the old law has been tempered. Charity rather than fear of punishment ought to be the weapon used to restore the wayward to the fold.[99] Thus does Erasmian prudence and charity advise concerning the use of the authority of the Church in regard to baptized infants.[100]

Wilhelm Maurer thinks that Erasmus' thoughts here, though moving out from the sacrament of baptism, are in actuality a reformation of the sacrament of confirmation. The sacramental effects have been replaced by a catechetical, psychological operation.[101] But, contrary to what Maurer assumes, Erasmus nowhere speaks of this ceremony of renewal of the baptismal vow as confirmation, nor does he ever connect it, as far as I can judge, with that rite.[102] As we shall notice, he seems to accept the sacrament of confirmation and regards it in a traditional way without placing much emphasis on it.

Rebaptism

In his replies to the attacks upon the ceremony proposed in the appendix to the Paraphrase of Matthew, Erasmus vigorously denied the charge that this rite would represent a repetition of baptism. He stated that the thought of a repeated baptism never even in a dream entered his head.[103] Erasmus was doubtless correct and sincere in his denial that he advocated the necessity of rebaptism because of a supposedly invalid infant baptism, although he did admit that the ceremony of renewal of the baptismal vow would simulate a repetition of baptism. However, he was not quite correct in asserting without qualification that the thought of rebaptism had never entered his mind. For in the first preface to the edition of Cyprian, Erasmus held that, were it a matter for human argumentation and except for the sake of unity, Cyprian's opinion on the necessity of the rebaptism of heretics and schismatics could be affirmed rather than the traditional view of the Church.[104]

Of course for Cyprian it was not a matter of *re*baptism but simply of *baptism,* for he denied the validity in the first place of the heretics' baptism. He argued with keen logic that since there is one Church and one faith, there can be only one baptism, and between these three there is an indissoluble unity so that where the true Church and true faith are, there is also the one true baptism. Where the former are not present, baptism is necessarily also lacking. Cyprian argued relentlessly that if the heretics have baptism, then they must have the Church and the gifts of baptism and the Church, which are the remission of sins and the Holy Spirit. Since such is manifestly not the case, they cannot have baptism. Cyprian rejected a purely objective understanding of the sacrament, and placed the emphasis on the personal and ethical factors of the faith and worthiness of the minister and recipient of the sacrament.[105]

Cyprian's sentiment, though it became the prevailing one in the East, failed to carry the day in the West. The Roman understanding with its emphasis upon the objective and sacramental over against the subjective and personal factors became victorious with the decisions of the Councils of Arles, 314, and of Nicea, 325.[106] The Western persuasion was given its classical formulation by Augustine, who made the famous distinction between "having" and "having salubriously." Heretics have the sacrament of baptism but without beneficial effect until they return to the unity and charity of the Church. The important matter is not "who gives, but what he gives; not who receives, but what he receives; not who has but what he has."[107] Since the sacrament belongs to Christ, not to any man, it is holy in itself and confers a "character" which cannot be destroyed and which therefore does not require repetition. The objective, sacramental element of baptism was thus secured against anxious considerations concerning the personal attitude and worthiness of the administrator and even the degree of faith of the recipient.

Understandably in the light of Erasmus' own stress on the personal and ethical quality of baptism, the arguments of Cyprian might well have seemed more compelling to him than the traditional view of the Church.

Beda and the Spanish monks saw a connection between the opinion expressed in the preface to Cyprian and the proposal of the appendix, for they cited both as evidence that Erasmus was unorthodox on the question of rebaptism.[108] In the very interesting answer to Beda, Erasmus stressed the hypothetical nature of his remarks in the preface: "*If* the matter depended on human arguments . . ." But, he says, the question does not depend on human arguments but upon the definition of the Church, which he accepts to the contempt of human arguments. He continues with this revealing statement:

> What I say here concerning the repetition of baptism can be piously said about many other decrees of the Church, with which I would disagree if it depended upon human reasoning. I think it is appropriate for a pious mind to attribute more to the rules of the Church than to human arguments.[109]

Thus, in the end, human reason gives way to fideism and ecclesiastical positivism. Such was Erasmus' position on other sacraments and the authority of the Church.

Infant Baptism

Erasmus' works contain no extended treatment of infant baptism. His remarks on the subject are few and scattered. Some of them we have already touched upon in other connections. The presuppositions for his understanding we have also already considered: his idea of original sin and the necessity of a personal appropriation in faith of the baptismal grace. Both of these facets of his thought work against the necessity for him of infant baptism. We remember that he did not regard what is called original sin as properly speaking any sin at all but rather as an inclination to sin or a seedbed of future sins. Such a point of view means that unbaptized infants not yet accountable are not deserving of the punishment of damnation. In two separate passages he refers to the opinion of Gerson that unbaptized babes of Christian parents may be saved by the immense mercy of God through the supplications of their parents.[110] Also his catechetical and voluntaristic principles militate against infant baptism. In view of the non-necessity of infant baptism because of the no-guilt character of original sin and the importance for him of the personal understanding and appropriation of the meaning of baptism, it is not surprising that in one place he recommends that it be left to parents to determine whether children are to be baptized immediately or later during adolescence.[111] Somewhat in contradiction to this thought, however, is the advice elsewhere that mothers do well to make haste to baptism, which is of absolute necessity in contrast to either confirmation or Eucharist. These latter two, he thinks, can be given in their own time, more profitably after a little admonition.[112] However, in spite of these thoughts which would obviate infant baptism, Erasmus never, as far as I can judge, opposed the practice. Rather, he expressly said that it should be retained as one which has come down from the ancient authority of the Church.[113] In the *De amabili Ecclesiae concordia* (1533), he critizes the Anabaptists by asking, "Does not the baptism which has been sufficient for the Catholic Church for one thousand four hundred years suffice for them?" He thinks the custom of baptizing infants was already an ancient one at the time of Augustine and that it probably dates back to Apostolic times. Infant baptism is not explicit, to be sure, but implicit in the accounts of Paul's baptism of the families of Crispus, Gaius, and Stephanas (I Cor. 1) as well as of Peter's baptism of the family of Cornelius and the others who were present with him (Acts 10).[114]

We have already seen, however, that though Erasmus grants that infant baptism will avail for the salvation of children, it will not avail for adults unless it is supplemented by the spiritual and moral assimilation of the sacrament in faith and love. Necessary for such an appropriation of the sacrament is catechetical instruction. Thus, without denying the validity of infant baptism, Erasmus makes its effectiveness for adults contingent upon the personal consciousness of the meaning of the sacrament and the personal acceptance of its obligation. We can conclude, then, that infant baptism plays no essential role in his thought. In fact, it seems to be an embarrassing fragment of his baptismal theology which is not easily reconciled with the other elements and which he integrates not intrinsically but rather primarily on the basis of the authority of the Church.

IV. Confirmation

Erasmus' remarks on confirmation are also quite limited, usually occurring in connection with baptism. In large measure they relay the traditional medieval understanding of the sacrament as a strengthening and anointing for battle with the evils of this world.[115] I do not find him using the expression *augmentum gratiae,* but the thought seems present in his words on the sacrament.[116] Already in the poem *Institutum Christiani hominis* (1514), Erasmus says: "Sacred confirmation establishes us in the love of God and makes firm our mind by an invincible strength."[117] In the later and longer prose exposition of the Apostles' Creed Erasmus refers to that "sacred unction by which the novice is confirmed against the temptations of Satan."[118]

The medieval theme of anointing for battle is present in two late works.[119] One can understand Erasmus' fondness for this meaning of confirmation in the light of his understanding of the Christian life as a continual struggle. Most of Erasmus' attention was thus given to what the scholastics call the "effect" of the sacrament. He does not treat other items, such as the *materia* and the *forma*. Though Erasmus does speak of confirmation as an anointing, he does not call it the matter of the sacrament. Neither does he mention the reservation of the bestowal of the sacrament to the bishop.[120] Finally, the only mention of the "indelible character" of confirmation occurs in a passage already cited where he speaks primarily concerning the "character" of baptism but names also confirmation, extreme unction, and orders. As we have already noted, Erasmus was understandably cool toward this idea.

More important than the objective quality of the sacrament was its subjective realization:

> What was the use of having the sign of the Cross outlined on your forehead unless you were to live by it and campaign under His standard? What point in being sprinkled with holy oil unless you were to wage unremitting war upon your vices?[121]

In order to insure a more profitable use of this sacrament he urges that some instruction be added to confirmation, as also to the Eucharist. In line with this thought he requests that the custom in some places of granting confirmation to infants be changed, just as the Church has changed the custom of Augustine's day of requiring baptized infants to partake of the Eucharist, because these sacraments are not, like baptism, of absolute necessity.[122]

As with baptism, so with confirmation, Erasmus recommends a catechetical instruction concerning its meaning in order to bring about its inward appropriation. He makes no connection between this act and the ceremony of the renewal of the baptismal vow which he set forth in the appendix to the Matthean paraphrase. Again, we must insist against Maurer that there is no ground for maintaining that the proposed ceremony after catechism represents for Erasmus himself a catechetical and psychological reformation of the sacrament of confirmation, however it may have been so interpreted by Bucer and the other Reformers.

We conclude, then, that Erasmus seems to have accepted the Roman sacrament of confirmation[123] without placing much emphasis upon it. Although he could speak of its objective aspect in a traditional way, typically he has more interest in the personal application and realization of the meaning of the sacrament. For him, as for the early Church, the military character of confirmation was actually already contained in baptism. In the *Enarr. Ps. XIV* (1536), Erasmus connects kingship and priesthood with baptism and says that it is the office of kingship to battle with and conquer the devil.[124] Actually, both amount to the same thing, since priesthood means the mortification of one's earthly members, i.e., the fleshly desires. Thus, both have to do with the spiritual and ethical struggle of the Christian man. This struggle, as we have seen, commences at baptism but continues throughout one's life. Presumably, confirmation signifies for Erasmus a help and reminder at one stage of this process.

X

PENANCE AND EXTREME UNCTION

———————◆·◄◆►·◆———————

Though for Erasmus baptism represents only a first step on the road to salvation, it signifies, nevertheless, a decisive beginning. A genuine moral transformation ought to have taken place. As Christ's death and resurrection together constitute a once-and-for-all event, so do our burial and resurrection with him. There must be no return to the former life. Yet Erasmus recognizes that even baptism does not destroy the old nature. An inclination to sin remains which may again erupt into evil deeds. He thinks that hardly anyone can live after baptism without committing the lighter sins but that one should be able to live without gross sins. Since, however, unfortunately, mortal crimes do occur, God in his mercy has prepared a remedy. Penance represents still another accommodation of God's mercy to human frailty.[1]

I. Institution

The question of its divine institution is the one which more than any other drew Erasmus into controversy over this sacrament. The humanist's philological and historical criticism causes him to raise a serious doubt concerning its establishment in the New Testament. Through his translations and annotations of passages which were thought to be bases for penance, Erasmus both indirectly and directly criticizes the institution of the sacrament *de iure divino*. This fact raises once more the issue of the relation of his critical, philological reason and his allegiance to the authority of the Church.

In the 1516 edition of his *Novum Testamentum* Erasmus changed Jerome's translation of Matthew 3:2 and 4:17 from *Poenitentiam agite* to *Poeniteat vos;* in his note on 3:2 he allows as other possible translations *Resipiscite* or *Ad mentem redire.*[2] These, Erasmus thinks, are more appropriate translations for μετανοεῖτε, which signified a change of mind, not what people ordinarily understand in the expression *Poenitentiam agite,* associated as it is with satisfaction. Because of criticism Erasmus changed his translation of Matthew 3:2 in the 1522 edition to *Poenitentiam agite vitae prioris,* ". . . in order that we might as far as possible gratify everyone."[3] However, the translation of Matthew 4:17, which was changed in 1519 to *Resipiscite,* is retained as such in the succeeding editions.

Another passage from the Gospels which was customarily used to buttress the sacrament of penance was the command of Jesus to the leper (Matt. 8:4, Mark 1:44, Luke 5:14) or to the ten lepers (Luke 17:14), "Go, show yourself [*ves*] to the priest." Erasmus makes no significant comment on this passage in the 1516 edition nor in any of the following editions of the *Novum Testamentum.* His remarks on the passage occur in the long reply to Lee's criticism of the 1519 note on Acts 19:18. Erasmus opposes Lee's use of Jesus' command to the lepers to support the law of confession. The historical sense of "Go, show yourself to the priest" has to do with the confirmation of Jesus' miraculous cleansing of the lepers by the priest who had previously pronounced them unclean. Next, if anyone maintains that the allegorical sense supports confession, he interprets in a forced manner which goes beyond the example of the ancients. Besides, allegory is insufficient proof for a sacrament. Finally, even if allegory is attempted here, it is to be noted that the Fathers, and among them Augustine, let leprosy stand for heresy, not sin.[4] Erasmus' paraphrases of these words reflect this historical understanding of the passage. Of interest is only the paraphrase of Luke 5:14, which stresses that "Jesus alone removes every disease from everyone, demanding no other sacrifice than pure and simple trust in him."[5] Beda criticizes this remark, which to him implies that Erasmus thinks that priests today do not absolve from sins.[6] Erasmus may well have intended such an implication even though he denies that any such thing was in his mind. He was probably very much aware of scholastic discussion concerning the passage, for he points out that "theologians think that sin is remitted by contrition before the priest absolves, who really more pronounces than absolves since Christ is the true author of absolution."[7] In his last words on this passage in the *Ecclesiastae* (1535), he repeats what he said to Lee, that confession cannot be established from Christ's words here because the historical understanding of the passage has nothing to do with this sacrament and that if allegory is applied to it, heresy rather than sin is the more appropriate hidden meaning for leprosy on the basis of the witness of the Fathers.[8]

In his 1516 note on II Corinthians 7:10 Erasmus denies that the three aspects of penance—contrition, confession, and satisfaction—can be drawn from this passage. He states that Valla was also entirely of this opinion. In the 1522 edition he adds:

> But when we say these things, we do not remove contrition nor confession nor satisfaction, but we show the force of the Evangelical word. For these three things accompany true repentance: grief, confession, which in my judgment is a part of satisfaction, and satisfaction, which pays for bad deeds with good deeds.[9]

Erasmus also rejects as false the interpretation which connects James 5:16 with sacramental confession. He states that if the writer had had in mind auricular confession he would not have said "to one another" but "to the priests."[10]

The note, however, which involved the humanist in the sharpest controversy was the one in 1519 on Acts 19:18. In 1516 Erasmus had admitted that there was some confession in Christian antiquity, but it was public and general. In 1519 he adds that present secret, auricular confession seems to have arisen from private consultations with the bishops, whenever some anxiety burdened the soul.[11] Nothing more was added to this annotation in the succeeding editions.

Erasmus' comments on this passage were severely attacked by Lee, to whom Erasmus replied at length in 1520 with one of his most important discussions of confession. At this point we shall consider only those matters in his response which touch on the question of the institution. Erasmus makes more explicit than in his annotation his view that "this confession" or "this method of confession" or "this law of confession" was not instituted by Christ, unless one can say that what the Church through the Spirit of Christ has established has been instituted by Christ. The law of confession is then *de iure humano,* not *de iure divino.* But what the Church has established by the Spirit of Christ and what has been approved by a public consensus ought to be preserved as if established by Christ himself. However, what the Church has instituted by the Spirit of Christ can also be changed by the same Spirit for the sake of the salvation of men just as the prohibitive decree of the Apostolic Council concerning the abstention "from things strangled and from blood" (Acts 15:20) was lifted. If someone objects that this was a temporary law, the same can be said about the law of confession, Erasmus asserts. In the end, however, the humanist bows to the authority of the Church. He does not think that the Church has clearly pronounced that "this confession" was instituted by Christ, but—

> If the Church establishes by a certain decree that this confession is *iuris divini,* if it thinks that it was instituted by Christ, if it thinks that it cannot be abolished, I shall not resist the judgment of the Church and will adapt my understanding, even protesting, to its declaration.[12]

The important elements of his view as expressed here are: (1) his philological and historical criticism which perceives that sacramental confession was not instituted by Christ nor by the Apostles nor indeed by the early Church Fathers;[13] (2) his historical sense which judges that what has been established by the Church and is therefore *de iure humano* is not necessarily permanent, but can be changed and adapted for varying times and circumstances; (3) his moralism which desires that the burden of the law of confession (i.e., the obligation to annual confes-

sion) and the abuses of confession be removed for the sake of
the salvation of men; (4) his traditionalism, i.e., his willingness
to accept confession as handed down by the Church even
though not instituted by Christ, indeed to accept it as established by Christ if the Church so decrees. These are certainly
not easily compatible factors in his thought. It seems that here
as elsewhere he seeks to allow his critical, historical, and moral
reason as much free play as possible, but that in the final analysis his conservatism wins out.

In later remarks on his note on Acts 19:18 and his defense
against Lee, Erasmus consistently maintained the position expressed in that apology, except that he was sometimes careful
to say that he did not deny, but only doubted, that present
auricular confession had been instituted by Christ. In a letter of
1520 to Godescalc Rosemondt he refers to his discussion on the
institution of confession in the Apology to Lee, which had come
under attack by a Carmelite preacher named Nicolaus Egmon-
danus. He states that he had conducted his argument for the
human institution of this sacrament in such a way that he
defined nothing.[14] In a letter of 1521 to Peter Barbirius, Erasmus mentions that he submitted his *Novum Testamentum* to Atensis (John Briard), vice-chancellor of Louvain, for scrutiny. He
says that Atensis examined it carefully and only wished that
Erasmus had added that this confession as now practiced was
instituted by Christ. Erasmus answers that "because this dogma
was not yet clear to me, I did not wish to be its author."[15]

In two apologies—one in 1522, the other in 1524—to
Stunica, his principal Spanish theological critic,[16] Erasmus ad-
dresses himself to the former's criticism of his words on the
institution of confession in the 1519 note on Acts 19:18. In the
first, he defends himself briefly by pointing out that though he
did suggest somewhere that confession as presently practiced
had arisen out of the secret consultations of the bishops, he has
also indicated his willingness to submit himself to the judgment
of the Church.[17] In the second, somewhat longer response
Erasmus insists that by qualifying his remarks in the annotation
by *ut opinor* and *ut videtur* he shows that he asserts nothing. He

emphasizes that he is not questioning the obligation to confession, but the divine institution of this present confession with all its circumstances. He supports his position to Stunica as he had to Lee with the fact that Gratian, after collecting the various opinions on both sides of the issue of whether we are obligated to confess, allowed freedom of decision to the individual. If confession had been divinely instituted, says Erasmus, "that writer was not sober." And yet no one has thought to attack this passage in Gratian in all this time. Nevertheless, as before, Erasmus shows his willingness to submit his understanding to the authority of the Church.[18]

Erasmus includes in his defense to Stunica the opinion that before the Bull of Leo ("Exsurge Domine," June 15, 1520, which cited as the fifth error of Luther his rejection of the scriptural and patristic foundation of the sacrament of penance) one was permitted to doubt whether this confession was instituted by Christ. The intent of this remark may be that, since his note was written before the publication of this bull, he is not culpable, or it may simply be to note the diversity of opinion on this subject before the outbreak of the storm about Luther.[19] In any case Erasmus did not alter his views because of this edict. He apparently did not highly regard its authority.[20] He did not think that Leo was really responsible for it, but rather certain mendicant monks who surrounded the Pope.[21] But even if he had thought that it actually represented the papal view, it is doubtful that he would have held it as regulative of belief in the light of our discussion of his opinion on the authority of the papacy.

Erasmus' last words in defense of the Acts 19 note are to be found in the *Apologia adversus monachos quosdam Hispanos* (1528), in which he answers criticism of this and other passages in his writings on confession. There he again stresses that he did not insist that this present auricular confession had not been instituted by Christ, but that it seemed to him to have been established by the Fathers *ex occasione*. Nevertheless, repeating what he had said to Lee, he says that it should be preserved as if it were instituted by Christ. He cannot teach that it was so instituted, because he has not yet been sufficiently instructed as to be able to prove it, but when he has been, he will profess that, too.[22]

In a letter addressed probably to Lorenzo Campegio in January 1524, Erasmus says once more that when he states that "this" confession seems to have arisen out of secret consultations, he means confession as it has developed with all its circumstances. As in the Apology to Lee, he maintains that nevertheless he embraces it as if instituted by Christ and, finally, that he does not deny, but only doubts, that it was instituted by Christ.[23]

Of special interest to us because they appear in an informal writing are some remarks made by Erasmus in the person of the youth Gaspar in the colloquy *Confabulatio pia* (1522):

> ERASMIUS. But whom do you call the rulers of the Church?
> GASPAR. Popes, bishops, apostles.
> ERAS. And you include Christ with these?
> GASPAR. He is indisputably the head of them all.
> ERAS. And author of the customary confession?
> GASPAR. Assuredly he is the author of all good; but whether he
> instituted this confession such as the Church now
> uses, I leave to theologians to decide.[24]

In response to attacks made on this colloquy, particularly the words on confession, Erasmus wrote three letters, probably all at about the same time. He prefaces his comments in two of the letters by stating that the colloquies are intended not to treat dogmas but rather to teach the method of speaking correct Latin.[25] Even though that was undoubtedly their primary purpose, it certainly was not their only one, because Erasmus expresses himself on too many topics which are dear to his heart, and in a manner not at all unlike what he says elsewhere in his writing. For these reasons, what he says in these informal writings must be considered seriously as representing his views. We shall notice especially that what he says on confession in the colloquies duplicates what he says in other works on this subject.

In the defense of the above words on the institution of confession, his language is ironical and evasive, but continues to display his doubt concerning the institution *de iure divino*.[26] As in his defense of the Acts 19:18 note, he steadfastly maintains that it is not evident to him that the Church has clearly spoken on this issue, but when it does, he will bow to the authority of the Church. He thinks that the boy's willingness to obey the princes of the Church reveals his deference to authority so that there is nothing at all culpable in the passage. Apparently, he had been reminded of the anathema in the Bull of Leo, for he says in the letter to the theologians of Louvain:

> But if the bull had exactly expressed this [that confession was instituted by Christ], and I either did not know or did not remember, it would meanwhile be sufficient to submit to the authority of the Church with the intention of obeying, even if that were evident.[27]

This bull seemingly caused him some concern, but he meets the criticism of those who wave it before his face by questioning the clarity of its language, by professing ignorance, and by expressing a general willingness to submit to authority. However, as we have already noted, Erasmus evidently had little respect for what he considered a despicable proclamation. In any case, he continued to express his doubts concerning the divine institution of confession and yet also his willingness to submit to the authority of the Church when it has unambiguously spoken.

In later defenses of this colloquy Erasmus consistently maintains this position. In the *De colloquiorum utilitate* (1526), Erasmus states that he teaches that confession ought to be upheld as if it were instituted by Christ but that he can neither affirm nor deny that it has been actually instituted by him.[28] In a letter to his friend and patron John Longland in 1528, Erasmus says that the youth "hints" (*subindicat*) but does not assert that confession as it is now practiced was established by men. Erasmus goes on to say:

> That it has been instituted by Christ is not probable, nor has anyone been able to demonstrate [*docere*] it up to now. If anyone were to demonstrate it, he will certainly have me as an applauder. Nevertheless, I teach that it ought to be preserved as if Christ had instituted it.[29]

Finally, in his response to the censure by the Sorbonne of this passage Erasmus reaffirms that he thinks that confession ought to be reverently preserved as having been approved by the authority and the custom of the Church, even if it cannot be proved that it is based on Scripture or the institution of Christ.[30]

Erasmus has more important words on the institution of this sacrament in his 1524 treatise on confession, *Exomologesis seu modus confitendi*:

> Now since there are those who believe that this confession was instituted by Christ, those who hesitate in this matter, those who think that though it was instituted by men, confession ought to be no less religiously preserved than if it had been instituted by Christ's very words, those who think that it is arbitrary but urge that it not be spurned since it is salutary, for all these I have prepared this little book. I completely disagree with those who teach that it is arbitrary. With those who contend that it was instituted by mere men, I neither agree nor disagree, but am more inclined to the side which believes that it was instituted by Christ and will willingly do battle for this opinion when I have been furnished with the proper armor of Scripture and arguments, lest I should undertake an inferior cause and even in trying be unsuccessful.[31]

On the basis of our previous discussion we cannot help thinking that Erasmus is hedging here in this treatise, which was intended as a mediating work on the subject of confession and which, because of its author and subject, was bound to have a wide circulation. In a treatise dealing with confession which would doubtless be carefully examined by theologians, Erasmus had to be extremely careful about what he said. Also, in a letter to the theologians of Louvain in defense of the *Exomologesis,* Erasmus states that he accepts the opinion of Henry VIII (in his *Assertio septem sacramentorum adversus Martinum Lutherum,* July 1521) as probable, which the English king supports with probable arguments, that confession was instituted by Christ.[32] Before these theologians, I think, again he is being not quite candid, for in the later letter written to John Longland, which we have just examined, Erasmus wrote what more truly represented his view, namely, that it is not probable that confession was instituted by Christ.

In the last few years of his life his statements on the institution of sacramental confession are infrequent but largely consistent with his previous thoughts on the subject. He continues to say that he has never doubted concerning sacramental confession, but only whether as presently practiced it proceeds from Christ. However, if it were proved by irrefutable arguments that it was instituted by Christ, he again says he would very much favor it.[33] In the *Detectio praestigiarum libelli cuiusdam* (1526), the question of the divine institution of confession illustrates the second kind of "dogmas," those "concerning which the authority of the Church has not yet clearly pronounced and concerning which theologians disagree."[34] He thinks therefore that he cannot be blamed for suspending his judgment on this issue, meanwhile observing it as if Christ had instituted it.

The humanist's final words on the subject were in the conciliating treatise, *Liber de sarcienda ecclesia concordia* (1533):

> Let those in these times who are not yet persuaded that sacramental confession was instituted by Christ preserve it as a thing salutary and commendable for many uses and confirmed by the use of many ages. . . . Let those who believe that it was instituted by Christ observe it all the more religiously and allow the others to remain in their understanding until a sacred synod pronounces concerning it more expressly.[35]

Here, of course, his traditionalism and his concern for Church unity are abundantly clear.

In conclusion, we can say that though Erasmus occasionally before an audience of conservative theologians overstretched his view to say that he was inclined to believe that confession was instituted by Christ or that he regarded it as a probable opinion that confession was instituted by Christ, he generally doubted its institution *de iure divino* on the basis of his philological and historical study. He states frequently, however, that he will openly teach confession as divinely established when he is persuaded by the arguments of Scripture and reason. Without much doubt he does not think any such arguments can be brought forth. Because no foundation in Scripture or in the early tradition can be found for the sacrament, he would probably prefer that no dogma be established concerning the divine institution of the sacrament. As we have noticed, Erasmus prefers a coinherence of Scripture and tradition. However, the implication of his reply to Lee and of his discussion in the *Detectio* and the *Liber de sarcienda ecclesia concordia,* as well as of his general understanding of authority, is that, even though no foundation in Scripture or early tradition can be discovered, he would accept a decision of a rightly constituted universal council.[36] He would bow to the authority of the Church in this sense. But he does not allow his judgment to be shaped by a questionable papal bull. The results of our study on this question are thus entirely in keeping with the conclusions reached in the discussion of Scripture and tradition.

II. Flesh and Spirit—*Sacramentum* and *Virtus*

In the light of Erasmus' usual emphasis upon the inner, subjective, spiritual factor in the sacraments as opposed to the outer, objective, physical element, it is not surprising that in penance he stresses not the *sacramentum* but the *virtus,* i.e., contrition. From this point of view he may be related to the early scholastic tradition as represented by Abelard and Lombard and also to the late nominalistic tradition of Occam and Biel. All of these theologians were contritionists, that is, they insisted that the act of contrition, including sincere remorse for one's sins out of love of God and the intention to amend one's life and make satisfaction, was the only indispensable condition of divine forgiveness.[37] On the basis of contrition one is already forgiven before he goes to the priest. According to the example of the healing of the lepers and the allegory of Lazarus, the priest does not himself forgive sins but only indicates that they have already been forgiven. However, the act of contrition includes also the intention to confess to the priest, the *votum confessionis,* so that these theologians have reason to think that justice has been accorded to the sacramental aspect of penance.[38]

Erasmus repeatedly states that contrition and confession to God are the first, chief, or necessary matters in penance.[39] Especially in the colloquies, Erasmus refers to confession to God while neglecting to mention confession to the priest. For example, in *Naufragium* (1523) Adolph reports to Anthony that in the midst of the shipwreck an old priest preached to them a sermon from Gerson on the five truths concerning the benefit of confessing and that there was a Dominican priest there also to whom, as well as to the other priest, anyone who wished could confess. Upon being asked by Anthony what he did, Adolph replies: "Seeing everything in an uproar, I confessed silently to God, condemning my unrighteousness before him and imploring his mercy."[40] Likewise in Γεροντολογία (1524), without mentioning confession to a priest, Glycion says: "But if I'm at fault for any reason, I don't go to bed until I've first reconciled myself with God."[41] Again, at the end of the *Epicureus* (1533), Hedonius speaks of the repentance possible for the lifelong sinner without referring at all to sacramental confession:

> If he cries with his whole heart, "Have mercy on me, O God, according to the multitude of thy tender mercies," the Lord will take away the Tantalean stone, will grant him the sound of joy and gladness, and *his bones broken by contrition shall rejoice for sins forgiven.*[42] [My italics.]

Except for those in the *Naufragium,* these passages seem not to have drawn fire immediately from the orthodox.[43] But the passage which apparently greatly offended some was this one from the *Confabulatio pia* (1522):

> ERASMIUS. But how does confession please you?
> GASPAR. Very much, for I confess every day.
> ERAS. Every day?
> GASPAR. Yes.
> ERAS. Then you should keep a priest of your own.
> GASPAR. But I confess to him who alone truly remits sins and who has all power.
> ERAS. Who is that?
> GASPAR. Christ.
> ERAS. You think that's sufficient?

GASPAR. It would be quite sufficient for me if it were so for the rulers of the Church and accepted custom.[44]

Of course, it was not only the question of confession to God vis-à-vis confession to the priest which concerned Erasmus' critics, but also his uncertainty about the divine institution of confession as expressed in the immediately following lines which we have already discussed. However, these two questions are closely related. The necessity of sacramental confession rests in large measure on the fact of the divine institution. Because Erasmus doubts the institution of auricular confession *de iure divino,* he can also raise a question concerning the necessity of confession to the priest.

His replies to the attacks on this passage emphasize the condition "if it were so for the rulers of the Church and accepted custom" and the acknowledgment made by the boy later that he also confesses to a priest.[45]

Not only does Erasmus place the emphasis on contrition and inner confession while sometimes entirely neglecting sacramental confession, but he goes further and criticizes the current practice of confession. He satirizes confessions which are mechanical, too frequent, or on the deathbed.[46]

On the basis of his criticism of the idea of the divine institution of confession, his emphasis upon contrition and confession to God, and his ridicule of confessional practice, one might think that Erasmus has entirely surrendered the *sacramentum* to the *virtus* of penance. However, such is not the case. He says that he accepts it, that he goes to the priest especially before communion,[47] and recommends that one confess to God every day and to the priest three or four times a year.[48]

He accepts it not only on the basis of ecclesiastical tradition and authority but also on account of the nature of man as composed of body and soul and of the necessity of a visible, corporeal ceremony as an accommodation to our weakness. In the *Exomologesis* under the rubric of the first use of confession (to crush pride), Erasmus states that since the whole man rebelled against God, it is fitting that the body also submit itself in confession. Also, "just as the body often offers the occasion of

sinning, so also it frequently either causes or aids the virtue of
the soul." For this reason, says Erasmus, the ancient leaders of
the Church displayed certain visible ceremonies that men might
be deterred from sinning and provoked to repentance. "The
weakness of the human mind needs many incitements to catch
fire with love, to persevere, to be transformed after gathering
strength."[49] Erasmus' spiritualism is thus partially balanced by
an awareness of the appropriateness of a sacrament's matching
man's bodily nature and of its necessity as an accommodation
to human weakness.

The sacramental aspect of penance is further secured by the
votum confessionis just as it was for the early scholastic and late
medieval nominalist contritionists. Erasmus says in his treatise
on confession that no true contrition is present unless there is
also a willingness to confess to the priest.[50] In the *De praeparatione ad mortem* (1534), he says that if the sacramental signs are
not available to one who is dying, God will supply what is lacking
by his special grace as long as faith and a ready will are present,
and neglect and contempt of the sacraments are absent.[51] He
continues:

> A Christian will certainly want the sacraments to be present, for
> they are a great solace to our minds, and aids of our faith, but
> it is even more Christian to wish for faith and love, without
> which the sacraments are of no use.

The usefulness of confession is also underlined by the fact
that though contrition is necessary in order that confession may
be of advantage, nevertheless it sometimes happens that confession to the priest awakens in us a legitimate contrition.[52]
Confession thus effects not a sacramental but a psychological
change in us.[53]

III. Contrition

In the previous section we have considered the prime necessity of contrition in the process of penance. Actually, contrition
is only one of two indispensable presuppositions for receiving

the pardon of God. The other is beneficence toward the neighbor.[54] The vertical dimension of forgiveness is dependent upon the horizontal.

Now we wish to examine more closely the nature and the possibility of contrition. Contrition is, first of all, out of love for God a sincere sorrow or bitterness for all sins—not simply for this or that one—committed against him. Included in this feeling is also the desire, especially important for Erasmus, not to commit sin again.[55] If this will is not present, one can question whether genuine contrition is present. Although contrition is initially characterized by a sorrow for sins, it is succeeded by joy as the sign of divine forgiveness.[56]

Contrition is sharply contrasted with attrition, a hatred of sins which is born out of fear of the wrath of God and of hell.[57] Attrition may be the first stage of a true sorrow for sins, but contrition must follow in order to secure the divine forgiveness. In one place he says that he leaves to the Scotists to dispute whether attrition can be converted to contrition by confession,[58] but it is clear from what he says elsewhere that Erasmus actually permits only a psychological, not a sacramental, change as the result of confession.

The possibility of contrition is grounded both in God's grace and in human endeavor. No one can bestow upon himself this feeling. It is a gift of God, yet one which must be striven for with tears, prayers, and pious deeds. The gracious God does not grant his gifts to those who are idle.[59] Although he does not use the term here, Erasmus thus seems to insist on a *meritum de congruo* in order to receive the gift of contrition, which is the indispensable prerequisite for forgiveness. His thought on this subject therefore accords with his ideas on grace and free will as we have already outlined them.

From the human side, contrition is born not only out of the consideration of a badly conducted life but also out of the contemplation of the divine mercy as displayed in Scripture. God's gracious words and deeds are to be discovered in both Testaments, but, of course, especially in the doctrine, life, and death of Jesus Christ.[60] It is characteristic of Erasmus not to talk of

God's grace abstractly, but to point concretely to many scriptural examples. It is a particular source of consolation and a stimulus to repentance that there are so many examples of great men in the Bible who sinned yet repented; David, Peter, and Paul are those he mentions specifically.

Another method of arousing contrition is the consideration of what will be confessed to the priest. He who meditates on what he will say to the priest will consider more acutely the depth of his depravity.[61] Confession is thus of use in inducing contrition not only in that during the process a genuine hatred of sins may arise, but also in that even before confession the consideration of what will be confessed to the priest may awaken in the sinner a deeper awareness of his condition. In spite of his acknowledgment of the use of confession in bringing about a true contrition, Erasmus does not recommend generally that one who has some feeling of attrition run immediately to the priest. Rather he should persevere in tears and prayers "until he senses that another kind of fear has been joined with a certain will to change one's life and with an expectant love."[62] His ambivalence here stems from a desire not to neglect the sacrament as well as from a wish to insure against a hypocritical confession and a too easy reliance on the external act of confession.

The possibility of repentance is not negated by the size, number, or endurance of sins. God in his gracious mercy does not consider the multitude or the magnitude of the crimes as long as true contrition is present.[63] As long as life lasts, there is the possibility of repentance. Yet one should not rely on this fact and put off repentance until his deathbed, for he cannot know when death will strike or whether God will grant him a contrite heart on his deathbed.

In view of our previous discussion on the relation of sin to forgiveness, it is somewhat surprising that Erasmus stresses as much as he does that no sin prevents the possibility of repentance and forgiveness. We remember that he also holds that sin committed out of weakness or ignorance deserves mercy, whereas sin perpetrated out of intended malice deserves pun-

ishment—or that such would be the case except that the divine
mercy exceeds the divine righteousness.[64] Only the one who
remains in sin, obstinately refusing the remedy of penance,
deserves truly to perish. The difference in terms of repentance
between the lighter sins and the graver ones is that the former
require only the easier remedy of daily prayer, whereas the
latter require the more radical cure of penance. Moreover, although we should undertake penance with the determination of
never returning to our former sins, God in his mercy again
adapts himself to our weakness in offering us this remedy as
many times as we may fall.[65]

IV. Confession

Prior to *Exomologesis* (1524)

In connection with the discussion of penance as virtue and
as sacrament, we have already touched on the nature of confession in Erasmus' penitential theology. Now it is our task to
analyze his thought on this subject in greater detail.

Most of his words on confession prior to the *Exomologesis* are
in criticism of contemporary confessional practice. In the note
on Matthew 11:30 written in 1519 Erasmus includes confession
among the burdens which now shackle men.[66] Similarly, during
the same year, in a celebrated letter to Albert of Brandenburg
on behalf of Luther, he remarks that Luther "dared to dispel
some anxieties on the subject of confession, but in which the
monks endlessly chain the consciences of men."[67] In his first
longer discussion of confession in the 1520 note to Lee, which
is chiefly a defense of his 1519 annotation on Acts 19:18 concerning the institution of the sacrament, Erasmus lodges several moral objections to the practice of confession that are
repeated in the *Exomologesis*. He is careful to preface and conclude his words of criticism with an approval of confession. He
says he does not intend to criticize the sacrament but only some
abuses of it. He complains that many priests feed their curiosity
by what they hear in confession, others commit base deeds out

of contagion from what they learn from the recital of evil
desires ("when a major part of innocence is not to know evil"),
still others make use of confession as a weapon to exercise their
tyranny over the common people, to whom they ought rather
to be fathers. They chain the souls of the simple to prevent
anyone from having a calm and serene conscience. As in
the note on Matthew 11:30 and elsewhere, Erasmus calls the
present custom of confession a heavy burden, a yoke that has
been imposed on men.[68]

In the well-known letter to Jodocus Jonas of 1521 concerning the lives of John Vitrier and John Colet, Erasmus in-
timates his attitude toward confessional practice by his description of the customs in this regard of these two figures whom
he so admired. He says that they both abhorred anxious and
continually-repeated confessions. While of Vitrier he says that
the Franciscan friar did not hear secret confessions gladly but
served also in this matter the dictates of charity, of Colet he
remarks that the Dean of St. Paul's "strongly approved secret
confession and affirmed that there was nothing from which he
received so much consolation and spiritual benefit."[69]

In the colloquy *Confabulatio pia* (1522), the youth Gaspar says
he goes to confession especially before Holy Communion but
makes sure he chooses a priest he can trust with the secrets of
his heart. Erasmus adds:

> A wise thing to do, for experience proves there are a great
> many who blab about what they hear in confession. There are
> some unworthy and shameless priests who demand to know of
> the person confessing what it would have been better to keep
> silent about. There are ignorant and dense ones who for sordid
> gain offer their ear rather than their mind, since they do not
> distinguish between an injury and something done rightly; nor
> are they able to teach, console, or advise. I've often heard from
> many persons that this is so; and I myself have to some extent
> experienced it.[70]

Exomologesis

Not until 1524 with the *Exomologesis,* however, did Erasmus write a very extensive discussion of confession. In this treatise he sets forth both the advantages and the disadvantages of the sacrament, as well as a method for its proper use and means by which its disadvantages can be overcome.

The disadvantages of confession arise, says the humanist, not from the sacrament itself but from the vices of men. Erasmus enumerates nine, the first five of which arise from the behavior of priests, the last four from that of penitents.

Among the disadvantages as related to priests he includes the following: danger of corruption of young, innocent, inexperienced priests by what they hear in confession; the self-deception resulting from a too easy comparison of the vices of the penitent with those of the priest himself; the tyranny exercised by some priests in the confessional; the spread by contagion of evil deeds enumerated in confession; and, finally, the betrayal of the secrecy of the confessional.[71]

The evils of confession as connected with the penitent embrace the following: a loss of sense of shame from too frequent confession; the anxiety and burden of a solicitous enumeration of secret sins, which prevents the birth of love and a peaceful conscience; the noxious confidence in the perfunctory observance of the sacrament without sincere contrition and a serious intention to lead a new life; and, finally, the danger of hypocrisy from confession out of fear of disgrace or of excommunication rather than out of a genuine feeling of repentance. In order that the practice of confession might not become mechanical, hypocritical, superstitious, or lead to a loss of sense of shame, Erasmus strongly opposes going to the priest too frequently.

His discussion of the burden of confession is lengthier than that of the other evils and requires more extended treatment. He goes so far as to compare the yoke of confession with that of the Mosaic law, which he says Peter and Paul refused to impose on the Gentiles. His reasoning here is interesting. He says that not even Christ demanded celibacy of anyone, and yet does a man require so grave a matter as confession of another man? Paul out of consideration of human weakness relaxed somewhat a precept of the Lord (presumably the commandment concerning divorce, with his judgment that a pagan is free to separate from his or her Christian spouse—I Cor. 7:15):

> With what impudence do they who are not to be compared with Paul impose such a weight beyond the precept of the Lord? Especially when one considers confession as it is now practiced, entangled as it is by so many perplexities and anxieties that one scarcely departs from the priest with a tranquil conscience?[72]

Here Erasmus definitely acknowledges that the present law of confession is of human origin, and very much regrets that such a burdensome human ordinance has been inflicted on men. This practice is more in keeping with Jewish legalism than with evangelical freedom and charity. It contrasts sharply with the *philosophia Christi,* whose yoke is easy and whose burden is light, just as is that of nature. Christ did not demand virginity, because that would have conflicted with the law of nature. Paul somewhat lightened the burden of the law of divorce. The implication is that if even Christ did not impose a burden on us that would have gone contrary to nature (the commandment of divorce is, as we have seen in an earlier chapter, an exception), and if Paul, indulgent of human frailty, can slightly modify a commandment of the Lord, then a law imposed by men on men not only can but ought to be removed or at least modified for the sake of the salvation of men. His moralism, philological criticism, and sense of history again reinforce one another here in his censure of the present practice of confession.

Immediately following his discussion of the disadvantages of confession and again at the end of the treatise Erasmus suggests some remedies for correcting the abuses by confessor and penitent alike. The second discussion nearly repeats the major points of the first.

First of all, Erasmus stresses the need for priests who are mature, learned, prudent, of sound doctrine and integrity—men who will act as wise and compassionate pastors, fathers, and physicians to their people. He urges that the priestly office be undertaken only by individuals who are aware of its arduousness and its heavy responsibility and who therefore assume it with seriousness and trepidation.[73] He insists that a large part of the blame for unworthy priests lies with the bishop who is not sufficiently careful that only worthy individuals enter the priesthood.

Most of the abuses of the sacrament could be corrected if the character of the confessor could be radically improved. He says prudent and upright priests hear confessions only with caution. They do so only when love or authority or the necessity of the office presses the task upon them.

Since Erasmus' emphasis is not upon the priest's sacramental power but rather upon his pastoral and intercessory functions in confession, he is concerned about the priest's intellectual and moral quality. The beneficial effect of confession in its pastoral aspect is contingent upon the integrity of the confessor. In his emphasis upon this element of penitential practice Erasmus again follows his favorite of the Fathers, Origen.[74] The question of the power of the priestly absolution we shall treat in a later section of this chapter.

In addition Erasmus gives out some advice to those who go to confession. In line with the above remarks he indicates that the first necessity is the selection of an appropriate priest. As in the healing of the body, so in the healing of the soul, a physician of the first rank is indispensable.[75] The next requirement is to enter confession not lightmindedly or habitually but with sincere remorse for one's sins out of love of God and with the serious intention to lead a new life.[76] One should undertake confession only with the will never to relapse into the former sin, and this is not so difficult with the help of the grace of Christ. The emphasis, in accord with his total sacramental theology, is clearly upon the inner and moral dimensions of confession. Although contrition is necessary for confession to be advantageous, he allows one to go to the priest out of obedience to the Church and with some degree of hatred of his sins, for it is possible that in confession he may realize a true contrition.

The anxiety and burden of confession can be partially removed by a brief examination and revelation to the priest of only those crimes which clearly weigh upon our consciences, certainly "capital, or strongly suspected, crimes."[77] Venial or light sins born of bodily weakness ought to be fought lest they become gross, but they do not require confession. He especially criticizes those who advocate confession of those things which relate not to genuine sins but merely to the natural human constitution, such as nocturnal pollutions. He accuses Gerson of having written too scrupulously along these lines.[78] He rejects the need for a continually repeated general confession. One's intensity of contrition and will to reform ought to be such that it will not be necessary for him immediately to return to the priest, but if he happens to relapse, he should disclose only what he has committed since the last confession.[79]

Along with the nine disadvantages of confession, Erasmus enumerates in the *Exomologesis* nine advantages, or uses. The first and chief value is as a means of crushing pride, the source of all evil. As pride was the first step to sin, so acknowledgment of one's turpitude and submission to God are the first step to a recovered righteousness. To this end the act of submitting oneself to a man and revealing one's faults to him is most helpful.[80] As we have already noticed, for Erasmus the willingness to go to the priest is a sign of true contrition. One who refuses to go is not sufficiently repentant. As we have already pointed out, Erasmus observes that since the whole man rebelled against God, it is fitting that the whole man, including the body, surrender to God. This bodily submission is accomplished in the act of confession. A corollary of this thought is the idea that a bodily sacrament is needed because of our bodily weakness to deter us from sinning, to provoke us to repentance, and to incite in us a true love of God.

A second value of confession is that it may provide a more accurate knowledge of one's sins. Since many, because of age, inexperience, or ignorance, misjudge their sins, finding a crime where there is none, or not recognizing a mortal sin when they have committed one, confessors are needed who as wise, learned, and faithful physicians are able to spot the disease, recommend the proper remedy, and advise how it can be avoided in the future.[81]

Related to the above uses of confession is a third, concerned with the correction of two opposite evils—a pernicious security or glorying in one's sins and an even more dangerous despair of the divine mercy. For the one, the priest in confession seeks to induce a salutary shame and grief; for the other, a confidence and hope in the divine mercy and promises. Near the end of the treatise Erasmus says that many more are endangered by a too excessive confidence than by despair.[82] As Tentler correctly points out,[83] this thought is not necessarily contradictory to the idea expressed above that despair is more dangerous than both an overconfidence and a boasting about one's sins. Despair is more dangerous because, since it calls into question the nature of God as gracious and merciful, it is the more serious sin. But Erasmus thinks that in actual fact there are more cases in his day of presumption than of despair, and thus it is more frequently needful for the priest to incite the penitent to a proper fear of God than to call him away from desperation by pointing to the divine mercy. This observation, however, ought not to obscure the fact that Erasmus is also genuinely concerned for anxious and despairing penitents, as the next use of confession indicates.

The fourth use of confession is to gratify those who are too scrupulously concerned about their minor faults until they can progress to a stronger mind. Erasmus has in mind those who are so anxiously concerned about imperfections having to do with their bodily natures or with sudden thoughts which only very lightly crease the surface of the mind that they think they can have no peace of conscience until they receive absolution from the priest. Such confessions arise out of fear, not out of love, and thus overburden both penitent and confessor. He would prefer that they not take place. However, he thinks that it belongs to Christian charity to adapt oneself to the weakness of these persons, but in such a way that they might be advised to progress to what is more perfect and learn to love more and fear less.[84] Here again the major theme of accommodation makes room for the sacramental and displays not only the aspect of pedagogy but also of mercy.[85]

The fifth advantage of confession, already discussed in the section on penance as virtue and as sacrament, is that the premeditation of what we will confess to the priest may help to create in us a proper hatred of our sins which may take its origin in attrition and then move to contrition. "This benefit urges a man to confess to the priest, even if confession were not necessary; how much more should he embrace it if necessity forces him to do so."[86]

The sixth advantage of confession is that the shame of confessing to a man restrains sin. This benefit is, however, easily lost when confession becomes too frequent.

The seventh value of confession, not substantially different from the second, is to assist with self-knowledge, which is the principal part of wisdom. In confession, sins which reside in the inner recesses of our heart are disclosed, and the ways by which we have either adhered to or strayed from the law of God are illuminated. This self-knowledge is for the humanist an important presupposition of virtue.

An eighth benefit is that one is aided by the counsel, encouragement, consolation, and prayer of the priest. Erasmus shows that he is interested not in his sacramental power but in his pastoral and intercessory functions in the confessional.

In his discussion of the last advantage Erasmus' traditionalism and concern for Church unity are apparent. Even though confession is not strictly necessary, since already through contrition one is freed from his guilt, nevertheless confession should be retained as a long-established ecclesiastical custom and as the means of reconciliation with the Church and of prevention of injury to the peace of the *res publica Christiana.* "This is also a part of piety, to fulfill all righteousness, to avoid all offense, and, as Paul says, to be pleasing in all things to all men." To what is his chief interest here Erasmus adds secondarily the thought that even though one is previously forgiven of sins, one ought not to spurn confession, since through it one receives additional "light and grace."

In his views on confession, as elsewhere, Erasmus pursues the middle course. His criticism of the divine institution of the sacrament, his emphasis upon the priority of contrition, and his description of the moral abuses, specifically of the burden, all serve to undercut its necessity and reduce its stature in the popular mind. These thoughts link him with the Protestant critique of the sacrament.[87] But with his view that confession ought to be retained as a sacrament even though only *de iure humano* out of respect for ecclesiastical tradition and out of a concern for its moral and spiritual value as an accommodation to man's weakness, he separates himself not only from the Protestants but also from those among the Roman orthodox who place the emphasis upon the sacramental power, that is, especially, the Thomists and the Scotists.

In line with his pedagogical interests, the humanist, who gives us methods of right study, of interpreting Scripture, of preaching, of prayer, of right living, and of dying, provides us in this treatise also with a method of confessing.

He prefaces his comments here with a short criticism of existing practice. He thinks the widespread promulgation of the little handbooks of penance which describe in full detail both actual and possible sins is dangerous and requires an exceptional maturity on the part of those who use them. He is also opposed to the indiscriminate and full interrogation on the part of priests of all penitents regardless of their sex, age, or natural disposition.

While noting that St. Thomas has written detailed catalogues of virtues and vices, Erasmus says that, since he is writing for laymen, his method is simpler. Like the Erasmian program for an inner understanding of the baptismal vow, so the Erasmian method of confession calls for clear and brief teaching on the Apostles' Creed and the commandments in yearly sermons and in compendiums written in the vernacular. A knowledge of these would be necessary for living well even if it were not mandatory to confess to any man. But also the frequent hearing of sermons and the reading of Scripture pre-

pare a man properly to confess, whether to God or to man.
Thus, Scripture and the Apostles' Creed, the mainsprings of
theological and moral reform, are also for Erasmus to be the
source of the reform of the confessional, making it simpler,
more tolerable, and hopefully without doubt less necessary.

The chief of all the commandments, says Erasmus, is faith
which works through love. Subjectively, faith is a deep inner
trust. Its object and content are all the promises and commandments of Scripture which are confirmed by a universal consensus of the Church. Although not expressly mentioned here, he
would undoubtedly include also the Apostles' Creed and all
those doctrines and practices in the tradition which are universally received by the Church even though not present in Scripture.

Erasmus points out that sixteenth-century men do not measure up to this norm. He says many do not believe in the resurrection of the body, some not even in the immortality of the
soul. Many admit, he says, that they do not believe in the Apostles' Creed. Most men, says Erasmus, especially those who are
rich in honors and dignities, act as if they do not believe in
Scripture. Catechism, so essential for an effective baptism, is
necessary also for an efficacious confession.

Faith and love are the measure of sin. Whatever does not
proceed from these roots is sin even if it has the appearance of
righteousness. On the other hand, what may appear to be sin
is not, if it flows from sincere faith and love. As always with
Erasmus, what is crucial is the inner direction and motivation
of one's life, not the outward activities. Thus he contrasts the
hypocrisy of those men who, while building monasteries and
giving alms, have as their real aim riches and worldly honors
with the genuine piety of those whose every action, whether at
work or at play, whether awake or sleeping, is directed by faith
and love.

In contrast with the casuistry of the medieval handbooks of
penance Erasmus supplies indeed a simple method. However,
while he thinks of all sins as issuing from the heart, he will
accept the traditional division into spiritual and fleshly sins. The

former include envy, hate, desire of revenge, pride, hypocrisy, ill will; the latter, debauchery, lust, violence, injury. Many sins may be referred to each of the five senses, but the most to the tongue, a favorite target of Erasmian moralistic criticism.

Erasmus himself engages in a certain amount of casuistry, however, when he comes to consider briefly the complicated topic of the circumstances of the sins. With characteristic care when dealing with a controversial subject, he says at the outset that he intends by his remarks not to teach but to advise. First, he says that those priests sin who inquire concerning the circumstance in order to discover accomplices of the crime. He is also critical of priests who out of filthy curiosity probe into all the circumstances of sexual sins. The humanist evinces a concern for the context of human sins. In evaluating the degree of sin, Erasmus suggests, the priest should consider the time, the place, the person, the amount of intentional malice, the magnitude of his temptation, and his station in life. The only rule is love and human need. For example, though usually adultery is looked upon as a more serious sin than simple fornication, it is actually worse, says Erasmus, for one with wicked design to entice into fornication a virgin of a fine family intended for a good marriage than for one accidentally to slip into adultery. It is likewise a graver sin to rob another's home without any necessity, especially that of a poor family, than to take out of need what one accidentally comes across in a sacred shrine. It is a much more serious crime to break divine precepts than human precepts. It is considerably worse to transgress the moral than the ceremonial law. One should consider the consequences of the sin, as in the murder of a prince upon whom the welfare of the whole commonwealth depends. One must view sins of omission as seriously as sins of commission. For example, a person is guilty of murder when he fails to act to save the life of one in danger. Moreover, he sins doubly who not only does not do what he ought but carries on abominable activities, as when one not only neglects to observe the Lord's Day in prayer, hearing sermons, meditation, and holy reading, but passes the day in silly pleasures, fornication, drunkenness, filthy

tales, quarrels, and fights. This point holds true especially for
those in authority, thinks Erasmus. The Pope sins doubly when
he not only does not exercise his office to reconcile warring
parties but engages in war himself. A prince is held accountable
not only for oppressing or plundering his commonwealth but
also for not ridding the country of oppressors of liberty when
it is in his power. It is a double sin when knowingly and de-
signedly he entrusts rule to a wicked magistrate for the sake of
gain. Likewise, a bishop sins twice when he not only does not
care for his flock but corrupts them by evil teaching and living
and by handing them over to wicked priests. Therefore, it is
important for the priest to notice the station in life of the penitent before judging the relative heinousness of the crime. Thus
in his discussion of the circumstances of sin does Erasmus have
the opportunity to bring within range of his fire favorite targets
of his searching moral attack—evil popes, bishops, princes,
who by virtue of their high offices have special responsibilities
to educate, to correct abuses, and to set an example for all to
follow.[88] We note, finally, that the contextual thinking which
shapes his understanding of Scripture and of the development
of Church dogma determines also his analysis of the circumstances of sins to be examined in the confessional.

After the *Exomologesis*

Erasmus' remarks on confession after this treatise add nothing new to his thought on the subject. He continues to speak of
the sacrament as salubrious, as bringing tranquillity, even as
necessary.[89] As we have already seen, he counsels that one go
to confession three or four times a year, before communion,
and especially before death.[90] But he continues to be critical of
the abuses of confession. In one of the colloquies he ridicules
not only a dying man who has lived an evil life for his false
reliance on confession and the other deathbed sacraments, unction and communion, but also the tyranny of the mendicants
and the priest who fight over the right to hear the man's confession.[91] The evil of which he complains the most, however, is that
of the anxiety or burden of confession.[92]

Erasmus sums up his views on this subject in the treatise which he intended as a contribution to the restoration of Christian unity, the *De amabili Ecclesiae concordia* (1533).[93] He urges that those who are not convinced that confession was established by Christ preserve it as salutary and useful and approved by the custom of many centuries. His emphasis upon the subjective aspect of the sacrament is easily discerned in the opinion that whether we receive benefit from confession depends largely on ourselves. We must choose an appropriate priest, one who is learned, upright, and can hold his tongue. We ought to confess only the "letalia vulnera," of which he gives us these examples: adultery, murder, theft, a great and voluntary drunkenness, malicious disparagement (in itself a kind of murder), or poisoning, perjury, deceit, plunder, and other kinds of crimes committed with a clear and intended malice. He expresses his perennial wish that a superstitious repetition and anxious enumeration of all crimes and circumstances be absent from the confession. What chiefly interests him here as elsewhere is that we have such a strong and sincere contrition and intention to lead a new life that we not fall back into mortal sin. His moralism is further shown in the previously uttered thought that although it is hardly possible for anyone to live without the lighter sins, it is not difficult with the help of God to escape the mortal sins if one is rooted in the love of God and of the neighbor. He who can do this is free from the burden of confession. But if anyone should commit a mortal crime, it is not necessary that he run immediately to the priest, but first confess to God. He ought then to confess also to the priest when there is opportunity. Erasmus concludes his remarks with the hope that those who regard confession as divinely instituted will observe it all the more religiously but will leave others not of the same mind to their own opinion until a general synod pronounces more clearly concerning it.[94]

V. Absolution

In the light of Erasmus' stress upon contrition as the one indispensable presupposition of divine forgiveness, it is not surprising that, as for the early scholastics and the late medieval nominalists Occam and Biel, absolution can have only a declarative, not a sacramental, meaning.[95] In the *Confabulatio pia* (1522), this point of view is implied in the statement of the boy: "But I confess to Him who alone truly remits sins and who has all power."[96] In the *Exomologesis* (1524), Erasmus states clearly that God alone forgives sins, both their guilt and their punishment.[97] Finally, in what must be regarded as his last word on the subject, he maintains this point of view: "The sins of the contrite are actually forgiven before they confess. The priest only confirms the gift of God, and, as it were, seals it."[98]

Moreover, since the contrition of the penitent is uncertain,[99] the formula of absolution is necessarily deprecative, not indicative.[100] He further calls into question the indicative formula by pointing out that not even Christ dared to say, "I forgive sins," but only "Your sins are forgiven you."[101]

Since the fundamental matter in absolution is contrition, of which in any case the priest cannot be sure when he declares the penitent absolved or wishes for his absolution, it is not necessary for the priest to know all the circumstances of the sin or sins before he pronounces. Erasmus sharply rejects the analogy of the priest to the judge who must know all the circumstances of the case before he can make a judgment.[102]   Besides, Erasmus points out, if remission of sins is contingent upon the priest's knowledge of all sins and all circumstances, how are sins forgiven through baptism, even those which have not been confessed?[103] Erasmus thus criticizes the judicial power of the priesthood. He rejects then implicitly the *clavis scientiae,* which the scholastics generally regarded as the presupposition for the operation of the other key, the *clavis potestatis.* The former is exercised in confession, whereby the priest learns of the kind of sins of the penitent as well as of the quality of his penitence and makes *"iudicium de idoneitate recipientis";* then the other is exercised in absolution.

But Erasmus is cool also toward the *clavis potestatis,* though he does not explicitly deny it.[104] Like Origen and Abelard Erasmus seems to ground the sacerdotal power of absolution in the spiritual and moral integrity of the priest.[105]

More than the powers of absolution Erasmus emphasizes the pastoral and intercessory function of the priest. Because this is the primary role of the priest, the choice of an appropriate or good priest is a very important one.

VI. Satisfaction

Traditionally, the priestly powers were exercised not only in loosing, absolution, but also in binding, prescription of satisfaction. Along with contrition and confession, satisfaction was regarded as a third important part of penance. Peter Lombard considered satisfaction in deed along with contrition of the heart and confession of the mouth as three essential steps in the perfection of penance.[106] Penance then was commonly thought to have both an exterior and an interior aspect.

The question of the role of satisfaction, if through contrition and absolution the guilt and eternal punishment of sin were remitted, was resolved by the distinction between eternal and temporal punishment. Though the former is remitted by interior penance and confession, at least a portion of the latter remains to be exacted by exterior penance, voluntary works of satisfaction. The theological reasoning behind this assumption was that in the sacrament of penance both the mercy and the justice of God are revealed—his mercy in the act of absolution, his justice in the necessity of satisfaction in order proportionately but not quantitatively to make up for the offense against God's honor.[107] Furthermore, sin constitutes an offense not only against God but also against the Church and the neighbor. Satisfaction is thus regarded in the first place as voluntary punishment for past sin. Whatever amount of the debt of temporal punishment is not paid in this life by works of satisfaction is exacted by suffering here and in the fires of purgatory to come. Thus, the motive of performance of acts of penance was as much the avoidance of future punishment in purgatory as re-

moval of the offense against God. In addition, however, satisfaction was thought of not only as punishment for past sins but
also as medicine to avoid future sins. Works of satisfaction
consisted chiefly of prayer, fasting, and almsgiving. Finally, at
least by the thirteenth century, it was thought that vicarious
satisfaction on the basis of the unity of the charity existing
among the members of the mystical Body of Christ was possible
for the vindictive, but not for the medicinal, aspect of penance.[108]

On the one hand, Erasmus is critical of satisfaction. He
stresses that contrition is the prior and fundamental fact in
penance, removing all guilt and punishment. In the colloquy
Adolescentis et scorti (1523), Sophronius reported that a wise
confessor had imposed on him for his acts of incontinence only
the penance of reciting a psalm and giving a florin to a needy
person. When he expressed surprise that the penance was so
light, the confessor replied: "Son, if you truly repent and
change your way of life, I don't care much about penance."[109]
In line with the fundamental principle of his thought, Erasmus
places the emphasis upon an interior rather than an exterior
penance.

Furthermore, Erasmus finds no basis for satisfaction in the
New Testament. We have already seen that he rejects Matthew
3:2 as a basis for any part of the sacrament. In addition, by his
translation and annotation he implicitly overturns a favorite
scholastic proof text for satisfaction, namely, Matthew 3:8—
Luke 3:8, translated in the Vulgate "Facite fructum dignum
poenitentiae." Erasmus translates it thus: "Facite igitur fructus
qui deceant poenitentiam." Satisfaction is more appropriately
suggested by the former than by the latter translation. His note
on the Matthean text indicates that the true meaning of the
passage is that true repentance ought to be demonstrated in a
new life.[110]

Not only is it impossible to ground satisfaction in the New
Testament, but the action and words of Christ seem to run
counter to it. He reveals that the mercy of God is infinitely
greater than that of men when, without inflicting satisfaction, he

said simply: "Your sins are forgiven."[111]

On the basis of his understanding of God Erasmus was naturally critical of satisfaction at least insofar as it is a punishment for sin. As we have already noticed, in Erasmus' theology the element of the divine justice recedes behind the divine mercy. Since there is no justice requiring satisfaction, there is no need for punishment. Of course, for obdurate sinners there will be punishment, but for earnest penitents inner anguish is sufficient penance.[112] There is no need for exterior works of satisfaction.

Finally, his opposition to satisfaction as punishment is to be understood also from the point of view of his criticism of the juridical powers of the priest which express themselves in the knowledge of sins and their attendant circumstances and in the acts of absolution and the prescription of satisfaction.

Yet Erasmus recommends that satisfaction also be preserved, presumably for four major reasons: (1) out of reverence for the tradition and the authority of the Church, (2) out of concern for the peace of the Church,[113] (3) out of concern that the removal of satisfaction would encourage excessive security and immorality,[114] and (4) out of regard for it as a helpful remedy against sin.

It is thus upon the medicinal aspect of penance and the priest as physician that Erasmus lays all the emphasis in his discussion of satisfaction in the *Exomologesis*. He urges that priests not prescribe simply any kind of satisfaction whatever but, like the experienced physician, consider the quality of person and disease before recommending the proper remedy. He especially commends the reading of books of the Fathers which would bear on the nature of the crime. He naturally values moral works more highly than ceremonial works. He is critical of the prescription of pilgrimages, especially for the young and for those who have wives and children at home. He also severely criticizes works of satisfaction which consist of gifts to build monasteries, churches, lavish shrines, altars, etc. Whatever works are performed ought always to be carried on in the spirit of love for them to have any value.[115]

VII. Indulgences

In the light of Erasmus' total penitential theology it is not surprising that he shows little sympathy for a practice which, while it is not a part of the sacrament of penance, stands in the closest relation to it, namely, indulgences.[116] His emphasis on the interiority of penance, his lack of interest in satisfaction as punishment, and his questioning of the jurisdictional power of the papacy and the priesthood all preclude his enthusiasm for a practice which had become so externalized and commercialized that it is generally admitted that it had become an open scandal well before Erasmus' time.[117]

In the *Enchiridion, Laus stultitiae,* and the *Colloquia,* Erasmus satirizes the popular superstition in contrast to the theory that one could purchase his salvation by indulgences. The references in the *Enchiridion* (1503) and the *Laus stultitiae* (1509) are noteworthy as the only pre-Reformation utterances of Erasmus that I have been able to discover on this subject. In the *Enchiridion* he says:

> Perhaps you believe your sins are removed once and for all by a wax seal, by giving a little money or by making a little pilgrimage. You are completely off the track. The wound has been inflicted within, and the remedy must be applied there.[118]

In the *Laus stultitiae* he pokes fun at those who hug themselves with *fictis scelerum condonationibus.*[119] But also in a colloquy written after the outbreak of the Reformation in 1522, he ridicules a drunken soldier who "though in other respects the most frivolous trifler . . . pinned his whole hope of salvation, so to speak, on a piece of parchment instead of on a moral life."[120]

In various letters beginning in 1518 Erasmus criticizes the impudence of the Roman curia in granting indulgences, the exaggerated claims made for them, their frequency, immoderation, and the connection of the profit motive. He refers to them as an evil traffic or as having become mere merchandise.[121]

By the ironical *utinam* Erasmus places in question the power of the Pope over purgatory. In the *Ratio* (1522) he expresses the wish: "Would that he [the Pope] could truly remove souls from the punishments of purgatory."[122] In the preface to I Corinthians (1519) he includes the question whether souls in purgatory are freed by the highest pontiff as one of the disputed matters concerning which he wishes the Apostle Paul had provided us enlightenment.[123] Thereby he ironically indicates that such a doctrine has no scriptural warrant. In answer to a censure by the Sorbonne theological faculty of this passage, Erasmus admits that the Pope can relax satisfactions imposed by men, but notes that

> . . . whether this power extends to purgatory has been doubted by a few, even pious men. Whether indeed holy councils have approved such indulgences is not yet sufficiently clear.[124]

Elsewhere he does not simply suggest but clearly states that indulgences have no basis in the Holy Scriptures nor in the early Fathers and that more recent theologians have had various opinions concerning them.[125] His major complaint against indulgences, which he expresses freely from shortly after the outbreak of the Protestant revolt to the end of his life, is that they engender a false assurance, a false sense of security. Repeatedly, he states that though he does not condemn indulgences as such, he has admonished those who trust in them superstitiously that it is safer to rely on the mercy of Christ and/or pious deeds.[126]

His attitude is summed up in these few words: "If love is absent, of what advantage is the bull? If love is sufficiently present, the diploma is superfluous."[127] The emphasis upon the inner, personal element of love and contrition as well as his neglect of the idea of satisfaction as punishment serves to negate the necessity and the usefulness of indulgences for Erasmus. However, Erasmus says he does not condemn indulgences, at least not entirely. He accepts them, though not gladly, primarily on the authority of the Church,[128] but also secondarily as an extreme accommodation to the weakness of some who are on the brink of desperation in order that they may be nourished and raised so that they may proceed to better things.[129] Erasmus' attitude on indulgences is thus in keeping with his understanding of the sacrament of penance as a whole and, indeed, in large measure with his whole sacramental theology, which accepts the sacraments, especially those which are not grounded in the New Testament, on the basis of the authority of the Church and also as accommodations to our weakness. It is understandable, however, that he shows so little enthusiasm and so much criticism for this institution, which had become so corrupt that many besides Erasmus were clamoring for its reform.

VIII. Extreme Unction

Extreme unction was traditionally regarded as standing in close relation to penance. The Council of Trent came to speak of it as the "completion" of penance. In the *Decretum pro Armenis* at the Council of Florence, 1439, it is placed immediately after penance. In his listing of the sacraments in the *Christiani hominis institutum* (1514) Erasmus names it after penance.[130] But just as he did not feel himself bound to the traditional order of the sacraments as a whole, so regarding this one he varied in his order of placement. In the *Symbolum* (1533) it is named, as we have seen, after the Eucharist.

Institution

Concerning the institution of the sacrament, Erasmus wrote brief notes on the two passages which were customarily cited as its New Testament basis, Mark 6:13 and James 5:14-15. In the 1516 edition of the *Novum Testamentum* Erasmus remarks on Mark 6:13 that apparently from this passage arose the present custom of anointing only those who are dangerously ill, but not that they might recover. In the 1522 edition he adds, "not exactly that they might recover but that they might depart more safely."[131] The difference between the contemporary and the Apostolic practices, which is implicit in the earlier note, is made explicit in the later one. His 1516 comment on James 5:14 f. also marks the difference between the present and the former custom by saying that the anointing of the sick "now takes place at the last moment of life."[132] In his 1522 note Erasmus adds that although we do not read that the Apostles were commanded by the Lord to anoint the sick, there is agreement that what they did, they did by order of the Lord. In other words, the institution of the practice is more implicitly than explicitly grounded in a divine command in this passage of James.[133] The result of a study of these texts is that though Erasmus points to the difference between the ancient and the modern practice, he does not call into question the divine institution of the sacrament.[134] He rejects out of hand an accusation of Stunica that he did so.[135] That he regarded the ancient practice as sacramental is indicated by his paraphrase on Mark 6:13:

> That oil was not a medicine (for who heals all diseases with the same medicine?) but a sacrament. The skin was anointed with visible oil so that the body was healed; but the souls, that they might be healed from their diseases of sins, were anointed by the oil of evangelical grace through Jesus, our anointed one.[136]

Flesh and Spirit

The above quotation reveals that Erasmus understands also the sacrament of extreme unction from the viewpoint of the contrasting flesh and spirit. As in his total sacramental theology he makes a sharp distinction between the visible sign and the invisible grace. He applies it explicitly to unction in the passage from the *Detectio* (1526), where he is defending himself against those Protestants who appeal to the emphasis upon the spiritual element in his writings. He feels compelled to argue that though he does indeed prefer the spiritual aspect of the sacrament, i.e., the gift of grace and the faith which receives this grace, he does not intend to negate the visible sign as his admirers imagine. Regarding this sacrament, he states: "In unction, does he who posits faith and the grace of the Holy Spirit before the oil deny that the oil is present?"[137]

As with the other sacraments Erasmus repudiates a merely fleshly, formalistic, magical understanding and usage. In the *Convivium religiosum* (1522) he includes extreme unction in his satire of the many ceremonies which accompany and protect us from cradle to grave. He concludes this speech by noting:

> Though these ceremonies, especially the ones sanctioned by ecclesiastical usage, are acceptable, yet there are also other, more interior means of helping us to depart from this life with cheerfulness and Christian trust.[138]

Likewise, in the *Enarratio in psalmum XXXIII* (1531) he pokes fun at the superstition of those who maintain that a person who has received the last rites necessarily dies well and that one dies badly who has not received them. He asks: "Why do we judge a neighbor, ignorant as we are of the faith in which he died?"[139] In his paraphrase of James 5:14-15, Erasmus emphasizes that the anointing is not magical, but is effective because of the prayers of the elders and the faith of the recipient. Although these thoughts were applied to the ancient practice, in the light of the rest of his sacramental understanding they can also be related to the modern sacrament of extreme unction and taken to mean that, as always, he emphasizes the *opus operantis* and the deprecative character of the formula.[140]

In fact, more important than the actual receiving of the sacraments at death are faith and love. Indeed, if these are present, the sacraments are not absolutely necessary so long as there is neither neglect nor contempt of them.

And yet a Christian will wish the sacraments to be present, for they are signs of the divine beneficence toward him. They are sources of consolation and aids of faith. Besides, it is fitting for the Christian to fulfill all righteousness,[141] that is, not to spurn the law and the custom of the Church.

The Effect of Extreme Unction

In the paraphrases Erasmus says that the effect of the New Testament sacramental practice of anointing was unity in the healing of body and soul. As vices of the soul lead to contagion of the body, so both body and soul are healed through faith and the prayers of the elders.[142] We have already observed that in his 1522 note on Mark 6:13, he points out the difference between the desired effects of the two anointings, although he acknowledges that it was from the ancient practice that the modern one developed. The former was observed that the sick one might recover; the latter, that he might depart more safely. In his brief verse on this sacrament in the early *Christiani hominis institutum* (1514), he describes as the effect of extreme unction only the aid it affords us for a safe journey to the beyond.[143] However, in his later and longer catechism of 1533, Erasmus allows his description of the effect of the sacrament to be shaped by the former practice to such an extent that he mentions as the first end of the sacrament that "the sick one may recover if it so seems best to God" before going on to say, "or that with faith and good hope he may sleep in the Lord."[144] Erasmus does not make any more precise his ideas of how the sacrament makes for a "safe" or "safer" journey to the beyond. He does not at all enter into the scholastic discussion concerning the exact nature of the chief effect of the sacrament as a healing of the soul.[145]

CONCLUSION

———————————◂◆▸———————————

Just as Erasmus' interests are more in Christ as teacher and example than as redeemer and more in the priest as teacher, preacher, and example than as administrator of the sacraments, so his interest is not so much in the sacraments as the mainspring of the Christian life as in the *philosophia Christiana* without which the sacraments are useless. However, just as he does not neglect the role of Christ as redeemer and the priest as administrator of the sacraments, so he does not neglect the role of the sacraments in the Christian life. They have a secondary yet significant place in his thought, even if the emphasis is more upon their subjective use than upon their objective meaning.

I. Flesh and Spirit

The fundamental principle of Erasmus' religious thought, the neo-Platonic contrast of flesh and spirit grounded in the nature of man, shapes Erasmus' understanding of Scripture, Christ, the Christian life, and also the sacraments. The movement is from the visible to the invisible according to the higher part of man; from the literal to the allegorical and tropological interpretation of Scripture; from the carnal to the inward, affective understanding of Christ; from the merely formal to the personal and moral appropriation and application of the sacraments. Indeed, the emphasis is so much upon the spiritual and moral element that some have questioned whether Erasmus' Platonism and moralism have not entirely obscured the physical and sacramental.

Without doubt there is in Erasmus' thought a definite tendency toward spiritualism and moralism which reduces the
necessity of the sacraments. This tendency is especially apparent in the early work, the *Enchiridion,* where he is severely critical of a formalistic sacramentalism. But just as in his later
writings Erasmus emphasizes more strongly the necessity of
the literal sense of Scripture as a foundation of the allegorical,
so also in his later works he gives greater weight to sacramental
participation, out of a sense of obedience to the Church and
of the use of the sacraments as aids of the spiritual and moral
life.

Yet even in the *Enchiridion,* however much he shows his
scorn for a superstitious reliance on ceremonies, even the great
mystery of the Eucharist, he does not deny the flesh or the
sacramental. He says: "I praise them [the crowd] for embrac-
ing the flesh of piety, but I do not praise them for stopping at
that point."[1] He also regards the sacraments as "evidence"
(*indicia*) and "supports" (*adminicula*) of piety, especially for the
weak; but even the strong do not spurn them lest they injure the
weak by their example. While later affirming more strongly the
sacramental element, Erasmus continues to stress throughout
his life the greater importance of the personal dimension.

The constitution of man out of flesh and spirit explains both
the necessity of the movement from a formal to a personal
appropriation of the sacraments and the necessity of their use
as supports of piety. Just as the language of Scripture and,
indeed, the incarnation itself are accommodations to our fleshly
weakness, so also are the sacraments—a theme which Erasmus
derives from the early Fathers, especially Origen. If we were
completely spiritual, we would not need the sacraments; but
since we are creatures of flesh, we require signs which remind
us of God's grace, nourish our faith, and excite our love.[2] However, God's gracious accommodation to our weakness in Scripture, incarnation, and sacraments is of no value if we are
content always to cling to the flesh and not allow ourselves to
be drawn by degrees to a more perfect piety. There is thus a
double movement in Erasmus' thought on flesh and spirit:

God's accommodation to our weakness, from the invisible to the visible; and our progress to a deeper religion, from the visible to the invisible.

Undoubtedly, for Erasmus there is less need for the sacraments on the part of the strong in faith and love. Yet out of obedience to the Church and consideration for the weak they will not neglect or disdain them. Besides, insofar as they are less than perfect, they stand in need of them, although this thought remains in the background.

II. Gift and Example

Erasmus acknowledges that we receive a gift of grace through the use of the sacraments. In a Franciscan manner he understands this grace as accompanying or paralleling the sacramental action rather than as channeled through it. The sacraments do not cause and contain grace, but are signs of the invisible grace which necessarily accompanies their use. Grace is received inwardly while the sign is received outwardly.[3] His Platonism prohibits his admission of a natural, intrinsic connection between sign and thing signified. The emphasis, however, is not upon the objective act, the *ex opere operato,* but upon the subjective reception of the grace in faith and love, the *ex opere operantis.*

Just as in his understanding of Christ's work Erasmus does not leave out of view the objective redemption but does emphasize the role of teacher and example, so in his concept of the sacraments he does not neglect the gift of grace but does stress the sacrament as a task to be fulfilled.[4] However, as in his doctrine of justification, so in his understanding of the sacraments, the sheer gift aspect is impaired by its being made contingent upon the fulfillment of the demand, the psychological and ethical application of the meaning of the sacrament. For this purpose, Erasmus insists upon the importance of catechism. Here also the original Latin understanding of *sacramentum* as an oath of allegiance or obligation comes into view, especially in his thought on baptism. However, in contrast to Zwingli and

Oecolampadius, it is remarkable that Erasmus did not specifically apply this meaning of the term to the Eucharist. Rather there his emphasis is ever upon its meaning as mystery.

III. The Sacraments and the Process of Salvation

Erasmus accepts all seven sacraments and finds a place for them in the movement of the Christian life. He seems to question marriage alone as being a sacrament in the narrower sense of the word, as conferring grace, but says he is willing to accept that opinion, which has become a universal consensus in the Church.

Within the order of salvation, however, marriage, by which we are born into the world, has its importance as the representation of nature (*pulchri, pulcherrima portio, mundi*), which, though corrupted, is the positive presupposition for the rebirth in baptism. Because there is for Erasmus no original sin in the sense of an inherited depravity passed on in procreation, but only an inclination to sin, weakness, and ignorance, it is possible *ex puris naturalibus* to produce a *meritum de congruo* before the reception of justifying grace in baptism, at least for adults. Erasmus accepts infant baptism largely on the authority of the Church, but thinks that on the basis of the wide mercy of God and a human nature not radically corrupted by sin, the immediate baptism of infants is not necessary, and that infants of Christian parents who of necessity die unbaptized may be redeemed. Normally, however, baptism is regarded as the condition *sine qua non* of the Christian life. He is careful to emphasize that baptism, which suffices for the salvation of infants, will not be sufficient for the salvation of adults unless it is supplemented by the spiritual and moral appropriation of the sacrament in faith and love. Necessary for such a reception of the sacrament is catechetical instruction. Indeed, he regards catechetical instruction as so important for an effective use of the sacrament that he proposed that it be instituted even for adolescents who were baptized as infants in order that they might have a more personal understanding of the meaning of their baptismal profession.

Baptism, through which we are reborn through grace and set on the path toward Christian perfection, is the foundational sacrament. It signifies the decisive beginning of the struggle of the Christian life under the banner of Christ the commander, who furnishes the aid and example for this battle.

Though baptism marks the decisive origin of the Christian life, it is only the first step. One must not rely upon it, but strive to make continual progress toward perfection. Erasmus thinks that, though all inclination to sin has not been erased by baptism, one ought to be able with the help of Christ and the effort of the will to abstain from mortal sins, that is, overt sins committed with an obstinate and perverse malice. Hardly anyone is free of venial sins, however. For washing them away, prayer, almsgiving, and, principally, the Eucharist are sufficient.

For mortal sins God has prepared a more radical cure, penance. Those who have been resurrected with Christ to a new life ought to sin no more, but God in his mercy accommodates himself to our weakness and provides the remedy of penance. Erasmus' anthropological optimism nearly undercuts the necessity of penance. Since penance is essentially only for those who fall into mortal sin and since it is possible to avoid mortal sin, it is in principle possible to avoid sacramental penance. But in spite of this optimism, his historical criticism of the divine ground of the sacrament, and his attack on the abuses of confessional practice, Erasmus recommends, out of obedience to an ecclesiastical institution but also out of consideration for its salutary use to deter from sinning and incite to love (provided one chooses a learned and good priest), that one make confession three or four times a year, especially before communion and before death.

For those who do commit mortal sin, confession is necessary, even though sin is already forgiven in contrition, for genuine contrition includes also the will to confess. Those who come to confession without sufficient contrition, which is the one indispensable condition for the divine forgiveness, may experience it during the process. In this thought it is clear that, as with the fourteenth-century nominalists and some of the early

scholastics of the Abelardian school, confession has not a sacramental but a psychological effect. The possibility of contrition
is grounded both in God's grace and human endeavor. The gift
comes from God, but is given only to those who strive for it—
that is, to those who produce a *meritum de congruo,* although
Erasmus does not use this term in this specific context.

For venial sins, prayer, almsgiving, and especially participation in the Eucharist are necessary. For Erasmus the Eucharist
stands next to baptism as the most important sacrament, for in
this mystery are represented the death of Christ, the source of
our salvation; our union with him; and our communion with one
another. Here through commemoration and contemplation of
the wonder of the deed upon the cross our faith is nourished,
we are given strength for the battle of the Christian life, and we
are stimulated to respond in love to God and our neighbor.
Though not neglecting the vertical dimension of the Eucharistic celebration, Erasmus places the emphasis upon the horizontal, the Eucharist as the symbol of friendship and unity which
calls for fulfillment in our lives. For this reason even the perfect
do not spurn this sacrament, for otherwise the communion in
love which includes both the weak and the strong would be
broken.

To confirmation and extreme unction Erasmus gives not
much weight. He accepts them, however, and talks about them
in a traditional manner, but stresses as always the personal,
inner assimilation. In confirmation we are established in the
love of God and given strength for the struggle of the Christian
life. In extreme unction we receive aid for a safe journey into
the beyond. More important than receiving this sacrament at
death or even than confession or the Eucharist are faith and
love, without which the sacraments are useless, but a Christian
will want them to be present out of obedience to the Church and
out of a sense of their value as aids of faith and sources of
consolation in the final hour. But, since the focus is on the inner
subjectivity, there is in the end uncertainty of salvation, for one
may not know whether his faith and love are sufficient for eternal salvation.

Erasmus thinks then that baptism is the only sacrament which is normally indispensable. But he accepts all the others out of obedience to the Church and out of a sense of their value to excite, strengthen, and preserve faith and love. Erasmus thus accords to the sacraments a certain objective value as a means of grace. However, especially from a Thomistic point of view, Erasmus so emphasizes the personal and subjective dimension that he threatens to undercut their objective, sacramental character.[5] Sacramentalist indeed he was not, but neither was he a thoroughgoing radical antisacramental spiritualist.

IV. The Authority of the Church Vis-à-vis Humanistic Reason and the Sacraments

Erasmus accepts all the sacraments on the authority of the Church, even those that his philological, historical reason cannot find grounded in Scripture. The authority of the Church is not simply a manner of speech, nor simply a piece of apologetic, nor a last refuge before the Inquisition, but an important, operative, formal principle in his sacramental thought. Of course, it is important to understand what he means by that authority. In the first chapter we noted that Erasmus defines the authority of the Church as constituted not primarily by the papal hierarchy but by the universal and perpetual consensus of the Christian people, the marks of which are first the decisions of rightly constituted universal councils and second the universal agreement among the doctors. Although he prefers that the Church define only those things which are clearly scriptural, he expresses his willingness to accept dogmas and practices which cannot be found in Scripture, if they are received by a universal and perpetual consensus. He prefers a coinherence of Scripture and tradition, but he is willing to accept extrascriptural truths. Thus we found that he accepts sacramental confession, although for him it was not grounded in Scripture. On the same basis he receives marriage as a sacrament, even in the special sense of the word, as conferring grace. Likewise, he acknowledges the Real Presence as a clear fact of the tradition.

However, Erasmus allows his critical, historical reason as much room as possible to point out the lack of a scriptural basis for some of these doctrines, such as those concerning auricular confession and marriage, and to trace the variations in the tradition before bowing ultimately to the authority of the Church.

But, as we have seen, his critical reason does not bow completely to this authority. It sometimes assesses how much of a definition is to be received. For example, although he admits the Real Presence, he never accepts the doctrine of transubstantiation. He notes simply that it is sufficient to believe *in genere* what the Church prescribes. Likewise, he raises a doubt implicitly about the clarity of the Church's decision on marriage as a sacrament in the special sense of the word, possibly because he did not think the Council of Florence was a legitimate council or because he did not think the universal consensus had been perpetual enough. He thus sometimes allows his humanistic reason to qualify the definitions of the Church.[6] He also permits it to give advice to that authority, as on the questions of the law of confession and divorce, which he regards as heavy burdens for men. Some dogmas and laws have been so received by the Church that they can be adapted to changing times and circumstances. His historical thinking comes to the aid of his moral sense, which desires a modification of certain laws which he believes oppress the consciences of men.

Without doubt, Erasmus' wish for a greater freedom for the human spirit, his qualifications concerning the exact formulations of ecclesiastical authority, and his sense of historical change do not easily fit into the framework of an authoritarian institution. Yet not only his horror of tumult but also his respect for the value of ecclesiastical traditions, especially ancient and universal, albeit provisional, prevented his leaving the Roman Church, however tyrannical and corrupt he might have regarded the sacerdotal hierarchy. He wished to be a member of that Church and therefore for the most part submitted himself to its authority, understood in his own manner, even on those points which went against his understanding of Scripture and his historical and natural reason. Although additional study is needed to ascertain this subject, it seems that the authority of the Church and his critical, humanistic reason are mutually operative, though not easily compatible, principles which shape his thought. Because of this fact, he is neither as orthodox nor as heterodox as he has sometimes been depicted.

V. Erasmus and the Tradition

The subject of Erasmus and the preceding tradition is an immense and complex one because the influences upon his religious thought were many and varied. They include, of course, the early Fathers, notably Origen and Jerome, but also Tertullian, Chrysostom, the Cappadocians, and others; the early scholastics of the Abelardian school; the late medieval nominalists, especially Durandus and Gerson; the *Devotio Moderna;* Italian humanism, particularly Valla; Florentine Platonism, principally through Colet. We have not sought to disentangle the various influences upon his sacramental theology but have focused on that theology as such. We have limited ourselves to drawing certain parallels with these various traditions.

If among the early Fathers we have emphasized the connections with Origen, it is because he was Erasmus' favorite and because the links between them are numerous indeed. We have noticed that Erasmus' Origenism is especially apparent in his anthropology; his hermeneutics, although here it is qualified; his understanding of the Trinity; his doctrine of the work of Christ; his conception of the Christian life as a struggle of flesh against spirit; his understanding of baptism as the beginning of this struggle; and his emphasis on the pastoral role of the priest in confession. As Telle has already indicated, a study devoted to the theme of Erasmus and Origen would be most useful.[7]

If among the later writers we have pointed frequently to the scholastics, it is because this tradition has been largely neglected as a background for Erasmus' thought. We have noticed that, far from universally repudiating scholasticism, however much he may have detested the subtleties of scholastic argument, Erasmus had considerable knowledge of and appreciation for some of the scholastics, especially the late medieval nominalistic tradition. He enlists the support especially of Gerson and Durandus, but also of Biel, for his views on baptism, confession, marriage, and Eucharist. On the subjects of faith and reason, Scripture and tradition, justification and predestination, the relation of sign and thing signified in the sacraments, Eucharist as memorial, and penance, we have shown that Erasmus' thought bears many resemblances to the nominalistic tradition.[8]

ABBREVIATIONS

Allen   *Opus epistolarum Des. Erasmi Roterodami.* Edited by P. S. Allen, H. M. Allen, and H. W. Garrod. 12 vols. Oxford, 1906-1957. Cited by volume, letter, and lines.

ARG   *Archiv für Reformationsgeschichte.* Leipzig and Gütersloh, 1903- .

BE   *Bibliotheca Erasmiana. Répertoire des oeuvres d'Érasme.* Nieuwkoop, 1961. (Photo-reprint of Ghent edition, 1893.)

CSEL   *Corpus Scriptorum Ecclesiasticorum Latinorum.* Vienna, 1866- .

Denzinger   Denzinger, Heinrich. *Enchiridion Symbolorum.* Edited by A. Schönmetzer, S.J. 32nd ed. Freiburg im Br., 1963. Cited according to both the old and the new numbering, first the old, then the new in parentheses.

DG, III   Seeberg, Reinhold. *Lehrbuch der Dogmengeschichte.* 5th ed. Darmstadt, 1959. (Reprint of Leipzig edition, 1953.) Vol. III.

DTC   *Dictionnaire de théologie catholique.* Paris, 1909-1950.

GCS   *Die griechischen christlichen Schriftsteller der ersten drei Jahrhunderte.* Leipzig, 1899- .

HDG   *Handbuch der Dogmengeschichte.* Edited by H. Schmaus *et al.* Freiburg im Br., 1951- .

Holborn   Desiderius Erasmus Roterodamus, Ausgewählte Werke. Edited by Hajo Holborn and Annemarie Holborn. (Veröffentlichungen der Kommission zur Erforschung der Geschichte der Reformation und Gegenreformation.) München: C. H. Beck'sche Verlagsbuchhandlung (Oscar Beck), 1933. Cited by page and lines.

LB   *Desiderii Erasmi Roterodami opera omnia.* Edited by J. Clericus. 10 vols. Hildesheim, 1962. (Photo-reprint of Leiden edition, 1703-1706.) Cited by volume, column, and position in column.

PG   *Patrologia Graeca.* Edited by J. P. Migne. Paris, 1857-1912.

PL   *Patrologia Latina.* Edited by J. P. Migne. Paris, 1844-1890.

WA   *D. Martin Luthers Werke: Kritische Gesamtausgabe.* Weimar, 1883- .

NOTES

CHAPTER I

ERASMUS AS THEOLOGIAN

1. "Pour tout dire d'un mot, Érasme était né pour les lettres et non pour la théologie." H. Durand de Laur, *Érasme: Précurseur et initiateur de l'esprit moderne* (Paris, 1872), II, 539. "Il n'était pas théologien, et maintes fois avait déclaré que, sur ces questions [i.e., on free will and the Eucharist], il s'en tenait à la plus simple croyance." A. Renaudet, *Études érasmiennes (1521-1529)* (Paris, 1939), p. 45. "Érasme ne veut être qu'un simple moraliste..." *Ibid.,* p. 147. "Erasmus belongs to the world of the moral philosopher; he has no doctrine, only the desire to reform men." T. Tentler, "Forgiveness and Consolation in the Religious Thought of Erasmus," *Studies in the Renaissance,* 12 (1965), 115. Lortz speaks of Erasmus' adogmatism and his shrinking from all dogmatic definitions. Joseph Lortz, "Erasmus-kirchengeschichtlich," in *Aus Theologie und Philosophie, Festschrift für F. Tillman zu seinem 75. Geburtstag,* ed. Th. Steinbüchel and Th. Müncker (Düsseldorf, 1950), p. 297. Pineau also points to what he considers Erasmus' opposition to theological definitions, his adogmatism, and even his agnosticism. J. B. Pineau, *Érasme, sa pensée religieuse* (Paris, 1924), pp. 63, 65, 184.

2. The point of view of Seebohm [*The Oxford Reformers* (London, 1887, 3rd ed.), p. 128], echoed by J. Huizinga [*Erasmus of Rotterdam,* tr. F. Hopman (London, 1952), p. 33] and by K. Bauer ["John Colet and Erasmus von Rotterdam," *ARG,* Erg. Band 5 (Leipzig, 1929), p. 18], that Erasmus was changed from largely humanistic to chiefly theological studies under the decisive influence of his encounter with Colet has been accepted most recently by A. Auer [*Die vollkommene Frömmigkeit des Christen* (Düsseldorf, 1954), p. 45] and J. W. Aldridge [*The Hermeneutic of Erasmus* (Richmond, 1966), p. 10]. This interpretation was already rejected by A. Hyma ["Erasmus and the Oxford Reformers, 1493-1503," in *Voordrachten gehouden ter herdenking van den sterfdag van Erasmus* ('S-Gravenhage, 1936), pp. 132 ff.] who, disregarding important theological motifs in Erasmus' earliest writing, maintained that Erasmus

retained his dominantly humanistic interests after the meeting with Colet as before. Most recently, however, E.-W. Kohls [*Die Theologie des Erasmus*, 2 vols. (Basel, 1966)] has shown that Erasmus had developed important theological views prior to the England visit in the pre-*Enchiridion* writings—especially the *De contemptu mundi* and the *Antibarbari*, but also the smaller prose and poetic pieces. See especially I, 28 ff., 35 f., and 43 ff. Cf. II, p. 50, n. 105. It is probable that the friendship with Colet strengthened his resolve to engage chiefly in theological pursuits and to allow his humanistic studies to assume a propaedeutic role. In addition he probably received through Colet the Florentine neo-Platonic renaissance.

3. ⟨August 1497⟩, Allen, I, 64.

4. Christian Dolfen, *Die Stellung des Erasmus von Rotterdam zur scholastischen Methode* (Osnabrück, 1936), pp. 64-94.

5. *Symbolum sive catechismus* (1533), LB, V, 1133-1196E; *Inquisitio de fide* (1524), LB, I, 728A-732E; *Christiani hominis institutum* (1514), LB, V, 1357D-F.

6. Auer, pp. 51-52.

7. *Methodus* (1516), Holborn, 151, 17-21, and LB, V, 77B. This work, first published as an introductory writing to the New Testament in 1516, was greatly expanded and published separately at Louvain in November 1518, under the title *Ratio seu methodus compendio perveniendi ad veram theologiam*. The latter work was revised and expanded in subsequent editions up to 1523 (see Holborn, pp. XIV ff.). I have made use of both the Holborn critical edition (see Abbreviations) and the Leiden edition, which is a reproduction of the text of 1522 (Holborn, p. XVII). The date after the title indicates the year in which the passage quoted or referred to first appeared in the work. Because the 1518 Louvain edition was inaccessible to the editors of the critical edition, they used the second oldest, that of Basel, January 1519. As Holborn points out (p. XV), one can be sure that these two editions are identical from a letter of Erasmus of May 1519 (Allen, III, 976, 12 ff.). In a note added to the 1964 reprint the editor reveals that a later examination of a 1518 edition confirmed this judgment.

8. My translation of Erasmus' Latin translation, I Tim. 1:5, *Nov. Test.* (1516), pt. 2, p. 120, and in LB, VI, 926A. (References to the *Nov. Test.* are given according to the first edition in which the material cited appeared. The original title of the *Nov. Test.* was *Novum Instrumentum*. Unless otherwise noted, all translations in the text are mine.)

9. LB, V, 141EF. Cf. *ibid.*, 140E, and *Methodus* (1516), Holborn, 161, 18-20, and LB, V, 133F.

10. James 3:17. *Ratio* (1519), Holborn, 181, 11-14, and LB, V, 77D.

11. *Apologia in dialogum Iac. Latomi* (1519), LB, IX, 89E.

12. Note on I Tim. 1:6, *Nov. Test.* (1519), pt. 2, p. 464, and in LB, VI, 926E. Cf. *Imitatio Christi,* I, 1.

13. To John Carondelet, 5 January 1522/3, Allen, V, 1334, 207-213.

14. Note on I Tim. 1:6, *Nov. Test.* (1519), pt. 2, p. 465, and in LB, VI, 927F-928D.

15. Note on I Tim. 1:6, *Nov. Test.* (1527), pt. 2, p. 593, and in LB, VI, 926D.

16. *Ratio* (1522), Holborn, 300, 7-8, and LB, V, 135C. Cf. note on I Tim. 1:6, *Nov. Test.* (1519), pt. 2, p. 464, and in LB, VI, 926F-927B.

17. *Pio Lectori,* an "appendix" prefixed to the *Paraphrasis in evangelium Matthaei* (1522), LB, VII, **3 (called such by Erasmus himself in To Natalis Beda, 15 June 1525, Allen, VI, 1581, 741; see also Allen, V, 1255, Intro.). Cf. *Adag.* 569, LB, II, 250AB, quoting Lactantius *Inst.* 3. 20; cited by Allen, V, p. 177n.

18. To John Carondelet, 5 January 1522/3, Allen, V, 1334, 178-179, 189-207.

19. Huizinga, p. 116.

20. *Paraphr. in evang. Ioannis* (1523), 1:1, LB, VII, 497C-E; *Symbolum* (1533), LB, V, 1150F. Cf. *Paraphr. in epist. Pauli ad Rom.* (1517), 11:33; LB, VII, 816E.

21. *Antibarbari* [written in substance by 1495, but not published until 1520; Allen, I, p. 121, n. 16, and R. Pfeiffer, "Die Wandlungen der 'Antibarbari,'" in Rudolf Pfeiffer, *Ausgewählte Schriften,* ed. Winfried Bühler (Munich, 1960), pp. 192 f. (originally published in *Gedenkschrift zum 400. Todestage des Erasmus von Rotterdam*)], LB, X, 1717AB: ". . . quanto satius erat Academicorum verecundiam imitari, ad quos cum isti ne componendi quidem fuerant, nihil tamen scire professi, omnibus de rebus pudenter disputare, quam confidenter affirmare maluerunt." Paul Mestwerdt, *Die Anfänge des Erasmus* (Leipzig, 1917), p. 262. Cf. *Methodus* (1516), Holborn, 297, 23-24; LB, V, 134A; and *De libero arbitrio* (1524), LB, IX, 1215D. Renaudet mentions ancient Pyrrhonism as an important source of Erasmus' thought. *Études érasmiennes,* p. 125.

22. *Symbolum* (1533), LB, V, 1150C, E.

23. LB, IV, 462C-463A; tr. H. H. Hudson, *The Praise of Folly by Desiderius Erasmus* (Princeton, 1941), p. 77.

24. Allen, V, 1334, 173-174; *Dulce bellum inexpertis* (1515), LB, II, 961A-D.

25. *Ratio* (1519), Holborn, 210, 33 ff., and LB, V, 92B. Cf. *Convivium religiosum* (1522), LB, I, 681F-682AB.

26. *Declarationes ad censuras facultatis theologicae Parisiensis* (1532), LB, IX, 919E.

27. *Concio in psalmum IV* (1525), LB, V, 286B. Cf. *Ratio* (1519), Holborn, 280, 4 f., and LB, V, 126A.

28. *Ratio* (1522), Holborn, 299, 25-28, and LB, V, 135B.

29. *Symbolum* (1533), LB, V, 1150BC.

30. *Ibid.*, 1146EF.

31. Allen, V, 1334, 170-172.

32. *Ratio* (1520), Holborn, 299, 7 ff., and LB, V, 134F-135A.

33. *Symbolum* (1533), LB, V, 1143F.

34. *Paraclesis* (1516), LB, V, 139F. Cf. *Ratio* (1519), Holborn, 213, 26 ff., and LB, V, 93B.

35. For Occam the monotheism of the first article was indemonstrable and the mystery of the Trinity completely incomprehensible. "Confronted with this impenetrable datum, the mind stops in a pure and simple faith. A similar criticism seems to extend to the idea of *fides quaerens intellectum,* by putting an end to all speculative theology." Paul Vignaux, *The Philosophy of the Middle Ages,* tr. E. C. Hall (New York, 1959), p. 176. Though speculative reason is rejected, yet "dialectic remains." Though certainty and demonstration are inaccessible, there are "probabilities capable of persuading" (p. 177). Cf. Vignaux, "Nominalisme," in *DTC,* XI, 776 ff., and Seeberg, *DG,* III, 718. On Biel see Heiko A. Oberman, *The Harvest of Medieval Theology* (Cambridge, Mass., 1963), p. 81.

36. "Aber sein Masshalten wird zu einer Skepsis, die sich an der Wahrheit selbst desinteressiert." Lortz, p. 297.

37. To Paul Volz, 14 August 1518, Allen, III, 858, 144.

38. 1 June 1523, Allen, V, 1365, 104-107.

39. 23 January 1535, Allen, XI, 2988, 70-72.

40. *Ratio* (1522), Holborn, 299, 27 ff., and LB, V, 135B.

41. Allen, III, 858, 146. Cf. note on Matt. 11:28, *Nov. Test.* (1519), pt. 2, pp. 43 f., and in LB, VI, 63DE.

42. Allen, V, 1334, 362-369.

43. *Pio Lectori* (1522), LB, VII, **3b. See below for the catechetical purpose of this yearly summary of essential doctrine, pp. 171 ff.

44. *Methodus* (1516), Holborn, 159, 30 ff., and LB, V, 132CD.

45. *Paraclesis* (1516), LB, V, 144CD.

46. *De amabili Ecclesiae concordia* (1533), LB, V, 480B.

47. Allen, IV, 1039, 222-223.

48. *De praep. ad mort.* (1534), LB, V, 1296F. Cf. *Enchiridion* (1503), LB, V, 6F-7A.

49. *Symbolum* (1533), LB, V, 1135E-1136C. A similar list of arguments is given in *Ecclesiastae* (1535), LB, V, 1078B-D. As early as the *Enchiridion* (1503), Erasmus presents in no clear order most of these reasons for the authority of Scripture. Here he mentions its inspiration from above, its revelation by the prophets, its confirmation by the blood of martyrs, miracles, and the consensus of righteous men, its harmony with natural equity, the agreement of the books of Scripture with one another, its capacity to engage our attention and move and transform us. LB, V, 21E-22A.

50. *Paraphr. in evang. Matt.* (1522), 19:8, LB, VII, 103C: ". . . Evan-

gelica doctrina renovat ac perficit naturae sinceritatem." Erasmus notes his agreement with St. Thomas on the interpretation of I Tim. 5:8. "Etenim qui quod dictat fides Christiana, quae naturae doctrinam non abrogat, sed perficit, non praestat, is hac parte descivit a fide." LB, VI, 940E; first appeared in *Nov. Test.* (1519), pt. 2, p. 473.

51. *Adv. epist. Lutheri* (1534), LB, X, 1552D: "Mea sententia vehementer confirmat Christi doctrinam, quod cum Prophetis consentiat et a naturae sensu non abhorreat."

52. *Hyper. I* (1526), LB, X, 1294C.

53. LB, V, 697D-F.

54. *Ratio* (1519, 1520), Holborn, 211, 14 ff., and 294, 8 ff., and LB, V, 92D and 132C. *Paraphr. in evang. Marci* (1523), 1:6, LB, VII, 217BC.

55. *Symbolum,* LB, V, 1162AB. Here he notes that the only article not expressly contained in Scripture is the one concerning the descent into hell.

56. *Ratio* (1520), Holborn, 211, 20 ff.; *Declar. ad cens.* (1532), LB, IX, 870F.

57. *Symbolum,* LB, V, 1136D. Cf. C. R. Thompson, *Inquisitio de fide* (New Haven, 1950), pp. 39-42. On *consensus omnium* as a criterion of truth in Erasmus and its background in antiquity and in the patristic period, cf. G. Gebhardt, *Die Stellung des Erasmus von Rotterdam zur Römischen Kirche* (Marburg a.d. Lahn, 1966), pp. 52 ff. Gebhardt draws on Klaus Oehler, "Der Consensus omnium als Kriterium der Wahrheit in der antiken Philosophie und der Patristik," in *Antike und Abendland,* 10 (1961), 103-129.

58. Thompson, *Inquisitio de fide,* pp. 38-39.

59. LB, I, 732C; Thompson, *Inquisitio de fide,* p. 72, ll. 341-351. See also *Declar. ad cens.* (1532), LB, IX, 944A; and *De colloq. utilitate* (1526), LB, I, 905AB. Cf. Gottfried Krodel, "Luther, Erasmus, and Henry VIII," *ARG,* 53 (1962), 76, n. 96.

60. LB, X, 1291E.

61. *Ibid.,* 1263DE.

62. LB, IX, 1219C.

63. LB, X, 1263CD.

64. *Commonitorium* II, 3, ed. Reginald S. Moxon (Cambridge, England, 1915), p. 10. I have found, however, no explicit reference of Erasmus to this definition of Vincent.

65. In the *Antibarbari* (1520), Erasmus places Jerome before Augustine. LB, X, 1717F-1718A. In a letter written to Greverade, probably in 1500, Erasmus sings praises to Jerome. Allen, I, 141, 16-49. See Allen, II, pp. 210-211 nn. Cf. To John Eck, 15 May 1518, Allen, III, 844, in which Erasmus defends himself against Eck's charge that Erasmus too much prefers Jerome to Augustine and that he evidently has not read Augustine. From John Maier of Eck, Allen, III, 769, 80-99.

66. *Ratio* (1519), Holborn, 295, 17 ff., and LB, V, 133A. He includes also Tertullian and Cyprian along with the above in the *Eccles.* (1535), LB, V, 857AB.

67. Mestwerdt, p. 261.

68. See the sarcastic derision of scholastic corruption and ostentation in the *Laus stult.*, LB, IV, 463D-471A, and the defense of this satire in To Martin Dorp, ⟨ May fin.⟩ 1515, Allen, II, 337, 307 ff. Cf. *Nov. Test.* (1519), pt. 2, p. 43, and in LB, VI, 63EF; To Lorenzo Campegio, 5 February 1519/20, Allen, IV, 1062, 28-34.

69. To Wolfgang Fabricius Capito, 26 February 1516/17, Allen, II, 541, 118-120. To Louis Platz, 31 July ⟨ 1520⟩, Allen, IV, 1127, 12-16.

70. Holborn, 303, 23 ff., and LB, V, 136F.

71. "Wie manche seine Darlegungen über Eucharistie, Ehe, Beichte verraten durch die Bemerkung 'iuxta neotericum sententiam,' 'ut moderni volunt,' dass er die vorliegende Frage eingehend studierte, bevor er sie niederschrieb." Dolfen, p. 82. I must therefore reject as unfounded the contentions of Renaudet that "Il [Erasmus] n'estime guère l'oeuvre spéculative du Moyen Âge et ne l'a guère étudiée" (*Études érasmiennes*, p. 123), and most recently of Aldridge that ". . . Luther, by his great knowledge of the Scholastics, used them to help his exposition, while Erasmus rarely quotes them, but usually satirizes their method and theology" (p. 35). Aldridge shows no knowledge of this basic work of Dolfen. Cf. my review of Aldridge's book in *The Journal of Ecumenical Studies*, 5 (1968), No. 1, 177, and the criticism of Kohls, II, 133, n. 12.

72. Other scholastics mentioned but seldom: Anselm (LB, IX, 118C), Richard of St. Victor (LB, V, 922F), Albert the Great (LB, IX, 187F-188A), Bonaventure (LB, IX, 188B, and V, 1270BC). Occam is often placed alongside Scotus as having burdened theology with too many subtle, thorny arguments. *Ratio* (1520), Holborn, 301, 17-18; note on Luke 6:20, *Nov. Test.* (1516), pt. 2, p. 330, and in LB, VI, 254F; *Resp. ad notat. Ed. Lei* (1520), LB, IX, 163B. The *Inceptor Venerabilis* is mentioned along with Gerson as having sometimes "carped at the authority of the Roman Pontiff." *Resp. ad Albertum Pium* (1529), LB, IX, 1105A. As Dolfen observes, it is striking that Peter d'Ailly, the teacher and friend of Gerson, is rarely cited. He notes only the above-cited reference on the Trinity. *Die Stellung des Erasmus*, p. 92.

73. *Methodus* (1516), Holborn, 152, 26, and LB, V, 78E: ". . . neotericorum omnium diligentissimus Thomas Aquinas . . ."; note on Rom. 1:4, *Nov. Test.* (1516), pt. 2, p. 413, and in LB, VI, 554E; *Apol. ad Iac. Fabrum*, LB, IX, 24E. Cf. *Apol. in dialogum Iac. Latomi* (1519), LB, IX, 103B: ". . . *Thomae* inter neotericos plurimum alicubi tribuo, ita nusquam mihi dictum arbitror, quod solus legendus sit"; and *Antibarbari* (1520), LB, X, 1739A.

74. *Declar. ad cens.* (1532), LB, IX, 919E.
75. Dolfen, p. 87.
76. *Ibid.*
77. In this connection we shall find it necessary to disagree sharply with the opinion of Louis Bouyer, *Autour d'Érasme* (Paris, 1955), and Rudolf Padberg, *Erasmus als Katechet* (Freiburg, 1956), and most recently and most strongly argued by Ernst-Wilhelm Kohls, *op. cit.*, that Erasmus was deeply influenced by St. Thomas. See Bouyer, pp. 134, 143; Padberg, pp. 125, 129 ff., 137, 140 f., 158; and Kohls, p. 86, n. 14, for a list of Kohls' notes in which he tries to document his thesis.
78. Allen, VI, 1581, 87 f.
79. LB, I, 12EF; III, 868 (Allen, VI, 1581, 87 f.); III, 1178F (Allen, VIII, 2136, 120-126); V, 151BC, 622C, 857D; VI, 228E, 408F; IX, 457F, 556A, 568D, 594C, 648C, 828F, 946C. All of these references are also to be found in Dolfen, pp. 88-91, 125. Other references to Gerson in Erasmus' works are: Allen, VI, 1596, 17-18; 1679, 84; VII, 1902, 251-254; LB, I, 804C, 905AB (cf. Thompson, *Inquisitio de fide*, pp. 47 f., n. 3); VI, 697B; IX, 587F, 692C, 694C, 918F-919D, 1105A, 1182D; X, 1534E.
80. *Declar. ad cens.* (1532), LB, IX, 918F, 919AB. Cf. *Sermo Dom. XIX, post Pent. de IV domibus, Opera Omnia,* ed. L. E. du Pin (Antwerp, 1706), III, 1302B, and *Lectiones super Marcum,* IV, 216CD-217A.
81. Dolfen, p. 91. Seeberg, *DG,* III, 757.
82. Mestwerdt had already indicated the *Devotio Moderna* and Italian humanism as the *Ansatzpunkte* of Erasmus' theology (pp. 18-174). Cf. also Otto Schottenloher, *Erasmus im Ringen um die humanistische Bildungsform. Reformationsgeschichtliche Studien und Texte* (Münster i.w., 1933), Heft 61. K. Bauer and F. Seebohm have discussed (in their works cited above) the relationship between Colet and Erasmus. Both these authors somewhat exaggerate when they emphasize Colet's role in turning Erasmus to the study of theology. A full assessment of Colet's influence in detail upon Erasmus' theology has yet to be made. C. Dolfen (pp. 22-33) has supplemented their studies by research into the basis of Erasmus' practical theology in the reform movement within scholasticism headed by Gerson. Mestwerdt is rightly critical of Hermelink's undocumented thesis that Erasmus' reform ideals were given their impetus from contact with the reform movement within scholasticism carried on by the *via antiqua.* Mestwerdt, pp. 318-328; H. Hermelink, *Die religiösen Reformbestrebungen des deutschen Humanismus* (Tübingen, 1907), pp. 22-23. However, Mestwerdt overlooks the evidence that Erasmus may have received something positive from the reform movement within the *via moderna* led by Gerson and his disciples.

As early as the *Laus stult.* (1509), Erasmus pointed out that not all scholastic theologians indulge in curious speculations. There are some indeed who spurn such subtlety. "Nec mirum sane, cum sint et inter ipsos Theologos melioribus instituti litteris, qui ad has frivolas, ut putant, Theologorum argutias nausent. Sunt qui velut sacrilegii genus exsecrentur, summamque ducant impietatem, de rebus tam arcanis et adorandis magis quam explicandis, tam illoto ore loqui, tam profanis Ethnicorum argutiis disputare, tam arroganter definire, ac divinae Theologiae maiestatem tam frigidis, imo sordidis verbis simul et sententiis conspurcare." LB, IV, 468B. This statement of Mestwerdt therefore is too strong: "Wir müssen urteilen, dass die nähere Kenntnis, die Erasmus in Paris von der Scholastik gewann, ihn nur zu einem verstärkten Misstrauen und Widerspruch gegen die ganze Art ihrer Theologie getrieben hat" (p. 317).

Kohls, drawing on Dolfen, likewise maintains that Erasmus' strictures are not against scholasticism as such but against the curious subtleties of some scholastics. He also points to Erasmus' appreciation of Gerson. Kohls, I, 223, and II, 75, nn. 162-163. He exaggerates, however, Erasmus' appropriation of and dependence upon Aquinas, whom he sees as the favorite of the scholastics for Erasmus. Kohls, I, 193 and 196. It is all of one piece when he places Gerson along with Erasmus in the Thomistic line (I, 223; II, 75, n. 163), and thinks that Erasmus was led back to Thomas by Gerson (II, 75, n. 163). On the contrary, Gerson like Erasmus, as we shall see, bears more the influence of nominalism. Gerson's attack on the vain curiosity of the scholasic theology of his time and his quoting of Aquinas ought not to be construed as an attack on nominalism or as a return to Thomas. See Oberman, *Harvest*, pp. 331 ff., especially 334. Cf. *ibid.*, pp. 205 f., 233, and 334, for nominalistic aspects of Gerson's theology. Thus, rather than to Thomism, one ought to assume that Gerson would lead Erasmus to nominalism.

83. *Nov. Test.* (1519), pt. 2, pp. 464 f., and as expanded in LB, VI, 927-928. Cf. *Ratio* (1522), Holborn, 297, 30 ff., and LB, V, 134B-D.

84. Dolfen, pp. 64-82.

85. Renaudet qualifies the above-quoted remarks (n. 71) with the statement: "S'il en conservait quelque curiosité, ce serait sans doute la philosophie de Guillaume d'Ockham, toute critique et modestement positive, que, d'accord avec Luther, il préférerait." *Études érasmiennes*, p. 123. To be sure, Renaudet provides no substantiation for this assertion.

86. To Jacob Hochstrat, 11 August 1519, Allen, IV, 1006, 192-193. Cf. *Apol. adv. mon. Hisp.* (1528), LB, IX, 1041D: "His gradibus Deus voluit innotescere mundo." On the basis of such statements as these, Renaudet speaks of an evolution of dogmas. *Études érasmiennes*, p. 169. Here our point is rather an "evolution" of theological opinions.

Whether Renaudet is correct or not in describing Erasmus' view as an evolution of dogma is discussed below.

87. Mestwerdt, p. 274.

88. *Eccles.* (1535), LB, V, 1026E.

89. *Modus orandi*, LB, V, 1115C, 1116B; *Eccles.*, LB, V, 1026E.

90. H. A. Oberman has helped to clarify the problem of Scripture and tradition in the history of medieval theology by distinguishing between two understandings of tradition, which he calls Tradition I and Tradition II. By Tradition I he refers to the mutual coinherence of Scripture and tradition. All truth is contained in Scripture. Tradition, the interpretation of the doctors, simply unfolds or makes explicit this truth. (*Harvest*, pp. 366-367.) By Tradition II he means a concept of tradition which rests on two distinct sources, Scripture and extra-scriptural truths handed down from Christ and the Apostles but not contained in written Scripture. Both positions have their patristic and medieval advocates. Although the former was more widespread in the patristic period, there were champions then of the latter view, notably Basil the Great and Augustine (pp. 369-370). In the Middle Ages Tradition II increasingly gained the ascendancy, although even in the late Middle Ages there were upholders of Tradition I. He sees d'Ailly, Gerson, Occam, and Biel all as supporters of Tradition II, and Bradwardine, Wyclif, Hus, and Wessel Gansfort as notable exponents of Tradition I.

It is my judgment that Erasmus, in this classification, falls roughly under Tradition II. He stands very close to Occam and d'Ailly in stressing that dogmatic definitions ought to be based "chiefly" (Occam) or "as much as possible" (d'Ailly) on Scripture, but not entirely on Scripture and the interpretation of Scripture by the *doctores*. Oberman, *Harvest*, pp. 380 and 383. They may be based also on what is universally held by the Church even though not contained in Scripture. Therefore, Erasmus, however much he may have stressed the necessity of a return to Scripture, was not as much of a Biblicist as some have claimed, as, for example, C. Goerung, who wrote: ". . . la théologie n'est guère autre chose que la science de l'Évangile; l'Écriture, voilà fondement de la théologie." Goerung, *La théologie d'après Érasme et Luther* (Paris, 1913), p. 139.

George H. Tavard is likewise wrong in stating that Erasmus ". . . acknowledges the basic coinherence of the Church and Scripture." *Holy Writ or Holy Church* (New York, 1959), p. 78. Erasmus wishes that there were such a coinherence, but he recognizes that in fact there is not.

John Guarnaschelli is also in error when he says: "Clearly Erasmus saw no dichotomy between the Church's traditional consensus and Scripture, the very source of belief." "Erasmus' Concept of the

Church, 1499-1524: An Essay Concerning the Ecclesiological Conflict of the Reformation," unpublished doctoral dissertation, Yale University, 1966, p. 327. He is aware, however, of Erasmus' acceptance of extrascriptural traditions, which he judges an inexplicable contradiction in Erasmus' ecclesiology (pp. 336 ff.).

91. LB, V, 1171F. On the other hand, Gebhardt is not sufficiently circumspect when he stresses ". . . die Erhebung der Tradition zur gleichberechtigten Offenbarungsquelle neben der Bibel" (p. 66). Erasmus accepts tradition which is not grounded in Scripture, but it does not have for him the same weight as Scripture itself and tradition based on Scripture.

92. LB, I, 794E; tr. C. R. Thompson, *The Colloquies of Erasmus* (Chicago, 1965), p. 327.

93. *Detectio praestig.* (1526), LB, X, 1569F-1570A: "Dogmatum triplex est genus. Primum est eorum quae citra controversiam magnoque consensu tenet Ecclesia Catholica, qualia sunt quae expresse continentur in sacris Litteris, et in Symbolo Apostolorum, quibus adiungi patiar quae in Conciliis rite convocatis ac peractis decreta sunt. Secundum est eorum, de quibus nondum evidenter pronuntiavit auctoritas Ecclesiae, et de quibus inter sese etiamnum disceptant Theologi. Tertium est eorum quae nobis ut Ecclesiae oracula obtruduntur, cum sint opiniones hominum, frequenter multum conducentes ad rixas et dissidia, minimum aut nihil pietatem." It is possible here as at other points in his ecclesiology to detect the influence of conciliarism, which regarded general councils as the highest authority for defining articles of faith. According to Marsilius of Padua, it was the exclusive prerogative of a universal council as representative of the whole Church to determine the articles of faith necessary for salvation. *Defensor pacis,* II, xix. Less radical, John of Paris, drawing on the decretists, had held that ". . . the highest authority for defining it [the Chrisian faith] was not the Pope alone but a General Council of the whole Church." Brian Tierney, *Foundations of the Conciliar Theory* (Cambridge, 1955), p. 169. Likewise, Gerson maintained that "the Church or the Council representing it is the only infallible guide in matters of faith." John B. Morrall, *Gerson and the Great Schism* (Manchester, 1960), p. 109. For clear and succinct summaries of conciliarism, see Matthew Spinka, *Advocates of Reform: From Wyclif to Erasmus* (Philadelphia, 1953), pp. 91 ff.; Paul E. Sigmund, *Nicholas of Cusa and Medieval Political Thought* (Cambridge, Mass., 1963), pp. 67 ff.; Hubert Jedin, *A History of the Council of Trent,* tr. E. Graf (St. Louis, 1957), pp. 5 ff.; and E. F. Jacob, *Essays in the Conciliar Epoch* (Manchester, 1952), pp. 1 ff. On the canonistic background of conciliar theory, see the excellent study of Tierney cited above.

94. Ἰχθυοφαγία (1526), LB, I, 794E: "LA. Licetne de Evangeliis

dubitare? SA. Bona verba; ne de conciliis quidem rite in Spiritu Sancto congregatis, peractis, editis et receptis." *Detectio praestig.* (1526), LB, X, 1569F: ". . . quae in Conciliis rite convocatis ac peractis decreta sunt." Cf. this portion of the definition of a council by Conrad of Gelnhausen, one of the leading conciliarists at the time of the Schism: "Concilium generale est multarum vel plurium *rite convocatarum,* repraesentatium vel gerentium vicem diversorum statuum ordinum et sexuum et personarum totius Christianitatis. . . ." *Epistola concordiae,* in E. Martène and U. Durand, *Thesaurus novus anecdotorum,* II (Paris, 1717), 1217-1218; cited and quoted by Sigmund, p. 100 and n. 59. Cf. the similar definition of Occam, by whom Gelnhausen was influenced: ". . . diversae personae gerentes auctoritatem et vicem universarum partium (qui) ad tractandum de communi bono *rite conveniunt.*" *Dialogus,* Part I, Book VI, ch. lxxxv, in M. Goldast, *Monarchiae Sancti Imperii* (Frankfurt, 1668), II, 469; cited and quoted by Sigmund, p. 97 and n. 52. (My italics.)

95. LB, I, 799D: "LA. Videtur igitur et de conciliis dubitari posse. SA. Non arbitror, posteaquam fuerint Christianarum gentium iudicio consensuque recepta comprobataque." See also *Hyper. I* (1526), LB, X, 1262A; and *Lingua* (1525), LB, IV, 703E. Cf. Occam, *Dialogus,* Part III, Book III, ch. xiii, in Goldast, pp. 830 f., who similarly had insisted upon the necessity of the consent of the whole Church to the meeting and acts of a universal council; cited by Alan Gewirth, *Marsilius of Padua: The Defender of Peace,* Vol. I: *Marsilius of Padua and Medieval Political Philosophy* (New York, 1951), p. 289, n. 48. In contrast to Marsilius and the later conciliarists, Occam made a distinction between the universal Church and the universal council on the basis of the judgment that a representative does not enjoy all the prerogatives of those whom he represents. For a comparison between the views of Marsilius and Occam on this subject, see Gewirth, pp. 288 f. See also Brian Tierney, "Ockham, the Conciliar Theory, and the Canonists," *The Journal of the History of Ideas,* 15 (1954), p. 70, n. 104, for references to conciliarists who did not follow Occam in making a distinction between the powers of the Church and those of the council.

96. LB, I, 794F. In the *Dialogus, Iulius exclusus e coelis* [1516 or 1517; see *Erasmi Opuscula,* ed. Wallace K. Ferguson (The Hague, 1933), Intro., p. 41], the author suggests that this council, called to meet under the shadow of the Pope at Rome, presided over by Julius himself, and packed with his own friends, could scarcely be considered a genuine ecumenical council. Whether Erasmus is the author of this anonymously written, pungently sardonic dialogue is uncertain. Allen (II, 502 ⟨From Thomas More·⟩, Intro., pp. 418-420), J. B. Pineau [*Érasme et la papauté* (Paris, 1924), pp. 1-27], and Ferguson (Intro., pp. 42-48) all argue for the Erasmian authorship. Carl Stange [*Erasmus und Julius II, eine Legende* (Berlin, 1937)] argues forcefully against it. Renaudet

(*Études érasmiennes*, p. 85, n. 3) concludes ". . . rien n'autorise à le lui attribuer avec quelque certitude." In his later work, *Érasme et l'Italie* (Geneva, 1954), pp. 112 f., Renaudet entirely rejects the *Iulius exclusus* • as an authentic work of Erasmus. In a recent essay Roland H. Bainton has reopened the question and comes to the conclusion that Erasmus surely had a major hand in it. "Erasmus and Luther and the Dialog Julius Exclusus," in *Vierhundertfünzig Jahre lutherische Reformation* (Berlin, 1967), pp. 17-26.

97. To Willibald Pirckheimer, 30 March 1522, Allen, V, 1268, 35-36: "De conciliis non ausim aliquid dicere, nisi forte proximum Concilium Lateranense concilium non fuit." In the reply to Beda, *Supput. errorum N. Beddae* (1527), LB, IX, 560F, he hopes that the possible future council will be different from recent ones. Cf. Renaudet, *Études érasmiennes*, pp. 208-209, 283-284.

98. *Hyper. I* (1526), LB, X, 1297CD.

99. *Ibid.*, 1283A. Cf. To Henry Bullock, ⟨22?⟩August 1516, Allen, II, 456, 61-63. In the admission, in spite of his high regard for truly representative councils, that they can err, Eramus may again be related to Occam, who thought not only that councils can err but that the whole multitude of the faithful can err except one or that the true faith might exist only in baptized infants. *Dialogus*, Part I, Book V, ch. xxxv, p. 506; cited by Gewirth, p. 289. Cf. Jacob, p. 96. D'Ailly was the only one of the later conciliarists to follow Occam on this point. See Morrall, p. 116.

100. To Simon Pistorius, c. 2 September 1526, Allen, VI, 1744, 20-23.

101. *Hyper. I* (1526), LB, X, 1262AB: ". . . caeterum Ecclesiae Catholicae decreta, praesertim ea quae generalibus Synodis prodita sunt, et Christiani populi consensu comprobata, tantum apud me ponderis habent, ut etiamsi meum ingeniolum humanis rationibus non assequatur quod praescribit, tamen velut oraculum a Deo profectum sim amplexurus . . ."

102. Note on I Cor. 7:39, *Nov. Test.* (1519), pt. 2, p. 327, and in LB, VI, 696CD: "Idem videtur accidisse in conceptione beatae Virginis, si tamen hoc Ecclesia sic definiit, ut haereticus sit habendus qui dubitet: nam mihi nondum satis liquet, etiamsi sunt qui praedicent hoc esse definitum in Concilio Basiliensi." The last clause of this sentence, "etiamsi . . . Basiliensi," was added in 1527, p. 415. Of course, he doubted whether all the acts of this council were valid, and here he was not alone, as he himself realized. *Ibid.*, 696D: "Hic rursus oritur dubitatio gemina, an valeant omnia in eo Concilio acta, tum quibus verbis et quo animo hoc sit definitum. Quod si ut articulus fidei, quid fiet Dominicanis, quorum plerique persistunt in diversa sententia?" See also *Resp. ad notata per N. Beddam* (1526), LB, IX, 460D-F, and *Supput.*

errorum N. Beddae (1527), LB, IX, 569EF and 570AB. The doctrine of the immaculate conception was promulgated at the thirty-sixth session of the Council of Basel, 17 September 1439. See *Monumenta Conciliorum Generalium seculi decimi quinti,* ed. Ernestus Birk, III, pt. 1 (Basel, 1932), 364. Cf. C. J. Hefele and H. Leclercq, *Histoire des Conciles,* VII (Paris, 1916), 1071. However, since only the first twenty-two sessions of this council were approved by the Pope and therefore its authenticity was questioned, the doctrine of the immaculate conception set forth there was subject to doubt. Oberman, *Harvest,* p. 285. In an otherwise sound and illuminating chapter on Erasmus' religious thought, Lewis Spitz incorrectly cites the immaculate conception as an illustration of Erasmus' acceptance of the traditions of the Church in addition to Scripture. *The Religious Renaissance of the German Humanists* (Cambridge, Mass., 1963), p. 227. He is also not quite correct when he says that "Erasmus was perfectly orthodox and 'correct' on all matters of dogma" (p. 226). He was not entirely orthodox on the question of the mode of Christ's Presence in the Eucharist, i.e., transubstantiation, in his understanding of marriage, or in his views on divorce.

103. Seeberg points out that Duns Scotus held a view which was really a theory of consubstantiation even though because of the teaching of the Church he tried with his dialectical skill to interpret it along the lines of a kind of transubstantiation. *DG,* III, 523. He also notes a whole host of theologians, mostly nominalists, who recognized the possibility of the continuance of the substance of the bread and wine after the words of consecration. These include Occam, Durand, Thomas of Strassburg, Dionysius Carthusius, Biel, v. Wesel, d'Ailly, and Wessel. Seeberg remarks with regard to Occam that, although he remained with the dogma of transubstantiation as the Roman Church taught, he held a view of consubstantiation as not at all repugnant to reason or Scripture (p. 789). Seeberg concludes: "Die Transsubstantiation stand kirchenrechtlich fest, die Theologie des ausgehenden Mittelalters hat an ihr keine Freude gehabt" (p. 791).

104. "Aber im Grunde geht des Roterdamers Missbehagen nicht bloss gegen die Aufnahme neuer dogmatischen Worte, sondern gegen die Feststellung kirchlicher Lehreschlüsse, gegen die abschliessenden *dogmatischen Definitionen* der Kirche selbst." J. Kerker, "Erasmus und sein theologischer standpunkt," *Theologische Quartalschrift,* 41 (1859), 552. (Kerker's italics.)

"Car, je le répète, ce n'est pas seulement aux questions subtiles débattués dan l'École qu'Érasme s'attaque. . . . Il nie la valeur des doctrines défines elles-mêmes ou définissables parce qu'on les trouve pas dans l'Évangile." Pineau, *Érasme et la papauté,* p. 184.

105. *Hyper. II* (1527), LB, X, 1663AB.

106. *Ibid.,* 1263B. Cf. above the letters to Paul III and Slechta for

Erasmus' sense of the difference between essential and nonessential dogmas, nn. 39 and 47. See also Roland H. Bainton, "Erasmus and the *Wesen des Christentums,*" in *Glaube Geist Geschichte, Festschrift für Ernst Benz,* ed. Gerhard Müller and Winfried Zeller (Leiden, 1967), pp. 202 ff. Bainton sees Erasmus as the father of this idea in the sixteenth century.

107. *Hyper. I* (1526), LB, X, 1305AB.

108. *Ibid.*, 1258E.

109. With regard to the *homoousios* at Nicea, for example, he would have no doubt preferred to remain with the simple declaration of Jesus' divine sonship without using this philosophical term which for him has no biblical basis and which also represents speculation on the mystery of the Trinity. He constantly points, as we have noticed, to the reticence of the Fathers to speculate concerning the divine mystery and to use nonbiblical terms in describing it. He recognizes, however, that the temerity of the heretics—that is, their philosophical specula- tions—made a more precise definition necessary. There is, as far as I can see, no evidence that Erasmus did not accept the definition of Nicea. I think the same can be said for the Christological formulations at Chalcedon. I should therefore like to reject as exaggerated Lortz's contention that Erasmus "gerne über alle dogmatischen formulier- ungen überhaupt zurückschielen, und wie er die Nützlichkeit der alt- christlichen Dogmenformulierungen leugnet, so gerne auch deren Verbindlichkeit beseitigen möchte." Lortz, p. 297.

110. Bouyer is rightly critical of Renaudet for being unclear as to the distinction between dogma, i.e., definitions of the Church, and doctrine, i.e., the opinions of theologians. Bouyer, p. 143. It is true, I think, that Erasmus accepts both the evolution of theological opinions and the evolution of dogmas—at least of those not clearly based on Scripture and the Apostles' Creed—but the two matters, dogma and doctrine, must be carefully distinguished. But Bouyer much oversim- plifies matters when he states: "Mais alors que tout le souci d'Érasme était de distinguer ces differents cas pour opposer aux définitions de l'Église, qu'il accepte, les définitions arbitraires de certains théologi- ens, qu'il refuse. . . ." *Ibid.* In the first place, he opposed not only the arbitrary pronouncements of theologians but also the multiplication of articles of faith, i.e., definitions of the Church. Secondly, though he does appear to accept nearly all the definitions of the Church once promulgated and received by a universal consensus, he accepts more willingly those clearly based on divine Scripture and the Apostles' Creed than others not so evidently based.

111. For more detail on this question see Karl Schätti, *Erasmus von Rotterdam und die römische Kurie* (Basel, 1954).

112. *Hyper. I* (1526), LB, X, 1305B.

113. LB, I, 794E: "LA. Quod Pontifex decrevit, nemo potest

abrogare? SA. Nemo. LA. Unde igitur audimus rescissas Pontificum sententias, hoc titulo, quod parum recte fuerint edocti; et priorum constitutiones a posterioribus antiquatas, quod a pietate delirarent? SA. Ista subrepticia sunt ac temporaria. Nam et in Pontificem, ut hominem, cadit ignorantia personae factive. Caeterum quod ex auctoritate concilii universalis proficiscitur, coeleste oraculum est, et pondus habet par Evangeliis, aut certe proximum."

114. *Ratio* (1519), Holborn, 198, 1-8, and LB, V, 86C. Cf. *Nov. Test.* (1519), pt. 2, pp. 56 f.; LB, VI, 88D-F; and *Paraphr. in evang. Matt.* (1522), 16:16-18, LB, VII, 92E-93A.

115. *Nov. Test.* (1519), pt. 2, p. 382, and LB, VI, 785E.

116. *Ratio* (1519), Holborn, 198, 8-16, and LB, V, 86CD. Cf. note on John 21:15, *Nov. Test.* (1516), pt. 2, pp. 372 f., and LB, VI, 418EF. In the *Enchiridion* (1503) Erasmus already emphasized that the papacy does not mean power or dominion, but an office of charity. LB, V, 49AB. It was likewise the position of the conciliarists that true dominion rested with the total Church. The prelates, including the Pope, were not lords but servants and ministers. Tierney, *Foundations*, p. 6.

117. Note on Luke 22:36, *Nov. Test.* (1519), pt. 2, p. 156, and LB, VI, 319AB, and *Paraphr. in evang. Lucae* (1523), 22:38, LB, VII, 454BC.

118. Pineau, *Érasme et la papauté*, pp. 43 and 45.

119. LB, IV, 484C: "Quasi vero ulli sint hostes Ecclesiae perniciosiores, quam impii Pontifices, qui et silentio Christum sinunt, abolescere, et quaestuariis legibus alligant et *coactis interpretationibus adulterant*, et pestilente vita iugulant." (My italics.)

120. *Dulce bellum inexpertis* (1515), LB, II, 965C: "Hoc ipsum ius, quod habes, populi consensus dedit. Eiusdem autem, ni fallor, est tollere, qui contulit." Cf. *Sileni Alcibiadis* (1515), LB, II, 775C. Erasmus does not specifically apply this thought to the Church as the consensus of the Christian people and its ruler, the Roman pontiff, although in the latter work he goes on to talk about the Church and its prelates, including the Pope.

121. To ⟨ Lorenzo Campegio⟩, 19 January 1524, Allen, V, 1410, 19-22: "De monarchia Pontificis nunquam dubitavi; sed an haec monarchia fuerit agnita tempore Hieronymi aut exerta, dubito alicubi ex occasione loci, nimirum in scholiis meis quae aedidi in Hieronymum." Cf. *Apol. ad blasph. Iac. Stunicae* (1522), LB, IX, 370DE; *Resp. ad Albertum Pium* (1529), LB, IX, 1104D-F.

122. Ἰχθυοφαγία (1526), LB, I, 794E; *Enarr. in ps. XXXVIII* (1532), LB, V, 435B; *Ratio* (1519), Holborn, 203, 24 ff., and LB, V, 89BC.

123. To Albert of Brandenburg, 19 October 1519, Allen, IV, 1033, 166-170, and To Duke George of Saxony, 12 December 1524, Allen, V, 1526, 131-132.

124. *Ratio* (1522), Holborn, 206, 37-207, 1-3, and LB, V, 91A.

125. *Laus stult.*, LB, IV, 483-484; tr. Hudson, p. 100. See whole section 482E-485A. I omit similar satirical passages from the *Iulius exclusus* because of lingering uncertainty as to its authenticity as a work of Erasmus. Cf. *Sileni Alcibiadis* (1515), LB, II, 779CD, and *Dulce bellum inexpertis* (1515), LB, II, 967BC. In this connection Erasmus is understandably critical of the patrimony of Peter. *Laus stult.*, LB, IV, 484CD.

126. To ⟨Artlebus of Boskowitz ⟩, 28 January 1521, Allen, IV, 1183, 72-78.

127. *Sileni Alcibiadis* (1515), LB, II, 778B.

128. Allen, IV, 1039, 99-101: "Quid enim magis accedit ad imaginem coelestis hierarchiae quam ut digestis ordinibus summa redeat ad unum? aut quae res utilior ad excludenda mundi dissidia?"

129. Schätti, p. 76.

130. For the background of this idea in Italian humanism see Mestwerdt, pp. 74 f. One detects here the influence not only of Italian humanism but also of conciliarism, especially in the following statement: "Mihi in tantum non improbatur, quod Romanus Pontifex habetur totius Ecclesiae quaquaversum diffusa princeps, ut, etiamsi non esset institutum, suasurus sim instituendam, veluti necessarium ad excludenda vel coercenda dissidia, premendamque quorumdam tyrannidem, *modo meminerit hanc potestatem ipsi datam ad aedificationem domus Dei, non ad destructionem.*" *Apol. adv. Mon. Hisp.* (1528), LB, IX, 1067A. (My italics.) John of Paris had already expressed the idea which "was to become a stock argument in later conciliar works" that all ecclesiastical authority was given for the "edification," not the "destruction," of the Church. Tierney, *Foundations,* p. 168. Morrall, p. 53.

131. 'Ιχθυοφαγία (1526), LB, I, 804D. Here Erasmus draws a distinction between the laws of the Pope and the mind of the Pope. Regardless of his laws the Pope does not intend laws which harm men. Elsewhere he says the same thing, but adds that, even if he wanted to, the Pope does not have the right "constituendi quod perniciem adfert homini, non salutem." To Ulrich Zasius, ⟨23 March ⟩1523, Allen, V, 1353, 49-55.

132. In spite of a largely critical attitude toward canon law on the basis of his understanding of Scripture and natural equity and of the variations in its historical development, as with scholasticism so with canon law Erasmus does not desire its removal, but its reduction and reform. Cf. Wilhelm Maurer, "Reste des Kanonischen Rechtes im Frühprotestantismus," *Zeitschrift der Savigny-Stiftung für Rechtsgeschichte, Kanonistische Abteilung,* 51 (1965), 200, 204 ff.

133. *Hyper. I* (1526), LB, X, 1279B. Cf. Schätti, p. 128.

134. *Dulce bellum inexpertis* (1515), LB, II, 966C: ". . . quasi vero populus non sit Ecclesia, aut quasi tota Ecclesiae dignitas in sacerdotum opibus sita sit . . ."; and *Sileni Alcibiadis* (1515), LB, II,

775E: ". . . Ecclesiam vocant Sacrificos, Episcopos, ac summos Pontifices, cum hi revera nihil aliud sint, quam Ecclesiae ministri. Caeterum Ecclesia populus est Christianus, quem Christus ipse maiorem vocat . . ." Cf. *Non e quercu aut saxo,* LB, II, 1122A, and note on I Cor. 6:4 (pre-1525), LB, VI, 682C.

135. Thompson, *Inquisitio de fide,* p. 69. It is remarkable that Guarnaschelli does not mention these statements when he refers to the paucity of Erasmian definitions of the Church. "Erasmus' Concept of the Church, 1499-1524," pp. 161 f. In fact, his notes and bibliography indicate no use of the *Colloquia* or the *Adagia* or the *Annotationes.*

136. 30 July 1526, Allen, VI, 1729, 26-27: "Ecclesiam autem voco consensum populi Christiani per universum orbem"; 19 October 1527, Allen, VII, 1893, 59-60: "Ecclesiam autem voco totius populi Christiani consensum." The vesting of the supreme authority and power in the whole Christian people rather than in the papal hierarchy, the heart of Erasmus' ecclesiology, was also the center of the conciliar theory. "The appeal to the underlying authority of the Church, understood as the *congregatio fidelium,* was the very essence of the conciliar position." Tierney, *Foundations,* p. 4. Tierney supplies references for this idea from the works of several conciliarists on p. 4, n. 1. For the views of Marsilius of Padua, the most radical exponent of the theory of popular sovereignty, see Gewirth, p. 263, and his references in nn. 18-23. For Nicholas of Cusa, who, while retaining the objective hierarchy, emphasized strongly a theory of *consensus,* see Sigmund, pp. 119 ff., especially 137 ff. Though Erasmus certainly had no full-scale conciliar theory, in the light of all the evidences to which we have pointed, it must be confessed that his thought bears traces of conciliarism. Hence, one must disagree with Renaudet, who expressed the view that "Érasme n'était pas gallican, et la doctrine conciliaire lui demeurait assez indifférente." *Érasme et l'Italie,* p. 200. Gebhardt takes up the question of possible conciliar influence on Erasmus only to reject it, though he recognizes Erasmus' high regard for universal councils as representatives of the general consensus (pp. 269, 270, 274).

137. *Spongia adv. adsperg. Hutteni* (1523), LB, X, 1654DE. Cf. *Inquisitio de fide* (1524), ed. Thompson, p. 68, ll. 285-286: "Ecclesia vero proprie dicta, quanquam non *constat nisi ex bonis,* tamen ex hominibus constat, qui ex bonis possunt fieri mali . . ." (My italics.) In the *Symbolum* (1533), LB, V, 1172A, he indicates as one of the marks by which the holy Church can be discovered, the moral life of the members. In the *De amab. Eccl. conc.* (1533), Erasmus says that, even though what many maintain—that the Church is invisible—is not false, since only God truly knows who are his, "Multis tamen argumentis saepe deprehenditur ubi sit Ecclesia Dei, ubi Synagoga Satanae. Multorum enim peccata praecedentia sunt ad iudicium." LB, V, 477C. We note that the

main criterion here as to where the true Church is, is not so much dogma as the moral life. Compare, however, the above passage from the *Symbolum*, where he makes the authority of the ancient synods the first mark of the Church. Following the above passage from the late treatise on Christian unity, the *De amab. Eccl. conc.*, Erasmus sings praises also to this very visible Church "quae bonis habet admixtos malos quantum habet alacritatis ac maiestatis quoties ad pietatis convenit." LB, V, 477D. As our discussion of dogma and sacrament bears out, however much Erasmus is inclined to a pneumatic and moral conception of the Church, he does not repudiate the visible Church with its dogmas and sacraments. For pneumatic and moral aspects of Erasmus' ecclesiology, see Guarnaschelli, especially pp. 152 ff.

138. *Hyper. I* (1526), LB, X, 1258A.

139. *Érasme et l'Italie*, p. 200. Cf. p. 175.

140. Cf. the criticism of Renaudet's category of the "third church" by Myron P. Gilmore, *Humanists and Jurists* (Cambridge, Mass., 1963), p. 133.

CHAPTER II
ANTHROPOLOGY

1. Other recent writers have already pointed in this direction, especially A. Auer, pp. 63-79, and G. Krodel, "Die Abendmahlslehre des Erasmus von Rotterdam und seine Stellung am Anfang des Abendmahlsstreites der Reformatoren," unpublished doctoral dissertation, Erlangen, 1955, pp. 4-8. Cf. H. Ernst, "Die Frömmigkeit des Erasmus," *Theologische Studien und Kritiken*, 92 (1919), pp. 57-58. Ernst-Wilhelm Kohls takes issue with this line of interpretation, specifically that of Auer. Instead of seeing a Platonic metaphysical base of Erasmus' anthropology which is carried into his whole theology, Kohls posits a "heilstheologische Fundierung" and a "bibeltheologischer Ausgangspunkt" of Erasmus' anthropology, indeed of "aller theologischen Aussagen." II, p. 94, n. 98, and p. 96, n. 131. While recognizing that Scripture itself shapes Erasmus' anthropology and his whole theology, I cannot agree with Kohls that the principle of flesh and spirit is derived solely or even primarily from the Bible, as the ensuing discussion will demonstrate.

2. LB, V, 27D.

3. LB, IV, 500D-501C, 502B.

4. LB, V, 27E.

5. LB, V, 14AB; *Timaeus*, 42B-45B, 69B.

6. LB, V, 29B (*Symposium*, 215-217); 14F (*Phaedo*, 9B-12E, 64A); 28CD (*Phaedo*, 80-81); 15A (*Phaedrus*, 25B-C, 9B-12E).

7. In the *Enchiridion,* LB, V, 30A, Erasmus mentions that Augustine preferred the Platonists and the Pythagoreans over the Aristotelians. (*De civ. Dei,* VIII, 4-5.) It was Augustine who more than any other Father transmitted the Platonic tradition to the Middle Ages. See E. Portalié, "Augustinisme," in *DTC,* III, 2501 ff. Cf. for Augustine's influence on Renaissance humanism and Platonism, Paul O. Kristeller, "Augustine and the Early Renaissance," in his *Studies in Renaissance Thought and Letters* (Rome, 1955), pp. 360 ff.

8. See J. Colet, *Opuscula* (*In principium Genesios*), tr. J. Lupton (London, 1876), pp. 170 f., 179, where Colet divides the "mundus intelligibilis" into the "divinus" and "angelicus mundus," and the "mundus visibilis" into the "mundus coelestis, qui ex sempiternis orbibus conficitur" and the "mundus terrenus quem homines incolunt"; quoted by Auer, p. 65, and cited on p. 226, n. 14. Colet had read Plato, Plotinus, and Pseudo-Dionysius the Aeropagite at Oxford. Lupton, *Life of Dean Colet* (Hamden, Conn., 1961, reprint), p. 79. Later he studied the works of Ficino and Pico. In a recent study Sears Jayne has shown that Colet did not actually visit the Academy on his travels through France and Italy (c. 1493-1496). *John Colet and Marsilio Ficino* (Oxford, 1963), pp. 17 ff.

9. LB, V, 11EF.

10. LB, IV, 500B.

11. LB, V, 15F.

12. *Ibid.,* 16EF.

13. *Laus stult.,* LB, IV, 500B. *Paraphr. in epist. Pauli ad Cor. I* (1519), 15:45, LB, VII, 910F.

14. *Paraphr. in epist. Pauli ad Gal.* (1519), 4:26, LB, VII, 959F.

15. LB, I, 680B; tr. Thompson, *Colloquies,* p. 62.

16. LB, V, 13E, 14BC; *Timaeus,* 69 ff.

17. *Supput. errorum N. Beddae* (1527), LB, IX, 685CD.

18. *Enarr. ps. I* (1515), LB, V, 192A. Cf. *Epicureus* (1533), LB, I, 886CD.

19. *De amab. Eccl. conc.* (1533), LB, V, 484DE.

20. *Concio de puero Iesu* (1515), LB, V, 608F.

21. *Paraphr. in epist. Pauli ad Cor. I* (1519), 15:44, LB, VII, 910DE; *De amab. Eccl. conc.* (1533), LB, V, 488F.

22. *In Rom. Comm.* 1:5, 10, in *PG,* XIV, 850, 856.

23. *Enchiridion,* LB, V, 19A. He quotes I Thess. 5:23: "Ut integer corpus vestrum, anima, et spiritus, in die Dominic nostri Iesu Christi servetur," in support of a Pauline threefold division.

24. *Hyper. II* (1527), LB, X, 1464AB.

25. LB, V, 1024BC.

26. LB, X, 1459EF.

27. *De lib. arb.* (1524), LB, IX, 1235CD. Cf. *Hyper. II* (1527), LB, X, 1459E.

28. *Enchiridion,* LB, V, 34DE. Gal. 5:19-21.

29. LB, V, 1024BC.

30. *Enchiridion,* LB, V, 19BC. Cf. *De lib. arb.* (1524), LB, IX, 1235E.

31. *Enchiridion,* LB, V, 19B, E.

32. *Ibid.,* 19C. Cf. Pico della Mirandola, *De hominis dignitate,* in *Dignita dell'uomo,* ed. B. Cicognani (Florence, 1941), p. 8.

33. *Enchiridion,* LB, V, 12F, 13B.

34. *Symbolum* (1533), LB, V, 1154A. Cf. *Paraphr. in epist. Iac.* (1520), 1:15, LB, VII, 1121D: "Ex primorum parentum vitio insita est animis nostris quaedam ad vitia proclivitas, ea ceu peccati seminarium est: quod si in animum admissum coaluerit, iam mens veluti concepit peccatum." In his account of the Erasmian conception of original and actual sin, Kohls fails to point out that Erasmus prefers not to call the former "sin" at all. I, 154 f. Kohls thinks that in the annotation on Romans 5:12 Erasmus stresses the close connection between the *peccatum originis* and the *peccatum imitationis.* He neglects to mention that Erasmus' whole effort in that note is to defend his thesis that this passage may not be used to buttress the traditional concept of original sin and that it may more probably be understood as referring to the *peccatum imitationis.*

Kohls is likewise in error when he states that "Die Anschauung der Erbsünde zunächst hat Erasmus in bemerkenswerter Abweichung von Origenes festgehalten." I, 154. On the contrary, Erasmus names Origen as one of the early Fathers who favored his preferred interpretation of Romans 5:12, that there Paul does not speak of original sin in the proper sense of the word but rather of personal sin in imitation of Adam. *Nov. Test.* (1535), p. 368, and LB, VI, 586D-587A. On Origen's rejection of an inherited original sin in favor of a personal sin see Georg Teichtweier, *Die Sündenlehre des Origenes* (Regensburg, 1958), pp. 96 ff.

35. *Eccles.* (1535), LB, V, 1018BC.

36. *Paraphr. in epist. Pauli ad Rom.* (1517), 5:12, LB, VII, 793B.

37. LB, X, 1454F-1455A.

38. *Eccles.* (1535), LB, V, 909D.

39. *Paraphr. in evang. Matt.* (1522), 5:1, LB, VII, 23D. Cf. *Eccles.,* LB, V, 796D: ". . . ex perversis opinionibus enim nascitur perversa vita."

40. *Hyper. II* (1527), LB, X, 1493EF, 1459D.

41. *Eccles.,* LB, V, 1083A: "Fons autem omnium vitiorum hinc est, quod hominum imbecillitas magis obtemperat carni quam spiritui."

42. *Paraphr. in evang. Lucae* (1523), 11:4, LB, VII, 380E. Cf. *Paraphr. in I. epist. Ioannis* (1521), 5:16, LB, VII, 1159D.
43. *Paraphr. in evang. Lucae*, 12:10, LB, VII, 388F-389A.
44. *Paraphr. in evang. Matt.* (1522), 26:75, LB, VII, 138D. Cf. *Paraphr. in evang. Ioannis* (1523), 3:19, LB, VII, 522F.
45. *Paraphr. in evang. Marci* (1523), 14:31, LB, VII, 261B.
46. *Paraphr. in evang. Lucae*, 15:32, LB, VII, 410F.
47. *Ibid.*, 23:34, LB, VII, 462B.
48. *Paraphr. in acta apost.* (1524), 9:6, LB, VII, 703B.
49. *Ibid.*, 3:17, LB, VII, 677A.
50. *Paraphr. in evang. Ioannis* (1523), 3:19, LB, VII, 522F-523A.

CHAPTER III
HERMENEUTICS

*This chapter is based upon an article, "Toward the Hermeneutics of Erasmus," prepared for publication early in 1970 in the Louvain 500th anniversary *Mélanges, Scrinium Erasmianum*, Vol. II, ed. J. Coppens *et al.* For more particulars I refer the reader to that article.

1. *Paraphr. in epist. Pauli ad Gal.* (1519), 4:24, LB, VII, 959D: ". . . ut quemadmodum in homine, sub crasso corporis operculo latet animus corporis moderator, ita sub historia penitius quiddam ac sublimius tegatur." *Enchiridion* (1503), LB, V, 29AB, and *Eccles.* (1535), LB, V, 1043D.

2. *Sileni Alcibiadis* (1515), LB, II, 773C: "Iam habent et suos Silenos arcanae Litterae. Si consistas in superficie, ridicula nonnunquam res sit: si penetres usque ad anagogen, divinam adores sapientiam." See also *Enchiridion*, LB, V, 29AB.

3. B. Smalley, *The Study of the Bible in the Middle Ages* (Oxford, 1952), pp. 1-25.

4. *De principiis*, IV, 2, 4, in *GCS*, V, ed. P. Kötschau, pp. 312-313. Smalley, pp. 8 f.; H. de Lubac, *Exégèse médiévale* (Paris, 1959), pp. 199-201.

5. *Ep.*, 58, 9, in *PL*, XXII, 585; *Ep.*, 52, 2, in *PL*, XXII, 528; cited by Auer, p. 240, n. 131. Cf. *Enchiridion* (1503), LB, V, 8F.

6. On the controversial issue of the relation between history and allegory in Origen, see J. Daniélou, *Origène* (Paris, 1948), pp. 145-198; H. de Lubac, *Histoire et esprit* (Paris, 1950), pp. 278, 290, and 377; R. P. C. Hanson, *Allegory and Event* (London, 1959), pp. 242-258, 285-286; and R. Gögler, *Zur Theologie des biblischen Wortes* (Düsseldorf, 1963), pp. 337 ff. Whereas de Lubac and Gögler defend Origen's allegorical exegesis as standing in close relation with the historical sense, Hanson, admitting that Origen does not totally depreciate the letter, thinks that

his allegorical exposition has no necessary connection with the text and that the history is of value only because of the allegorical significance it contains. Daniélou distinguishes in Origen's spiritualistic exegesis a more traditional typological interpretation from a fanciful allegorization which is influenced by Philo in the exegesis of the Old Testament and by Gnosticism in the exegesis of the New Testament.

7. LB, V, 29F.

8. See the detailed study of the first two editions of this work by A. Bludau, *Die beiden ersten Erasmus-Ausgaben des Neuen Testamentes* (Freiburg im Br., 1902), for a critical estimate of Erasmus' scholarship. See also the notes in Allen, II, pp. 164 ff. and 181 ff., and cf. also Kenneth W. Clark, "Observations on the Erasmian Notes in Codex 2," *Studia Evangelica*, ed. Kurt Aland *et al.*, *Texte und Untersuchungen*, 53 (1959), 749-756.

9. *Ratio* (1519), Holborn, 196, 29 ff., and LB, V, 85E. See also *Eccles.* (1535), LB, V, 1019DE.

10. *Ratio* (1519), Holborn, 192, 8 ff., and LB, V, 83BC.

11. *Ratio,* Holborn, 286, 1 ff., and LB, V, 128BC.

12. *Enchiridion* (1503), LB, V, 25E; *Enarr. in ps. XXXIII*, LB, V, 373DE; *Ratio* (1519), Holborn, 294, 8 ff., and LB, V, 132C.

13. *Ratio* (1519), Holborn, 210, 4-6, and LB, V, 91F-92A: "Totus doctrinae circulus, ut secum consentit, ita cum ipsius vita consentit, etiam ipsius naturae iudicio consentanea." Cf. note on Matt. 11:28, *Nov. Test.* (1519), pt. 2, p. 43; and LB, VI, 63D: "Facile toleratur, quicquid est secundum naturam. Nihil autem magis congruit cum hominis natura, quam Christi philosophia, quae pene nihil aliud agit, quam ut naturam collapsam suae restituat innocentiae sinceritatique." Otto Schottenloher rightly criticizes Kohls for his failure to point out the hermeneutical significance of the arguments in the *Enchiridion*, especially of the agreement of Scripture with natural equity. Review of Kohls' *Die Theologie des Erasmus, ARG,* Jahrg. 58, Heft 2 (1967), 253 f. Cf. Kohls, I, 79 f. On natural equity in Erasmus, cf. Guido Kisch, *Erasmus und die Jurisprudenz seiner Zeit. Studien zum humanistischen Rechtsdenken. Basler Studien zur Rechtswissenschaft,* ed. E. Ruck *et al.*, Heft 56 (Basel, 1960), pp. 55 ff. and 117 ff.

14. Note on I Cor. 7:39, *Nov. Test.* (1519), pt. 2, pp. 326-327, and LB, VI, 695D, F, 696AB.

15. *De lib. arb.* (1524), LB, IX, 1219B.

16. See, for example, criticisms in *Ratio* (1519 *et seq.*) of distortions of Scripture by Origen in his allegorical interpretation, by Ambrose in his efforts to confute the Arians, by Augustine in his polemics against the Donatists. Holborn, 287 ff., and LB, V, 129 f. Cf. also *Nov. Test.,* LB, VI, 589B, for a criticism of Augustine's interpretation of Rom. 5:12 as original sin in his conflict with the Pelagians, and LB, VI, 685D, and

Eccles., LB, V, 1028C-1031C, for a censure of Jerome's twisting of Scripture in his attack on Jovinian, the champion of marriage.

17. *Hyper. I*, LB, X, 1301E-1302B. He also throws at Luther the variety of interpretations of the Reformers concerning the Eucharistic passages in the New Testament. *Ibid.*, 1302D.

18. *De lib. arb.*, LB, IX, 1216C, 1217A. "Quaedam voluit nos scrutari, sic ut ipsum in mystico silentio veneremur." In a review of the Holborn critical edition R. Pfeiffer already correctly pointed to Erasmus' awareness of the limits of his philological method: "Der oft gegen E. erhobene Vorwurf einer engen, im einzelnen haftenden Verbalkritik geht also im Prinzip fehl, ebenso der eines überheblichen 'Rationalismus' gegenüber den religiösen Urkunden. Denn die Grenzen menschlichen Wissens und Forschens hat der am schärfsten betont, der bis an diese Grenzen zu gehen forderte." *Gnomon*, 12 (1936), 630. Aldridge shows no recognition of Erasmus' sense of the limits of philological reason in his description of "erudition" and "philology" as the "means" and "method" of Erasmus' interpretation of Scripture. Aldridge, chapters 3 and 4.

19. *Eccles.*, LB, V, 1034DE. Cf. 1044AB, EF, and *Ratio* (1519, 1523), 277, 29 ff., where he implies that a number of statements of Jesus and Paul are allegory when they are really metaphor.

20. *Ratio* (1519), 198, 34 ff., and LB, V, 86F-87A.

21. On Origen see Daniélou, pp. 180 ff., and Gögler, p. 347. In this respect Erasmus' exegetical method represents a retrogression, for already with Hugh of St. Victor the figurative meaning "belongs to the literal sense." Smalley, pp. 93, 101.

22. *Eccles.*, LB, V, 1044A, DE; 869E. Cf. *Enchiridion*, LB, V, 29DE, and *Ratio* (1519), 277, 29-31, and LB, V, 125A.

23. *Eccles.*, LB, V, 1043E-1044A; *Enarr. in ps. XXXIII* (1531), LB, V, 373E.

24. *Eccles.*, LB, V, 1045E. Erasmus refers to Augustine's *Epistola ad Vincentium*.

25. *Ibid.*, 1047F-1048AB.

26. *Ibid.*, 1047BC. Cf. *Ratio* (1519), Holborn, 259, 33 ff., and LB, V, 117AB, and Augustine, *De doctrina Christiana*, II, 6; IV, 8, 22; in *PL*, XXXIV, 38 and 98-99.

27. *Ibid.*, 1047C-E. Cf. Gregory of Nazianzus, *Oratio theologica*, V, 25, in *PG*, XXXVI, 160-161.

28. Hanson, pp. 224-231; Daniélou, pp. 104 ff. and 274 ff.; Gögler, pp. 309 ff.

29. *Expos. concion. in ps. LXXXV* (1528), LB, V, 511EF. See also *Enchiridion* (1503), LB, V, 8EF; and *Ratio* (1519), Holborn, 274, 24-27, and LB, V, 124E.

30. *De lib. arb.* (1524), LB, IX, 1218AB.

31. John 6:63. Also Paul: "The letter kills, the spirit makes alive." II Cor. 3:6. LB, V, 9AB, 30B.

32. Allen, II, 373, 104 ff. In defense of attention to the minutiae of grammatical criticism Erasmus states: "Infima pars est quam vocant literam; sed huic ceu fundamento mysticus innititur sensus." Cf. *Expos. concion. in ps. LXXXV*, LB, V, 511AB; *De amab. Eccl. conc.* (1533), LB, V, 470C. Hugh of St. Victor was perhaps the first to emphasize the historical sense as the foundation of the allegorical and to criticize "the Gregorian tradition with its sublime disregard for the letter of Scripture." Smalley, p. 95. Cf. Spicq, *Esquisse d'une histoire de l'exégèse latine au moyen âge* (Paris, 1944), who points to the increasing influence of Jerome as over against that of Augustine and Gregory in medieval exegesis from the eighth to the eleventh centuries and especially to a more rational, historical, philological exegesis in the twelfth century with Abelard and Hugh of St. Victor. Spicq, pp. 59, 72 ff. Cf. however de Lubac, who differs with Smalley and Spicq in insisting upon the unity of the exegetical tradition from Paul, Origen, Augustine, and Gregory to Hugh of St. Victor. *Exégèse médiévale*, II, 1, 318, 358 f.

33. *Eccles.* (1535), 1029CD, 1027D, 1038E.

34. *Enarr. in ps. XXXIII* (1531), LB, V, 381C.

35. *Eccles.*, LB, V, 1028C. Cf. *Enarr. in ps. XXXVIII* (1532), LB, V, 468E.

36. LB, V, 1038E.

37. Holborn, 284, 23 ff.; 287, 27 ff.; and LB, V, 127D, 129AB.

38. *Ibid.*, 284, 26 f. Cf. another 1523 addition, Holborn, 280, 23 ff., where Erasmus is critical of those imitators of Origen ". . . qui nonnunquam studio inculcandae allegoriae sensum grammaticum submovent, cum nihil sit opus."

39. LB, V, 1028DE, 1029BC.

40. Gerhard Ebeling, *Evangelische Evangelienauslegung* (Darmstadt, 1962, reprint of Munich, 1942, edition), p. 139.

41. Pineau, *Érasme, sa pensée religieuse*, p. 113, n. 74, followed by Lucien Febvre, *Problème de l'incroyance* (Paris, 1942), p. 340, cited by de Lubac, *Exégèse médiévale*, II, 2, 473, n. 4. Pfeiffer had already pointed out that Erasmus ". . . folgt keineswegs (wie K. Holl, 'Luthers Bedeutung für den Fortschritt der Auslegungskunst,' *Gesammelte Aufsätze*, I, 1921, 422 behauptet) kritiklos dem Origenes." *Gnomon*, p. 629.

42. He mentions that recent theologians interpret scriptural passages also according to a fourth sense, anagogy, the eschatological sense (*Eccles.*, LB, V, 1034D, 1035A), but he pays no attention to the anagogical sense in his exegesis. In his exposition of the Psalms he regards only the literal, allegorical, and tropological senses.

43. *Concio in ps. IV* (1525), LB, V, 274D.

44. The whole exegesis of Psalm 1 (1515) is tropological (LB, V,

171-198B). His reasoning for so doing is ". . . vel quod ea melius quadret, *vel quod magis conducat ad vitae correctionem, quam praecipue spectamus.*" 174AB. (My italics.) Cf. *Enarr. ps. XIV* (1536), LB, V, 301B: "Nos tamen in praesentia maluimus tractare sensum moralem, qui, licet videatur humilior, est tamen, meo iudicio, utilior."

45. *Eccles.* (1535), LB, V, 1036D-F.

46. *Enarr. ps. II* (1522), LB, V, 232A.

47. *Eccles.* (1535), LB, V, 1050AB: "Tropologiae nusquam non est locus, ut interim his vocibus abutamur docendi gratia. . . . Neque enim mysticum sensum habent omnia, et sunt quae per Allegoriam aut Anagogen tractata frigent." See also *Enarr. ps. II* (1522), LB, V, 201D.

48. *Ratio* (1520), Holborn, 179, 12 ff., and LB, V, 26C; *Enarr. in ps. I* (1515), LB, V, 171A, 172A; *Eccles.,* LB, V, 774D.

49. *Eccles.,* LB, V, 825E, 870A.

50. I place quotation marks around "mystical" because I am using the term in a minimal sense. See below for a brief discussion of the "mystical" in Erasmus, Ch. VIII, n. 43.

51. Huizinga, pp. 101, 106, 136. Preserved Smith, *Erasmus* (New York, 1923), pp. 169, 173; Goerung, pp. 150, 186; Émile Telle, *Érasme de Rotterdam et le septième sacrement* (Geneva, 1954), p. 463; Aldridge, especially pp. 57-64. In his book on Erasmus' hermeneutics Aldridge almost completely ignores the allegorical and spiritualistic side of Erasmus' exegetical method.

CHAPTER IV
CHRISTOLOGY

1. Allen, II, To the Reader, ⟨c. December⟩1515, 373, 116-119.

2. *Sileni Alcibiadis* (1515), LB, II, 771D-F.

3. *Concio in ps. IV* (1525), LB, V, 246AB.

4. LB, V, 32C.

5. John 16:7.

6. II Cor. 5:6. *Enchiridion* (1503), LB, V, 32CD.

7. LB, VII, 612C: "Nec egebitis posthac mea praesentia corporali, quae pro tempore data est hominum crassitudini . . ." Cf. 619E, 620C.

8. LB, V, 1093EF: ". . . donec sublata corporis praesentia veniret Spiritus ille igneus, qui carnem vertit in spiritum."

9. *Paraclesis* (1516), LB, V, 142E: ". . . qui [Christus] quod pollicitus sese semper nobiscum fore usque ad consummationem seculi, in his litteris praecipue praestat, in quibus nobis etiamnum vivit, spirat, loquitur, pene dixerim, efficacius quam cum inter homines versaretur." *Praef. tertiae ed. Nov. Test.* (1524), LB, VI, *2b.

10. Note on Matt. 24:23, *Nov. Test.* (1527), pt. 2, p. 92, and in LB, VI, 125CD.

11. *Paraphr. in evang. Ioannis* (1523), LB, VII, 612C: ". . . praesentia

corporali, quae pro tempore data est hominum crassitudini, quo per gradus proficerent ad perfectiora." Cf. 619E, and *Eccles.* (1535), LB, V, 1093F. This theme, which is an integral part of his own thought, Erasmus undoubtedly derived from the Church Fathers, most especially from Origen. According to Origen the Word always accommodates himself to the capacity of those who receive him. See Daniélou, *Origène,* p. 257, and Rolf Gögler, *Zur Theologie des biblischen Wortes,* pp. 307 ff. and 381 ff.

12. *Paraphr. in evang. Lucae* (1523), 2:51, LB, VII, 308A.

13. *Paraphr. in evang. Ioannis* (1523), 16:7, LB, VII, 620B.

14. *Nov. Test.* (1527), pt. 2, p. 504, and in LB, VI, 798D; pt. 2, p. 611, and in LB, VI, 946E; *Apol. ad Iac. Stunicam* (1521), LB, IX, 309F.

15. Note 32 on I Tim. 1:17, *Nov. Test.* (1519), pt. 2, p. 467, and in LB, VI, 930F; *Apol. ad Iac. Stunicam,* LB, IX, 309F; *Adv. epist. Lutheri* (1534), LB, X, 1545A.

16. *Apol. adv. mon. Hisp.* (1528), LB, IX, 1041D; *Adv. epist. Lutheri,* LB, X, 1545B.

17. C. H. Dodd states that "It is first quoted as a part of I John by Priscilian, the Spanish heretic, who died in 385, and it gradually made its way into MSS of the Latin Vulgate until it was accepted as part of the authorized Latin text." *The Johannine Epistles* (New York, 1946), p. 127n.

18. *Resp. ad notat. novas Ed. Lei* (1520), LB, IX, 275B.

19. Smith (p. 166) accepts the opinion of Caspar René Gregory in *Biblical World* (April 1911), p. 256, that this manuscript was forged for this express purpose.

20. *Nov. Test.* (1522), pt. 2, p. 617, and cf. *Apol. ad Iac. Stunicam* (1521), LB, IX, 353DE. Smith, p. 166.

21. Note on I John 5:7, *Nov. Test.* (1527), pt. 2, p. 697, and in LB, VI, 1081D.

22. John Knox, "Exegesis of Romans," *Interpreter's Bible,* IX, ed. George A. Buttrick (New York, 1954), p. 540. Erasmus here anticipates the conclusions of modern New Testament criticism.

23. Note on Phil. 2:6, *Nov. Test.* (1519), pt. 2, p. 434, and in LB, VI, 868BC.

24. *Apol. ad Sanctium Caranzam* (1522), LB, IX, 401E.

25. John 20:28.

26. Note on John 20:28, *Nov. Test.* (1519), pt. 2, p. 196, and in LB, VI, 417DE.

27. *Apol. adv. mon. Hisp.,* LB, IX, 1034D. Erasmus gives this reasoning as valid for the orthodox formula. "Ex his oritur collectio, Si nascitur singulari ratione a Patre, non adoptione Filius est, sed natura. Si natura, nascitur e substantia Patris: sed Dei substantia dividi nullo modo potest, quemadmodum nec augeri nec minui. Consequitur igitur eamdem et individuam esse substantiam Patris ac Filii. Haec est illa ratiocinatio, de qua loquebar, quae non nititur hominum commentis,

ut isti calumniantur, sed ex Scripturis Divinis sumitur."1034F.

28. *Apol. adv. mon. Hisp.,* LB, IX, 1023F-1029B.

29. On Origen's subordinationism, see Daniélou, pp. 250-252, and Franz Heinrich Kettler, *Der ursprüngliche Sinn der Dogmatik des Origenes,* pp. 7, n. 29, and 24-26, n. 110.

30. Note on I Tim. 1:17, *Nov. Test.* (1519), pt. 2, p. 467, and in LB, VI, 930F.

31. Note on Col. 1:15, *Nov. Test.* (1522), pt. 2, p. 502, and in LB, VI, 884E-885C.

32. *Expos. concion. in ps. LXXXV* (1528), LB, V, 511BC.

33. *Eccles.* (1535), LB, V, 939A.

34. Note on John 1:1, *Nov. Test.* (1516), pt. 2, pp. 352-353, and LB, VI, 337CD. Cf. *Comm. in Ioan.,* II, 2, 13; cited by J. N. D. Kelly, *Early Christian Doctrine* (New York, 1958), p. 131. In this note, again like Origen, Erasmus uses the Platonic term "participation" for the relation between Son and Father, upon the meaning of which he had another debate with Lee. See *Ad notat. Ed. Lei* (1520), LB, IX, 171C-173B. For Origen on "participation" see *Comm. in Ioan.,* II, 2, 16, and *ibid.,* II, 10, 77; cited by Kelly, p. 130.

35. *Paraphr. in evang. Matt.* (1522), 28:16, LB, VII, 145A; *ibid.,* Matt. 26:37-38, LB, VII, 135CD. See also *Expos. concion. in ps. LXXXV* (1528), LB, V, 510EF, 512F-513A, 530DE.

36. LB, V, 1282C.

37. *Ad Lectorem,* LB, IX, 67AB. This is Erasmus' 1516 annotation (pt. 2, pp. 585-586) which is quoted for the benefit of the reader in the *Opera Omnia,* LB, IX, 67A-68C. For the sake of convenience I cite from this work.

38. LB, IX, 67B-68A. Cf. *Apol. ad Iac. Fabrum,* LB, IX, 42F-47E, 49DE.

39. Note on II Cor. 5:21, *Nov. Test.* (1519), pt. 2, p. 370, and LB, VI, 769C.

40. *Paraphr. in evang. Matt.* (1522), LB, VII, 16F.

41. *Ratio* (1519), Holborn, 203, 23 f., and LB, V, 89B.

42. *Resp. ad notata per N. Beddam* (1526), LB, IX, 460EF. Cf. *Symbolum* (1533), LB, V, 1154C.

43. *Nov. Test.* (1519), pt. 2, p. 76, and LB, VI, 126F.

44. LB, VII, 127A.

45. LB, IX, 460EF; *Supput. errorum N. Beddae* (1527), LB, IX, 569EF-570A.

46. Erasmus will sometimes refer to three different parts: body, soul, and deity. *Disputatio de taedio et pavore Christi* (1503), LB, V, 1286C; *Expos. concion. in ps. LXXXV,* LB, V, 526AB; *Eccles.* (1535), LB, V, 1057D.

47. *Paraphr. in evang. Marci* (1523), 14:33, LB, VII, 261D.

48. *De amab. Eccl. conc.* (1533), LB, V, 494C. See also *Christiani matrimonii institutio* (1526), LB, V, 620B-D, where Erasmus suggests that the union of the two natures in the incarnation is a model of the union of the sexes in marriage.

49. *Apol. ad Iac. Fabrum,* LB, IX, 28E. Ber and Capito also accuse Erasmus of dividing the person of Christ, which is denied by Erasmus. To Louis Ber, 6 December 1517, Allen, III, 730, 4-11; To Wolfgang Capito, 6 December 1517, Allen, III, 731, 9-21.

50. *Iac. Fabri disputatio in annot. Erasmi,* LB, IX, 70EF, 71C, 72D-F.

51. *Apol. ad Iac. Fabrum,* LB, IX, 35EF.

52. *Ibid.,* LB, IX, 39F-40A, 41C.

53. *Ratio* (1519), Holborn, 216, 7-29, and LB, V, 94EF-95AB. See also *Eccles.* (1535), LB, V, 1057C-1058F, where in a much more lengthy and detailed passage than the one quoted above, Erasmus shows the parallel indications of the human and divine natures throughout the gospel history.

54. I do not understand how John W. Aldridge can state: "Erasmus was impressed by the divinity of Christ rather than the humanity; the concept of a Jesus Christ, truly God, truly man, was foreign to him. . . . The divinity of Christ was so important for Erasmus and his concept of the philosophy of Christ that in pointing out its importance, he relegated the humanity of Christ to a place of secondary importance." *The Hermeneutic of Erasmus,* p. 41.

55. Bouyer, *Autour d'Érasme,* p. 133.

56. P. Wernle, *Die Renaissance des Christentums im 16. Jahrhundert* (Tübingen, 1904), pp. 14 f.; Mestwerdt, pp. 95 f.; Pineau, *Érasme, sa pensée religieuse,* p. 118; Ernst, "Die Frömmigkeit des Erasmus," pp. 63 f., 74 f.; Renaudet, *Études érasmiennes,* pp. 147, 171; *Érasme et l'Italie,* p. 201; W. Köhler, *Erasmus* (Berlin, 1917), p. 12; R. Kommoss, *Sebastian Franck und Erasmus von Rotterdam* (Berlin, 1934), pp. 54 f., 59 ff. Cf. Auer, pp. 103 ff.; Padberg, *Erasmus als Katechet,* pp. 47, 90; and Kohls, I, 103 ff.

57. *Expos. concion. in ps. LXXXV* (1528), LB, V, 532A.

58. *Enchiridion* (1503), LB, V, 22E.

59. *Paraphr. in evang. Matt.* (1522), 28:19, LB, VII, 145C.

60. Note on II Cor. 13:13, *Nov. Test.* (1527), p. 504, and LB, VI, 798D. Among other passages where the fact of redemption is expressed are the following: *Confabulatio pia* (1522), LB, I, 651C; cf. *Enarr. in ps. XXII* (1530), LB, V, 314C; *Inquisitio de fide* (1524), LB, I, 729D; *Concio de miseric. Dom.* (1524), LB, V, 577C; *Symbolum* (1533), LB, V, 1152BC; *De praep. ad mort.* (1534), LB, V, 1298B.

61. On this theme in Origen, see Kelly, p. 185, and Daniélou, pp. 267-268. See G. Aulén, *Christus Victor,* tr. A. Hebert (New York, 1951), pp. 16 ff., for a survey of what he calls the classical theme of conflict

and victory in Irenaeus and the later Greek and Latin Fathers. Aulén judges that though the idea is clearer and more dominant among the Greeks, it is nevertheless also to be found among the Latins.

62. *Paraphr. in evang. Lucae* (1523), 4:3, LB, VII, 319AB. This theme was especially prominent in Gregory of Nyssa among the Greek Fathers. See *Oratio catechetica*, XXII-XXIV, XXVI; Kelly, p. 382, and Aulén, p. 52.

63. *Symbolum* (1533), LB, V, 1151C: "Dignatus est nobis propius per eumdem Filium ac familiarius innotescere, ut vel sic in mutuum amorem illius reparemur, tot tamque mirandis provocati beneficiis . . . misit unicum Filium factum hominem, ut saltem hominem homines amaremus." Cf. *ibid.*, 1160F; *Concio de puero Iesu* (1514), LB, V, 602C.

64. *Paraphr. in evang. Lucae* (1523), 2:51, LB, VII, 307EF.

65. See *Paraphr. in epist. Pauli ad Rom.* (1517), 8:3, LB, VII, 801A; *Paraphr. in epist. Pauli ad Cor. II* (1519), 5:21, LB, VII, 925D.

66. The emphasis upon God's love and mercy, which runs through all of Erasmus' works, is especially present in the treatise *Concio de miseric. Dom.* (1524), LB, V, 557-588. The thought of Erasmus is that Christ comes as the gentle, merciful savior in the first advent, who by his gracious words and deeds evokes a responding love. Only an obstinate malice rejects such an amiable love. But in the second advent he comes as judge to those who stubbornly reject him and who therefore are deservedly condemned. He thus very nearly splits God's love and his wrath into two distinct moments, the first in the moment of the incarnation, the second in that of the *Parousia*. Cf. *Enarr. ps. II* (1522), LB, V, 206D.

67. *Paraphr. in epist. Pauli I. ad Tim.* (1520), 2:4, LB, VII, 1041AB. See also *Paraphr. in evang. Matt.* (1522), 28:19, LB, VII, 145B.

68. *Symbolum* (1533), LB, V, 1156C. Cf. *ibid.*, 1160E; *Paraphr. in evang. Matt.* (1522), 28:19, LB, VII, 145B.

69. Note on Luke 6:20, *Nov. Test.* (1516), pt. 2, p. 330, and LB, VI, 254F. Cf. *Paraclesis* (1516), LB, V, 139E: ". . . novum et admirabile Philosophiae genus sit, oportet, quod ut traderet mortalibus: is qui Deus erat, factus est homo . . ."; and *Precationes* (1535), LB, V, 1199B.

70. The *Epistola de philosophia evangelica* (date unknown), LB, VI, *4b.

71. *Adv. epist. Lutheri* (1534), LB, X, 1552F; cited by Auer, p. 234, n. 61.

72. LB, V, 25AB: "Christum vero esse, puta, non vocem inanem, sed nihil aliud, quam caritatem, simplicitatem, patientiam, puritatem, breviter, quidquid ille docuit."

73. *Paraclesis*, LB, V, 139D, 141F. Cf. note on Matt. 5:11, *Nov. Test.* (1519), pt. 2, p. 22, and LB, VI, 27E.

74. *Ibid.*, 139D; *Paraphr. in evang. Matt.* (1522), 1:1, LB, VII, 1D.

75. *Paraphr. in evang. Matt.*, 5:2, LB, VII, 23D.

76. LB, V, 142C.

77. *Paraclesis,* LB, V, 141F: "Quid autem aliud est Christi Philosophia, quam ipse renascentiam vocat, quam instauratio bene conditae naturae?" I am aware that part of the point of this passage is to indicate the continuity between the *philosophia Christi* and the teachings of nature as exemplified by some of the ancient philosophers, as is indicated by the discussion that follows. Yet Erasmus is also cognizant of the discontinuity between Christ's teaching and the law of nature, though he insufficiently emphasizes this difference. *Paraphr. in evang. Matt.* (1522), 5:45, LB, VII, 34F: "Naturae est, non Evangelicae virtutis, redamere amantem." Furthermore, this *renascentia,* or new manhood, is accomplished, as far as Erasmus is concerned, as we shall notice in the next chapter, both by grace and law, i.e., living both by the aid of Christ and according to his teaching and example. Cf. *Paraphr. in epist. Pauli ad Eph.* (1520), 2:10, LB, VII, 977A: ". . . et insiti Christo, innocentiae principi, ut posthac huius ope atque exemplo vacemus officiis verae pietatis, positoque vetere homine, novum hominem novis actionibus praestemus . . ." Auer (p. 104) points in this same direction but fails to explain the meaning of the *renascentia,* specifically that the term includes both the redemptive and the normative aspects of Christ's work.

78. *Paraclesis,* LB, V, 142D: "Sive vivendi formam requirimus, cur aliud nobis prius est exemplum, quam archetypus ipse Christus?" *Enchiridion* (1503), LB, V, 40C; *Praef. tertiae ed. Nov. Test.* (1524), LB, VI, *2b.

79. *Paraphr. in evang. Matt.* (1522), 4:11, LB, VII, 20A.

80. *Ibid.,* 9:21, 56C.

81. *Paraphr. in evang. Marci* (1523), 1:35, LB, VII, 166F-167A.

82. *Ibid.,* 169F-170A.

83. *Ratio* (1519), Holborn, 237, 17 f., and LB, V, 105E: "Duo quaedam peculiariter et perpetuo inculcat Christus, fidem et caritatem." Cf. *ibid.,* 239, 242, 28 ff., and LB, V, 106EF, 108D.

84. *Epist. de phil. evang.,* LB, VI, *5; *Pio Lectori,* appendix prefixed to *Paraphr. in evang. Matt.,* LB, VII, **3b.

85. Especially E. Rénan, *La Vie de Jésus* (Paris, 1863). See A. Schweitzer, *Quest of the Historical Jesus,* tr. W. Montgomery (New York, 1910), p. 185. Cf. Renaudet, *Études érasmiennes,* p. xxiv.

86. *Ratio* (1519), Holborn, 222, 9 ff., and LB, V, 98A.

87. *Enchiridion,* LB, V, 6AB; *De praep. ad mort.,* LB, V, 1297F, 1298F, 1301C; *Enarr. in ps. XXXIII* (1531), LB, V, 398EF.

88. *Paraphr. in evang. Matt.* (1522), 4:11, LB, VII, 20A: "Vicit illum Christus, ut nobis ostenderet vinci posse, et vincendi rationem docuit." In *Paraphr. in evang. Lucae,* 4:12, LB, VII, 322D, this whole idea of Christ the commander, who is redeemer and teacher-example, is

neatly summarized: "Sed horum vires semel fregit princeps noster, ac proinde nobis vincibiles tradidit, quos rursus victurus est in nobis, si modo nos pugnandi rationem, qua Christus eos devicit, imitemur." See also *De praep. ad mort.*, LB, V, 1296F.

89. Kohls goes too far in his corrective to the earlier rationalistic, moralistic interpretation of Erasmus' Christology when he stresses the objectivity of the event of the Cross for Erasmus: "Das Kreuz wird zum Heilsweg des Christen zu Gott, weil Gott selbst durch das Kreuz Christi das Heil der Erlösung zuvorgeschenkt hat. Erasmus will diese vorgegebene, göttlich gesetzte Heilsfaktizität des Kreuzes nie übersehen wissen: . . . Erasmus hat in seiner Herausstellung des Kreuzes Christi den Indikativ der in Christus persönlich geschenkten Heilsgüter und den von diesem vorgegebenen Heilshandeln ausgehenden paränetischen Imperativ Darzulegen versucht." *Die Theologie des Erasmus*, I, 107. Without having, to be sure, overlooked the divinely established ground of salvation, Erasmus certainly places much more emphasis upon the imperative than the indicative of Christian existence.

CHAPTER V
SOTERIOLOGY

1. *De lib. arb.*, LB, IX, 1222A; *Hyper. I*, LB, X, 1324EF, 1326A; *Paraclesis* (1516), LB, V, 141F-142AB. On this point see Thompson, *Inquisitio de fide*, pp. 113-119, especially pp. 118-119.

2. *Eccles.*, LB, V, 1075A.

3. *Supput. errorum N. Beddae* (1527), LB, IX, 688D; *Eccles.*, LB, V, 1076B.

4. *Eccles.*, LB, V, 1076B-D: ". . . quaedam [judicial laws] videmus et hodie servari a Christianis, quaedam prorsus sublata, quaedam mitigata, quaedam immutata, contracta quaedam, rursus alia dilatata."

5. *Paraphr. in evang. Matt.* (1522), 19:9, LB, VII, 103C; *Paraphr. in evang. Lucae* (1523), 16:17-18, LB, VII, 414D-F; *Declar. ad cens.*, LB, IX, 859E: ". . . de summa perfectaque charitate erga Deum et proximum, quae complectitur universam Legem, atque etiam Evangelii perfectionem."

6. *Paraphr. in epist. Pauli ad Rom.*, 8:3, LB, VII, 800F: "Quemadmodum (ut dictum est) in uno homine, veluti duo sunt homines, carnalis et spiritualis: ita in una Mosi Lege, ceu sunt duae Leges, altera crassa et carnalis, altera spiritualis." Erasmus defends this statement against Beda twice: *Ad not. per N. Beddam in paraphr. in Paulum* (1526), LB, IX, 470BC, and *Supput. errorum N. Beddae* (1527), LB, IX, 668F-669B. He supports his statement that there are, as it were, two laws in the one law by noting that Jerome and Origen likewise made such a distinction

on the same basis. Cf. *Paraphr. in epist. Pauli ad Gal.* (1519), 4:24, LB, VII, 959D: "Nam huiusmodi ferme est Lex Mosaica, ut quemadmodum in homine, sub crasso corporis operculo latet animus corporis moderator . . ." Cf. *ibid.,* 5:16, 964A. See Auer, pp. 171 and 247, n. 329, and Kohls, II, p. 116, n. 501. Kohls rejects out of hand Auer's suggestion of an anthropological base of Erasmus' understanding of law. He thinks that the Galatians paraphrase is ". . . in doch offensichtlich nur bildlicher Rede!" He does not note the Romans paraphrase and the answers to Beda which further corroborate Auer's contention, though this scholar likewise does not refer to these passages.

7. *Paraphr. in epist. Pauli ad Rom.* (1517), 8:3-6, 801AD. *Eccles.* (1535), LB, V, 1076B.

8. *Paraphr. in epist. Pauli ad Cor. II* (1519), 3:11-17, LB, VII, 920C-921A; *In epist. Pauli ad Gal. Argumentum* (1519), LB, VII, 943.

9. *Hyper. I* (1526), LB, X, 1325B. See also *Paraphr. in epist. Iac.* (1520), 4:6, LB, VII, 1135B.

10. *Summa totius Sacrae Scripturae* (date unknown), LB, VI, ****3.

11. *Hyper. I,* LB, X, 1350EF.

12. *De servo arbitrio* (1525), WA, XVIII, 680 ff., where Luther criticizes Erasmus' confusion of law and gospel. In its strange work the gospel intensifies the demands of the law, making them impossible to fulfill, but in its proper work it proclaims nothing but grace. WA, I, 105 ff.; cited by R. Seeberg, *Textbook of the History of Doctrine,* II, tr. Charles E. Hay (Philadelphia, 1905; reprint, Grand Rapids, 1954), p. 228. See Seeberg's discussion of Luther on law and gospel, pp. 228, 246-251.

13. *Paraphr. in epist. Pauli ad Gal.,* 3:19, 22, LB, VII, 954EF, 955CD; *Paraphr. in epist. Pauli ad Rom.* (1517), 7:7, LB, VII, 798F.

14. *Hyper. II* (1527), LB, X, 1498AB, 1530A.

15. *Declar. ad cens.,* LB, IX, 833CD, 861A.

16. *Paraphr. in epist. Pauli I ad Tim.,* 1:5, LB, VII, 1036E. See also *Enarr. ps. I* (1515), LB, V, 181B, E.

17. *Ratio* (1520), Holborn, 245, 10 f., and LB, V, 109E: "Ama, et fac quod vis: non enim peccat sincera caritas, ipsa sibi lex est, et ubique dictat, quid sit optimum factu."

18. See this passage from the *Antibarbari* (written by 1495 but not published until 1520), where Erasmus places the emphasis on human industry and endeavor as a prerequisite for the reception of divine grace, LB, X, 1741F-1742A: "Promissa erat sapientia coelesti oraculo Solomoni, promissum erat patri regnum Israeliticum, neuter tamen ita oraculo confisus est, ut vel hic quicquam humani conatus praeterierit, quo se dignum praestaret, vel ille sapientiam languidiore studio quaesiverit: intelligebant nimirum quod gravissime a quodam scriptum est, Deos omnia nobis laboribus vendere. Dabunt igitur, sed laboranti, addent sapientiam, sed annitenti, praestabunt continentiam, sed

conanti, docebunt, sed studiosos, adiutabunt, sed dimicantes." Erasmus here underlines his stress upon the necessity of human effort by reference to the myth of Prometheus, LB, X, 1742B: "Auget enim ille, quae nostra peperimus industria, promovet studia nostra, adspirat nostris conatibus. Quod si fas est hoc loco Poetarum fabulas admiscere, Prometheus est nobis imitandus: qui simulachro illi suo luteo, vitam ex astris ausus est petere, sed tum demum ubi quicquid humano artificio praestari potuit, adhibuisset. Nos rudem massam offerimus, et Spiritum omnia nobis dormientibus confecturum speramus? . . . Videtis ut operam humanam Spiritus huius munus non excluserit, sed adiuverit." Erasmus' statements here are in line with his mature position as expressed in the *Hyperaspistae II*, where the humanist indicates his acceptance of the Scotist and late-medieval nominalist affirmation of Occam and Biel concerning a *meritum de congruo* prior to the reception of justifying grace (*gratia gratum faciens*). I must therefore disagree with Kohls who remarks concerning this passage, "Erasmus legt mit diesem Bild nicht den Nachdruck auf das humanum artificium, auf die 'freie Schöpfung aus eigener menschlicher Kraft' (so Rudolf Pfeiffer, *Humanitas Erasmiana*, a.a.O., S. 15, ähnlich Richard Newald, *Erasmus Roterodamus*, a.a.O., S. 58), sondern sucht in diesem Bilde, wie der Zusammenhang zeigt, die vom Hl. Geist gesteigerte und geförderte Fähigkeit und Kraft des Christen zu verdeutlichen." II, 63, n. 76.Though Erasmus indeed does not deny the role of divine grace, he surely places the emphasis here upon human effort as a necessary condition for the reception of this grace. His thought here is in line with the maxim of Occam and Biel: ". . . facienti quod in se est, Deus non denegat gratiam." See P. Vignaux, "Nominalisme," in *DTC*, cl. 776, and Oberman, *Harvest*, pp. 135 ff.

Cf. these passages from the *Enchiridion* (1503) and the *Paraphrases* where free will seems to have the larger place. LB, V, 16C: "Magna pars Christianismi est, toto pectore velle fieri Christianum." *Ibid.*, 23C: "Quod si non omnibus contingit ad perfectam imitationem capitis pertingere, omnibus tamen huc manibus, pedibus est enitendum. Bonam Christianismi parten habet, qui certo animo decrevit fieri Christianus." *Paraphr. in evang. Matt.* (1522), 23:37, LB, VII, 124B: "At cui semel data est arbitrii libertas, invitus servari non potest. Oportebat meae voluntati, vestram respondere voluntatem."

19. *Paraphr. in evang. Matt.*, 6:13, LB, VII, 37E: "Primum, docet vos totos non aliunde pendere quam a Patre coelesti . . . cui debetis quod estis a peccatis redemti; cui debetis quicquid habetis virtutum." Cf. *Paraphr. in evang. Marci* (1523), 5:20, LB, VII, 195D: "Agnosce et confitere qualis fueris: et quod nunc alius subito factus es, ne tribuas meritis tuis, sed gratuitae Dei misericordiae qui miseretur, quorumcumque vult ipse: nulli debitor, neque obnoxius." *Paraphr. in evang. Lucae*

(1523), 5:14, LB, VII, 338B: "Nec enim nostra sunt, quae Deus per nos operatur."

20. See the *De contemptu mundi* (written c. 1486 but first published c. 1521; Allen, IV, 1194, Intro.), where, as pointed out by Kohls (II, 51, n. 111), Erasmus deals with grace and free will under the rubric of the *militia Christi*: "Postremo durissimum illud Pharaonis teterrimi iugum, Deo opitulante excussimus, improbissimis dominis, vitiis dico, parere desivimus, non ita quidem, ut nihil umquam peccemus, quod haud scio an nemini mortalium in vita contigerit: sed ut miles is plurimum sibi laudis victorisque nomen e certamine merito suo ferre potest, qui consertis cominus dextris gnaviter dimicans, non sine vulneribus quidem suis, sed tamen hostem aut capit, aut iugulat: contra vero victus iudicaretur, si etiam citra vulnera, et salva cute se capi, atque in servitutem abduci pateretur: ita nobis, si quando evenerit, quod, ut dixi, ab homine praestari fere nequit, quid nostra refert, si nonnihil labamur, certe vincimus, certe libertatem, certe vitam tutamur." LB, V, 1253DE. Cf. *Enchiridion,* LB, V, 6B: "Pro te pugnabit, et liberalitatem suam tibi pro merito imputabit. Victoriam omnem illi feras acceptam oportet, qui primus et solus a peccato immunis, peccati tyrannidem oppressit, verum ea tibi non sine tua continget industria." *Paraphr. in epist. Pauli ad Rom.* (1517), 8:28, LB, VII, 804C: ". . . tantus est Dei favor in eos, quos ex destinata animi sui voluntate delegit, ac vocavit in hanc felicitatem. Noster conatus est, caeterum eventus pendet a decreto Dei." *Paraphr. in evang. Matt.* (1522), 20:15, LB, VII, 108B: "Hoc praemium ut non debetur omnino meritis nostris, sed potius beneficentiae divinae, tamen non contingit citra conatum nostrum." *Paraphr. in evang. Ioannis* (1523), 6:45, 548F: "Donum est Dei, sed vester est conatus." In the *Paraphrases,* just as in the much earlier *Antibarbari,* Erasmus occasionally uses language which approximates his mature position as found in the *Hyperaspistae II* concerning the necessity of a *meritum de congruo* before the reception of justifying grace. *Paraphr. in evang. Ioannis* (1523), 6:44, LB, VII, 548DE: "Non impartit ille tantum munus, nisi volentibus et avidis. Quisquis autem promeruit sua promta voluntate, pioque studio, ut attrahatur a Patre, per me vitam aeternam consequetur."

21. *De lib. arb.* (1524), LB, IX, 1236D: ". . . semina quaedam honesti; tradunt insita mentibus hominum, quibus aliquo modo vident et expetunt honesta . . ."

22. *Ibid.,* 1224F-1225A, 1227CD.

23. *Ibid.,* 1242B.

24. *Ibid.,* 1223E. Durandus, Occam, and Biel all held to a purely natural basis as sufficient preparation for the reception of the *gratia gratum faciens.* As Oberman remarks regarding Biel: "One thing is clear: when the term *gratia gratis data* is used, it is thoroughly natural-

ized and barely distinguishable from man's natural endowments." *Harvest,* p. 138. On the other hand, Gregory of Rimini and Thomas Aquinas, at least in the *Summa theologica* and *Summa contra Gentiles,* held to the necessity of the *auxilium speciale.* However, there is a certain ambiguity in Thomas. Some interpreters note that in his commentary on the *Sentences* Thomas' view is much nearer the other position of a purely naturalistic basis for the preparation for justifying grace. Oberman, *Harvest,* pp. 142-145. See his whole discussion of this question with special reference to Biel and Biel's understanding of the medieval tradition at this point, pp. 135-145. On Occam and Biel, see also Seeberg, *DG,* III, pp. 766 f., especially n. 4, and C. Feckes, *Die Rechtfertigungslehre des Gabriel Biel und ihre Stellung innerhalb der nominalistischen Schule,* Münsterische Beiträge zur Theologie, VII (Münster i.w., 1925), 125 ff. Scotus is likewise not altogether clear on this matter but seems to presuppose the *auxilium speciale,* as Minges points out. See below, n. 42.

25. *De lib. arb.,* 1231A, 1235F, 1240F, 1244B.

26. *Ibid.,* 1223F-1224B. Three kinds of grace are signified for Erasmus by the parable of the prodigal son: the gift of property to the son, the grace of nature; his return home, the human response to prevenient or stimulating grace; the running of the father to meet his son, cooperating grace, which furthers our will to enable us to accomplish what we wish. 1240EF.

27. LB, X, 1327C.

28. LB, IX, 1224C, and X, 1327CD.

29. *De lib. arb.,* LB, IX, 1224D. Cf. 1245A, C.

30. LB, IX, 1224C. The opinion of Ole Modalsi [*Das Gericht nach den Werken* (Göttingen, 1963), pp. 181 f.] taken over by Kohls (II, p. 24, n. 154, and p. 64, n. 78) that Erasmus here in the *Diatribe* expresses agreement with Thomas concerning "ein durch die Gnade befreiter Willen" is in the main correct. However, both these authors overlook the inconsistencies in Erasmus' position as expressed even in the *Diatribe,* as well as Erasmus' inclination to accept in the *Hyperaspistae II* not the Thomist but rather the Scotist-nominalist point of view. Kohls goes so far as to interpret Erasmus' statements from the *De contemptu mundi* (c. 1486) through the *Antibarbari* (c. 1495) and *Enchiridion* (1503) to the *De libero arbitrio* (1524) as consistently revealing a Thomist interpretation on the issue (II, pp. 51-52, n. 111; pp. 63-64, n. 77; p. 64, n. 78). As already pointed out, Erasmus' statements prior to the *De libero arbitrio* are not so consistent as Kohls imagines, nor are they all necessarily to be interpreted along Thomist lines, but rather at least some of them may easily bear a Scotist-nominalist interpretation. In any case, Erasmus indicates in the end his preference for the Scotist-nominalist position.

31. LB, IX, 1235F. It is not clear when he says here "adiutus auxilio Dei" whether he has in mind the *gratia naturalis* or the *gratia specialis.* Of course, if he means the former, he is closer to the Occamist position; if the latter, he is closer to the Scotist position, at least as interpreted by Minges. See below, n. 42.

32. His definition (1220F-1221A) indicates an exalted view of free will: ". . . *Liberum Arbitrium* hoc loco sentimus vim humanae voluntatis, qua se possit homo applicare ad ea quae perducunt ad aeternam salutem, aut ab iisdem avertere." Yet in 1221E he also says that the will lost its freedom in sin: ". . . sed amissa libertate cogebatur servire peccato, cui se volens semel addixerat"; in 1221F that it is ineffective for good works without divine grace; in 1243F that we owe the whole work of salvation to God without whom we could do nothing and that the contribution of the free will is very little (*perpusillum*). Luther points to these contradictions in WA, XVIII, 635 ff. and 668 ff.

33. Oskar J. Mehl rightly points to the unfortunate neglect of the *Hyperaspistae* in Erasmus research. "Erasmus' Streitschrift gegen Luther: Hyperaspistes," *Zeitschrift für Religions- und Geistesgeschichte,* 12 (1966), 144. Cf. *ibid.,* "Erasmus contra Luther," *Luther-Jahrbuch,* 29 (1962), 52 ff.

34. *Hyper. I* (1526), LB, X, 1293E, 1315A, 1343DE; *Hyper. II* (1527), LB, X, 1441D, 1471C.

35. The following quotation is an example of a statement which overestimates the role of free will in Augustine: "Etenim Augustinus cum facit gratiam operantem et cooperantem, satis fatetur esse liberum homini applicare se ad gratiam exstimulantem, si naturae vires ad eam accommodet: eum conatum imperfectum adiuvat et absolvit gratia cooperans, quae cooperans, non recte diceretur, si nihil omnino operaretur nostra voluntas . . ." LB, X, 1331E. Cf. *Hyper. II,* LB, X, 1480A and 1487B. Augustine's position was rather that the will's application for and cooperation with grace was itself a consequence of God's initiating grace. *De gratia et lib. arb.,* 24. See Paul L. Lehmann, "The Anti-Pelagian Writings," in *A Companion to the Study of St. Augustine,* ed. Roy Battenhouse (New York, 1955), pp. 224 f.

36. *Hyper. I,* LB, X, 1323DE. If Minges is correct Erasmus incorrectly interprets the Scotist position, which, as he describes it here, is actually the Occamist position.

37. *Hyper. I,* LB, X, 1327DE, 1330E; *Hyper. II,* LB, X, 1339CD, 1356EF, 1358A, 1457B, 1472BC, 1473F, 1476DE. He sometimes oversimplifies the matter when he simply identifies this opinion as the present scholastic opinion: 1339C and 1479F.

38. *Hyper. II,* LB, X, 1487AB: "Iam saepius testatus sum Scholasticorum opinionem, quod liberum arbitrium suis viribus possit promereri, saltem de congruo, gratiam iustificantem, me nec probare

nec improbare: *proclivior tamen ad probandum quam ad improbandum.* " (My italics.)

39. *Ibid.,* 1500E.

40. *Hyper. II,* LB, X, 1528E.

41. *Ibid.,* 1531C: "Quod si huiusmodi operibus moraliter bonis, sive quocunque nomine vocare placet, praeparatur homo gratiae divinae, sive, ut Scholastici loquuntur, merito congruo promeretur eam, quid habet absurditatis sententia?"

42. *Ibid.,* 1531E. The problem of the necessity of the *gratia gratis data* for the *meritum de congruo* is here in view. With Scotus, the former probably is presupposed, but with Occam and Biel, only a *concursus generalis;* or we can say that for the latter the *gratia gratis data* is identified with the *concursus generalis.* Oberman, *Harvest,* pp. 164, 210-211, and Seeberg, *DG,* III, p. 666, n. 1: "Im übrigen wird hier wie bei den älteren Franziskanern die *gratia gratis data* als Grund des *meritum de congruo* anzusetzen sein, wiewohl Duns hiervon nicht spricht." Seeberg refers here also to Minges, *Die Gnadenlehre des Duns Scotus auf ihren angeblichen Pelagianismus und Semipelagianismus geprüft* (Münster i.w., 1906), pp. 45 ff., 69. Minges thinks that even in passages where it is not expressly mentioned, prevenient or exciting grace is presupposed by Duns Scotus in order to produce the *meritum de congruo* preceding the reception of the *gratia gratum faciens. Ibid.,* p. 69. This grace is available to all men; it belongs to the *influentia communis,* but is to be distinguished from the *concursus naturalis* insofar as it is a supernatural gift. *Ibid.,* pp. 69 and 96.

On Scotus and Occam, see further P. Vignaux, *Justification et prédestination au XIVᵉ siècle* (Paris, 1934), pp. 12 ff., 123 ff., and 188; "Nominalisme," *DTC,* XI, 770 ff.; and "Occam," *DTC,* XI, 878 f.

43. *Ox.* I d 41 q l n 12; cited by W. Pannenberg, *Die Prädestinations lehre des Duns Scotus* (Göttingen, 1954), p. 96, n. 84. See his discussion of this important theory in Scotus, pp. 95 ff. Cf. Vignaux, *Justification et prédestination,* pp. 23-31, and Oberman, *Harvest,* p. 212.

44. "Although these terms [*potentia absoluta* and *potentia ordinata*] had been employed since the beginnings of scholasticism, they had been more or less peripheral. Only in Duns Scotus, and after him in the nominalistic tradition, did the terms become key words for theological method and for the understanding of an increasing number of dogmatic *loci.*" Oberman, *Harvest,* p. 36. See also Seeberg, *DG,* III, 654 and 715. The term *potentia absoluta* signifies that God can do whatever does not go against the law of contradiction. With this aspect of his being is contrasted what God has actually decided to do. "There are many things God can do which he does not want to do." Oberman,

Harvest, p. 37. Cf. P. Vignaux, "Nominalisme," p. 764.

45. *Justification et prédestination,* pp. 139 ff.

46. Oberman, *Harvest,* pp. 210 f. See the whole chapter on the views of Occam and Biel on predestination and their relation to Scotus, Gregory of Rimini, and Holcot.

47. *Hyper. II,* LB, X, 1412DE, 1436C, *et passim.*

48. With the difference between Scotus and the nominalists (Occam and Biel) being that Scotus seems to presuppose special grace for even the *meritum de congruo,* whereas Occam and Biel posit the *meritum de congruo* on a purely naturalistic basis.

49. *Hyper. II,* LB, X, 1447DE. In the next column he states that the merits are not commensurate with the reward but that the reward is not given without merits. The merits are therefore not *causa efficiens,* but *causa sine qua non* of the reward. 1448B.

50. H. Humbertclaude, *Érasme et Luther, leur polémique sur le libre arbitre* (Paris, 1909), p. 225.

51. See Allen, VI, 1667, Intro., and VII, 1853, Intro., for the dates of the writing of the two *Hyperaspistae.*

52. Allen, VII, 1804, 75-82, 91-95. Erasmus must surely have meant by the last clause that "not even *all* the scholastics receive this opinion." Note that his description of the opinion not displeasing to him is more characteristic of the Occamist than the Scotist formulation of the basis of the *meritum de congruo.* Karl Heinz Oelrich likewise points to this letter as revealing, in contrast to his views as expressed in the *Diatribe,* Erasmus' appreciation for the "Scotist" opinion and yet also his continuing uncertainty as to the proper exact formulation. Resting his analysis largely upon the letters, Oelrich fails to note that Erasmus' inclination to the "Scotist" opinion is corroborated by his discussion in the *Hyperaspistae II.* Oelrich, *Der späte Erasmus und die Reformation* (Münster, 1961), pp. 125-126.

53. *Expos. concion. in ps. LXXXV* (1528), LB, V, 512B, E; 553CD.

54. *Ibid.,* 522D: "Pollicitus est misericordiam suam, sed conversis, sed timentibus, sed invocantibus, sed diligentibus."

55. LB, V, 394B.

56. *Enarr. in ps. XXXIII* (1530), LB, V, 394D. (My italics.)

57. *Ibid.,* 410F-411A. (My italics.)

58. LB, V, 500BC.

59. LB, V, 1296F-1297A, 1297F.

60. Thus I should like to qualify Humbertclaude's judgment by noting that Erasmus' seeming acceptance of the Scotist, more precisely the Occamist, position on grace and free will in the *Hyperaspistae* is corroborated by his scattered remarks on the subject in later works.

61. *Concio in ps. IV* (1525), LB, V, 257C: ". . . non ex operibus iustitiae quae fecimus nos, sed secundum misericordiam suam salvas nos fecit." See also the note on Luke 2:14 in *Nov. Test.* (1519), pt. 2, p. 122, and greatly expanded in 1527, pt. 2, pp. 155 f.; and in LB, VI, 231F-233F, where Erasmus argues that "good will" refers to God's gracious favor toward undeserving men and "peace" to the reconciliation of men with God as a result of his gracious will toward them.

62. *Concio in ps. IV,* LB, V, 283C. Cf. *Paraphr. in epist. Pauli ad Rom.* (1517), 3:22, LB, VII, 786E; 4:5, LB, VII, 788E.

63. *Paraphr. in evang. Marci* (1523), 2:12, LB, VII, 173EF.

64. *Resp. ad notata per N. Beddam* (1526), 5:2, LB, IX, 476CD.

65. *Elenchus in cens. erron. Beddae,* LB, IX, 498A: "Imo haeresis est dicere, quod homo suis operibus mereatur vitam aeternum *de condigno. De congruo* non sum loquutus." See also *ibid.,* 505C.

66. *Paraphr. in evang. Lucae* (1523), 24:27, LB, VII, 473A.

67. *Resp. ad notata per N. Beddam* (1526), LB, IX, 494B, and *Supput. errorum N. Beddae* (1527), LB, IX, 620E-621E. LB, VII, 473A: "Hanc cum auditis redimendam in iudicio, videtis sublatam legilium ceremoniarum fiduciam. Deus enim non iudicat ex operibus, sed ex fide: non ex cibo aut potu, non ex veste aut otio, sed ex animi pietate."

68. *Concio in ps. IV* (1525), LB, V, 265A; *Enarr. ps. XIV* (1536), LB, V, 293F. See also *Paraphr. in evang. Matt.* (1522), 5:3, LB, VII, 24A; *Paraphr. in evang. Marci* (1523), 2:12, LB, VII, 173F.

69. *Concio in ps. IV,* LB, V, 252D; *Eccles.* (1535), LB, V, 1079EF.

70. *Ratio* (1520), Holborn, 242, 25 ff., and LB, V, 108CD. See also note on Rom. 1:5, *Nov. Test.* (1516), pt. 2, p. 417, and LB, VI, 558D; *Paraphr. in evang. Lucae,* 5:3, LB, VII, 334E.

71. *Eccles.,* LB, V, 1078F-1079A. Cf. *Symbolum,* LB, V, 1144A.

72. *Enarr. in ps. II* (1522), LB, V, 227E.

73. *Enarr. ps. XIV* (1536), LB, V, 293F: *Eccles.,* LB, V, 1079B.

74. *Paraphr. in evang. Lucae,* 17:5, LB, VII, 418A.

75. *Ratio* (1520), Holborn, 242, 21, and LB, V, 108C; *Paraphr. in evang. Lucae,* 11:36, LB, VII, 385A.

76. *De amab. Eccl. conc.* (1533), LB, V, 489C, 500C.

77. *Symbolum,* LB, V, 1135BC; *Eccles.,* LB, V, 1079AB, 1080B.

78. *Enarr. ps. I* (1515), LB, V, 176D; *Enarr. ps. XIV,* LB, V, 303EF. Cf. *Symbolum,* LB, V, 1135B, and *Eccles.,* LB, V, 1078F.

79. Sometimes when he talks of the *fides quae,* Erasmus mentions only the content of Scripture, as in the passage from *Eccles.* referred to above, n. 71: ". . . certam persuasionem de iis quae narrant ac docent Scripturae sacrae." See also *Symbolum* (1533), LB, V, 1135D. Sometimes he mentions only tradition which is grounded in Scripture: ". . . sed quod e Scripturis divinis tradidit nobis Ecclesia Catholica firma fide teneamus . . ." *De amab. Eccl. conc.* (1533), LB, V, 497C. Near

the end of the *Symbolum,* after having summarized what is essential for all to believe, Erasmus mentions that the *Erudite* must hold all "... quae sacris Voluminibus expressa sunt, aut quae illinc evidenter colliguntur: praeterea quidquid universali perpetuoque consensu comprobavit Ecclesia Catholica ..." LB, V, 1179B. From our previous discussion of the problem of dogma it is clear that Scripture, or what the Church evidently draws from Scripture, e.g., the Apostles' Creed, is the primary content of faith, but that the content of faith includes also, at least for the learned and advanced, whatever the Church with universal consensus approves.

80. *Vidua Christ.* (1529), LB, V, 744C. See also *Symbolum,* LB, V, 1179C: "... in contentiosis autem et obscuris dogmatibus, tui similibus suffecerit hac cautione profiteri, de his credo sicuti credit Ecclesia. Hoc tutius quam asseverare, de quo dubites, aut quod non intelligas." That this thought is, however, not new to Erasmus in his old age is indicated by this passage from a work written in 1515, *Enarr. ps. I,* LB, V, 177A: "Felix igitur, qui semper constitit in Christo, semper adhaesit divinae Scripturae testimoniis, *semper Ecclesiae decretis* assensus est." (My italics.)

The first quotation maintains more a *fides implicita,* a general belief in whatever the Church believes; the second, more a *fides explicita,* a conscious assent to concrete testimonies of Scripture and decrees of the Church. On this distinction in late medieval thought see Oberman, *Harvest,* pp. 82 ff., 468 f., and Seeberg, *DG,* III, 725 f. Whether Erasmus actually had in mind these distinctions, however, is doubtful. I never find him using these terms.

81. *Paraphr. in evang. Ioannis* (1523), 6:44, LB, VII, 548D; *Enarr. in ps. XXXIII* (1530), LB, V, 394D. See also *Hyper. II* (1527), LB, X, 1511B, 1526B.

82. LB, IX, 1227D.

83. LB, X, 1413DE.

84. *Paraphr. in epist. Pauli ad Col.* (1520), 1:10-11, LB, VII, 1006C.

85. *De lib. arb.* (1524), LB, IX, 1243D: "Nec admodum digladiabor cum his, qui ad fidem velut ad fontem caputque referunt omnia, etiamsi mihi fides ex charitate, charitas ex fide vicissim nasci alique videtur: certe charitas alit fidem, quemadmodum in lucerna lumen alitur oleo." See also *Eccles.* (1535), LB, V, 1080BC, and *Symbolum* (1533), LB, V, 1181AB.

86. *Concio in ps. IV* (1525), LB, V, 283D: "... non satis est vacare culpa, nisi succedant fructus bonorum operum, quae fides per dilectionem operatur..." Cf. *De amab. Eccl. conc.* (1533), LB, V, 500CD. The interpretation of Telle is therefore to be rejected that Erasmian spiritualism meant the disapproval not only of ceremonial but also of moral works insofar as they are tangible expressions of charity. *Érasme*

de Rotterdam et le septième sacrement, pp. 27-28. The texts cited by Telle —Allen, I, 181, 46-52, and *Enchiridion,* LB, V, 37C-D—do not support his conclusion. *Ibid.,* p. 28, n. 15. In fact, I find no texts which support the contention that Erasmus, however much he may have emphasized the inner and spiritual vis-à-vis the outward and physical in religion, intended to deny the necessity of good works, i.e., tangible expressions of love to the neighbor.

87. *Paraphr. in evang. Matt.* (1522), 3:12, LB, VII, 16B. See also *Paraphr. in evang. Lucae* (1523), 3:11, LB, VII, 312A.

88. *Paraphr. in evang. Matt.,* 5:7, LB, VII, 25C.

89. *Paraphr. in evang. Matt.,* 6:14, LB, VII, 38A. See also *Prec. Dom.* (1523), LB, V, 1226A.

90. *Enarr. in ps. XXXVIII* (1532), LB, V, 447A.

91. *Ratio* (1520), Holborn, 235, 4 ff., and LB, V, 104C: ". . . tanto alacriores ingrediemur hoc stadium, ab eodem et cursus initium et *progressum* et exitum felicem exspectantes." *Paraphr. in epist. Pauli ad Rom.* (1517), 6:3, LB, VII, 795B: ". . . iam novam agentes vitam, versemur in pietatis vestigiis, *semper ab honestis ad honestiora progedientes."* (My italics.)

92. *Paraphr. in epist. Pauli ad Cor. I* (1519), 13:11, LB, VII, 901D; *Expos. concion. in ps. LXXXV* (1528), LB, V, 527F.

93. *Paraphr. in evang. Lucae,* 2:52, LB, VII, 308F.

94. LB, V, 28C; tr. Himelick, p. 103.

95. *Ratio* (1519), Holborn, 253, 12 ff., and LB, V, 113E: ". . . in factis, non verbis: in affectu, non cultu: in obedientia, non cerimoniis sitam esse veram pietatem . . ." This, of course, was a prominent thought of the *Devotio Moderna.* Cf. *Imitatio Christi,* I, 11, *Opera* II, p. 19, ll. 23 ff., and Mestwerdt, pp. 86 f.

96. *Enarr. ps. XIV* (1536), LB, V, 308D.

97. *Eccles.* (1535), LB, V, 784C.

98. *Enchiridion* (1503), LB, V, 32E: ". . . saepius mihi testandum est, me nequaquam taxare corporales cerimonias Christianorum, et studia simplicium, praesertim ea quae Ecclesiastica comprobavit auctoritas: sunt enim nonnumquam tum indicia, tum adminicula pietatis . . ." See also *Ratio* (1520), Holborn, 252, 4 ff., LB, V, 113AB: " 'Quid igitur,' inquiet aliquis, 'damnas cerimonias?' Absit. Laudo ritus, quibus et olim et hodie chorus ecclesiasticus peragit sua mysteria. Repraesentant aliquid, et addunt maiestatem cultui divino; quamquam in his quoque modus esse debet." See also *Paraphr. in epist. Iac.* (1520), 1:26, LB, VII, 1124EF; and *Apol. ad blasph. Iac. Stunicae* (1522), LB, IX, 368D.

99. *Enarr. in ps. II* (1522), LB, V, 209F: "Habet et nostrum quisque suam quamdam infantiam in Christo. Habet et Ecclesia suas quasdam cerimonias, quibus fovet aetatem imbecillem, donec robur colligat

augescens in fide et caritate Evangelica. Tolerat Deus ad tempus car-
nales, si paulatim extenuentur in spiritum, at non tolerat in aeternum.
Portentum est infantia perpetua." *Concio in ps. IV* (1525), LB, V, 270F.

100. *Resp. ad notata per N. Beddam* (1526), LB, IX, 473A.

101. *Enchiridion,* LB, V, 32E. Cf. *ibid.,* 37BC, and 'Ιχθνοφαγία
(1526), LB, I, 799F.

102. *Resp. ad notata per N. Beddam,* LB, IX, 473A.

103. This was an important theme in the Church Fathers and the
Devotio Moderna. On the patristic background see especially Adolf von
Harnack, *Militia Christi: Die christliche Religion und der Soldatenstand in den
ersten drei Jahrhunderten,* 1905. As representative of the *Devotio Moderna*
see *Imitatio Christi,* I, 11, and III, 6, 47, 56. See below the reference to
Origen as the background for Erasmus' treatment of baptism as the
beginning of this spiritual struggle, Ch. IX, n. 74.

104. LB, V, 1251C-E, 1253D. See Kohls, II, pp. 30-31, n. 27.

105. *Enchiridion,* LB, V, 10A, 54EF; *Symbolum* (1533), LB, V,
1160EF; *De praep. ad mort.* (1534), LB, V, 1312F-1313A, EF. Cf. *Imitatio
Christi,* I, 25; II, 1.

106. The themes of *contemplatio* and *imitatio* are joined together in
the following passages: *Paraphr. in evang. Lucae* (1523), 23:34, LB, VII,
462D: "Nos vero ne dimoveamus oculos nostros ab hoc exemplo, et
imitemur Regem nostrum in cruce debellantem omnem potestatem
tyranni Satanae . . ." *Expos. concion. in ps. LXXXV* (1528), LB, V, 530AB.

107. *Eccles.* (1535), LB, V, 1024B.

108. *Expos. concion. in ps. LXXXV,* LB, V, 518B. See also *Supput.
errorum N. Beddae* (1527), LB, IX, 667D, and *De praep. ad mort.* (1534),
LB, V, 1298B.

109. *Paraphr. in epist. Pauli ad Eph.* (1520), 4:13, LB, VII, 982C.

110. LB, V, 23C; tr. Himelick, p. 90. (My italics.)

111. LB, V, 1171AB.

112. *Enchiridion,* LB, V, 17F, and *De praep. ad mort.,* LB, V, 1301EF.

113. See *Expos. concion. in ps. LXXXV,* LB, V, 516E, and *Enarr. ps. XIV*
(1536), LB, V, 298BC, on Christ's unique perfection.

114. LB, V, 16C; tr. Himelick, p. 71.

115. *De praep. ad mort.,* LB, V, 1297AB.

116. *Ratio* (1519), Holborn, 195, 20 ff., LB, V, 85A. Cf. *Eccles.*
(1535), LB, V, 1024AB.

117. *Paraphr. in evang. Matt.* (1522), 5:33-37, LB, VII, 33A-D. Erasmus defends this paraphrase in a lengthy response to a censure of the
Paris faculty of theology, *Declar. ad cens.* (1532), LB, IX, 834D-837F.

118. *Vidua Christ.* (1529), LB, V, 733E; see also n. 116 above.

119. *Declar. ad cens.,* LB, IX, 837EF, 838A.

120. *Paraphr. in epist. Pauli ad Cor. I* (1519), 15:44, LB, VII, 910DE.

121. *Expos. concion. in ps. LXXXV* (1528), LB, V, 519BC: "At perfec-

tus non ero, nisi totum servaris, totum restituas in resurrectione. . . .
Prior erat animae cura, quia potior hominis pars est: nunc corpus
etiam, quod fuit quasi socius ac minister laboris, vult esse consors
gloriae."

122. The *meditatio vitae futurae* was a prominent theme in Erasmus'
writings from the *De contemptu mundi* (written c. 1486) to the *De praep.
ad mort.* (1534). I cite only this summarizing statement in the latter
work: "Atque haec est magna Christianae Philosophiae pars, quae nos
morti praeparat, ut contemplatione rerum aeternarum ac coelestium,
discamus temporariarum ac terrenarum contemtum." LB, V, 1295D.
See also *Concio de puero Iesu* (1514), LB, V, 605A; *De amab. Eccl. conc.*
(1533), LB, V, 485F, 496F; *Symbolum* (1533), LB, V, 1185A.

123. *De contemptu mundi*, LB, V, 1255B; *Enchiridion* (1503), LB, V,
3EF, 22B; *Concio de puero Iesu*, LB, V, 607CD.

124. *De contemptu mundi*, LB, V, 1257C: ". . . tota vitae nostrae ratio
Epicurea est"; *Epicureus* (1533), LB, I, 882D: "Quod si de veris loqua-
mur, nulli magis Epicurei quam Christiani pie viventes." Cf. *Concio de
puero Iesu*, LB, V, 607F, 608C; *Enarr. ps. I* (1515), LB, V, 191EF. See
Mestwerdt, p. 234, who alleges Valla's influence upon Erasmus at this
point. Cf. Kohls (I, 26, and II, 48-49, n. 93), who denies any material
influence of Valla on Erasmus here. Kohls maintains that Valla's conception of a *voluptas* of *natura* in his dialogue *De voluptate ac de vero bono*,
which was set over against a Stoic and monastic asceticism, was transformed by Erasmus in a religious-ethical, eschatological direction. On
Valla's central intention in his treatise see Eugenio Garin, *Italian Humanism*, tr. Peter Munz (New York, 1965), pp. 50 ff. But this was also
a thought of the *Devotio Moderna*. Cf. *Imitatio Christi*, I, 20; II, 6.

125. E. Troeltsch, "Die christliche Religion," in *Kultur der Gegen-
wart*, 1, 4, ed. P. Hinneberg, 1906, pp. 473 ff.; W. Köhler, "Neuere
Kirchengeschichte" in *Theologische Rundschau*, 1909, pp. 214 ff., cited by
Ernst, "Die Frömmigkeit des Erasmus," p. 49.

126. M. Schulze, *Calvins Jenseitschristentum in seinem Verhältnis zu den
religiösen Schriften des Erasmus* (Görlitz, 1902). See on this debate Ernst,
pp. 49 f., and Hermelink, *Die religiösen Reformbestrebungen des deutschen
Humanismus*, pp. 20, 31.

127. *De praep. ad mort.* (1534), LB, V, 1308F.

CHAPTER VI

THE SACRAMENTS IN GENERAL

1. LB, V, 1175D. See also *Responsio ad annotationem Stunicae ex Cap.
V ad Ephesios a Sanctio Caranza defensam* (1522), LB, IX, 429C. In classical
usage *sacramentum* had at first to do with the money which was deposited at the temple treasury by the losing party in a suit and which was
dedicated to the divinity and used for religious purposes. It also desig-

nated in military language the oath of allegiance made by recruits upon entrance into military service. But, as Erasmus seems to know, in either case, whether the deposit at the *aerarium* or the military oath, the action takes place before the god so that the money deposited or the person bound by oath is *res aut persona consecrata.* Charlton T. Lewis and Charles Short, *A Latin Dictionary* (Oxford, 1958), pp. 1611 f.

Tertullian, the shaper of the theological vocabulary of the Christian West, was the first to apply the term *sacramentum* to what the Greeks called μυστήριον, although prior to him there was already a period of assimilation of the two terms. Émile de Backer, "Tertullien," in *Pour l'histoire du mot "sacramentum" I. les anténicéens,* ed. J. de Ghellinck *et al.* (Louvain, 1924), pp. 145 ff.

2. LB, V, 1175EF.

3. *Ad notat. Ed. Lei in epist. ad Eph.,* 5:32 (1520), LB, IX, 227C. Erasmus admits that he is simply bringing forth the definition of Peter Lombard's *Sentences,* IV d 1 cap. 4. He recites this definition of Lombard again to Stunica, *Apol. ad prodromon ad Iac. Stunicae* (1522), LB, IX, 376E.

4. *Apol. ad Iac. Stunicam* (1521), LB, IX, 338D. Cf. *Apol. ad prodr. Iac. Stunicae,* LB, IX, 375F-376A: ". . . hanc vocem *Sacramentum* in Theologorum libris bifariam accipi, nonnunquam ut sit sacrae rei signum, nonnunquam ut sit signum sacrum visibilibus formis constans, sed quod invisibilem ac peculiarem gratiam gignat in nobis, velut ex pacto divino"; and *Apol. ad concl. Iac. Stunicae* (1524), LB, IX, 390B: ". . . per signa sacramentalia ex pacto infundatur gratia sacramentalis."

5. Erasmus can say, as in the quotations from the *Symbolum* and from the *Apol. ad concl. Iac. Stunicae* (preceding note), that grace is infused *through* the sacramental signs, but that is not his characteristic thought. In any case, the words do not carry a Thomistic sense, as is clear by the qualification in *Apol. ad concl. Iac. Stunicae,* "ex pacto." Erasmus' aversion to definition shows itself in a typical lack of consistent expression.

6. Thomas held that the primary cause was God and the instrumental cause was the sacraments, which were more than mere signs, since a divine power resides in them. Seeberg, *DG,* III, 510. *Summa* III, 62, 1c, and III, 62, 4c; cited by F. Loofs, *Leitfaden zum Studien der Dogmengeschichte,* ed. K. Aland (Tübingen, 1959), p. 471, n. 3.

7. Bonaventure, IV *Sent.* d 1 a 1 q 3. "Causalitas sacramentorum non est aliud, quam quaedam efficax ordinatio ad recipiendam gratiam ex pactione divina"; and *ibid.,* d 1 a 1 q 5; cited by Loofs, p. 471 and n. 2. Cf. Duns Scotus, IV *Report.* d 2 q 1, 2, and IV *Sent.* d 14 q 4, 6; cited by Seeberg, *DG,* III, 511. On Duns Scotus' understanding of the causality of sacraments and the relation of the sign to the thing signified, see further R. Seeberg, *Die Theologie des Duns Scotus* (Leipzig, 1900), pp. 345 ff. For similar thoughts on this subject in post-Scotistic

scholasticism as represented by Aureolus, Durandus, and Occam, see Karl Werner, *Die Scholastik des späteren Mittelalters, Die nachscotistische Scholastik* (Vienna, 1883, r.p. 1960), II, 381, 384, 387.

8. LB, X, 1447E: "Erit igitur et incerta vis sacramentorum. Et tamen hoc libere fit ad quod volens esse obstringit." Cf. Bonaventure, IV *Sent.* d 1 p 1 a 1 q 3: ". . . ex tali pactione dominus astrinxit se quodammodo ad dandam gratiam suscipienti sacramentum"; quoted and cited by Seeberg, *DG,* III, 511.

9. Somewhat at variance even with the Franciscan tradition, however, Erasmus did not think that God had necessarily limited himself to the bestowing of even sanctifying grace only through the sacraments. In the *Symbolum* (1533) Erasmus expresses the view that "Utrumque quum aliis modis, tum vero praecipue per Ecclesiae sacramenta suggerit gratia Dei." LB, V, 1140B. Erasmus does not at all explain his meaning here. But since he makes this statement in connection with the article in the Apostles' Creed on the forgiveness of sins and mentions shortly thereafter baptism and penance as the means for the reception of remission of sin (*ibid.*), it is probable that he had in mind not only assisting but sanctifying grace. His meaning is perhaps indicated by his thought (to be discussed later) that unbaptized infants of Christian parents may be saved through the parents' supplications by God's grace. (We shall note that he twice mentions this as Gerson's opinion. Actually Erasmus carries Gerson's words a step further, for this author speaks not of unbaptized infants but of unborn infants.) Such a sentence is also not surprising in view of Erasmus' warm regard for virtuous pagans like Socrates, Seneca, and Cicero. If they are not excluded from salvation, one must assume also in their case an extrasacramental grace. In the *Hyper. II* (1527), LB, X, 1529E, Erasmus says that the good deeds of virtuous pagans ". . . nec gignebant gratiam iustificantem, sed tamen reddebant animam gratiae capaciorem . . . Quod si quis haec quoque quae Gentes vel cognoverunt, vel praestiterunt, velit adscribere gratiae Dei, non refragabor, sic ut fateantur hominis liberum arbitrium per gratiam adiutum huc pervenisse, in quibus si profecissent, per eandem gratiam assequi poterant aeternam salutem." See Thompson, *Inquisitio de fide,* pp. 101 ff., for an excellent discussion of the Erasmian passages on this subject and of the variations among the patristic and medieval literary and scholastic authors. Cf. Hans Baron, "Erasmus-Probleme in Spiegel des Colloquium *Inquisitio de Fide,*" *ARG,* 43 (1952), 254-263, and Gebhardt, pp. 198 ff. In any case, Erasmus considered the sacraments as the chief means of grace and normally the *sine qua non* of salvation.

10. The Latin word for the Greek ἀρραβών meaning a "pledge" later returned, a "deposit" on the total debt, or "earnest money" ratifying a contract. Paul uses it figuratively in II Cor. 1:22 and 5:5 in

connection with the Spirit—τὸν ἀρραβῶνα τοῦ πνεύματος. See J. Behm, "ἀρραβών," in *Theologisches Wörterbuch zum Neuen Testament*, ed. G. Kittel (Stuttgart, 1933), I, 474.

11. LB, V, 620B.

12. *Nov. Test.* (1519), pt. 2, p. 464, and retained in LB, VI, 926E-927A.

13. This thought is not contained in the notes in the several editions of the *Nov. Test.* but is found in some of the apologies which defended the early notes of 1516 and 1519: *Resp. ad notat. novas Ed. Lei* (1520), LB, IX, 227C; *Apol. ad Iac. Stunicam*, LB, IX, 338D; *Apol. ad prodr. Iac. Stunicae* (1522), LB, IX, 376AB.

14. See below, Ch. VII, n. 44.

15. *Enarr. in ps. XXII* (1530), LB, V, 337C. Cf. note on John 1:31, *Nov. Test.* (1519), p. 169.

16. *Precatio Erasmi Roterdami ad Virginis Filium Iesum* (1498-1499), LB, V, 1211E: ". . . quot efficacibus sacramentis assidue de tuae sacrosanctae mortis fonte subscatentibus confirmavit." Cf. *Symbolum* (1533), LB, V, 1141A.

17. *Enarr. in ps. XXII*, LB, V, 337C and 339EF; *Symbolum*, LB, V, 1177D.

18. *Eccles.* (1535), LB, V, 820E-821A.

19. He likes to call attention to John 6:63: "Caro non prodest quidquam, spiritus est qui vivificat." *Enchiridion* (1503), LB, V, 30B.

20. *Enchiridion*, LB, V, 30D-32F, 37A-38B; *Conviv. relig.* (1522), LB, I, 683EF-684C. Cf. *Laus stult.* (1509), LB, IV, 502B-D, 504A.

21. LB, V, 65C.

22. *Apol. adv. mon. Hisp.* (1528), LB, IX, 1070A.

23. LB, I, 683EF; tr. Thompson, *Colloquies*, p. 68. It is clear from his manner of writing that Erasmus makes no sharp distinction here between ceremonies and sacraments. He includes sacraments among ceremonies. "Ch. Nec mirum, eos sic mori, qui per omnem vitam tantum philosophati sunt in caerimoniis. Neph. Quid isthuc verbi est? Ch. Dicam, sed illud etiam atque etiam praefatus, me non damnare, imo vehementer probare sacramenta et ritus Ecclesiae; sed quosdam vel improbos vel superstitiosos, vel, ut mollissime dicam, simplices et indoctos, qui docent populum hisce rebus fidere, praetermissis his quae nos vere reddunt Christianos. Neph. Nondum satis intelligo quorsum eas. Ch. Faxo ut intelligas. Si vulgus Christianorum spectes, nonne prora et puppis vitae illis in caerimoniis est? In baptismo quanta religione repraesentantur prisci ritus Ecclesiae?"

24. *Declar. ad cens. colloq.* (1532), LB, IX, 935D-936A.

25. *Des hochgelerten Erasmi von Roterdam unnd Doctor Martin Luthers maynung vom Nachtmal unnsers herren Ihesu Christi*, by Leo Jud; Allen, VI, Intro., and 1737, n. 1. This work and Erasmus' reply will concern us

in greater detail when we consider Erasmus' understanding of the Eucharist.

26. *Detectio praestig.* (1526), LB, X, 1562AB. See the entire passage, 1562A-1563A.

27. *Detectio praestig.*, LB, X, 1562E: "Imo ne quis suspicaretur a me damnari quod est in sacramentis aut exercitamentis pietatis visibile, nominatim his verbis admoneo lectorem: *Quod carnem pietatis amplectuntur laudo, quod illic consistunt non laudo.* Rursus aliquanto post: *Non damnantur opera corporalia, sed praeferuntur invisibilia. Non damnatur cultus visibilis,* sed non placatur Deus nisi pietate invisibili." LB, V, 31B and 37C.

28. For ready documentation I list the following references in their order of date, most of which I have already given: *Enchiridion* (1503), LB, V, 30B-31C, 32EF, 37BC; *Laus stult.* (1509), LB, IV, 502B-D, 504A; *Sileni Alcibiadis* (1515), LB, II, 773C; *Conviv. relig.* (1522), LB, I, 683E-684C; *Detectio praestig.* (1526), LB, X, 1562A-1563A; *Apol. adv. mon. Hisp.* (1528), LB, IX, 1069EF; *Enarr. in ps. XXII* (1530), LB, V, 340A; *Declar. ad cens. colloq.* (1532), LB, IX, 935EF-936AB.

29. LB, V, 1358DE. Noted by J. Lupton in *Ioannis Coleti opus de Sacramentis Ecclesiae,* tr. and ed. J. Lupton (London, 1867), p. 23. According to Lupton, the exact date of Colet's catechism is unknown, but it was probably composed shortly after the founding of St. Paul's School in 1509. J. Lupton, *Life of Dean Colet,* p. 177. Lupton gives this catechism of Colet as Appendix B in the latter book. See Colet's description of the sacraments on p. 287. See Padberg, pp. 54 ff., for a brief comparison of Colet's *Catechyzon* and Erasmus' *Christiani hominis institutum* on the sacraments.

30. LB, V, 1175F.

CHAPTER VII

ORDERS AND MARRIAGE

1. *Enarr. ps. II* (1522), LB, V, 206B; *Modus orandi* (1524), LB, V, 1130F, 1131CD.

2. LB, V, 1131CD; *Symbolum* (1533), LB, V, 1176AB; *Apol. adv. mon. Hisp.* (1528), 1067F-1068A. On orders, cf. Gebhardt, pp. 243 ff., who places too much emphasis on the *potestas iurisdictionis* in Erasmus' thought on the subject. See especially pp. 251 and 254 ff.

3. *Christiani hominis institutum* (1514), LB, V, 1358D; *Symbolum,* LB, V, 1176A.

4. To Paul Volz, 14 August 1518, Allen, III, 858, 233 ff.; *Ratio* (1519), Holborn, 202, 7 ff., and LB, V, 88CD. We have already seen that Erasmus does not place the Pope at the head of this hierarchy by divine right. He is rather *primus inter pares de iure humano.* On the highest standing of bishops within the ecclesiastical hierarchy, see

Eccles. (1535), LB, V, 801C, and Gebhardt, pp. 263 ff.

5. LB, V, 49AB; tr. Himelick, pp. 155 f.

6. *Sileni Alcibiadis* (1515), LB, II, 775EF. Cf. LB, II, 778C, and To Paul Volz, 14 August 1518, Allen, III, 858, 352-360.

7. Note on Luke 10:16, *Nov. Test.* (1519), pt. 2, p. 139, and in LB, VI, 273EF. Cf. To Paul Volz, 14 August 1518, Allen, III, 858, 592-598; and *Eccles.* (1535), LB, V, 824D.

8. LB, V, 820EF.

9. LB, VII, 215B.

10. Ἰχθυοφαγία (1526), LB, I, 803F-804A; tr. Thompson, *Colloquies*, p. 347. In the letter to Paul Volz, Erasmus satirizes those who think it is the greatest crime for a priest who has touched the body of a prostitute to handle the body of Christ, but who are not likewise shocked at the administration of the sacred mysteries by those who are totally worldly. Allen, III, 858, 420 ff.

11. To Balthasar Mercklin, 15 March 1530, Allen, VIII, 2284, 147-148.

12. *Eccles.* (1535), LB, V, 831CD.

13. Note on I Tim. 3:2, *Nov. Test.* (1516), pt. 2, p. 567, and in LB, VI, 934DE; *Enarr. ps. I* (1515), LB, V, 188E; Ἰχθυοφαγία (1526), LB, I, 804B.

14. *Enarr. ps. I*, LB, V, 189; note on I Tim. 3:2, *Nov. Test.* (1527), pt. 2, p. 601, and in LB, VI, 934E; *Eccles.*, LB, V, 802D.

15. *Supput. errorum N. Beddae* (1527), LB, IX, 581B: "At Episcoporum est, quod quidem in ipsis est, docere, corrigere, mederi. Qualis autem est Episcopus, qui nihil aliud possit quam vincire, torquere, flammis tradere?" Cf. *Eccles.*, LB, V, 822A, and *Paraphr. in epist. Pauli ad Titum* (1520), LB, VII, 1069AB.

16. *Enarr. ps. I*, LB, V, 188E.

17. *Paraphr. in epist. Pauli I ad Tim.* (1520), 3:2-3, LB, VII, 1043DE, 1044B.

18. *Eccles.*, LB, V, 817D.

19. Ἰχθυοφαγία (1526), LB, I, 807EF-808AB; *Laus stult.* (1509), LB, IV, 485; To Paul Volz, 14 August 1518, Allen, III, 858, 352-353; note on I Peter 5:3, *Nov. Test.* (1519), pt. 2, p. 533, and LB, VI, 1055C.

20. *Eccles.* (1535), LB, V, 808E-809D. *Epistola apologetica* (1522), LB, IX, 1201DE.

21. Note on I Tim. 3:4, *Nov. Test.* (1519), pt. 2, p. 469, and LB, VI, 934BC; note on I Cor. 7:1, *Nov. Test.* (1519), pt. 2, p. 321, and LB, VI, 685F; *Encomium matrimonii* (1518), LB, I, 419E; *Epistola apologetica*, LB, IX, 1201AB. On the degenerate condition of clerical celibacy in the fifteenth century and proposals of marriage as a remedy, see H. C. Lea, *A History of Sacerdotal Celibacy*, 3rd rev. ed., Vol. II (London, 1907), pp. 1 ff., 26 ff. Cf. Telle, pp. 189 ff., n. 1. As Telle points out, in the *Encomium matrimonii* Erasmus suggests marriage even to monks who

find it impossible to be continent. Telle, p. 192. Telle, who is impressed—indeed overly impressed—with Erasmus' antimonasticism, thinks the question of sacerdotal celibacy is quite secondary to monastic celibacy in Erasmus. See pp. 190 ff.

22. To Paul Volz, 14 August 1518, Allen, III, 858, 415 ff. While Erasmus does not favor the incontinence of priests (Allen, III, 858, 425), nevertheless he recognizes sexual desire as natural and not evil.

23. *Epistola apologetica* (1522), LB, IX, 1201C. He does not accept the traditional interpretation of I Timothy 3:2, that "one wife" in the phrase "It is necessary for a bishop . . . to be married to one wife" refers to "one Church." See note on I Tim. 3:2, *Nov. Test.* (1519), pt. 2, p. 469, and in LB, VI, 933F.

24. *Epistola apologetica,* LB, IX, 1201EF. Telle thinks Erasmus only feigns his wish for a truly celibate clergy here since it is Telle's thesis that Erasmus entirely opposes celibacy, whether sacerdotal or monastic. Telle, p. 197. In spite of Telle's claims, however, it is not so clear that Erasmus wholly repudiated sacerdotal and monastic celibacy.

25. It was published with the *Querela pacis* in 1518. Beginning in 1522, it appeared as chapter 47 of the *De conscribendis epistolis* as an example of an *epistola suasoria.* See Allen, III, p. 17, n. 10, and Telle, p. 156. It appears as a part of this latter work in LB, I, 414E-424C.

26. LB, I, 415BC-416E, 417D. Some of these arguments in praise of marriage are quite old. N. Paulus in his short but substantial article "Mittelalterliche Stimmen über den Eheorden," in *Historisch-politische Blätter für das katholische Deutschland,* CXL (Munich, 1908), p. 1012, points especially to William Perauld, a French Dominican in the thirteenth century who set forth these arguments for the high dignity of marriage: The order of marriage was established by God, while the other orders were established by men; in the holiest place on earth, Paradise; before all the other orders; and while man was still in the state of innocence. It was maintained by God during the flood. The Mother of God wished to enter into this order. Christ honored it at the wedding feast of Cana, where Jesus performed his first miracle. The Church blesses it; from marriage children are born who then become children of God in Christian baptism. Marriage is one of the seven sacraments. It permits acts which outside of marriage would be mortal sins. See for similar arguments by a contemporary of Perauld, Robert of Sorbon, Paulus, p. 1013, and G. Le Bras, "La doctrine du mariage chez les théologiens et les canonistes depuis l'an mille," in *DTC,* IX², 2181. According to these scholars, although virginity was always regarded as the higher state, there were many preachers and writers, especially in the late Middle Ages, who granted to marriage a very lofty rank.

27. LB, I, 418B.

28. *Ibid.*, 419B-D. Cf. note on I Cor. 7:39, *Nov. Test.* (1519), pt. 2, p. 326, and in LB, VI, 695D: "Christus virginitatem non exigit, ne videatur cum natura pugnare, licet beatos pronunciet, quo hoc possint capere, sed addit, *propter regnum Dei.* Regnum autem Dei vocat Evangelii praedicationem, ut hoc ipsum ad ea tempora magis pertineat"; *Paraphr. in evang. Matt.* (1522), 19:11, LB, VII, 103F-104A.

29. On Mountjoy's actual state when Erasmus wrote this oration, see Allen, I, 79, Intro. Allen does not think that Mountjoy was necessarily single when Erasmus wrote the *Encomium.* On the basis of a reference to "novis nuptiis" in Ep. 117.7, he thinks that it is "likely that though the marriage ceremony took place in 1497, Mountjoy may not have received her as his wife till his return to England in 1499." Cf. also A. Hyma, "Erasmus and the Sacrament of Matrimony," *ARG,* 48 (1957), p. 161, n. 42.

30. Cf. *Paraphr. in epist. Pauli ad Cor. I,* 7:7, LB, VII, 879C: "Eximia quadam res est perpetua castitas, ob Christi negotium suscepta"; *Vidua Christ.,* LB, V, 733F-743F. Notice that in this work, however, Erasmus follows the tradition in granting virginity the first rank of dignity, if it is spontaneous; to widowhood, the second; and to marriage, the third. LB, V, 734C-E. However, although virginity is more honored, marriage is safer. He also bestows the first praise on the widow who abstains from a second marriage for devotion to Christ; the second praise on the widow who does so for love of her children; and the third praise to those who decide on remarriage because of weakness of the flesh. LB, V, 763A-C.

31. LB, I, 419D-420A, 423C.

32. Cf. *Paraphr. in epist. Pauli ad Cor. I* (1519), 7:1, LB, VII, 878C; *Christiani matrimonii institutio* (1526), LB, V, 698AB; *Vidua Christ.* (1529), 741B, 744B.

33. *Apologia pro declamatione matrimonii* (1519), LB, IX, 107F-108F.

34. See especially *Christiani matrimonii institutio,* LB, V, 615 ff., 628, and above, nn. 28, 30, and 32. See Telle, pp. 233 ff., 293 ff., 423 ff.

35. See *Vidua Christ.,* LB, V, 733 AB, E: "Vestis quae tangit corpus, non inquinat animum, nisi tangat animum, quemadmodum cibus non polluit animum, si tantum corpus tangat. Animus autem contingi non potest, nisi accedat affectus. . . . Sileant linguae in hoc tantum disertae, ut virtutis studium ad paucitatem relegent, nec aetas, nec sexus, nec conditio, nec status, nec fortuna, nec locus, nec vitae genus obstat, quo minus pie vivamus in Christo Iesu, qui nec hic est, nec illic, sed intra nos est, et ubicumque ille est, ibi est regnum Dei."

36. *Christiani matrimonii institutio* (1526), LB, V, 615C, 616AB. Though Erasmus sees procreation as the chief end of marriage, he sees as a secondary end the remedy for incontinence, a weakness of nature. LB, V, 697D, 698A. Erasmus breaks with the Augustinian tradi-

tion in regarding the sex drive as a matter of natural necessity, not of concupiscence, although perverse desire may attend the sexual act. See LB, V, 698A. Ever since Augustine the tradition had seen these as the primary and secondary ends of marriage. For Augustine, however, conjugal relations for the prevention of incontinence were only a concession. They are really intended by God and by nature only for procreation. Sexual activity even in marriage apart from this end proceeds from "pravi mores," but is, of course, preferable to illicit behavior. Intercourse for the sake of begetting has no fault, but if it is undertaken to satisfy concupiscence, it is a venial fault. Adultery or fornication is a mortal fault. *De bono coniugali*, 6, in *PL*, XL, 377-378. In the early scholastic period, in the twelfth and even in the early thirteenth century, many expressed the view that the marriage act could not take place without venial sin. In the early thirteenth century a reaction set in to this severe judgment. A number of theologians such as Hugh of St. Cher held that not every marital act is sinful, indeed that some may be meritorious. Thomas, on the basis of greater optimism concerning the powers of nature, held also that the conjugal act for the sake of procreation was not sinful; indeed, that it was meritorious. He nevertheless continued to hold with Augustine that "Si autem moveat libido sistens infra bona matrimonii, ut scilicet nullo modo ad aliam accedere vellet, est peccatum veniale." *Summa theol. suppl.* q 41 a 4. See Le Bras, cls. 2177, 2178. Erasmus does not suggest that it is even a venial sin for intercourse to take place as a remedy for incontinence. He advises only that intercourse be moderate and controlled, as much as necessity demands but not more than necessity demands. LB, V, 698A.

37. *Christiani matrimonii institutio* (1526), LB, V, 622B. Cf. *Symbolum* (1533), LB, V, 1175F; *Christiani hominis institutum* (1514), LB, V, 1358D.

38. *Nov. Test.* (1516), pt. 2, p. 92.

39. *De bono coniugali*. Augustine does use the term "sacramentum" to refer to the third good of marriage: *proles, fides, sacramentum. De bono coniugali*, 32, in *PL*, XL, 394. However, *sacramentum* is certainly not used in the later sense, but has to do with the indissolubility of marriage, as is clear in another passage where he talks about these three goods, *De nuptiis et concupiscentia*, I, 13, in *PL*, XLIV, 421: "Prolem cognoscimus ipsum Dominum Iesum: fidem, quia nullum adulterium: sacramentum, quia nullum divortium." It is, however, also clear that he thinks this indissoluble union is an image of the permanent union between Christ and his Church as in the passage in the following note. See L. Godefroy, "Mariage dans les pères," in *DTC*, IX², 2107-2108.

40. *De nuptiis et concupiscentia*, I, 23, in *PL*, XLIV, 427.

41. *Nov. Test.* (1519), pt. 2, p. 428. Erasmus was not the only Roman

Catholic theologian in the sixteenth century who thought that the sacrament of marriage could not be based on this passage. Cardinal Cajetan was of the same opinion. See Le Bras, cl. 2230. The Council of Trent said that Paul only insinuated (*insinuit*) the sacrament of marriage in this passage. Denzinger, 969 (1799).

42. *Nov. Test.* (1522), pt. 2, p. 486.

43. *Resp. ad notat. Ed. Lei* (1520), LB, IX, 225A, C, 226E, 227C; *Apol. ad Iac. Stunicam* (1521), LB, IX, 338D; *Apol. ad prodr. Iac. Stunicae* (1522), LB, IX, 376A; *Resp. ad annotat. Iac. Stunicae ex cap. V. ad Eph. a Sanctio Caranza Defensam,* LB, IX, 429A, D.

44. LB, IX, 226AB. Cf. *ibid.,* 228D: "Quod si quis me roget, Unde igitur credis esse de numero septem, si ex hoc loco colligi satis non potest, nec superest alius unde colligatur? in promtu est quod respondeam, Me movet auctoritas et consensus Ecclesiae, sed non hac in re tantum, verum in aliis quoque compluribus."

45. *Resp. ad notat. Ed. Lei,* LB, IX, 227CD. Here Erasmus is somewhat vague in his description of Lombard's opinion. He says that on the basis of the definition of sacrament which Lombard gives in IV *Sent.* d 1 ("Sacramentum enim proprie dicitur, quod ita signum est gratiae Dei, et invisibilis gratiae forma, ut ipsius imaginem gerat et causa exsistat" [in *PL,* series secunda, I, 329]) and the fact that in IV *Sent.* d 2 he expresses the opinion that marriage does not confer grace, the Master of the Sentences must not have regarded marriage as a sacrament in the special sense of the word. In the *Apol. ad prodr. Iac. Stunicae,* LB, IX, 376A-F, Erasmus is more specific concerning what he means when he was attacked by Stunica for misinterpreting Lombard. He recites exactly Lombard's opinion in IV *Sent.* d 2 (*PL,* series secunda, I, 332), where Lombard states: "Quorum alia remedia contra peccatum praebent et gratiam adiutricem conferunt, ut Baptismus, alia in remedium tantum sunt, ut Coniugium, alia gratia et virtute nos fulciunt, ut Eucharistia et Ordo." LB, IX, 376E. He then maintains that if the definition which Lombard gives in the first distinction (he repeats that definition) applies to marriage, then that contradicts what he says here in the second distinction, that marriage ". . . tantum esse in remedium, hoc est, non conferri gratiam, neque adversus peccatum, neque confirmantem ad profectum pietatis. Si non competit, sequitur matrimonium iuxta exactam sacramentorum rationem non esse sacramentum." I fail to understand on what basis Telle can say that in his recitation of Lombard's view Erasmus ". . . révélait son incompréhension de la théologie scolastique et son parti pris de ne pas bien lire Lombard." Telle, p. 290.

46. IV *Sent.* d 26 q 3. Erasmus is correct in his judgment concerning Durandus, who is the major representative of a theological point of view in the early fourteenth century which opposed the position

which had by that time largely taken hold—namely, that grace is conferred in marriage as in the other sacraments. He was impressed by the view of the canonists which denied that grace was conferred in marriage largely because of the role of money in the establishment of marriages. Le Bras, cl. 2213. See on the denial of grace in this sacrament this author's discussion in cl. 2208. He says further that "L'opinion des canonistes devait se maintenir jusqu'à la fin du Moyen Âge." Not only the canonists but also the majority of the early scholastic theologians saw marriage as a sacrament only in the larger sense of the word, as a sign of a sacred thing. They attributed to it exclusively a medicinal function *in remedium.* Peter Lombard is merely the most illustrious example of most early scholastics who, though accepting marriage as one of the seven sacraments, did not think of it as conferring grace like the others. According to Le Bras, Abelard was the only one who denied that marriage was at all a sacrament, whereas there were two important twelfth-century figures who regarded it as a sacrament even in the special sense of the word as conferring grace, Hugh of St. Victor and Anselm of Laon. *Ibid.,* cls. 2148, 2209. Even in the thirteenth century there were important hesitations, such as those of Hugh of St. Cher and Bonaventure. Bonaventure thinks only that "aliquid gratiae donum" is conferred on those who receive it worthily. IV *Sent.* d 26 a 2 q 2 concl.; cited by Le Bras, cl. 2210. He also makes the bestowal of grace dependent upon the nuptial, priestly blessing rather than upon the power of the sacrament itself as with the other sacraments. On the other hand, Albert the Great and Thomas both thought that grace was conferred in this sacrament. Le Bras, cl. 2211. This view became the common one by the latter half of the thirteenth century in spite of some rather strong resistance by Peter John Olive and some hesitation by Duns Scotus. *Ibid.,* cls. 2212-2213. Durandus, however, is an indication that even by the early fourteenth century the viewpoint was by no means universal. By the sixteenth century, the opinion that marriage conferred grace was held by everyone, according to Le Bras (cls. 2230), a fact which Erasmus seemed to recognize; but as a historical critic he could not resist pointing out that it was not always so. Telle, who is anxious to prove Erasmus a rank heretic on the subject, gives scarcely any indication of the variations among the scholastics. He mentions only Hugh of St. Victor and Durand de St.-Pourçain as being opposed to the collation of grace in the sacrament and bases his judgment upon this article in the *DTC,* one which he must have read hurriedly because this author names Hugh of St. Victor as being one of the few scholastics in the twelfth century who held that grace was conferred in marriage. Telle, p. 267 and n. 19.

47. *Resp. ad notat. Ed. Lei* (1520), LB, IX, 227E.

48. In the *De captivitate Babylonica ecclesiae* (1520), Luther had com-

pletely rejected marriage as a sacrament. Without much question he drew upon Erasmus' 1516 note on Ephesians 5:32. See WA, VI, 551, 6 ff. With some justification, therefore, Erasmus' critics accuse him of having accorded to Luther the occasion for rejecting the seventh sacrament. In the *Apol. ad prodr. Iac. Stunicae* (1522), LB, IX, 377F-378A, Erasmus protests his innocence by arguing that Luther could not have drawn that opinion out of his works, because they so often speak of marriage as a sacrament, but more likely from Lombard, Durandus, or Jerome.

49. The *Decretum pro Armenis,* which was also the Bull of Eugenius IV, "Exultate Deo" (22 November 1439), stated at the beginning concerning all the sacraments: "Novae Legis septem sunt sacramenta: videlicet baptismus, confirmatio, Eucharistia, paenitentia, extrema unctio, ordo et matrimonium, quae multum a sacramentis differunt Antiquae Legis. Illa enim non causabant gratiam, sed eam solum per passionem Christi dandam esse figurabant: haec vero nostra et continent gratiam, et ipsam digne suscipientibus conferunt." Denzinger, 1310 (695). As far as I can judge, Erasmus does not question the legitimacy of this council, although he might well have, because, especially after the departure of the Greeks, it was dominated by the Pope and the Dominicans and did not represent the viewpoint of the whole Church because a separate council was taking place simultaneously at Basel, where the conciliarist cause was being espoused. The *Decretum pro Armenis,* issued in the name of the Pope, rests largely on Thomas' treatise *De articulis fidei et Ecclesiae sacramentis.* Denzinger, p. 332. Cf. Carl Andresen, "Geschichte der abendländischen Konzile des Mittelalters," in *Die ökumenische Konzile der Christenheit,* ed. H. J. Margull (Stuttgart, 1961), pp. 173 ff., 182 ff., 196; Hefele and Leclercq, *op. cit.,* VII (2), 1072, 1079 ff.; M. A. Schmidt, "The Problem of Papal Primacy at the Council of Florence," *Church History,* 30 (1961), 35-49.

50. *Apol. ad blasph. Iac. Stunicae* (1522), LB, IX, 369C: "Matrimonium multis locis testor me recipere in numerum eorum, quae proprie dicuntur Ecclesiae Sacramenta; si tamen recepit Ecclesia, de quo mihi nondum constat ad plenum. Tametsi video consentire Scholasticos, et video citari Concilium *Florentinum . . .*"

51. *Apol. ad concl. Iac. Stunicae* (1524), LB, IX, 390B.

52. *Resp. ad notat. Ed. Lei* (1520), LB, IX, 225A, 225F, 226B, 227C; *Apol. ad Iac. Stunicam* (1521), LB, IX, 338E; *Apol. ad prodr. Iac. Stunicae* (1522), LB, IX, 377F-378A, 378C; *Apol. ad concl. Iac. Stunicae* (1524), LB, IX, 390A.

53. *Christiani hominis institutum* (1514), LB, V, 1357F, 1358D:

Hoc quoque persuasum est. Ecclesia mystica septem
Munera dispensat, quae Sacramenta vocantur.

Hinc variae dotes, et gratia plurima menti
Coelitus inseritur, si quis modo sumserit apte.

. . . .

Munere Coniugii nati hunc prodimus in orbem,
Usque adeo pulcri, pulcherrima portio, mundi.

54. Telle, p. 281.

55. Lombard, IV *Sent.* d 27 c 3: "Efficiens autem causa Matrimonii est consensus, non quilibet, sed per verba expressus; nec de futuro, sed de praesenti." He adds also "vel aliis certis signis." In *PL,* I, series secunda, 400. Le Bras, cl. 2152.

56. Le Bras, cls. 2160 ff., 2184 ff. Thomas solved the problem by the distinction between primary and secondary causes: "Dicendum quod sacramentorum prima causa est divina virtus, quae in eis operatur salutem; sed causae secundae instrumentales sunt materiales operationes ex divina institutione habentes efficaciam et sic consensus in matrimonio est causa." *Summa theol. suppl.* q 45 a 1. See Le Bras, cls. 2196 f. The *Decretum pro Armenis* of 1439 assumes simply that "Causa efficiens matrimonii regulariter est mutuus consensus per verba de praesenti expressus." Denzinger, 702 (1327).

57. Le Bras, cls. 2206, 2211, 2231 ff. See above on the debate concerning a gift of grace in this sacrament, n. 46.

58. *Ibid.,* cls. 2203, 2204.

59. Thomas, *Summa theol.* q 48 a 1. However, even if the marriage is undertaken for some base motive, rather than for the purpose of offspring, the sacrament is not destroyed, but those who do so commit mortal sin.

60. Thomas, *Summa theol. suppl.* q 49 a 2 and 3; Bonaventure, *Brevil.* VI, 4.

61. Bonaventure, *Brevil.* VI, 2.

62. Bonaventure gives a summary of these in *Brevil.* VI, 5. A more detailed enumeration is given in Thomas, *Summa theol. suppl.* q 50-62.

63. LB, V, 617F-618A.

64. *Ibid.,* 620E. Cf. 618A and D.

65. *Ibid.,* 649F. Erasmus was not the only Roman Catholic in the sixteenth century who was clamoring for reform of this evil. According to Le Bras, "Non seulement Érasme, mais les théologiens comme Delphinus, Berthold" thought clandestine marriages ought to be declared invalid. Le Bras, cl. 2232. This subject occasioned a protracted and warm debate at Trent, where the fears of undermining the sacrament, of creating novelties, and of being in accord with the heretics all played a part, but where the majority pressed for some reform. The result was that, while the role of parents and the invalidity of past and present clandestine marriages were denied, future marriages would

require for their validity a solemn mutual consensus in the presence of the parish priest or another priest authorized by him or by the bishop of the diocese and two or three witnesses. Denzinger, 990-992 (1813-1816). Le Bras, cls. 2246-2247. Erasmus would have undoubtedly wished that the Tridentine Fathers had gone further in their reform, but would have nonetheless surely rejoiced at the result.

66. LB, V, 654B.

67. *Ibid.*, 650A. Consent of parents had been necessary for valid marriages in ancient Roman law. Cf. Le Bras, cl. 2192.

68. *Ibid.*, 651F-652B, 654BC.

69. *Ibid.*, 634B-637B, 643B, 645A.

70. *Ibid.*, 621A-622A, 622D-F.

71. *Ibid.*, 620C-F.

72. *Detectio praestig.* (1526), LB, X, 1562D: "An qui in matrimonio praefert coniunctionem animorum, tollit coniunctionem corporum?"

73. Cf. To Paul Volz, 14 August 1518, Allen, III, 858, 390-394. In *Coniugium* (1523) Erasmus seems to give to the sexual relation a more positive role in the marital union. He speaks of it as a medicine to cure ills and a means of restoring love. LB, I, 706C.

74. LB, V, 623A, B, F.

75. *Ibid.*, 1176B: "Si quis ea sicut decet acceperit, per *Matrimonii* sacramentum accedente Sacerdotali precatione, confertur donum Spiritus, quo vir diligat uxorem amore casto, sicut Christus dilexit Ecclesiam . . ."

76. *Christ. matr.*, LB, V, 623BC, 624A: "Sacramentum igitur hoc primum significat tibi quod et venereris et imiteris, fontem indicans omnium charismatum, et archetypum omnis Christianae concordiae: commonstrat et officium, quod ex imitatione archetypi debet utrimque praestari, et addit coeleste donum, cuius auxilio possis etiam praestare quod debetur. Paratum est donum, si tu praebueris doni capacem animum."

77. Pt. 2, pp. 325-334. This note was further expanded in succeeding editions. For convenience I cite from LB, VI, 692D-703C.

78. LB, VI, 692D-694E.

79. *Ibid.*, 695A. On Erasmus' knowledge and use of canon law in this regard see W. Maurer, "Reste des Kanonischen Rechtes im Frühprotestantismus," pp. 211 ff.

80. LB, VI, 695F.

81. *Ibid.*, 695D.

82. *Ibid.*, 697F-698C.

83. *Ibid.*, 696A-E, 698D.

84. *Ibid.*, 695F: "Excutiamus, quando, quibus, qua occasione dic-

tum sit, et fortassis veram germanamque sententiam deprehen-
demus."

85. *Ibid.,* 699D-F. Although he will allow marriage to be *called* a
sacrament even where the personal and moral union is absent, it is
questionable whether he really thinks that it *is* a sacrament unless this
most essential aspect is present.

86. *Ibid.,* 700A.

CHAPTER VIII
THE EUCHARIST

1. "Die Abendmahlslehre des Erasmus von Rotterdam und seine
Stellung am Anfang des Abendmahlsstreites der Reformatoren."
(Hereafter, "Die Abendmahlslehre.")

2. Cf. Thomas Aquinas, *Summa theol.* III q 78 a 1, where Thomas
argues for the "Hoc est meum corpus" as Christ's words of consecration on the basis of the present participle "benedicens."

3. *Nov. Test.* (1516), pt. 2, p. 311.

4. Pt. 2, p. 109.

5. "Quanquam hac in re nolim esse perverse contentiosus, cum
locus excusari possit per figuram πρωθύστερον." Pt 2, p. 124.

6. Krodel, "Die Abendmahlslehre," pp. 66 f., and "Figura Prothys-
teron and the Exegetical Basis of the Lord's Supper," *Lutheran Quar-
terly,* 12 (1960), 154 ff.

7. *Nov. Test.,* pt. 2, p. 473. His brief remark is quite general:
"τοῦτο μου σῶμα id est, hoc meum corpus, absque verba substantivo
est: quanquam in quibusdam additum reperio." Having looked at the
critical apparatus of Nestle and Tischendorf, I fail to discover any
variations on this text. I find it also strange that Erasmus would discover any manuscripts of the late Koine text that he used which omit
the copula. It is possible that he allows his interpretation of the passage, perhaps shaped by Oecolampadius' knowledge of Hebrew, to
influence his textual criticism. However, he retains the verb both in his
Greek text and in the Latin translation.

8. *Summa theol.* III q 75 a 1 and q 78 a 1.

9. *Nov. Test* (1519), pt. 2, p. 342. Cf. also the preface to *Paraphr. in
epist. Pauli ad Cor. I* to Erard de la Marck, 5 February 1519, Allen, III,
916, 60-63: "Utinam illud saltem aperuisset, a quibus, quo tempore,
quo cultu, quo ritu, quibus verbis consecrari soleat panis ille mysticus
ac sacrosanctum Dominici sanguinis poculum!"

Erasmus' note was immediately attacked by Vincent Theodorici, a
Dominican theologian at Louvain, for impugning the definition of the
Real Presence, especially in these final words of the note: "Mihi in
totum videtur consultiius de rebus huiusmodi, quae certis sacrae scripturae testimoniis doceri non possunt, sed ab humanis pendent coniec-
turis non adeo fortiter asseverare, ut nostram opinionem oraculi vice

haberi postulemus. At fortasse tutius sit, ecclesiasticos proceres non pronunciare de quibuslibet, quae docere non possint, cum et ipsi sint homines, et labi queat."

See To Hermann Busch, 31 July 1520, Allen, IV, 1126, 237 ff., 305 ff.; and To Vincent Theodorici, ⟨c. March 1521⟩, Allen, IV, 1196, 63 ff.

10. *Nov. Test.* (1527), pt. 2, p. 442.

11. A modern Roman Catholic scholar observes that the liturgical texts of the institution, not only the modern but also the most ancient, "are never simply a Scripture text restated," but "go back to a pre-Biblical tradition which explains the variations within the Biblical texts themselves." J. A. Jungmann, S.J., *The Mass of the Roman Rite,* tr. Francis A. Brunner (New York, 1953), II, 195. See his whole discussion of the development of the liturgical tradition on the words of institution, pp. 195 ff. Cf. G. Dix, *The Shape of the Liturgy* (Glasgow, 1945), p. 49.

12. Council of Florence, 1442, *Decretum pro Graecis et Armenis* [Denzinger, 715 (1352)]: "In consecratione corporis Domini hac utitur forma verborum: 'Hoc est enim corpus meum'; sanguinis vero: 'Hic est enim calix sanguinis mei, novi et aeterni testamenti, mysterium fidei, qui pro vobis et pro multis effundetur in remissionem peccatorum.' "

The earlier *Decretum pro Armenis* (1439) at this Council had said that the "Forma huius sacramenti sunt verba Salvatoris, quibus hoc confecit sacramentum . . . ," but failed to say what these words were [Denzinger, 698 (1321)]. The 1442 additional decree, though it explains what words of consecration are to be used in the Roman Church, does not explicitly connect them with the words used by Jesus.

13. Leo Jud, in his *Des hochgelerten Erasmi von Roterdam unnd Doctor Martin Luthers maynung vom Nachtmal unnsers herren Ihesu Christi* (1526), although Erasmus suspected the author was Conrad Pellican when he wrote his reply.

14. LB, X, 1564F-1565B, 1569BC.

15. Erasmus does not give a reference, but see *Gabrielis Biel Canonis misse expositio,* Lectio XXXVI, Pars II, ed. H. A. Oberman and W. J. Courtenay (Wiesbaden, 1965), pp. 42-44. Biel takes the view that the opinion held in common by Alexander, Albert, Thomas, and others "quod Christus in ultima cena consecravit per eadem verba per que nos conficimus" is the more universal and probable one.

16. LB, IX, 1065B. The reference to the Decretals is Gratian, *Decretum,* 3, 2, 35, *Quia corpus.* Erasmus has reason to be uncertain of the author of this text, which has finally been established as belonging to Faustus of Riez.

17. LB, IX, 1065BC. This is the first opinion mentioned by Thomas and Biel. *Summa theol.* III q 78 a 1, and *Canonis misse expositio,* Lectio XXXVI, p. 43. Both refer to Innocent III as seeming to support it with

the words "Sane dici potest quod Christus virtute divina confecit, et postea formam expressit sub qua posteri benedicerent." *De Sacro Altaris Mysterio,* IV, 6, in *PL,* CCXVII, 859.

18. LB, IX, 1065D.

19. That Erasmus has in mind here not the priestly form as such but rather the identity of the priestly words of consecration with those of Jesus seems clear from this passage at the end of the reply: "Non enim hic agitur verbis consecret sacerdos, sed quibus consecrarit Dominus." *Ibid.,* 1066A.

20. *Declar. ad cens.* (1532), LB, IX, 852CD. See above n. 9.

21. *Nov. Test.* (1527), pt. 2, p. 269, and in LB, VI, 446D.

22. LB, VII, 674AB.

23. *Detectio praestig.* (1526), LB, X, 1566A.

24. *Nov. Test.* (1527), pt. 2, p. 442.

25. *Ibid.,* p. 443.

26. *Ibid.*

27. Allen, VIII, 2175, 24-26.

28. *Ibid.,* 2263, 77-81.

29. *De veritate corporis et sanguinis domini nostri Iesu Christi in Eucharistia* (Paris, 1554). According to A. F. Pollard in the *Dictionary of National Biography* (New York, 1899), LVII, 312, Tunstall's attitude during the religious struggles was one of "invincible moderation." "He retained until his death an unshaken belief in Catholic dogma," yet opposed persecution.

30. To Justus Decius, 8 June 1529, Allen, VIII, 2175, 21-26: "Nisi me moveret tantus Ecclesiae consensus, possim in Oecolampadii sententiam pedibus discedere; nunc in eo persisto quod mihi tradidit Scripturarum interpres Ecclesia. Alioqui nullum reperio locum in Scripturis divinis, unde certo constet Apostolos consecrasse panem et vinum in carnem et sanguinem Domini." Cf. Krodel, "Die Abendmahlslehre," pt. 1, p. 116. See on confession pp. 183 ff.

31. *Enchiridion,* LB, V, 30EF. Cf. *Enarr. in ps. XXXIII* (1531), LB, V, 398C. Here Erasmus takes John 6:55 in a Eucharistic sense and applies it to John 6:64. Usually, however, his preferred interpretation of "his flesh and blood" is that the phrase means Jesus' teaching. (This is the heavenly bread eaten in faith of which Jesus speaks throughout John 6. LB, VII, 547CD, 549A-D.) His paraphrase (LB, VII, 551C), as he tells us in the *Detectio* (LB, X, 1568F-1569A), gives this as the first understanding, but adds also a Eucharistic phrasing. "Flesh and blood" as "teaching" or "word" is the interpretation in the following places: *Enarr. in ps. XXII* (1530), LB, V, 322D; *Enarr. in ps. XXXIII* (1531), LB, V, 388A; *Eccles.* (1535), LB, V, 826D.

The stress upon an inner spiritual eating which does not deny a sacramental eating and the emphatic application of John 6:63 to the

Eucharist are to be found especially in the *Devotio Moderna.* See Mestwerdt, pp. 91 f. In fact, Wessel Gansfort in his stress upon the necessity
and usefulness of a spiritual eating goes so far as to say: "To the
spiritually faithful he is also given—even in bodily presence—outside
of the Eucharist and apart from the forms of bread and wine, since he
is given to those who believe in him." *The Sacrament of the Eucharist,*
XXIII, tr. L. W. Scudder, in E. W. Miller, *Wessel Gansfort: Life and Writings,* II (New York, 1917), 57. To my knowledge so radical a statement
cannot be duplicated in Erasmus.

32. *Enchiridion* (1503), LB, V, 31B: ". . . quod illic oculis repraesen-
tatur: repraesentatur mors capitis." *Laus stult.* (1509), LB, IV, 502C:
"Repraesentatur autem mors Christi . . ." Note on Mark 14:22, *Nov.
Test.* (1516), pt. 2, p. 311: "Iam enim hoc repraesentabat, quod paulo
post esset futurum." *Paraphr. in epist. Pauli ad Cor. I* (1519), 11:25, LB
VII, 897B, C; *Paraphr. in evang. Matt.* (1522), 26:26, LB, VII, 133E;
Paraphr. in evang. Marci (1523), 14:22, LB, VII, 260B.

33. *Enchiridion,* LB, V 31B; *Ratio* (1520), Holborn, 265, 10 ff., and
LB, V, 119F-120A.

34. *Modus orandi* (1524), LB, V, 1102C.

35. *Paraphr. in evang. Matt.* (1522), 26:26, LB, VII, 134B; *Paraphr. in
evang. Lucae* (1523), 22:19, LB, VII, 451A.

36. *Modus orandi,* LB, V, 1102C.

37. *Spongia adv. adsperg. Hutteni* (1523), LB, X, 1663AB.

38. LB, IX, 1064F-1065A.

39. *Expos. concion. in ps. LXXXV* (1528), LB, V, 509E.

40. *Symbolum* (1533), LB, V, 1176A. Cf. *De amab. Eccl. conc.* (1533),
LB, V, 503CD. On the complex question of the understanding of the
Eucharistic sacrifice prior to and during the time of the Reformation
see the recent excellent study of Francis Clark, S.J., *Eucharistic Sacrifice
and the Reformation* (Westminster, Md., 1960). The author shows that
ever since Lombard there was in scholasticism a general unanimity on
this subject. The Eucharistic sacrifice was for the scholastics a representation and commemoration of the original unique sacrifice on the
cross; yet it was not only a memorial but a real sacrifice. The offering
on the altar was regarded as dependent upon the first offering so that
it is the selfsame Christ who is re-presented there but not in the same
manner. As Lombard put it, whereas on the cross Christ was immolated *in semetipso,* on the altar he is immolated *in sacramento.* IV *Sent.*
d 12 c 5; cited by Clark, p. 76. The major difference between the
schools on the eve of the Reformation was that the Scotists and the
nominalists emphasized more the commemorative nature of the Eucharistic sacrifice and "attributed less absolute efficacy to the Mass
than did the Thomists." Clark, p. 325. Erasmus is certainly closer to
the Scotists and nominalists than to the Thomists in his emphasis on

the commemorative and representative character of the Eucharist. Indeed, he undoubtedly goes beyond them in this emphasis. He never refers to the Eucharistic sacrifice as the selfsame sacrifice as that of Calvary. Indeed, he prefers to avoid applying that term to the Eucharist as such. Finally, as we noticed in our treatment of Erasmus' conception of the work of Christ, because he has little sense of any tension between God's mercy and his justice, he would see little necessity of a continual propitiatory sacrifice. For one who stressed the manward rather than the Godward side of the atonement, we would expect that he would not see the need of a daily offering on the altar to God.

41. *Enchiridion* (1503), LB, V, 31B: ". . . peragatur in te, quod illic oculis repraesentatur . . ."; *Laus stult.* (1509), LB, IV, 502C. *Paraphr. in epist. Pauli ad Cor. I* (1519), 11:25, LB, VII, 897BC: ". . . sed ad arcanae rei repraesentationem, ne vobis veniat in oblivionem, quo pretio sitis a pristinae vitae vitiis redemti." *Ibid.,* 11:26, 897C. Cf. *Paraphr. in evang. Matt.* (1522), 26:26, LB, VII, 133EF; *Paraphr. in evang. Lucae* (1523), 22:19, LB, VII, 451A.

42. *De praep. ad mort.,* LB, V, 1306B, 1313A. Cf. *Symbolum* (1533), 1160E, 1187D, and *Paraphr. in evang. Lucae,* 23:34, LB, VII, 462DE.

43. Since the important themes of *repraesentatio* and *commemoratio, contemplatio* and *imitatio,* as applied to the Eucharist have already been richly detailed by Krodel, "Die Abendmahlslehre," pt. 1, pp. 91 ff., we have limited ourselves to a cursory review of them. In this connection Krodel talks about the mystical-ethical character of Erasmus' conception of the Eucharist—mystical, because of the subjective, commemorative *Vergegenwärtigung* of Christ; ethical, because of the moral representation in life of the objectively given love of Christ (pt. 1, p. 127). However, he places more emphasis than I would on the mystical element. In spite of his neo-Platonic background Erasmus is not a mystic in the technical sense of one who yearns for immediate union with God, whether this union is an essential or affective one. (See on these two distinct varieties of mysticism in the late Middle Ages, Oberman, *Harvest,* pp. 329 ff.) His thought is mystical primarily in his stress on a radical inwardness in religion and in his sense of a mysterious depth, whether in God, Christ, Scripture, or Eucharist, which cannot be grasped by reason but which is contemplated in faith. As in his understanding of Scripture the mystical, contemplative element is very much subordinated to the moral, so in his Eucharistic conception the mystical, contemplative aspect is subordinated to the ethical representation, the union with Christ in faith to the union with one another in love.

Cf. Mestwerdt (p. 229), who, in comparing Erasmus to the *Devotio Moderna* in this respect, says: "So fallen die beiden Elemente, die sich in der devotio moderna die Wage hielten, das religiösemystische und

das ethisch-praktische, bei Erasmus auseinander. Nur das letztere
nimmt er auf und sucht von hier aus die Verbindung mit den ethischen
Werten der ihm von anderer Seite her am Herzen liegenden antiken
Poesie." Also, see A. Renaudet, *Érasme, sa pensée religieuse,* p.
10: "Rien
ne le séduit moins que la mystique, passionement cultivée chez les
Windeshémiens et les Frères de la Vie commune." These statements
are too strong. There is some remnant of the mystical in Erasmus, but
it is not prominent. Even Krodel in his note in defense of the application of this category to Erasmus' religious thought must confess that
his mysticism is "ethisch bestimmt." Pt. 2, p. 36. Because of the ambiguity of the term and because of the limited nature of the mysticism
of Erasmus, I have preferred to avoid the term. Moreover, Krodel is
in error, as we shall see later, in designating the Real Presence for
Erasmus as merely mystical-ethical. Kohls likewise is not sufficiently
circumspect when he suggests without qualification that Erasmus like
Gabriel Biel embodies the spirit of the *Devotio Moderna* "in seiner Ein-
stellung zur Mystik." *Die Theologie des Erasmus,* II, 35, continued note.

44. *Enchiridion* (1503), LB, V, 31B.

45. *Detectio praestig.* (1526), LB, X, 1562C. The Abelardian view of
the atonement shines through in this thought. See above on Christology, pp. 64 ff.

46. *Paraphr. in evang. Lucae* (1523), 22:20, LB, VII, 451A: *"Hoc est
novum testamentum,* non vituli aut hirci, sed *meo sanguine consecratum, qui
pro vobis* servandis effunditur. Habetis summum argumentum ac pignus meae erga vos caritatis."

I leave open the question of what constitutes the signs, even though
in this passage it would seem to be in some sense the consecrated
blood of Christ, because I wish to treat this whole question later. See
below the discussion of symbols and the Real Presence, pp. 135 ff.

47. *Symbolum* (1533), LB, V, 1175F-1176A; *De praep. ad mort.* (1534),
LB, V, 1306B, 1317BC.

48. *Christiani hominis institutum* (1514), LB, V, 1358E:

> Mysticus ille cibus (Graeci dixere Synaxin)
> Qui panis vinique palam sub imagine, Christum
> Ipsum praesentem vere exhibet intima nostri
> Viscera coelesti saginat, et educat esca,
> Inque Deo reddit vegetos, et reddit adultos.

Cf. *Enarr. in ps. XXII* (1530), LB, V, 329C: "Quid enim honorificentius,
quam ut homo communione carnis et sanguinis dominici fiat unum
cum Christo, quemadmodum cibus ac potus corporalis transformatur
in substantiam vescentis ac bibentis, quamquam hic potius qui vescun-
tur et bibunt transformantur in id quod sumunt." However, the em-

phasis is more on the Eucharist as symbolizing than as actualizing the union of the members with Christ.

49. *Enarr. in ps. XXII,* LB, V, 332C. See also *Paraphr. in evang. Lucae* (1523), 23:28, LB, VII, 461C, and *Declar. ad cens.* (1532), LB, IX, 823CD.

50. *Detectio praestig.* (1526), LB, X, 1562CD: "Exempli, ut in Eucharistia significatur immensa Christi caritas erga genus humanum, pro cuius salute semetipsum in mortem tradidit, ut nos mutua caritate Redemtori respondeamus: significatur arctissima societas Christianorum inter ipsos, vel quod ex multis granis unus conficitur panis, et ex multis uvis confluit vinum: vel quod cibus potusque communis amicitiae sodalitatisque symbolum sit." *Paraphr. in evang. Lucae,* 22: 20-21, LB, VII, 451AB: "Habetis summum argumentum ac pignus meae erga vos caritatis. Deberet autem amor esse mutuus . . ."

51. As in the above citation from the *Detectio.* Cf. *ibid.,* 1569A; *Supput. errorum N. Beddae* (1527), LB, IX, 681DE; *Enarr. in ps. XXII* (1530), LB, V, 329C. The supper is sign, pledge, or representation of both Christ's love to us and the concord or love among Christians. To John Slechta, 1 November 1519, Allen, IV, 1039, 248-249; *Detectio praestig.,* LB, X, 1568CD; *De praep. ad mort.* (1534), LB, V, 1306B.

52. On the origin and growth of the *synaxis* idea (from σύναξιs — assembly) in the early Church, see H. Leclercq, "Synaxe," in *Dictionnaire d'archéologie chrétienne et de liturgie,* ed. F. Cabrol and H. Leclercq (Paris, 1953), XV, 1834 ff., and A. Fortescue, "Synaxis," in *The Catholic Encyclopedia,* vol. XIV, ed. C. G. Herbermann *et al.* (New York, 1912), p. 383. Erasmus uses the expression only for the Eucharist with the weight not as in Pseudo-Dionysius upon the vertical but upon the horizontal dimension of the fellowship, as in this passage from the *Modus orandi* (1524), LB, V, 1102D: "Unde et huic rei proprie nomen inditum *Eucharistiae,* quamquam eadem Graecis dicitur *synaxis,* id est, *conciliatio,* quod pariter ibi repraesentetur foedus caritatis inter omnia Christi membra, unde et Latini communionem vocant."

53. *Querela pacis* (1517), LB, IV, 632DE. Cf. *Dulce bellum inexpertis* (1515), LB, II, 959D.

54. *Paraphr. in evang. Matt.* (1522), 26:26, LB, VII, 134C. Cf. To John Slechta, 1 November 1519, Allen, IV, 1039, 246-247: "Scio Christi corpus et sanguinem purum pure a puris esse sumendum . . ." See also *Paraphr. in epist. Pauli ad Cor. I* (1519), 11:27-28, LB, VII, 897CD; To Balthasar Mercklin, 15 March 1530, Allen, VIII, 2284, 115-117, 159-160.

Cf. Origen in Erasmus' trans., *Commentarii Origenis Adamantii in evang. Matt.,* 15:15-16, LB, VIII, 468E: "Proinde etiam in pane Domini tum utilitas est vescenti, cum impolluta mente puraque conscientia, particeps est panis illius."

Cf. also Colet, *Enarr. in epist. I Pauli ad Corinth.,* 11 (c. 1496-1497, according to Lupton), ed. J. H. Lupton (London, 1874), pp. 243 f.: "Dignitas est in innocentia; ut innocentes sint, sicut Christus innocens; ut innocentes convescentes innocentissimi Iesu mortem representent."

55. *Paraphr. in evang. Matt.* (1522), 26:26, LB, VII, 134C.

56. With perhaps one exception. The mystical, even bodily, union with Christ is more prominent in passages which talk realistically about the presence of Christ in the Eucharist, e.g., To Balthasar Mercklin, 15 March 1530 (the preface to Erasmus' edition of Alger's treatise *De veritate corporis et sanguinis Dominici in Eucharistia*), Allen, VIII, 2284, 5-11: "Nihil enim habet illa sublimius quam quod per communionem corporis et sanguinis Dominici fit, etiam iuxta naturam ac substantiam, unum cum Christo, et quodammodo in Deum transformatur; nihil autem ad perfectam indissolubilemque concordiam efficacius, quam quod eodem corpore vescens, eundem sanguinem bibens, per eundem spiritum in unum corpus redigitur, et Christo capiti viuo viua connectitur." See also *Enarr. in ps. XXII* (1530), LB, V, 329C, quoted above, n. 48.

57. *Paraphr. in epist. Pauli ad Cor. I* (1519), 11:25-29, LB, VII, 897B-D.

58. 1 November 1519, Allen, IV, 1039, 246-255. From the very beginning Erasmus shows no pleasure in the doctrine of transubstantiation. See also *Laus stult.* (1509), LB, IV, 465A, 466AB, and note on I Cor. 7:39, *Nov. Test.* (1519), pt. 2, p. 327.

59. We cannot be as sure as Krodel is ("Die Abendmahlslehre," pt. 1, pp. 127 ff.) that Erasmus intends only a spiritual or mystical presence, in spite of the emphasis on a spiritual eating. Cf. W. Köhler, *Zwingli und Luther: Der Streit über das Abendmahl nach seinen politischen und religiösen Beziehungen,* I, in *Quellen und Forschungen zur Reformationsgeschichte* (Leipzig, 1924), VI, 144: ". . . seine Betonung des geistigen Genusses hatte den leiblichen nicht ausgeschlossen, sondern nur mystisch verhüllt."

60. Krodel ("Die Abendmahlslehre," pt. 2, p. 68, n. 14; p. 69, n. 5) points to another passage where Erasmus seems to agree with Theophylact, who "admonet fuisse verum corpus, non corporis figuram, quod panis ineffabili modo transformetur." Note on Matt. 26:26, *Nov. Test.,* LB, VI, 133E. However, since this note was not added till the 1527 edition, it cannot be used as evidence for Erasmus' early understanding of the Presence.

61. I apply this category of the later *Detectio praestig.* (1526), LB, X, 1562C, to his early conception.

62. *Paraphr. in evang. Matt.* (1522), 26:26, LB, VII, 133EF; *Paraphr. in evang. Marci* (1523), 14:22, LB, VII, 260D; *Paraphr. in evang. Lucae* (1523), 22:19, LB, VII, 450F. Cf. on the connection between symbol

and reality Köhler, *Zwingli und Luther,* I, 51 f., and Krodel, "Die Abendmahlslehre," pt. 1, p. 125.

63. *Querela pacis* (1517), LB, IV, 632D; *Paraphr. in epist. Pauli ad Cor. I* (1519), 11:25, LB, VII, 897B.

64. To John Slechta, 1 November 1519, Allen, IV, 1039, 247-249; *Paraphr. in evang. Lucae,* 22:20, LB, VII, 451A.

65. *Paraphr. in evang. Matt.,* 26:26, LB, VII, 133EF: "In hac igitur extrema coena . . . instituit sacrosanctum illud symbolum mortis suae." *Paraphr. in evang. Marci,* 14:22, LB, VII, 260D: "Sub haec Iesus commendavit suis sacrosanctum illud symbolum mortis suae, perpetuique foederis . . ." *Paraphr. in evang. Lucae,* 22:19, LB, VII, 450F: "Sub haec Dominus Iesus mystico symbolo suis consecraturus novum Testamentum . . ." Erasmus does not tell us exactly what the antecedents are for these demonstrative pronouns.

66. See note 65. *Paraphr. in evang. Lucae,* 22:20, LB, VII, 451A; *Paraphr. in epist. Pauli ad Cor. I,* 11:25, LB, VII, 897B.

67. *Querela pacis* (1517), LB, IV, 632D; Allen, IV, 1039, 247-249; *Paraphr. in evang. Matt.,* 26:26, 133F; *Modus orandi* (1524), LB, V, 1102CD.

68. *Detectio praestig.* (1526), LB, X, 1560, 1568B-1569B.

69. In three letters of early October he puts all three in one camp as denying the Real Presence. To N. Beda, 2 October 1525, Allen, VI, 1620, 81-85; To Peter Barbirius, 3 October 1525, Allen, VI, 1621, 15-22; To Thomas Lupset, ⟨ c. 4 October ⟩ 1525, Allen, VI, 1624, 29-35.

70. Allen, V, 1523, 97-99.

71. *Zwingli und Luther,* I, 69.

72. Allen, VI, 1624, 33.

73. Köhler, I, 16 ff. See, concerning the influence of Erasmus on Zwingli's conception of the Eucharist, *ibid.,* I, 49 ff., and Krodel, "Die Abendmahlslehre," pt. 1, pp. 205 ff.

74. Allen, VI, 1621, n. 18.

75. *Zwinglis Sämtliche Werke,* III, 335 ff. and 345 ff.; Köhler, I, 74 f.

76. *Werke,* III, 785, 34-36.

77. *Ibid.,* III, 761; Köhler, I, 81 f.

78. Allen, VI, 1616, 19-20.

79. *Ibid.,* 1618, 7-10.

80. To Thomas Wolsey, 25 April 1526, Allen, VI, 1697, 89-93; To Willibald Pirckheimer, 19 October 1527, Allen, VII, 1893, 77-82, cited by Renaudet, *Études érasmiennes,* p. 45, n. 7. Cf. *Detectio praestig.* (1526), LB, X, 1564A.

Allen says, "It may be conjectured that as the result of the correspondence with Pellican . . . and the conversation which followed . . . Erasmus came to some agreement with them [Pellican and Oecolampadius]: perhaps that he would not write against them, and that on their side they should abstain from asserting that he shared their views." VI, p. 177, n. 17.

81. To the Town Council of Basel,⟨October 1525⟩, Allen, VI, 1636. These words are reported in *Detectio praestig.* (1526), LB, X, 1564B.

82. ⟨C. 15 October 1525⟩, Allen, VI, 1637, Intro. This letter was immediately passed around against Erasmus' wishes. It was soon printed, at first under the title *Expostulatio ad quendam amicum admodum pia et Christiana Erasmi Roterodami.*

83. Allen, VI, 1637, 30-115. Erasmus later reports an interview he held with Pellican about this time in which he denied to Pellican's face that he shared the latter's views. To John Lasky, 8 March 1526, Allen, VI, 1674, 43-58. Erasmus also gives accounts of this conversation in two later works: *Epist. in pseudevang.* (1529), LB, X, 1580CE, and *Resp. ad fratres* (1530), LB, X, 1600C-F; cited by Allen, VI, p. 280, n. 43.

84. Allen, VI, 1708, Intro., and To Conrad Pellican,⟨c. 27 August 1526⟩, Allen, VI, 1737, 5-6; and Allen, VI, pp. 382-383, nn. 1 and 5.

85. *Maynung,* pp. Aii-Aiiii.

86. *Ibid.,* p. Av-B: "Da hat et gnug und mit vil worten zu versteen geben, das da seye brot und weyn, die er symbola nennet, das ist, bedeutliche zaichen."

87. Allen, VI, 1708, 16, 24-26, 38-42, and Intro.

88. LB, X, 1560BC, 1566F-1567A.

89. LB, X, 1562F-1563A. Thomas does not put it quite this way, but does state that the sacrament has no beneficial effect unless to the sacramental eating there is added the spiritual eating in faith and love. *Summa theol.* III q 80 a 1. The sinner who receives Christ's body only sacramentally commits mortal sin. *Summa* III q 80 a 4. The spiritual effect of the sacrament is even hindered by present venial sins. *Summa* III q 79 a 8. Cf. IV *Sent.* d 9 q 1 a 2, for description of a spiritual eating which is extrasacramental and a spiritual eating which is also a sacramental eating, whether *in voto* or *in actu;* cited by Köhler, *Zwingli und Luther,* I, 89, n. 1.

90. LB, X, 1563C.

91. Besides the letter to Pellican and the *Detectio,* these include especially the letter to Balthasar Mercklin, 15 March 1530, Allen, VIII, 2284 [the preface to Erasmus' edition of *De veritate corporis et sanguinis Dominici in Eucharistia,* by Alger of Liege (c. 1131)], and scattered passages in letters and other late writings to which we shall make specific reference.

92. Allen, VI, 1637, 75-76, 79-80.

93. LB, X, 1560F, 1567A, 1568C, D.

94. *Ibid.,* 1560DE. Notice the difference in expression concerning

the corporeal presence in this passage from the one in the letter to
Pellican. Here it is "corpus et sanguinem . . . quodammodo sensibus
nostris expositum . . ." There it is: "Caro est, sed nullis obnoxia
sensibus . . ." Allen, VI, 1637, 75. We shall discuss this point when we
take up the question of the nature of the Real Presence.

95. *Supput. errorum N. Beddae* (1527), LB, IX, 681DE; To Cuthbert
Tunstall, 31 January 1530, Allen, VIII, 2263, 85-88.

96. To Balthasar Mercklin, 15 March 1530, Allen, VIII, 2284, 59-68:
"Ac prisci quidam Ecclesiae doctores, interim obscurius, interim
varie, ne dicam diverse, loqui videntur de hoc sacramento. Obscuritas
vel ineffabili huius mysterii profunditati tribuenda est, vel illorum cau-
tioni, qui loquentes frequenter apud multitudinem ex Iudaeis, Gen-
tibus et Christianis permixtam, noluerunt sanctum dare canibus.
Varietas hinc nata est, quod interdum ipsae species sacramentales
dicuntur symbola, interdum ipsa sumptio symbolum dicitur: postremo, corpus ipsum sui alteriusve rei symbolum nonnunquam appel-
latur."

97. See To Cuthbert Tunstall, 31 January 1530, Allen, VIII, 2263,
69-72: "De Eucharistia prisci religiose loquuti sunt, priusquam hoc
veniret in quaestionem: fortasse ne nunc quidem evidenter definivit
Ecclesia quomodo sit ibi corpus, sub accidentibus an sub vero pane."
To Boniface Amerbach, 25 March 1532, Allen, IX, 2631, 3-6: "De
veritate Corporis Dominici nihil ambigendum est. De modo praesen-
tiae licet aliquo pacto dubitare, quoniam de hoc Ecclesia disputat
verius quam pronunciat, aut certe in genere credere quod credit Ecclesia, praesertim homini laico." Cf. To Balthasar Mercklin, 15 March
1530, Allen, VIII, 2284, 89-102.

Erasmus shows that he is aware that the Church had made the
doctrine of transubstantiation into dogma (Fourth Lateran Council,
1215 [Denzinger, 430 (802)]) in his note on I Cor. 7:39, *Nov. Test.*
(1519), pt. 2, p. 327, and in LB, VI, 696C: "In synaxi *Transsubstantia-
tionem* sero definivit Ecclesia: diu satis erat credere, sive sub pane
consecrato, sive quocumque modo adesse verum corpus Christi."

Bouyer attacks Renaudet for detecting a rationalistic doubt concerning transubstantiation in the statement from the *Novum Testamentum.* Bouyer, *Autour d'Érasme*, p. 130; Renaudet, *Études érasmiennes*, pp.
171-172. Renaudet is perhaps not justified in finding such a doubt on
the basis of this statement alone, which says nothing about how Erasmus regarded the definition. But on the basis of the statements to
Tunstall and Amerbach, one is certainly justified in noticing a doubt.

I must also reject Ernst's contention that, although Erasmus earlier
repudiated the doctrine of transubstantiation, "Später hat er sich
wieder der Transsubstantiationslehre angeschlossen." Ernst, "Die
Frömmigkeit des Erasmus," pp. 71-72.

98. Although the idea was present earlier, I do not find the actual term until the letter to Pellican ⟨ c. 15 October 1525⟩, Allen, VI, 1637, 37-38, where he says: "... eos voluerit eiusdem carne et sanguine modo quodam ineffabili pascere ..." Krodel mistakenly applies this expression to his thought in the pre-1525 period because he finds it in the note on Matt. 26:26, which was, however, not added until 1527.

99. To Balthasar Mercklin, 15 March 1530, Allen, VIII, 2284, 115-117: "Quantam enim puritatem, quantam reverentiam ac tremorem requirat hoc terque quaterque adorandum mysterium, quis digne verbis assequatur?"; 142-143: "Nam ineffabilibus mysteriis nulla res magis convenit quam silentium ..." The word "mysterium" occurs again and again in ll. 61, 84, 125, 147, 155, 162, 171.

100. "Die Abendmahlslehre," pt. 1, pp. 198, 217, 254.

101. Allen, VI, 1637, 74-75.

102. Allen, VI, 1674, 43-53.

103. *Epist. in pseudevang.* (1529), LB, X, 1580D: "Corpus, inquit, esse Christi. Hoc, inquam, sane mihi tecum convenit. Sed sentis illic esse corpus Christi substantialiter? Negavit cum aversatione. Atqui hoc mihi tecum non convenit, inquam."

104. To Michael Boudet, 13 March 1526, Allen, VI, 1678, 33-36.

105. LB, X, 1562E.

106. Allen, VIII, 2284, 81-82: "... concorditer sensisse in Eucharistia esse veram substantiam corporis et sanguinis Dominici." Wilhelm Maurer suggests the possible influence of this "Einheitsformel" on the Melanchthonian formulation at Augsburg. Both leave open the question of transubstantiation or consubstantiation and do not expressly bind the bodily presence to the elements of bread and wine. "Zum geschichtlichen Verständnis der Abendmahlsartikel in der Confessio Augustana," in *Festschrift für Gerhard Ritter* (Tübingen, 1950), pp. 205 ff., n. 148. For the participation of Erasmus in the story of Augsburg see further Peter Rassow, *Die politische Welt Karls V* (Munich, n.d.), pp. 40 ff.

107. Allen, VIII, 2284, 77-83.

108. *Ibid.,* 70-71. In his treatise (the title in *PL,* CLXXX, is *De sacramentis corporis et sanguinis dominici*), Alger held that at the consecration the elements are converted into the flesh and blood of Christ so that the flesh is "... praesentem in coelo et in terra vere et substantialiter esse; et cum vero caro comesta, et sanguis eius bibitus fuerit a populo, ipsum tamen Christum vivum et integrum suo permanere in regno." Prol. in *PL,* CLXXX, 741. However, he also holds that the body of Christ, which in the Eucharist is eaten by faith and spiritually, is itself "spirituale ... et incorruptible, nec tamen minus substantiale." I, 11, in *PL,* 771, 772. See on Alger's conception of the Eucharistic presence Darwell Stone, *A History of the Doctrine of the Eucharist* (London, 1909),

pp. 270-271. This was also the common view. See for the views of
Lombard, Peter of Poitiers, Alexander of Hales, Thomas Aquinas,
Stone, pp. 306, 307, 316, and 331.

109. Allen, VIII, 2284, 101-102. This was the view of Alger (I, 11,
15, in *PL*, CLXXX, 773, 783), as indeed it was the common scholastic
teaching. See for Hugh of St. Victor and Lombard, Stone, pp. 286 and
306.

110. *Enarr. in ps. XXII* (1530), LB, V, 329A.

111. *De amab. Eccl. conc.* (1533), LB, V, 504C; *De praep. ad mort.*
(1534), 1315A, 1317BC.

112. 6 June 1536, Allen, XI, 3127, 26-32. *Defensio Doctrinae Christianae adversus axioma catholicum, id est criminationem R. P. Roberti Episcopi
Abrincensis*, Strasbourg, 1534. Allen, XI, p. 333, n. 21, and p. 46n. On
this complex and much debated question among the scholastics concerning the mode of Christ's presence in the Eucharist, see Seeberg,
DG, III, 525 ff., 789 ff., and Gabriel Buescher, *The Eucharistic Teaching
of William Ockham* (St. Bonaventure, N.Y., 1950), pp. 65 ff. The usual
teaching was that Christ's body was present with quantity, but not
through quantity, i.e., not through a local or dimensive or circumscriptive mode as he is in heaven. Buescher, p. 67. Thomas held "quod
corpus Christi est in hoc sacramento per modum substantiae et non
per modum quantitatis." *Summa* III q 76 a 1; quoted and cited by
Seeberg, p. 525. This teaching supposes that quantity is a reality distinct from substance or quality. Durandus, who could conceive of
quantity only in a quantitative or local mode, denied that the quantity
of Christ's body was at all present in the Eucharist. Seeberg, p. 526,
and Buescher, p. 92. On the other hand, the nominalist Occam, who
held that quantity is not a reality separate from substance but only a
connotative term, thought likewise that Christ's body is not quantitatively or circumscriptively present on the altar as he is in heaven, but
that he is nevertheless definitively present, and, according to Buescher,
"equally as perfect and integral on the altar as he is in heaven" (p. 93).
For virtually the same teaching in Biel, see Oberman, *Harvest*, pp. 275
f. The terms "quantitative," or "circumscriptive," and "definitive"
mean here respectively: a presence whereby the thing in each of its
parts is wholly commensurate with the space it occupies and a presence
whereby the whole thing is in the whole space it occupies, but not
commensurate part for part with that space, as, for example, the soul
in the body.

113. To Martin Bucer, 2 March 1532, Allen, IX, 2615, 286-288:
"Quis autem nescit ab Ecclesia definitum in pane consecrato esse
verum Domini corpus, in vino verum sanguinem?" Here he is answer-
ing Bucer's charge that in the letter to Tunstall he denied the Real
Presence when he said that "De Eucharistia prisci religiose loquuti

sunt; fortasse ne nunc quidem evidenter definivit (Ecclesia) [Allen's insertion], quomodo sit ibi corpus, sub accidentibus an sub vero pane." Erasmus answers: "Hic appello tuam conscientiam, Bucere: declarat hic locus me de Eucharistia idem sentire quod vos docetis? Addubito de definitione ecclesiae, sed hec dubitatio pro fundamento habet illic esse verum corpus dominicum iuxta substantiam. Et hoc credo sequutus Scripturarum Ecclesieque autoritatem, nec unquam scripsi diversum neque sensi" (ll. 281-286). Then follows the quotation given at the beginning of this note.

114. Cf. Allen, VI, 1620, 80-85; 1621, 22-24; and 1624, 34-35. Perhaps here we see the main reason for Erasmus' failure to complete his book against Oecolampadius.

115. Allen, VI, 1717, 52-56: "Mihi non displiceret Oecolampadii sententia, nisi obstaret consensus Ecclesiae. Nec enim video quid agat corpus insensibile, nec utilitatem allaturum si sentiretur, modo adsit in symbolis gratia spiritualis. Et tamen ab Ecclesiae consensu non possum discedere, nec unquam discessi." Cf. Allen, VI, 1729, 25-27, and VII, 1893, 56-60.

116. I have been helped in discovering the heart of Oecolampadius' rather ponderous treatise by the discussions of Köhler, *Zwingli und Luther*, I, 117 ff., and E. Staehelin, *Das theologische Lebenswerk des Johannes Oecolampadius*, in *Quellen und Forschungen zur Reformationsgeschichte*, XXI (Leipzig, 1939), 277 ff. See the latter for Oecolampadius' earlier development on this question, pp. 267 ff. This writing represents Oecolampadius' first full discussion of a wholly symbolic understanding of the Eucharist, though in August 1525 he had briefly hinted at it in writing *Ellebron pro Iacobo Latomo*. See Staehelin, p. 276.

117. Fol. Av. Cf. Erasmus on the meaning of *sacramentum* and on baptism as a *sacramentum*, pp. 97 and 166. As far as I can judge, Erasmus does not apply this sense of the word to the Eucharist, as do both Oecolampadius and Zwingli.

118. Fol. Av-B.

119. Fol. B. Staehelin, p. 277, and Köhler, I, 118 f.

120. Fol. B. Oecolampadius contrasts the simplicity of the Apostolic rite of breaking bread with the growth of the present astonishment-evoking ritual. Fol. B-Biij.

121. Fol. C5-D. Staehelin, p. 279. *Adv. Marcionem* IV, 40, in *PL*, II, 491B. Tertullian's words are: ". . . acceptum panem, et distributum discipulis, corpus illum suum fecit, *Hoc est corpus meum* dicendo, id est, figura corporis mei." See C. W. Dugmore, *The Mass and the English Reformers* (London, 1958), pp. 4 f., for a brief discussion of the debate on Tertullian's meaning in this passage.

122. Fol. D5-E. Köhler, I, 121.

123. Fol. D5-E. Staehelin, p. 279.

124. Fol. Lij.

125. Fol. E5-F.

126. Fol. F5. He refers elsewhere to Zwingli as having already shown this truth that the spiritual eating in faith needs no bodily eating. Fol. Kiij-L. Cf. *De vera et falsa religione commentarus,* in Zwingli's *Sämtliche Werke,* III, 761 and 785 ff.

127. Fol. G-Giij.

128. Fol. K-K8.

129. Fol. E3.

130. Köhler, I, 124-125.

131. Cf. To Conrad Pellican, ⟨c. 15 October 1525⟩, Allen, VI, 1637, 66-70; To Willibald Pirckheimer, 19 October 1527, Allen, VII, 1893, 62-70; To Balthasar Mercklin, 15 March 1530, Allen, VIII, 2284, 109-111: "Breviter, adversus omnes humanae cogitationis scrupulos occurrat nobis primum immensa Dei potentia, cui nihil impossibile, cui nihil non facile . . ." *De praep. ad mort.* (1534), LB, V, 1315A: "Quomodo idem corpus possit esse diversis in locis eodem tempore, et quomodo in Eucharistia verum hominis corpus possit in minimo spatio contineri? Respondeat, sicut credit Ecclesia."

132. See above, n. 115.

133. To Conrad Pellican, ⟨c. 15 October 1525⟩, Allen, VI, 1637, 59-66: "Scio quam levis sit apud vos conciliorum autoritas: ego vero nec Ecclesiam Romanam contemno, multo minus quum illa habet sibi consentientes omnes ecclesias. . . . Ecclesia mihi persuasit Evangelio credere; eadem magistra didici Evangelii verba interpretari. Hactenus cum omnibus Christianis adoravi Christum pro me passum in Eucharistia." 112-116: "Si tuus animus vacillat, ut solebas profiteri, quia nihil tribuis autoritati pontificum et conciliorum, meum animum hactenus confirmavit Ecclesiae catholicae consensus." In the *Detectio praestig.* (1526), LB, X, 1569F, he implies that the Real Presence belongs in the first category of dogmas which the Catholic Church holds by a large consensus. Cf. also To John Vlatten, 25 July 1533, Allen, X, 2845, 25-30, and *De amab. Eccl. conc.* (1533), LB, V, 504BC.

I must therefore disagree with Krodel's judgment ("Die Abendmahlslehre," pt. 1, p. 262), that "Die Anerkennung der Lehrautorität der Kirche war aber alles andere als die Übernahme der katholischen dogmatischen Abendmahlslehre; er wahrte durchaus seine eigene Position des mystisch-ethischen Abendmahlsverständnisses." It is true that he did not take over the doctrine of transubstantiation concerning the mode of the corporeal presence, but he did accept the corporeal presence as such, so his understanding of that presence was not simply mystical-ethical.

I find myself in more basic agreement with Karl Heinz Oelrich that the writings of Oecolampadius aroused in Erasmus doubts concerning the corporeal Real Presence, but that, assisted and confirmed by the authority of the Church, in the end Erasmus explicitly confessed his faith in that dogma, although he remained critical of speculations concerning the "how" of the mystery *Der späte Erasmus und die Reformation,* pp. 135 ff. However, I am critical of his account for its failures (1) to place Erasmus' views on the Real Presence squarely within the context of his overall Eucharistic theology; (2) to treat at all adequately the important concept of the authority of the Church; (3) to explicate sufficiently the position of Oecolampadius so that it might be clearer in what respects Erasmus was attracted by the Reformer's teaching; (4) to consider the important previous secondary literature on the subject, e.g., the dissertation of Krodel, which, as this scholar himself suggests in a review, varies considerably in its conclusions from that of Oelrich (cf. *Theologische Literaturzeitung,* 1962, No. 10, p. 738). In addition I criticize his attempt to show that the year 1529 marks a decisive change in Erasmus' outlook on the Eucharist.

134. LB, X, 1563C. We have noticed that though Erasmus does not at all emphasize the Real Presence in his earlier writings, on the other hand, neither does he call it into question. Whether the authority of the Church was needed even earlier to prevent him from wavering in his faith, as it surely was after 1525, cannot be ascertained with assurance since there are no texts prior to 1525 which join the authority of the Church with the Real Presence. The implication of the above statement is that only now, that is, in 1526, after the questioning of the Real Presence by Carlstadt, Zwingli, and Oecolampadius, did Erasmus need the confirmation of the authority of the Church; but in the light of his symbolistic and spiritualistic tendency from the beginning, grounded in his neo-Platonic outlook, it is probable that even prior to the Eucharistic controversy he needed the confirmation of the authority of the Church just as he did with other issues which went counter to his humanistic reason. Perhaps his doubts on this score were only fully aroused by the treatises of these men, especially that of Oecolampadius.

At this point I must take issue with Oelrich's contention that in 1529 Erasmus changed from a skeptic disturbed by doubts concerning the Eucharist to a convinced and confident believer in the Church dogma. "Mit dem Jahre verstummen bei Erasmus die Bekenntnisse einer Neigung zur Abendmahlslehre Okolampads." Beginning with the publication of the preface to Alger's treatise in March 1530, Erasmus' utterances on the Eucharist are no longer characterized by uncertainty and hesitation but are "von innerer Geschlossenheit." *Der späte Erasmus,* p. 148. Oelrich overlooks, in a letter as late as June 1529, Erasmus' inclination toward Oecolampadius' view if it were not for the authority of the Church. Even in the preface to Alger Erasmus mentions the

variations and obscurities of the Fathers and the many difficult questions which have emerged concerning this sacrament. Also in the letter
to Tunstall of January 1530, Erasmus expresses his doubt, not concerning the Real Presence, to be sure, but concerning the dogma of
transubstantiation as well as the New Testament foundation of the rite
of the consecration of the bread and wine into the body and blood of
the Lord. Allen, VIII, 2263, 69-83. Oelrich is cognizant of these continuing difficulties of Erasmus, but he quickly passes over them (p.
149). He is likewise aware of the expression of doubt concerning the
dogma of transubstantiation in the letter to Amerbach (pp. 151 f.), but
allows himself nevertheless to describe Erasmus' post-1529 view simply as a "Bekenntnis zum kirchlichen Eucharistiedogma" (p. 149). That
Oelrich's judgment concerning the firm conviction and inner certainty
of the Erasmian statements from 1530 to 1536 on the Eucharist is an
exaggeration is clear from Erasmus' continued need to refer to the
authority of the Church to confirm his faith. Furthermore, Oelrich
exaggerates not only the unambiguity of Erasmus' pre-1529 certainty
but also the extent of his pre-1529 skepticism. Oelrich makes light of
Erasmus' description of his views in the letter to Pellican and scarcely
elucidates the content of the *Detectio,* in both of which one can find
statements in harmony with the post-1529 utterances. After 1529, as
before, Erasmus exhibited a faith in the Real Presence, but one which
required confirmation by the authority of the Church. One can, however, agree with Oelrich to this extent: that expressions of doubt are
more seldom and statements of faith are more frequent and more
explicit in the post-1529 period, probably in order that Erasmus may
clearly distinguish himself from the Reformed understanding.

CHAPTER IX

BAPTISM AND CONFIRMATION

1. *Paraphr. in evang. Matt.* (1522), 28:19, LB, VII, 145B-146D.
2. *Eccles.* (1535), LB, V, 827AB.
3. *Paraphr. in evang. Marci* (1523), LB, VII, 271C.
4. *Paraphr. in evang. Ioannis* (1523); LB, VII, 520BC.
5. *Ratio* (1519), Holborn, 199, 32 f., and LB, V, 87BC.
6. *Paraphr. in evang. Ioannis,* LB, VII, 525DE.
7. *Ibid.,* 523D.
8. *Paraphr. in evang. Matt.,* 3:15, LB, VII, 17C. See the same in the
Paraphrases of the other Gospels, LB, VII, 161D, 315B, 509B. Already
to be found in Ignatius (Eph. 18:2) is the idea that Christ "was born
and baptized that by his Passion he might hallow water." *Early Christian
Fathers,* ed. C. C. Richardson (Philadelphia, 1953), Vol. I in *Library of
Christian Classics,* ed. John Baillie *et al.,* p. 93. Without mention of the

Passion this thought was present also in Tertullian and Clement of Alexandria. See. A. Benoit, *Le baptême chrétien au second siècle* (Paris, 1953), p. 67.

9. Note on John 1:31, *Nov. Test.* (1519), p. 169, retained in later editions; see LB, VI, 345D. Erasmus is, however, critical here of what he considers Augustine's forced exegesis of this passage in order to use it against the Donatists. Cf. *Ratio* (1519, 1520), Holborn, 289, 21 ff., and LB, V, 130. See other passages which emphasize Christ, not the minister, as the source of the power and effect of baptism: *Paraphr. in evang. Ioannis* (1523), 1:33, LB, VII, 510B; To Henry VIII (the Preface to *Paraphr. in evang. Lucae*), 23 August 1523, Allen, V, 1381, 177-179.

10. He lists the terms of a careful rhetorical definition and description, most of which he illustrates with a treatment of baptism, in LB, V, 932A. He says that Cicero and Themistius took these terms from Aristotle. 931F.

11. We have already noticed, however, that in two lists of the seven sacraments he did not place it first in order but second or third after marriage.

12. LB, V, 933CD.

13. *Declar. ad cens. colloq.* (1532), LB, IX, 947EF.

14. B. Neunheuser, *Handbuch der Dogmengeschichte*, vol. IV, 2, *Taufe und Firmung* (Freiburg im Br., 1956), pp. 95-96. See also R. Seeberg, *Die Theologie des Johannes Duns Scotus*, pp. 351-357, especially 352-354.

15. The *Didache* is the first witness to baptism by aspersion. Later in the patristic period this method of baptism was practically limited to the "clinici," was sometimes regarded as having less value than baptism by immersion, and, as at Rome, had to be regularized by episcopal imposition of hands. Benoit, p. 9, and A. Stenzel, *Die Taufe* (Innsbruck, 1958), p. 46, n. 2. Apparently this name, "clinici," was attributed in jest to the sick or dying who received baptism by aspersion by those who did not highly regard such a baptism. Cf. *Concio de miseric. Dom.* (1524), LB, V, 581B: "Quidam olim ingenti periculo differebant baptismum usque ad extremum vitae diem, quos alii clinicos, alii adspersos appellabant, veluti Christianos parum γνησίως . . ." That Erasmus does not himself view highly such a practice is apparent from this statement which shortly follows: "Nec sine causa dubitatum est, an efficax esset ille baptismus, quo iam desperata vita, ac tantum non animam agentes adspergebantur, verius quam tingebantur."

16. Alexander of Hales (d. 1245) was the first to apply the Aristotelian concept of the four causes to the theology of baptism. *Summa theol.* IV q 8, 1-12; cited by Neunheuser, p. 84. The formal cause, in contrast to Erasmus, is understood as the immersion and the accompanying word, i.e., the utterance of the Trinitarian formula. Neunheuser, pp. 84-85. For Thomas the formal cause was simply the

utterance of the Trinitarian formula of Matt. 28:19. *Summa theol.* III q 66 a 5. Scotus understands the matter and form of baptism differently from the usual scholastic teaching (Neunheuser, p. 94, and Seeberg, *Die Theol. des Duns Scotus,* pp. 349 f.). The Thomistic view, however, became the general teaching fixed at the Council of Florence, 1439 [*Decretum pro Armenis,* Denzinger, 696 (1314)]. Of course, the Trinitarian formula had long been regarded as the necessary method of baptizing. At the Council of Arles, 314, it was judged that the only condition for the validity of heretical baptism was the satisfactory use of the Trinitarian formula. Denzinger, 53 (123).

17. *Eccles.,* LB, V, 934AB.

18. *Ibid.,* 934C-F.

19. *Paraphr. in epist. Pauli ad Gal.* (1519), 5:3-6, LB, VII, 961C-962A. Cf. 945A, 957F-958A. See above on law and gospel, pp. 70 ff.

20. *Paraphr. in epist. Pauli ad Col.* (1520), 2:11, LB, VII, 1010CD.

21. *Ratio* (1519), Holborn, 199, 1 ff., and LB, V, 86F.

22. *Eccles.,* LB, V, 830E.

23. Ἰχθυοφαγία (1526), LB, I, 792AB.

24. *Ratio* (1519), Holborn, 199, 13 ff., and LB, V, 87AB.

25. *Paraphr. in evang. Marci* (1523), 1:4, LB, VII, 158E-159A; note on Mark 1:4, *Nov. Test.* (1527), pt. 2, p. 109, and LB, VI, 153D; *Paraphr. in evang. Matt.,* 3:6, 7, LB, VII, 13F-14A, C; *Paraphr. in evang. Ioannis* (1523), 1:26, LB, VII, 508C.

26. *Paraphr. in evang. Marci,* 1:5, LB, VII, 159CD. Cf. *Paraphr. in evang. Lucae,* 1:77, LB, VII, 296F.

27. *Enchiridion* (1503), LB, V, 31C. *Paraphr. in evang. Marci* (1523), 1:10, LB, VII, 161E; *Paraphr. in evang. Ioannis* (1523), 5:4, LB, VII, 533F; *Declar. ad cens.* (1532), LB, IX, 862B. In this last passage Erasmus explicitly connects the corporeal aspect of baptism with the carnal part of man, his body: "Iuxta hanc partem Legem appellare crassam aut carnalem, nihilo contumeliosius est, quam si quis corpus appellet, quod sensibus magis patet, ut in baptismo aqua, sal, et unctio."

28. *Supput. errorum N. Beddae,* LB, IX, 688B. As in the definition of *Eccles.* above, he says that these are distinguished by the terms "matter" and "form." He even says here that "theologi" are accustomed so to distinguish them. I do not know what theologians he has in mind, because, as noted above, this was not the customary scholastic usage.

29. *Detectio praestig.,* LB, X, 1562F; *Paraphr. in evang. Marci,* 1:10, LB, VII, 161E; *Paraphr. in acta apost.* (1524), 11:16, LB, VII, 713C. The emphasis on moral renewal as the spiritual aspect of baptism is especially strong in the *Enchiridion* (1503), LB, V, 31BC. Cf. *Paraphr. in evang. Ioannis* (1523), 5:4, LB, VII, 533F, where he mentions both the works of the baptized and the heavenly power (grace) as accompanying an effective baptism.

30. In his stress upon the inner, spiritual meaning of baptism as

over against the external rite, Erasmus is again quite close to his favorite of the Fathers, Origen. See Neunheuser, p. 30. Cf. G. W. H. Lampe, *The Seal of the Spirit* (London, 1951), p. 163, and Daniélou, p. 67. Likewise, Colet under the caption of "spiritalis speculatio baptismi" spoke of the visible and invisible in the sacraments and, like Erasmus, made the connection with the soul and body in man: "Ut enim invisibilia sunt sensibilium initia, ita sensibilia sacramenta insensibilium sunt significamenta, quae sacramentis spiritualibus, ut corpus animae, adhibenter." *Ionnes Coletus super Opera Dionysii,* tr. and ed. J. H. Lupton (London, 1869), p. 211; cited by Auer, p. 246, n. 286. In his emphasis upon the distinction between inner and outer baptism Erasmus may have been influential upon Zwingli and such an Anabaptist as Hübmaier. See Rollin S. Armour, *Anabaptist Baptism* (Scottdale, Pa., 1966), pp. 26 f., 30 f.

31. *Paraphr. in evang. Lucae* (1523), 22:12, 13, LB, VII, 450BC; *Concio in ps. IV* (1525), LB, V, 282F; *Concio in ps. XXII* (1530), LB, V, 325B; *De amab. Eccl. conc.* (1533), LB, V, 489C: "Aditus in Ecclesiam fides, sine qua nihil prodest baptismus."

32. *Paraphr. in evang. Marci* (1523), 1:10, LB, VII, 161E.

33. *Enarr. in ps. XXII* (1530), LB, V, 325A.

34. *Paraphr. in acta apost.* (1524), 11:17, LB, VII, 713D. Cf. *Paraphr. in evang. Marci* (1523), 16:16, LB, VII, 271C-272A: "Quicunque crediderit Evangelio, per quod omnibus in me fidentibus, per mortem meam offertur gratuita remissio peccatorum omnium, et huius gratiae signum acceperit, aqua tinctus, salvus erit"; and *Paraphr. in evang. Matt.* (1522), 28:19, LB, VII, 146B.

35. *Concio de miseric. Dom.* (1524), LB, V, 581BC.

36. *Paraphr. in epist. Pauli ad Cor. I* (1519), 6:11, LB, VII, 876D; *Paraphr. in evang. Lucae* (1523), 3:21, LB, VII, 315D; *Hyper. II* (1527), LB, X, 1506EF.

37. *Expos. concion. in ps. LXXXV* (1528), LB, V, 518C; *Symbolum* (1533), LB, V, 1176C.

38. *Hyper. II* (1527), LB, X, 1401D.

39. *Enchiridion* (1503), LB, V, 21B. Himelick mistranslates "morbus" as "guilt" in this passage. *The Enchiridion of Erasmus,* p. 84. Cf. *De praep. ad mort.* (1534), LB, V, 1298A.

40. *Expos. concion. in ps. LXXXV* (1528), LB, V, 518B; *De praep. ad mort.,* LB, V, 1298B.

41. *Enarr. ps. I* (1515), LB, V, 174C; *Paraphr. in epist. Pauli ad Rom.* (1517), 6:5, LB, VII, 795B; *Paraphr. in evang. Lucae,* 3:22, LB, VII, 315E.

42. *Paraphr. in epist. Pauli ad Gal.* (1519), 3:28, LB, VII, 956B; *Concio in ps. IV* (1525), LB, V, 257C; *De amab. Eccl. conc.* (1533), LB, V, 491D.

43. *De amab. Eccl. conc.* (1533), LB, V, 480D; *Enarr. ps. XIV* (1536), LB, V, 301D.

44. *Eccles.,* LB, V, 772AB.

45. *Nov. Test.* (1519), p. 429, and retained in LB, VI, 857CD. Cf. *Christ. matr.* (1526), LB, V, 669F-670C.

46. *Paraphr. in epist. Pauli ad Cor. II* (1519), 5:17, LB, VII, 925AB; *Eccles.* (1535), LB, V, 1022C. In this last passage he is especially critical of the monks' appropriation of this term "brother" when it belongs to all who have been reborn in Christ by baptism. Cf. *Enchiridion*, LB, V, 45A-D.

47. *Symbolum* (1533), LB, V, 1137C; *Enarr. ps. XIV* (1536), LB, V, 310B.

48. *Paraphr. in epist. Pauli ad Cor. I* (1519), 6:19, LB, VII, 878A; *Concio in ps. IV*, LB, V, 257C, 282F; *De amab. Eccl. conc.* (1533), LB, V, 491DE.

49. *Symbolum*, LB, V, 1169D.

50. On the gradual growth of an independent rite of confirmation, at which moment the gift of the Spirit is bestowed by episcopal chrism and laying on of hands, see W. Maurer, "Geschichte von Firmung und Konfirmation bis zum Ausgang der lutherischen Orthodoxie," in *Confirmatio, Forschungen zur Geschichte und Praxis der Konfirmation,* ed. Kurt Frör (Munich, 1959), pp. 9-32, 46-57; Neunheuser, pp. 100-109; G. Dix, *The Theology of Confirmation in Relation to Baptism* (London, 1946); Lampe, pp. 149-192. On the influence of the supposed teaching of the texts from Acts concerning the gift of the Spirit by the laying on of hands, see Lampe, pp. 152, 161, 173-174, 177, 182. The culmination of this development is reached in the *Decretum pro Armenis* of the Council of Florence, 1439, concerning confirmation, which cites the Acts 8 passage as a New Testament basis for this sacrament and states that "in eo datur Spiritus Sanctus ad robur." Denzinger, 697 (1318, 1319).

51. The Reformers Luther, Zwingli, and Calvin all rejected confirmation as a sacrament, although they allowed a ceremony of confirmation or blessing to remain, what Luther called a *ceremonia sacramentalis* (*De captivitate Babylonica*, WA 6, 549). Maurer, "Geschichte von Firmung und Konfirmation," pp. 23 ff.

52. *Paraphr. in epist. Pauli ad Gal.* (1519), 5:24, LB, VII, 964D; *Paraphr. in ps. III* (1524), LB, V, 239B; *De amab. Eccl. conc.* (1533), LB, V, 481E.

53. *Supput. errorum N. Beddae* (1527), LB, IX, 630CD; *Declar. ad cens.* (1532), LB, IX, 885A. Even the merits which follow baptism do not necessitate the gift from God of eternal life. There is no equality between the reward and the merit. *Ibid.,* 886A-C.

54. *Paraphr. in epist. Pauli ad Rom.* (1517), LB, VII, 795 AB. Cf. a similar rapid change from the indicative to the imperative with emphasis upon the latter in Colet's commentary on Romans 6, *I. Coleti Enarratio in epistolam S. Pauli ad Romanos,* tr. and ed. J. H. Lupton (London, 1873), pp. 144-145.

55. Kohls fails to mark this emphasis when he states: "Erasmus

umschreibt auf diese Weise mit der ganz an den Gebrauch der Militär-
sprache angeglichenen Verwendung des Begriffes sacramentum das
objektive und das subjektive Heilsgeschehen der Taufe, die für ihn
unlöslich miteinander verbunden sind." *Die Theologie des Erasmus*, II, 88,
n. 22. Cf. *ibid.*, I, 73.

56. *Paraphr. in evang. Marci* (1523), 1:13, LB, VII, 162D; *Concio de
miseric. Dom.* (1524), LB, V, 565A; *Christ. matr.* (1526), LB, V, 680F. The
renunciation of Satan was the counterpart of the baptismal confession
in the ancient church's ceremony prior to the actual immersion in the
water. See *Constitutiones apostolorum*, VII, 41, in *Didascalia et constitutiones
apostolorum*, ed. F. X. Funk (Paderborn, 1895), p. 444. Cf. Tertullian,
De spect., 4, in *PL*, I, 709B; and Origen, *In Num. homil.*, V, 1, in *GCS*,
VII, ed. W. A. Bährens, 26, 14 ff.; cited by O. Heggelbacher, *Die christliche Taufe als Rechtsakt nach den Zeugnis der frühen Christenheit* (Freiburg,
Switzerland, 1953), p. 96, n. 431.

57. These three foes, which, as we have already noticed in connection with Erasmus' Christology and soteriology, are frequently cited
together as having been conquered by Christ and therefore as con-
querable by the Christian soldier, are associated with the act of renunciation in baptism in the *Enchiridion* (1503), LB, V, 23CD.

58. *Enchiridion*, LB, V, 3AB, 23BC; *Paraphr. in evang. Lucae* (1523),
4:12, LB, VII, 322D; *Christ. matr.* (1526), LB, V, 714B; *Exseq. seraph.*
(1531), LB, I, 868C.

59. See Heggelbacher, pp. 97 ff.

60. *Enchiridion*, LB, V, 2C. Cf. *Paraphr. in evang. Marci*, 12:17, LB,
VII, 249EF, and *De amab. Eccl. conc.*, LB, V, 498EF.

61. *De contemptu mundi* (1521), LB, V, 1262EF: "Nec imagineris tibi
quidquam in votis deesse, si votum, quod Christo professus es in
baptismo, praestiteris . . ."; cited by Mestwerdt, p. 66. This passage
comes from the final chapter, which was probably added some time
after the first eleven chapters were written (c. 1486, Allen, IV, 1194,
Intro.), presumably shortly before publication. Telle, p. 16. Telle takes
the view that there is no flagrant contradiction between the first eleven
chapters and the twelfth because the first eleven were written only
ostensibly in praise of the monastic life (pp. 16 ff.). On the other hand,
A. Hyma thinks that Erasmus is serious in his regard for the monastery
in the first eleven chapters but that his praise for monastic life is from
his point of view as a humanist, not as a true monk; chapter twelve must
be seen then as a later contrasting reflection, after the ascetic life had
become entirely repugnant to him. *The Youth of Erasmus* (Ann Arbor,
1930), pp. 173-174; "Erasmus and the Sacrament of Matrimony," pp.
146 ff. In his review of Telle's book, Hyma is critical of the French
scholar for having paid no attention to the results of the research of
earlier scholars such as Fruin, Ruden, Lindeboom, Mestwerdt, and

Allen, which had shown that Erasmus' final chapter does represent a fundamental change in attitude toward monasticism as over against the rest of the work. "Erasmus and the Sacrament of Matrimony," pp. 145 ff. and 148, n. 16.

62. *Eccles.* (1535), LB, V, 1020F, 1024C-F, 1025C-E; *Paracl.* (1516), LB, V, 142F-143A; appendix prefixed to *Paraphr. in evang. Matt.* (1522), LB, VII, **3b; *Christ. matr.* (1526), LB, V, 647D.

63. *Virgo* μισόγαμος (1523), LB, I, 700B: "Negotium pietatis potissimum agitur in baptismo: heic tantum agitur de veste mutanda, deque genere vitae, quod per se neque bonum est, neque malum." *Ibid.,* 700D. Cf. *Declar. ad cens. colloq.* (1532), LB, IX, 939F-940A.

Cf. *Enchiridion* (1503), LB, V, 65C: "Monachatus non est pietas, sed vitae genus pro suo cuique corporis ingeniique habitu, vel utile, vel inutile." Kohls points out that already in the *Oratio funebris* (c. 1489), composed for the death of Berta de Heyen, is to be found this thought of a "Mönchtum in der Welt." LB, VIII, 555EF, cited by Kohls, II, 52, n. 120. See also I, 200 ff.

As Mestwerdt has shown, L. Valla, who made a vivid impression on Erasmus, had already insisted that because of the baptismal vow, no second vow is necessary; that because of the perfection of the rule of Christ and the Apostles, no second rule is necessary; and that therefore Christian morality is independent of the forms in which it realizes itself. "De professione religiosorum," *Opusc. tria,* v. 62, pp. 123, 127 ff.; Mestwerdt, pp. 65 ff. See also Charles Trinkhaus, "Humanist Treatises on the Status of the Religious: Petrarch, Salutati, Valla," *Studies in the Renaissance,* XI (1964), 36 ff.

64. Telle, pp. 6 f. and 131 ff. Cf. Hyma's criticism of Telle based on the much earlier research of Jan Lindeboom [*Erasmus, onderzoek naar zijn theologie en zijn godsdienstig gemoedsbestaan* (Leiden, 1909), pp. 193-195]: "Strange though it may seem, Erasmus did not fully turn against the monastic life nor condemn celibacy always after 1514. On the contrary, as Professor J. Lindeboom has pointed out, he often argued in favor of both." "Erasmus and the Sacrament of Matrimony," p. 159. Without mentioning Telle, Kohls thinks that with his concept of a "Mönchtum in der Welt" Erasmus does not intend in the *De contemptu mundi* (LB, V, 1261D-F) nor elsewhere a "grundsätzliche Ablehnung des Mönchtums." I, 32.

65. Thompson, *Colloquies,* p. 101. See especially Πτωχοπλούσιοι (1524), LB, I, 744DE, and *Militis et Cartusiani* (1523), LB, I, 708 ff. Erasmus had the greatest respect for the order of the Carthusians. See To Vincent Theodorici, ⟨ c. March ⟩ 1521, Allen, IV, 1196, 425 ff.; *Apol. adv. debacch. P. Sutoris* (1525), LB, IX, 740A,D; cited by Allen, IV, 1196, 425 n. In this note Allen points to Epp. 308, 570, 1239, and 1646, where friends of Erasmus among the Carthusians are mentioned.

66. Thompson, *Colloquies*, p. 204. They were John Vitrarius, in To Jodocus Jonas, 13 June 1521, Allen, IV, 1211, 13-245, and Theodoric Coelde, in To Jodocus Gaverius, 1 March ⟨1523⟩, Allen, V, 1347, 104-117.

67. To a Monk, 15 October 1527, Allen, VII, 1887, and To John of Heemstede, 28 February 1533, Allen, X, 2771.

68. Hans Hillerbrand suggests the similarity of Erasmus' view to that of the Anabaptists "in its insistence that to be valid baptism must be accompanied by true discipleship." "The Origin of Sixteenth Century Anabaptism: Another Look," *ARG*, LIII (1962), 160. He draws here upon Krodel's brief discussion, "Die Abendmahlslehre des Erasmus," pp. 73, 78.

69. *Paraphr. in evang. Matt.* (1522), 28:19, LB, VII, 146BC; *Paraphr. in epist. Iac.* (1520), 1:18, 19, LB, VII, 1122C, F; *Paraphr. in epist. I. Ioannis* (1521), 3:6, LB, VII, 1152A.

70. *In Ioannis Comm.*, 1:27, in *GCS*, IV, ed. E. Preuschen, 142, 19-20. Cf. *In Rom. Comm.*, 5:8, in *PG*, XIV, 1040B; cited by Neunheuser, p. 30, n. 40. Cf. Lampe, pp. 163 f., and Daniélou, p. 67.

71. *Paraphr. in epist. Pauli ad Rom.* (1517), 13:14, LB, VII, 822CD: "Nunc posteaquam per baptismum Christo estis insiti, hunc ipsum induite. Eluceat in omni vita, quem sitis professi. Exprimite quem imbibistis . . ." *Paraphr. in epist. Pauli ad Cor. I*, 6:8, LB, VII, 876BC.

72. *Paraphr. in epist. Pauli ad Rom.*, 6:6, LB, VII, 795C; *Paraphr. in ps. III* (1524), LB, V, 239BC.

73. *Paraphr. in evang. Lucae* (1523), 1:12, LB, VII, 322D: "In baptismo damus nomina duci nostro, sub illius vexillis adversus Satanae copias bellaturi." *Exseq. seraph.* (1531), LB, I, 868C. Cf. Colet, *De ecclesiastico hierarchia*, ed. J. Lupton (London, 1869), pp. 201, 208, 209, 214.

74. *Paraphr. in epist. Pauli I ad Tim.* (1520), 3:6, LB, VII, 1044E: "Baptismus aperit aditum in Ecclesiam: verum hic superest, ut pro se quisque certatim contendat ad sanctimoniae metam." *Paraphr. in evang. Marci* (1523), 1:13, LB, VII, 162DE. Cf. Origen, *In Iudic. hom.*, IX, 2, and *In Ex. hom.*, VIII, 4, in *GCS*, VII, ed. W. A. Baehrens, 520, 15 ff.; VI, 223, 16; cited by Neunheuser, p. 31, n. 51. "Die Taufe ist damit auch Beginn und Prinzip des geistlichen Kampfes." *Ibid.*, p. 31.

75. *Paraphr. in evang. Lucae* (1523), 4:12, LB, VII, 322D.

76. Daniélou, p. 71. Daniélou refers to P. Hugo Rahner, "Taufe und geistliches Leben bei Origenes," *Zeitschrift für Aszese und Mystik* (1932), pp. 205-223.

77. *Paraphr. in epist. Pauli I ad Tim.*, 3:6, LB, VII, 1044E. Cf. *Paraphr. in epist. ad Col.* (1520), 2:6, 7, LB, VII, 1009DE.

78. *Paraphr. in evang. Marci*, 4:29, LB, VII, 190F; *Eccles.* (1535), LB,

V, 941C. Cf. *Expos. concion. in ps. LXXXV* (1528), LB, V, 537F-538C, where Erasmus sets catechism, baptism, and profession of Christian service in the second stage of the journey on the road to salvation, after a natural knowledge of God. Consequently, the third step is progress; the fourth, perfection.

79. *Paraphr. in epist. Pauli ad Cor. I* (1519), 10:12, LB, VII, 892D.

80. On baptism as the *signaculum infragile* among the Fathers see F. J. Dölger, *Sphragis. Eine altchristliche Taufbezeichnung in ihren Beziehungen zur profanen und religiösen Kultur des Altertums* (Paderborn, 1911), pp. 133 f., n. 2.

81. *Paraphr. in evang. Lucae* (1523), 11:24, LB, VII, 383CD: "Huic ad pristinam vitam revoluto, ad nihil aliud proderit baptismus ac cognitio sacrae doctrinae, nisi ut graviorem damnationem sibi accersat in die iudicii, videlicet ad pristinos errores ingratitudinem etiam, ac malitiam adiungens." *Paraphr. in II epist. Petri* (1520), 2:20, LB, VII, 1107B. Cf. Cyril of Jerusalem, *Cat.* III, 8, in *PG*, XXXIII, 440A; cited by Dölger, p. 134, n. 2.

82. *Paraphr. in epist. Pauli ad Rom.*, 6:9-11, LB, VII, 795EF; *Paraphr. in I epist. Petri* (1520), 3:21, LB, VII, 1094F-1095A.

83. *Symbolum* (1533), LB, V, 1171AB. Cf. Augustine, *De symbolo ad catechumenos*, c. 7, in *PL*, XL, 636; cited by Dölger, p. 134, n. 2.

84. Origen, *Hom. Luc.*, IX, 146; XXI; XXII; *Hom. Ezech.*, VI, 7; *Hom. Levit.*, VI, 2, cited by Daniélou, p. 67. See also Lampe, p. 163.

85. *Paraphr. in acta apost.* (1523), 2:42, LB, VII, 674A; *Paraphr. in epist. ad Heb.* (1521), 5:12, LB, VII, 1174A; *Expos. concion. in ps. LXXXV* (1528), LB, V, 537F. By rudiments Erasmus means what can be comprehended in a few articles (LB, V, 537F), presumably what is summarized in the Apostles' Creed. See the sections in the first chapter concerned with a simple theology based on Scripture and the Apostles' Creed. Erasmus' *Symbolum* (1533), which is largely an exposition of the Apostles' Creed, is an example of such a catechism. For an analysis of the *Symbolum* and its importance as a catechism, see R. Padberg, *Erasmus als Katechet.* At the end of his discussion of the Creed, before taking up the Ten Commandments, Erasmus states: "Ad consequendum Baptismum ista credere satis est homini laico: eruditis ac profectioribus omnia credenda sunt, quae sacris Voluminibus expressa sunt, aut quae illinc evidenter colliguntur: praeterea quidquid universali perpetuoque consensu comprobavit Ecclesia Catholica." LB, V, 1179BC. For the catechumen the essentials of faith as given in the Apostles' Creed suffice, but the more mature should believe all that is contained in Scripture and tradition as defined by him ("whatever the Church has approved by a universal and perpetual consensus"). See the whole discussion of Scripture and tradition above.

86. R. Padberg thinks that Erasmus in his catechisms, *Institut.*

Christ. hom. (1514), LB, V, 1357C ff., and the *Symbolum,* LB, V, 1133 ff., over against the medieval disinterest in the kerygmatic material of the catechism, may be regarded along with Colet, "als Erneuerer der kate-chetischen Verkündigung." Padberg, p. 157.

87. *Paraphr. in evang. Matt.,* 28:19, LB, VII, 145B, 146BC; *Expos. concion. in ps. LXXXV,* LB, V, 538AB.

88. *Eccles.,* LB, V, 831D.

89. *Expos. concion. in ps. LXXXV,* LB, V, 538A.

90. LB, VII, **3b. I quote the important elements of this text: "Quin et illud mihi videtur non mediocriter ad hanc rem conducturum, si pueri baptizati, quum iam ad pubertatem pervenerint, iubeantur huiusmodi, concionibus adesse, in quibus illis dilucide declaretur, quid in se contineat professio baptismi. Deinde diligenter privatim examinentur a probis viris, satis ne teneant, ac meminerint ea, quae docuit Sacerdos. Si comperientur satis tenere, interrogentur ratum ne habeant, quod susceptores illorum nomine polliciti sunt in baptismo. Si respondeant se ratum habere, tum publice renovetur ea professio, simul congregatis aequalibus, idque ceremoniis gravibus, aptis, castis, seriis, ac magnificis: quaeque deceant eam professionem, qua nulla potest esse sanctior." W. Maurer analyzed this important text in his *Gemeindezucht, Gemeindeamt, Konfirmation* (Cassel, 1940), pp. 43 ff. He summarized and partly revised his discussion there in a more recent essay already referred to, "Geschichte von Firmung und Konfirmation bis zum Ausgang der lutherischen Orthodoxie," pp. 19-23.

91. Not altogether novel, however, since the Bohemian Brethren already had something very much like it, as found in their confession of 1468 and as amplified under the leadership of Lukas von Prague in the Confessions of 1503 and 1511. See Georg Rietschel-Paul Graff, *Lehrbuch der Liturgik* (Göttingen, 1951), I, 629 f.; for a brief description of their rite, see Maurer, "Geschichte von Firmung und Konfirma-tion," p. 18. See also his *Gemeindezucht,* pp. 45-46. Erasmus had ample opportunity to learn of the Bohemian position. He received two visitors of the Brethren in 1520 at Antwerp who brought him a copy of their *Apologia* of 1507. For an account of this visit see Allen, IV, 1117, Intro. He acknowledges having received this book, but confesses that he has not had time to examine it thoroughly, although he has had it for six months—in a letter probably to Artlebus of Boskowitz, 28 January 1521, Allen, IV, 1183, 8-9. Artlebus of Boskowitz sent him a copy of a *Regula* of theirs probably in 1520. From Artlebus of Bosko-witz, ⟨c. October (?), 1520 ⟩ Allen, IV, 1154, 8-9, and n. 8.

92. Maurer thinks that this thought is "für die Ideengeschichte der Sentimentalität im abendländischen Kulturkreise nicht ohne Bedeutung." *Gemeindezucht,* p. 47, n. 3, and "Geschichte von Firmung und Konfirmation," p. 21.

93. LB, VII, **3b: "Haec si fierent, quemadmodum oporteret, aut ego fallor, aut haberemus aliquanto sinceriores Christianos, quam habemus. . . . Nunc multi sunt quinquagenarii, qui nesciant quid voverint in baptismo: qui ne somniarint quidem, quid sibi velint articuli fidei, quid precatio Dominica, quid Ecclesiae sacramenta." Cf. *Apol. adv. mon. Hisp.* (1528), LB, IX, 1061AB: "Ut paucis rem absolvam, *Christiani* generali nomine dicuntur, quicunque baptizati sunt, ut haec vox complectatur etiam haereticos, et apostatas, et parricidas: sed vere Christiani sunt, qui sacramento respondent innovatione vitae." (Erasmus' italics.) And cf. *Declar. ad cens.* (1532), LB, IX, 821AB.

94. LB, VII, **3b. Cf. *Supput. errorum N. Beddae* (1527), LB, IX, 562E: "Fides enim persuasio est, cogi non potest, nec debet"; and *Declar. ad cens.* (1532), LB, IX, 821B.

95. *Apol. adv. mon. Hisp.*, LB, IX, 1061C-E: "Puer vere baptizatus hactenus est Christianus, quod insitus in corpus Ecclesiae servatur, supplente per Ecclesiae fidem Dei bonitate quod deest aetati, non tamen ista sufficerent eidem, si perveniat ad aetatem adultam. In adultis autem baptismus non est perfectus Christianismus, nisi praeter sacramentum accipiant sacramenti gratiam, sed initium ac rudimentum Christianismi . . . In pueris tantum valet sacramentum, ut, si decesserint infantes, sufficiat illis ad salutem, et si adoleverint, non sit opus altero baptismo." Andrén correctly states that "Der Akt selbst ist jedoch nicht als eine Wiederholung, sondern als eine Aktualisierung der Taufe aufzufassen. . . . Was er erstrebt, lässt sich am besten als ein erweiterter Taufakt charakterisieren." Carl-Gustaf Andrén, "Die Konfirmationsfrage in der Reformationszeit," in *Zur Geschichte und Ordnung der Konfirmation in den lutherischen Kirchen,* ed. Kurt Frör (Munich, 1962), p. 51.

96. These are the passages in the apologies in which he answers attacks upon the proposal in the appendix: *Prologus in supput. Beddae* (1526), LB, IX, 445C-F; *Resp. ad notata per N. Beddam* (1526), LB, IX, 459, 484BC; *Supput. errorum N. Beddae* (1527), LB, IX, 557-563B; *Apol. adv. mon. Hisp.* (1528), LB, IX, 1062A-C; *Declar. ad cens.* (1532), LB, IX, 820A-822E.

97. *Prologus in supput. Beddae,* 445C: "Mentitur me veluti novum Evangelistam temerare ritus et sacramenta Ecclesiae Catholicae, cum ego de Baptismo non agam, sed de Catechismo, qui solet olim praecedere Baptismum: nunc propono considerandum, an quoniam infantes baptizamur, expediat ut ex Ecclesiae constitutione catechismus peragatur in adultis, quo cognoscant quid in Baptismo sint professi." Cf. *Supput. errorum N. Beddae,* 558D, 560D, and *Apol. adv. mon. Hisp.,* 1062AB, C.

W. Maurer says that Erasmus defends himself from the charge of introducing a new sacrament by the "Hinweis auf die altkirchliche

Skrutienpraxis, die er nur wieder aufgenommen hat." *Gemeindezucht,* p. 45, n. 3; also "Geschichte von Firmung und Konfirmation," p. 21. But I find in the texts no specific reference to this practice (Maurer gives no reference), although Erasmus' proposal bears a resemblance to that rite which was, however, in contrast with what Erasmus had in mind, more a liturgical and sacramental than a catechetical occurrence. Not the child but the acolyte, a member of the clergy, gave answer to the questions of the priest. (Vischer, p. 51.)

98. *Resp. ad notata per N. Beddam,* 459E; *Supput. errorum N. Beddae,* 563A.

99. *Declar. ad cens.,* LB, IX, 820F-821D.

100. Erasmus' entire proposal was expressly anathematized by the Council of Trent. Denzinger, 870 (1627). See H. Jedin, *A History of the Council of Trent,* tr. E. Graf, II (St. Louis, 1961), 388.

101. Maurer, *Gemeindezucht,* pp. 43 ff.; "Geschichte von Firmung und Konfirmation," p. 20. Kohls follows Maurer in calling Erasmus' proposal here a "Konfirmationsentwurf." *Die Theologie des Erasmus,* I, 124; II, 110, n. 370.

102. Maurer is somewhat more cautious in his second essay on Erasmus' thoughts in this connection. He says: "Er hat das alte Sakrament der Firmung nicht durch ein neues ersetzen wollen. Er hat die sakramentalen Züge, die diesem ursprünglich eigen waren, keineswegs völlig ausgetilgt. . . . Alles, was die Tradition über das 'augmentum gratiae' im Zusammenhang mit der Firmung gesagt hatte, findet auch bei Erasmus seine Stätte. Aber der Nachdruck liegt für ihn nicht auf dem sakramentalen Charakter seiner Reformfirmung, sondern auf ihren *subjektiven Zügen.*" "Geschichte von Firmung und Konfirmation," p. 21. Even though Maurer here, in contrast to his earlier essay, recognizes that Erasmus can speak in a traditional manner about confirmation, he still insists on regarding the proposal of the appendix to the Paraphrase of Matthew as having to do with confirmation, only here the subjective aspects receive all the emphasis. What he does not acknowledge is that the word "confirmatio" or anything like it does not at all appear here or in any other place where Erasmus talks of this proposal. On this point Carl-Gustaf Andrén is more nearly correct than Maurer: "Was Erasmus vorschlägt, ist kein Ersatz für die Firmung, noch auch eine Veränderung derselben. Nirgends in den Texten, die den oben angeführten Akt erwähnen, findet sich auch das Wort confimatio." "Die Konfirmationsfrage," p. 50. Of interest, but beyond the scope of this book, is the influence of Erasmus' thoughts concerning the renewal of the baptismal vow following catechetical preparation on the development of a Protestant catechetical confirmation, especially by Bucer. This influence has been clearly shown by Maurer, *Gemeindezucht,* pp. 72 ff., and "Geschichte von Firmung und

Konfirmation," pp. 28 ff.; by Andrén, "Die Konfirmationsfrage," pp.
51-52, and *Konfirmationen i Sverige under medeltid och reformationstid*
(1957), pp. 206 ff., cited by Andrén, "Die Konfirmationsfrage," p. 38,
n. 4; and by Vischer, pp. 58 ff. See also W. Caspari, *Die evangelische
Konfirmation* (1890), pp. 13 ff., cited by Andrén, "Die Konfirmationsfrage," p. 51, n. 34.

103. *Prologus in supput. Beddae* (1526), LB, IX, 445D. Cf. *Resp. ad
notata per N. Beddam* (1526), LB, IX, 459C; *Supput. errorum N. Beddae*
(1527), LB, IX, 558F; and *Apol. adv. mon. Hisp.* (1528), LB, IX, 1062AB.

104. To Lorenzo Pucci, 31 July 1519, Allen, IV, 1000, 145-147:
"Quod si res ab argumentis humanis penderet, et nisi concordia favo-
rem ubique mereretur, potius haberi poterat quod sequitur Cyprianus
quam quod est receptum." In the fourth and last edition (1530; see
Allen, Intro.), probably under the weight of orthodox attack, Erasmus
treats Cyprian's opinion as a definite error refuted later especially by
Augustine in *De baptismo* which Cyprian himself would have doubtless
changed in the light of superior arguments: "Nec ille repertor fuit eius
erroris, sed a maioribus acceptum tuebatur, haud dubie mutaturus
sententiam si melioribus argumentis veritatem fuisset edoctus; quemadmodum post episcopi caeteri priorem opinionem meliore sententia mutarunt. Nam testimonia Scripturarum et rationes quibus illi
fuerunt in eum errorem inducti, eleganter refellit Augustinus in libris
De baptismo contra Donatianos, praesertim libris tertio, sexto, sep-
timo." Allen, IV, p. 28 and n. 146.

105. *Ep.* 70, 2-3; 71, 1; 74, 5; in *CSEL,* III, ed. W. Hartel, 768 ff.,
771, 803. On a similar basis Tertullian, Cyprian's principal authority,
had already rejected as valid the baptism of heretics. *De bapt.* 15, in *PL,*
I, 1324 f.

106. Denzinger, 53 (123) and 55-56 (127-128).

107. *De bapt.* IV, 16, in *PL,* XLIII, 164.

108. *Resp. ad notata per N. Beddam* (1526), LB, IX, 484A-D, and *Apol.
adv. mon. Hisp.* (1528), LB, IX, 1062A-C.

109. LB, IX, 484AB.

110. *Christ. matr. instit.* (1526), LB, V, 622C. Cf. *Hyper. II* (1527), LB,
X, 1534E. Presumably in *Sermo de nativitate Mariae virginis,* in L. E. du
Pin, *Opera Omnia* (Paris, 1706), III, 1350AB; where, however, Gerson's
remarks are confined to unborn infants: "Constat itaque, Deum
misericordiam salvationis suae non ita Legibus communibus traditio-
nis Christianae, non ita Sacramentis ipsis alligasse, quin, absque prae-
iudicio Legis eiusdem, possit pueros nondum natos extra uterem,
intus sanctificare gratiae suae Baptismo, vel virtute Spiritus sancti."

111. To (?),⟨August 1533⟩, Allen, X, 2853, 39-42. We recall that in
the colloquy Ἰχθυοφαγία (1526), Erasmus made fun of the practice of
immediate baptism of infants by saying that baptism has replaced

circumcision with a harder condition, in that the baby has to be baptized just after being born. LB, I, 792AB. Cf. Oecolampadius, who as late as 1527 was of the opinion that the time of baptism of children was at the discretion of the parents, who might wait until the child was three. Letter to Zwingli, *Zwinglis Sämtliche Werke,* IX, No. 644, pp. 195-196, cited by Armour, p. 149, n. 33.

112. *Symbolum* (1533), LB, V, 1176DE.

113. Allen, X, 2853, 38-39; *Expos. concion. in ps. LXXXV* (1528), LB, V, 538A.

114. *De amab. Eccl. conc.* (1533), LB, V, 505C.

115. ". . . sed in confirmatione accipit homo potestatem ad agendum ea quae pertinent ad pugnam spiritualem contra hostes fidei." Thomas, *Summa theol.* III, q 72 a 5. Cf. Bonaventure, IV *Sent.* d 7 a 3 q l, cited by Maurer, "Geschichte von Firmung und Konfirmation," p. 15.

116. Cf. Maurer, "Geschichte von Firmung und Konfirmation," p. 21: "Alles, was die Tradition über das 'augmentum gratiae' im Zusammenhang mit der Firmung gesagt hatte, findet auch bei Erasmus seine Stätte." I must therefore disagree with G. Krodel, "Die Abendmahlslehre," p. 79, who states: "Die Firmung als römisches Sakrament im Sinne einer Mehrung der Taufgnade und der Eingiessung der gratia gratum faciens kennt Erasmus nicht."

117. LB, V, 1358D.

118. *Symbolum* (1533), LB, V, 1175F.

119. *Christ. matr. instit.* (1526), LB, V, 644D: "In Baptismo renascimur, in Confirmatione velut adversus hostem pugnaturi donativum accipimus"; *Enarr. ps. XIV* (1536), LB, V, 310F-311A: "Unctus es in baptismo unctus in sacramento confirmationis, illic ad sacerdotium, hic ad praelium."

120. This was the general scholastic teaching which was set over against the Greeks at the Councils of Lyons, 1245 and 1274 [Denzinger, 450 (831) and 465 (860)] and the Armenians at the Council of Florence, 1439 [Denzinger, 697 (1318)]. See Maurer, p. 18 and nn. 30-31. On the other hand, the Eastern Church has allowed to the priest the granting of confirmation which is acknowledged by the Roman Church. Neunheuser, p. 109.

121. *Enchiridion,* LB, V, 3B; tr. Himelick, p. 40.

122. *Symbolum* (1533), LB, V, 1176DE.

123. Erasmus did not question the New Testament institution of this sacrament as he did that of marriage and penance, but neither did he refer to its New Testament basis, specifically the passages in Acts.

124. LB, V, 310AB.

CHAPTER X
PENANCE AND EXTREME UNCTION

1. *Concio de miseric. Dom.* (1524), LB, V, 581AB; *Symbolum* (1533), LB, V, 1176C; *De praep. ad mort.* (1534), LB, V, 1303A ff.; and *Eccles.* (1535), LB, V, 882E.

2. P. 241. The note had immediate impact on Luther's understanding of the verse. See *Resolutiones* (1518), WA, I, 530, 19-22.

3. *Nov. Test.* (1522), pt. 2, p. 18. Cf. the 1522 paraphrase of Matt. 3:2: ". . . superioris vitae poenitentia . . ."; and of Matt. 4:17: ". . . *Resipiscite,* poeniteat vos vitae prioris." (Erasmus' italics.) LB, VII, 13C and 21C.

4. *Resp. ad notat. Ed. Lei* (1520), LB, IX, 257AB, D. For a similar interpretation by Luther beginning in 1521, see Gerhard Ebeling, *Evangelische Evangelienauslegung* (Munich, 1942; reprint, Darmstadt, 1962), pp. 168, 175 f., and 180 ff. Whether Luther again took a hint from Erasmus, since the humanist had reached a similar conclusion earlier than did the Reformer, I have not attempted to establish.

5. LB, VII, 338AB.

6. *Supput. errorum N. Beddae* (1527), LB, IX, 611CD.

7. Such an interpretation of the lepers passage and the raising of Lazarus is to be found in Lombard, IV *Sent.* d 18 c 6; cited and quoted by P. Anciaux, *La théologie du sacrement de pénitence au XIIe siècle* (Louvain, 1949), p. 330, n. 3; and in Anselm of Canterbury, *Hom.* 13; cited by B. Poschmann, *Busse und Letze Ölung, HDG,* IV, 3 (Freiburg i. Br., 1951), 85. For a discussion of virtually the same thoughts in other early scholastic authors, see P. Schmoll, *Die Busslehre der Frühscholastik* (1909), pp. 35 ff. The story of the raising of Lazarus (John 11) had been similarly allegorized in the medieval tradition to refer to the sacrament of penance. See the lengthy note of H. C. Lea in which he describes the developing exegesis on this Johannine event. *A History of Auricular Confession and Indulgences* (Philadelphia, 1896), I, 138 ff. Erasmus makes no mention of this allegorization in his annotations in the *Novum Testamentum,* nor anywhere else in his corpus, as far as I can judge. The extent of his allegorizing in the *Paraphrases* is to suggest that the severe disease of Lazarus signifies the chronically sick condition of the man who has been so infected by sin that he can return to the life of innocence through the divine mercy only by many tears and by an earnest repentance. *Paraphr. in evang. Ioannis* (1523), 11:38, LB, VII, 591E. [Cf. *Eccles.* (1535), LB, V, 979E-980B.] Here, though there is mention of penitence, there is no reference to sacramental penance nor to the power of the keys.

The interpretation of the allegory of Lazarus was identical with that of the allegory of the healing of the lepers in medieval authors. Those in the Abelardian-Lombardian line stated that Lazarus, already made alive by Christ, offered himslf to the disciples to be loosed. Anciaux, pp. 329-330. Hugh of St. Victor, on the other hand, thought the allegory of Lazarus signified that though Christ remits the guilt, the priest remits eternal punishment. Anciaux, pp. 191 and 192, n. 2.

   8. LB, V, 1046E.

   9. Pt. 2, p. 427.

   10. *Nov. Test.* (1516), p. 606.

   11. Pt. 2, p. 227. "Caeterum quae nunc recepta est clancularia et in aurem fit, videtur ex consultationibus privatis esse nata, quae solent apud episcopos fieri, si qui scrupulus urgeret animum."

   12. LB, IX, 262DE. Cf. 259B: "Quod si quis me roget, quid sentis de hac ratione confitendi, qua numero referuntur etiam occultissima peccata, usque ad turpissimas cogitationes, usque ad somnia, quae nunc Sacerdotes interdum haud absque pudicitae periculo audiunt, in qua exprimuntur circumstantiae, praesertim si quae mutant speciem, an existimas a *Christo* fuisse institutam? Respondebo ingenue, mihi pro meo quidem sensu non videri, at hunc sensum libens etiam reclamantem submittam Ecclesiae iudicio, simulatque eius vocem audiero." It is apparent from this statement that what was especially abhorrent to him from a moral point of view concerning confession he wishes to undermine by calling into question the divine institution of the contemporary practice of confession.

   13. Erasmus lists several of the early Fathers who he says make no mention of auricular confession: Chrysostom, Origen, Cassian, Ambrose, Basil, Bede. 259F-261D. He thinks that it was not until the time of Gregory I (590-604) that mention of private confession is found. 262CD. The evidence for this, thinks Erasmus, is the decree of Gregory concerning the silence of priests who hear confession which is recorded, he says, in the *Historia* entitled *Fasciculus temporum* as well as in Gratian's *Decretum (Decreti secunda pars causa* xxxiii q 3 d 6 c 2, in *Corpus iuris canonici* [Leipzig, 1878], I, ed. A. Friedberg, col. 1244). Erasmus accurately recited the words of the *Decretum* as follows: "Sacerdos ante omnia caveat, ne de iis qui ei confitentur peccata sua, alicui recitet, quod ea confessus est, non propinquis, non extraneis." IX, 262C.

The decree of Gratian does not state specifically Gregory I, but simply Gregory. This citation may be found in the somewhat earlier canonical collection of Polycarpus (1118), VI, 20 (19), 9, 9, and Peter Lombard, IV *Sent.* d 2, cited by Friedberg, col. 1243, n. 83. He gives no earlier references. It is doubtful that it actually goes back to Gregory I or, if it does, that it refers to private penance, for Poschmann finds no evidence in Gregory's writings for auricular confession or private penance in the later sense. *Die abendländische Kirchenbusse im Ausgang des christlichen Altertums* (Munich, 1928), pp. 271 ff.

Erasmus points out that Gratian, after presenting the views of ancient authorities on both sides of the question, leaves the matter in doubt whether one is obligated to confess or not. *Decreti secunda pars causa* xxxiii q 3 d 1. *Decretum dictum post* c 89, in *Corpus iuris canonici,* col. 1189. On Gratian's discussion, see Anciaux, pp. 196-206. Erasmus says that even the gloss on the decretal on penance (*Gloss. sup. Decr. Caus.* xxxiii q 3 d 5; cited by Lea, I, 168, n. 5) states that we are obligated to confess only on the basis of the custom and institution of the Church. 261C-E. Durandus, who rejects the gloss, can find, says Erasmus, no other reason for the divine institution of sacramental confession than that no purely human law could command it, and only supposes that Christ established this confession after the resurrection with the words to his disciples: "Quorum remiseritis peccata . . ." (John 20:23). 262B. Durandus, IV *Sent.* d 17 q 8 a 9, 11, 12.

The question of the time of the rise of private sacramental confession and penance is a much debated one. See G. J. Spykman, *Attrition and Contrition at the Council of Trent* (Kampen, 1955), p. 32, n. 22. There have been Roman Catholic scholars who think they find evidence of auricular confession in the West in the patristic period (see Spykman, p. 32, n. 22). However, Poschmann, after sifting the evidence with extreme care, does not discover in the West until the late sixth century any mention of private penance in the later medieval sense of repeatable private confession of a priest, absolution by the priest, and private acts of satisfaction (penance) prescribed by the priest. The first certain witness of private penance, Poschmann says, is Canon 11 of the third synod of Toledo (589), which attacks this custom in certain Spanish churches (*HDG,* IV, 3, p. 45). Cf. *Die abendländische Kirchenbusse im Ausgang,* pp. 213 f.

Thus one modern scholar who has studied the question quite thoroughly seems to agree with Erasmus on the approximate time of the rise of private confession and penance, even though he would not agree with him on the specific evidence for this assertion. Poschmann sees the Celtic manuals of penance as exercising a decisive influence on the development of private confession and penance. *HDG,* IV, 3, pp. 65 ff., and *Die abendländische Kirchenbusse im frühen Mittelalter* (Breslau, 1930), especially pp. 76 ff. Cf. O. D. Watkins, *A History of Penance,* II (London, 1920), 762 ff.

Concerning the obligation to confession, Poschmann says in summary: "Seit dem Jahre 800 wird von den Gläubigen durch Diözesangesetze verlangt, dass sie jährlich einmal oder gar dreimal dem Priester die Sünden beichten und von ihm die Rekonziliation erbitten. Das 4. Laterankonzil erhebt die Sitte zu einem allgemeinen, streng verpflichtenden Kirchengebot." *Die abendländische Kirchenbusse im frühen Mittelalter,* p. 232. But Erasmus correctly points to the remarkable fact

of the great Gratian's opinion based on the ancient authorities as to
the uncertainty of the necessity of confession, an opinion which ante-
dates the Fourth Lateran Council by only three-quarters of a century.
See Watkins, II, 744 f. and 769. With the illustration of Durandus,
Erasmus correctly indicates the embarrassment of some scholastics
concerning the divine institution of this sacrament. On this subject see
Lea, I, 168 f.

14. Allen, IV, 1153, 72-76.

15. Allen, IV, 1225, 118-120.

16. See Allen, IV, p. 622, for a list with dates of the several attacks
Stunica made on Erasmus and the order of the Erasmian apologies.

17. *Apol. ad blasph. Iac. Stunicae,* LB, IX, 369C.

18. *Apol. ad concl. Iac. Stunicae,* LB, IX, 389BC. See also the words
to N. Beda, Erasmus' chief critic at the Sorbonne, in defense of the
1519 edition of the *Annotationes*: "Satisfactum est illis [Atensis and
Dorpius] in omnibus, hoc uno excepto, quod non addidissem hanc
confessionem institutam a Christo. Respondi non esse meum affirmare quod probare non possem, submittere tamen me meum
iudicium autoritate Ecclesiae: hoc interim mihi satis esse." 15 June
1525, Allen, VI, 1581, 283-287.

19. See Lea, pp. 168 ff., for the latitude of opinion on this subject
prior to the time of the Reformation. Lea rightly concludes: "From all
this it is evident that Erasmus was not especially culpable in assuming
that confession is a human institution, and his doing so did not detract
from his reputation until after the appearance of Luther." Lea, p. 170.

20. He refers to it variously as "formidabilis" (Allen, IV, 1141, 21),
"supra modum terribilis" (Allen, IV, 1183, 116), and "saevissima"
(Allen, V, 1313, 61).

21. Allen, IV, 1153, 126-127: "[The Bull] magis sapit quorundam
πτωχοτυράννων saeviciam quam mite nostri Leonis ingenium . . ."

22. LB, IX, 1062EF.

23. Allen, V, 1410, 30-34.

24. LB, I, 651F-654A; tr. Thompson, *Colloquies,* pp. 38-39.

25. To Josse Laurens, 14 July 1522, Allen, V, 1299, 55-56. To
Jerome Vander Noot, 14 July 1522, Allen, V, 1300, 14-15.

26. Allen, V, 1299, 60-65: "Confessionem etiam approbo; tantum
puer dicit suo animo satis fore confiteri Deo, si idem visum esset
proceribus Ecclesiae, et tamen fatetur sese confiteri etiam sacer-
dotibus. Quasi non sit satis puero obtemperare primatibus Ecclesiae
in confitendo, aut quasi Christus non sit unus ex proceribus Ecclesiae,
aut quasi mihi constet esse articulum fidei hanc confessionem esse
institutam a Christo! Et tamen hac in re sensum animi mei semper
submisi iudicio Ecclesiae."

Allen, V, 1300, 18-25: "Hoc ille sic interpretatur quasi pronunciem confessionem esse iuris humani. Constat hanc confessionem nostram magna ex parte esse iuris humani; quod enim semel in anno confitemur, quod huic aut illi, constat esse ex capitulo *Omnis utriusque sexus.* [Canon of the Fourth Lateran Council under Innocent III, 1215, Denzinger, 437 (812).] Ergo quod confitemur semel in anno, movet nos episcoporum autoritas. Nihil igitur peccat puer, si in confitendo sequitur autoritatem pontificum, etiam si dubitet an sit iuris divini an non; de quo, ut vere dicam, mihi nondum satis constat."

Cf. To the Theologians of Louvain, ⟨c. 14 July 1522⟩, Allen, V, 1301, 34-56.

27. Allen, V, 1301, 49-52.

28. LB, I, 903F.

29. Allen, VII, 2037, 33-38.

30. *Declar. ad cens. colloq.* (1532), LB, IX, 932E.

31. LB, V, 146C-147A.

32. 1 July 1525, Allen, VI, 1582, 90-92.

33. To Louis Ber, 30 March 1529, Allen, VIII, 2136, 214-220. Cf. *Ad Phimost. de divortio* (1532), LB, IX, 965BC.

34. LB, X, 1569F-1570B.

35. LB, V, 502A, D. Cf. To (?), ⟨August 1533⟩, Allen, X, 2853, 27-30: "Quibus persuasum est, Confessionem non esse partem Sacramenti, nec a Christo institutam; servent temen eam ut rem salutarem, a patribus inductam, et multorum seculorum consensu probatam, donec aliud de ea statuat Ecclesia."

36. In the *Detectio* he named as the first kind of dogmas those which the Church holds with a great consensus and which are grounded in Scripture and the Apostles' Creed and, in addition, those which are enacted in rightly assembled general councils. LB, X, 1569F. By his characterization of the question of the divine institution of sacramental confession in the second class of dogmas concerning which no authoritative decision has been made, he strongly implies that if in a truly universal council such a decree were promulgated, he would have to bow to its authority. The argument of Thomas Tentler, therefore, does not logically carry any weight, that ". . . once he [Erasmus] has accepted the remission of sins and the Holy Catholic Church as necessary articles [in the Apostles' Creed], and accepted the tradition as his principle of authority, it is difficult to see how he could deny that divine institution was an article of faith." "The Problem of Anxiety and Preparation for Death in Luther, Calvin, and Erasmus," unpublished Ph.D. dissertation, Harvard University, Cambridge, Mass., 1961, p. 198, n. 6. He can very well accept these two articles of the Apostles' Creed and a universal consensus as his authority and yet not accept the divine institution of confession, if this universal consensus in a general council has not yet defined confession as of divine institution.

37. See the following for discussions of early and late scholastic contritionism: Anciaux, pp. 176 ff.; Schmoll, pp. 29 ff.; Poschmann, *HDG*, IV, 3, pp. 84 f., 102; Oberman, *Harvest*, pp. 147, 151.

38. For Abelard, see Poschmann, *HDG*, IV, 3, p. 85. Anciaux says, "Plus clairement qu'Abélard il [Lombard] exige la présence de la volonté de se confesser dans la pénitence intérieure" (p. 230). For Occam, see Poschmann, *HDG*, IV, 3, p. 102, n. 17; for Biel, see Oberman, *Harvest*, p. 157, n. 39; p. 151, n. 19.

39. *Enchiridion* (1503), LB, V, 38A-C; *Apol. ad notat. Ed. Lei* (1520), LB, IX, 259EF-260A; *Exomo.* (1524), LB, V, 157C; *De amab. Eccl. conc.* (1533), LB, V, 502BC; *De praep. ad mort.* (1534), LB, V, 1306A.

40. LB, I, 714BC; tr. Thompson, *Colloquies*, p. 143.

41. LB, I, 734F-735A; tr. Thompson, *Colloquies*, p. 194.

42. LB, I, 890B; tr. Thompson, *Colloquies*, p. 551.

43. The Spanish monks accuse him of ridiculing confession in this colloquy, a charge which Erasmus denies. *Apol. adv. mon. Hisp.* (1528), LB, IX, 1062D, 1063BC.

44. LB, I, 651EF; tr. Thompson, *Colloquies*, p. 38.

45. Allen, V, 1299, 61-62; Allen, V, 1300, 17-18; Allen, V, 1301, 33-34; *Declar. ad cens. colloq.* (1532), LB, IX, 932D.

46. *Militaria* (1522), LB, I, 643AB; *Enchiridion*, LB, V, 38C; *Enarr. in ps. XXXIII* (1530), LB, V, 414D.

47. *Exomo.*, LB, V, 146A.

48. *De praep. ad mort.*, LB, V, 1306A.

49. LB, V, 149CD.

50. LB, V, 149A.

51. LB, V, 1310F-1311A. Cf. Master Herman, *Epitome* c 36, cited by Anciaux, p. 182, n. 4; Zacharie de Besançon, *Unum ex quatuor* in *PL*, CLXXXVI, col. 317, cited by Anciaux, p. 216, n. 1; Lombard, IV *Sent.* d 17 c 1, cited by Anciaux, p. 226, n. 2. For Erasmus as for these twelfth-century authors in the Abelardian line, the *votum confessionis* arises primarily out of a respect for an ecclesiastical institution rather than out of a sense of its intrinsic necessity, as with the Victorines. See Anciaux, pp. 176 ff.

52. *Exomo.*, LB, V, 170BC: "Nec id raro accidit, ut qui frigide poenitens accedit ad Sacerdotem, inter confitendum accipiat legitimum criminum odium." Cf. 151F-152AB. Cf. Gerson, *De parvulis ad Christum trahendis, Opera*, III, 289CD: "Conqueretur alius et dicet: Frigidus sum et indevotus quid mihi prodest Confessio? . . . Accede ad hunc ignem, calesces plus statis. Video saepe multos frigidos in initio, qui etiam colloquium tale super actibus suis vel horrent, vel rident, et discedunt calentes, consolati et ubertim flentes."

53. We observe that at this point Erasmus stands again in the nominalist tradition. His thought here is in line with that of Gabriel

Biel, for whom likewise confession had not a sacramental but a psychological effect. See Oberman, *Harvest*, p. 160. This idea was already present in the twelfth-century writer Zacharie de Besançon, *Unum ex quatuor*, in *PL*, CLXXXVI, 316; cited by Anciaux, p. 263, n. 4. On this thought in Zacharie, see Anciaux, pp. 216, 263 f., and 319. Tentler fails to point out this scholastic background in his comment on this passage, which he interprets as evidencing simply Erasmus' moralism and conservatism. "Forgiveness and Consolation," p. 116.

54. *Concio de miseric. Dom.* (1524), LB, V, 585C.

55. *Exomo.*, LB, V, 151F, 157A-D.

56. *Confabulatio pia* (1522), LB, I, 652A; *Epicureus* (1533), LB, I, 890B. But cf. *De praep. ad mort.* (1534), LB, V, 1309AB, where Erasmus says that the confidence of pious men is always joined with a religious fear, for who can be sure that he has a truly contrite heart which is the prerequisite for receiving the remedy of penance?

57. *Exomo.*, LB, V, 157B, D, 151F-152A.

58. *Ibid.*, 152E: "Nam quid sit attritio, et an ex attritione per Confessionem fiat contritio: et an Confessio efficiat, ut in primo statim instanti remittatur peccatum, Scotistis dispuntandum relinquo." See below for the view of Scotus on this point, n. 95.

59. *Exomo.*, 157CD. Cf. *Concio de miseric. Dom.*, LB, V, 578AB: "Illico ex vindice factus opitulator, adiuvabo conatus vestros, ut quod vestris viribus non potestis efficere, meo favore consequamini. Nemo potest salubriter odisse peccata sua, nisi Deus dederit, nisi auferat cor lapideum et inserat cor carneum: nisi pro corde polluto, creet in nobis cor mundum . . ." Cf. also *De praep. ad mort.*, LB, V, 1302E.

60. *Concio de miseric. Dom.*, LB, V, 578B-579A, 582 ff. Cf. *De praep. ad mort.*, LB, V, 1316BC.

61. *Exomo.*, LB, V, 151F-152A.

62. *Ibid.*, 157D.

63. *Concio de miseric. Dom.*, LB, V, 576A, 581B; *De praep. ad mort.*, LB, V, 1302DE.

64. *Concio de miseric. Dom.*, LB, V, 582D, 576B-E.

65. *Exomo.*, LB, V, 157A.

66. *Nov. Test.*, pt. 2, p. 44. Cf. Allen, IV, 1202, 221-222 and n. 221.

67. Allen, IV, 1033, 148-150.

68. LB, IX, 258C, F.

69. 8 June 1521, Allen, IV, 1211, 132-135, 489-491.

70. LB, I, 652BC; tr. Thompson, *Colloquies*, p. 39.

71. LB, V, 153C-154D.

72. *Ibid.*, 155BC.

73. LB, V, 156B-E, 168A-E.

74. B. Poschmann, *Poenitentia Secunda* (Bonn, 1940), p. 470.

75. LB, V, 168E.

76. *Ibid.*, 156F-157D; 169CD.

77. *Ibid.*, 159A. Cf. these earlier remarks in the *Confabulatio pia* (1522), LB, I, 652AB: "... confiteor et sacerdoti, sed paucis, et non nisi ea quae certo videntur crimina: aut eiusmodi, ut vehemens suspicio sit crimen esse. Neque vero protinus arbitror esse piaculum, hoc est, enorme crimen, quod admittitur adversus quaslibet constitutiones humanas, nisi contemptus accesserit malitiosus. Imo vix arbitror crimen capitale, cui non sit adiuncta malitia, hoc est, perversa voluntas." Erasmus' understanding of sin thus somewhat negates the urgency of confession. Since only the capital crimes require confession and since after baptism it is quite possible to avoid this kind of sin, confession is not of general necessity but only an accommodation to the weakness of those who happen to fall into mortal sins. Apparently, the theologians of Louvain saw in these words a Lutheranism from which Erasmus felt it necessary to distinguish himself. To the Theologians of Louvain, ⟨ c. 14 July 1522⟩, Allen, V, 1301, 28-32: "In primo loco puer quidam sedecim annorum ait se confiteri peccata, duntaxat certo mortalia aut vehementer suspecta: Lutherus docet non esse necesse confiteri peccata mortalia omnia, sed tantum manifesta. Proinde sermo pueri multum dissonat a dogmate Lutheri." Cf. Luther, *Sermo de poenitentia*, 1518, WA, I, 322; quoted by Allen, IV, 1033, n. 78: "Primum ut nullo modo praesumas confiteri peccata venialia, sed nec omnia mortalia, quia impossibile est ut omnia mortalia cognoscas." See also *Confitendi ratio* (1520), caps. 6-9; WA, VI, 161 ff. Luther and Erasmus both criticize the practice of confessing all sins because such an effort contributes greatly to the anxiety of the confessional but also for Luther because not even all mortal sins well below the surface of the human heart can possibly be known. For Erasmus, who lacks Luther's depth understanding of sin, it is not impossible to know mortal sins, since for him mortal sin is not hidden but an overt crime which results from a malicious will. Erasmus' limitation of confession to mortal sins not only reduces the anxiety and burden of the confessional but also eliminates for some the necessity of confession, since he believes it possible to live without mortal crimes.

78. LB, V, 151BC. See, for example, *Sermo contra luxuriam Dominica IV. Adventus*, in *Opera*, III, 932A.

79. *Ibid.*, 159BC.

80. *Ibid.*, 147C, E. For similar views among the early scholastics see Anciaux, pp. 182, 194, 230. For Hugh of St. Victor, in contrast to those in the Abelardian line, confession in correction of sin as pride was not only useful but necessary.

81. *Ibid.*, 150A-151A.

82. *Ibid.*, 170A.

83. "The Problem of Anxiety," p. 200, n. 30.

84. LB, V, 151A-F. Cf. 170A.

85. Therefore, Tentler's contention that for Erasmus' thought on confession it was "more important to reform men's lives than soothe their consciences in difference to the Protestants" ("The Problem of Anxiety," p. 126) requires some qualification. No doubt for him it was more important to improve men's lives, that is, to assist them on the road to perfection, but it was also important to soothe the consciences of the weak. Tentler fails to recognize the important patristic theme of accommodation and neglects almost entirely the element of grace and mercy in Erasmus' religious thought. Of course, it is true that his moralism prevents a genuine relief of the anxiety of the confessional.

86. LB, V, 151F-152B.

87. Cf. Luther, *Ratio confitendi* (1520), 3, 6, 8, where Luther advises that one first confess to God before confessing to the priest, emphasizes contrition and the will to lead a new life, and expresses concern about the vexing laws and questions about the cases of sins and the terror-provoking false distinction between venial and mortal sins when not even all of the latter ought to be confessed since they cannot possibly be known. WA, VI, 159, 21 ff.; 161, 15 ff.; 162, 12 ff. In the *De captivitate babylonica* (1520), Luther stresses that contrition itself is not a human work or merit, but a result of faith in the divine forgiveness of sin. Though rejecting any scriptural basis for private confession, he says that he accepts it as long as it is understood not simply as confession to a priest but as confession and the receiving of absolution from any Christian brother. He is especially critical of the tyranny of popes and bishops who disturb the consciences of men by reserving even secret sins to themselves and by all the questions about the circumstances of sins. WA, VI, 544, 25 ff.; 546, 11 ff.; 547, 1 ff.

88. LB, V, 160B-163E.

89. *Apol. adv. mon. Hisp.*, LB, IX, 1063F.

90. To Louis Ber, 20 March 1529, Allen, VIII, 2136, 216-218: "... nec unquam ausus sum aut auderem ad Christi mensam accedere, aut ex hac vita decedere, nisi sacerdoti confessus quae gravant conscientiam." In *Funus* (1526) Cornelius, who served as the example for dying well, shortly before his death confessed to his priest, partook of communion, yet immediately before dying, although he received extreme unction and communion, felt no necessity of repeating confession. LB, I, 815CD. 816A: "Negabat enim quidquam scrupuli resedisse in animo." Furthermore, he placed his trust not in these acts nor in a papal brief but in the mercy of Christ. 816BC. Concerning Erasmus' own practice of confession, at least during his later years, we have these words from his confessor, John of Breisgau, in a letter written not long after Erasmus' death: "Fui illi dum viveret, aliquoties a confessionibus: in quo non nisi Christo dignam vitam depraehendebam." Allen, VIII, p. 145, Intro., cited by R. G. Villoslada, "La muerte de

Erasmo," in *Miscellanea Giovanni Mercati,* IV (*Studi e Testi,* 124) (Vatican City, 1946), p. 404, n. 37. On the question whether Erasmus received the sacraments at death, see below, n. 141.

91. *Funus* (1526), LB, I, 811A ff.

92. Ἰχθνοφαγία (1526), LB, I, 792C: *Supput. errorum N. Beddae* (1527), LB, IX, 568D: "Pharisaeorum est reddere conscientias anxias, quo suam tueantur tyrannidem, *Christus* amat conscientias spiritu gratiaque liberas: atque ut fateor esse periculum, laxare habenas vulgo, ita contra *Christi Paulique* doctrinam est, spiritus libertatem opprimere, quod alicubi *Gerson,* quoque monet . . ." Though Erasmus does not mention confession here expressly, there can be little doubt that he intends to include it among the practices by which the Pharisees, i.e., especially the monks, preserve their tyranny and render consciences anxious. We notice his mention of Gerson here as supporting evangelical freedom, when before in the *Exomologesis* he criticized him for contributing to the anxiety of the confessional. We have already seen that Erasmus likes to enlist this, perhaps his favorite, of the scholastics to support his understanding of the wide grace and freedom of the gospel. I have not found a reference in Gerson which gives this specific thought, but cf. *De arte audiendi confessiones,* in *Opera,* II, 449C: "Denique quicquid in Confessione dixerit Sacerdos, sit ipse semper in fine mansuetus atque benignus, infundens oleum consolationis, et compassionis, et bonae spei"; and *Sermo de poenitentia factus in coena Domini,* in *Opera,* II, 512C, where in talking about the secrecy of the confessional, Gerson says of priests: "Inquirentes autem et revelantes graviter peccant et esset puniendi, praesertim ubi ex curiositate, non ex charitate discreta procedit inquisitio."

See also *Apol. adv. mon. Hisp.* (1528), LB, IX, 1063D-F, where Erasmus defends his words in the *Exomologesis* in criticism of a too solicitous confession; To John Botzheim, 13 August 1529, Allen, VIII, 2205, 105-106: "Iam arcana confessione quid salubrius? Et hanc dum nimis astringunt, nimisque reddunt anxiam." Cf. Tentler, "Erasmus on Forgiveness and Consolation," p. 117: ". . . he makes little of the anxiety of the penitent, and he certainly does not use it as an argument for the abolition of confession . . ."

93. He does have a few other words on this subject in the treatise of one year later, *De praep. ad mort.,* but these are concerned primarily with the question of penance as virtue and sacrament, which we have already considered under that heading. Concerning confession as such, because it brings much tranquillity, he recommends its use three or four times a year, with, however, the usual qualifications, that it be not anxious or repetitious but sincere and brief, an enumeration of only the chief crimes. LB, V, 1310F, 1311D.

94. LB, V, 502A-D. Cf. To (?), ⟨August 1533⟩, Allen, X, 2853, 27-33.

95. "This declarative theory remained *communis opinio* among theologians until the thirteenth century." Spykman, p. 37. The major exception to this view among the early scholastics was Hugh of St. Victor, who sought to make room for the efficacy of the power of the keys by making a distinction between the *culpa* and the *poena* of sin. God alone forgives the former, but the priest remits the latter. This distinction was rejected as invalid by Peter Lombard. Poschmann, *HDG*, IV, 3, p. 86. Likewise, the early Franciscans Alexander of Hales and Bonaventure failed to accord to absolution any genuine sacramental power, holding with Lombard that God forgives both the *culpa* and *poena* of sin. *Ibid.*, p. 88. Hugh of St. Cher (d. 1263), the first Cardinal of the Dominicans, and the most famous Dominican of all, Thomas, on the other hand, did ascribe to absolution an *ex opere operato* effect. *Ibid.*, p. 89. Without entering into a detailed discussion of the influential but complex Thomistic theory, we can say in brief that Thomas sought to hold together in his synthesis the subjective and the objective, penance as virtue and as sacrament, by insisting upon both a genuine contrition and an actual sacramental effect *ex opere operato* of absolution. The sacramental absolution he regarded as so important that he posited its proleptic working of contrition in the *votum sacramenti*. It is effectual therefore both *proposito* and *actu*. Furthermore, the grace of the sacrament may actually transform one from *attritus* to *contritus* and thus make possible justification. This view of Thomas must not be confused with the later opinion of Scotus that through the sacrament attrition is changed to contrition, so that only a minimal attrition (*parum attritus*) is the necessary presupposition of the priestly absolution. *Ibid.*, p. 92. Whereas Thomas ascribed to priestly absolution an instrumental cause in the remission of the guilt of sin, at least insofar as it is a part of the eternal punishment, Duns Scotus thought that the sacrament, not, to be sure, as an instrumental cause but *ex pacto Dei*, is effective for the remission of both the guilt and the eternal punishment. *Ibid.*, pp. 93 and 100. For Duns Scotus this priestly act was so central that he located the total significance of penance in absolution, rejecting Thomas' division of the sacrament into the three acts of contrition, confession, and satisfaction as the personal and material element of penance, and absolution as the formal cause of penance. *Ibid.*, p. 100. Against Thomas and Scotus, Occam and Biel, returning to Lombard, held that God alone forgives both *culpa* and *poena*. The priest merely shows that they have already been forgiven. The priestly act does not transmit but increases grace. *Ibid.*, p. 102; Seeberg, DG, III, 542 ff.; and Oberman, *Harvest*, p. 159.

96. LB, I, 651F; tr. Thompson, *Colloquies*, p. 38.

97. LB, V, 167E. Erasmus thus shares the position of Lombard, the early Franciscans, and the late medieval nominalists Occam and Biel, over against those of Thomas and Scotus.

98. *Eccles.* (1535), LB, V, 944D.

99. In the *Militaria* (1522), LB, I, 643AB, Erasmus by his satire places in doubt the priestly absolution of a soldier who had committed many crimes. In the *De praep. ad mort.* (1534), LB, V, 1308CD, Erasmus says: "Impium est dubitare, an sit absolutus a peccatis, qui rite suscepit hoc Sacramentum. Non est tamen haereticum dubitare, an hic aut ille sit absolutus, quoniam de peculiaribus impedimentis nobis non constat."

100. This was the dominant view among the early scholastics (Abelard and Lombard) and the early Franciscans (Alexander of Hales and Bonaventure). See Schmoll, p. 32, and Poschmann, p. 93, n. 15.

101. *Eccles.*, LB, V, 1015AB.

102. *Ibid.*, 944CD.

103. *Resp. ad notat. novas Ed. Lei* (1520), LB, IX, 256E.

104. In the *Exomologesis* (1524), Erasmus refers to the power of the keys as one of the chains of confession that he passes over. LB, V, 157F.

105. *Paraphr. in evang. Matt.* (1522), 18:18, 100F-101A: "Quod enim iudicatis spiritu Dei, non vestrum est iudicium, sed per vos illius. Quod si damnaveritis aliquem humano spiritu, iam est iudicium humanum, non Dei: et is qui vestra sententia fuerit eiectus a vestro consortio, non protinus est alienus a consortio coeli. Vis igitur vestrae auctoritatis in affectibus est, quos solus Deus intuetur." Cf. 16:18, *ibid.*, 93BC; Origen, *De oratione* 28, 8; and *Comm. in Matt.* 24, II, 40, 19Kl; cited by Poschmann, *Poenitentia Secunda*, p. 465; Abelard, *Ethica* 26; Anciaux, pp. 288-289, nn. 3 and 1. In the Πτωχπλούσιοι (1524), LB, I, 739D, Erasmus ridicules the absolution of a lupine priest: "Rursum videtis lupum absolventem confessum, sed prominet pars ovis occultatae sub veste."

106. IV *Sent.* d 16 c 1 n 159, cited by Joseph A. Spitzig, *Sacramental Penance in the Twelfth and Thirteenth Centuries* (Washington, D.C., 1947), p. 59, n. 120. With Thomas these constituted the matter of the Sacrament. (Poschmann, *HDG*, IV, 3, p. 89.) As such they entered into dogma in the *Decretum pro Armenis* at the Council of Florence in 1439. [Denzinger, 699 (1323).]

107. Lombard, IV *Sent.* d 20 c 2 n 204, cited by Spitzig, p. 42, n. 133. For similar views by Peter of Poitiers, Alexander of Hales, Bonaventure, and Thomas, see Spitzig, pp. 87, 119, 129, and 156 ff. The idea of satisfaction as paying back honor to God was derived from Anselm, *Cur Deus Homo*, I, 11. See Spitzig, p. 112.

108. Alexander of Hales, *Summa* IV q 23 m 1 a 2, cited by Spitzig, p. 122, n. 50. For Bonaventure and Thomas see Spitzig, pp. 135 and 162.

109. LB, I, 720B; tr. Thompson, *Colloquies*, p. 157.

110. *Nov. Test.* (1516), pp. 5 and 125; note, p. 242; retained in LB, VI, 20D. The scholastics understood the passage as demanding works

of satisfaction to pay the debt of temporal punishment due to sin. See, for example, Peter Lombard, IV *Sent.* d 16 c 2 n 160, cited by Spitzig, p. 70, n. 128.

111. *Eccles.* (1535), LB, V, 944D.

112. Like Abelard, Erasmus could speak of confession of sin as satisfaction. *Paraphr. in evang. Lucae* (1523), 15:24, LB, VII, 409D. Cf. Abelard, *Ethica* 24; cited by Spitzig, p. 41, n. 8.

113. *Symbolum* (1533), LB, V, 1178A: "De *Confessione* ac *Satisfactione*, et quondam magna fuit concertatio, et hisce temporibus renovata est. Ego ut tutissimum, ita ad tuendam publicam concordiam accommodatius arbitror, simplici obedientia id sequi quod nobis tradit Ecclesiae auctoritas, hoc est, vere iuxta Graecorum proverbium, *ad felicius inclinare latus,* et ab his abstinere de quibus dubites." (Erasmus' italics.)

114. *Eccles.,* LB, V, 1070F: "Eundem in modum quum vulgus audit non esse opus satisfactione, quod Christus pro nostris peccatis dederit poenas, sic interpretatur, quasi liceat impune peccare, et in malefactis securum esse. Hic error plus habet periculi, quam si quis credat satisfactionem esse tertiam partem poenitentiae sacramentalis . . ."

115. LB, V, 166C-167D. So also the majority of scholastics thought that contrition and love were necessary in order for satisfactory works to be of any value. Lombard, IV *Sent.* XIV c 1-2 n 136, cited by Spitzig, p. 78, n. 157.

116. An indulgence is an authoritative remission of temporal punishment for sins granted by the Church to those whose guilt has been already forgiven. Indulgences in this sense, says Poschmann, arose first in the eleventh century, although they had precursors in the so-called redemptions, whereby one kind of satisfaction could be substituted for another in the interest of lessening the severity of the work and also in the absolutions, which had only deprecative character and which were applied only to the lessening of purgatorial punishment and not, as with the indulgence, to a reduction of the earthly ecclesiastical penance on the basis of a jurisdictional act. *HDG,* IV, 3, pp. 112-113, and *Der Ablass im Licht der Bussegeschichte* (Bonn, 1948), pp. 43 ff. Both the redemption and the absolution entered into the composition of an indulgence insofar as the indulgence consisted of an act of forgiveness of a part or all of unabsolved temporal punishment on the basis of some pious work. The difficulty of how on this basis sins could really be considered punished was eventually solved by the theory of the *thesaurus ecclesiae,* now known to have been first proposed not by Alexander of Hales but by Hugh of St. Cher, as passed on by the canonist Henry of Susa, *Summa aurea* lib. V tit. de remissionibus, 6; cited by Poschmann, *Ablass,* p. 82, n. 390. The relationship between the jurisdictional act of absolution based upon the treasure house of merits and the required pious work as the precondition for the reception

of the benefit of this act was a hotly debated topic in the High Middle Ages. Poschmann, *HDG,* IV, 3 pp. 119-120.

117. Concerning the abuses in the late Middle Ages see the detailed discussion of N. Paulus, *Geschichte des Ablasses im Mittelalter* (Paderborn, 1922-23), III, 450 ff. and 470 ff.

118. LB, V, 38B; tr. Himelick, p. 128.

119. LB, IV, 444A.

120. *De votis temere susceptis* (1522), LB, I, 640B; tr. Thompson, *Colloquies,* p. 7. Erasmus is careful, however, to preface these remarks by "Ego vero nihil elevo indulgentias . . ." This qualification was apparently not satisfactory to his detractors, because he had to defend himself for his remarks in this colloquy. See To Josse Laurens, 14 July 1522, Allen, V, 1299, 57-60: "Non damno illic indulgentias, nec usquam alias; sed quidam irridet sodalem suum, qui, quum esset nugacissimus nugator, putaret sese bullae praesidio posse pervenire ad coelum"; and To the Theologians of Louvain, ⟨14 July 1522⟩, Allen, V, 1301, 75-80. Cf. *Funus* (1526), LB, I, 814B, 815A.

Lea notes that Erasmus' criticism of this aspect of indulgence traffic was "guilty of no exaggeration." *History of Confession and Indulgences,* III, 76. See his discussion of indulgences which promised remission *a culpa et poena* (pp. 54-82). Although the expression itself would not necessarily suggest it, these presupposed contrition and sacramental confession and absolution, but were greatly enhanced by some indulgence sellers who omitted any reference to contrition in their preaching. It is no wonder, then, that some actually thought that their salvation was procured by the purchase of an indulgence. N. Paulus admits that the expression *a culpa et poena* was inexact, but insists that it owes its origin "nicht dem Rechte, sondern dem Volke," who accorded this designation to the indulgences which promised complete remission of temporal punishment. Although some theologians adopted the expression, there were never lacking those in the late Middle Ages who criticizied its use. Paulus, III, 330 ff. He acknowledges, however, that the ambiguous formula could lead to misunderstanding (p. 350).

121. To Colet, ⟨c. 5 March 1518⟩, Allen, III, 786, 23-24. To Albert of Brandenburg, 19 October 1519, Allen, IV, 1033, 142-143. To John Botzheim, 13 August 1529, Allen, VIII, 2205, 78 ff. To Nicholas Everard,⟨c. March 1521⟩, Allen, IV, 1188, 39. To John Kinck, 17 March 1530, Allen, VIII, 2285, 86. A historical note on the letters: I find no mention of indulgences in the correspondence of Erasmus prior to the outbreak of the Reformation in 1517. Immediately afterward his remarks are infrequent and brief. By and large, he maintains a discreet silence. He apparently thought it wise temporarily to say little about indulgences, but believed that eventually there would be opportunity to attack them more openly and boldly, for he remarks in the letter to Nicholas Everard: "Adversus condonationes hoc erit remedium, si

nihil detur: donec dabitur melior occasio explodendi has impias cauponationes." Allen, IV, 1188, 37-39. Indeed, in the later letters mentioned above to John Botzheim and John Kinck, Erasmus launches into a more open and extended assault upon the traffic in indulgences. It is probable that he was emboldened to do so because by the late 1520's there was such widespread complaint concerning the abuses of indulgences, not only among Protestants but also among Roman Catholics, that Erasmus himself could say in a letter, probably of 1533: "Indulgentiae iam explosae sunt, quibus aliquot seculis impositum est mundo, adiuvantibus monachis, conniventibus theologis." To (?), ⟨August 1533⟩, Allen, X, 2853, 15-17. See Lea, III, 295, 403 ff. Cf. *Eccles.* (1535), LB, V, 942BC, for a frank discussion of the immoderate growth of indulgences.

122. Holborn, 207, 1-2, and LB, V, 91A.

123. To Erard de la Marck, 5 February 1519, Allen, III, 916, 288-289.

124. *Declar. ad cens.* (1532), LB, IX, 852D. Cf. also *Apol. adv. mon. Hisp.* (1528), LB, IX, 1090C. Poschmann concludes his discussion of the varying scholastic opinions on this question: "Grundsätzlich blieb indes die Frage, ob Ablässe für Verstorbene möglich seien, auch weiterhin offen. Um die Mitte des 15. Jahrhunderts stellte Antonius von Florenz fest, dass die Mehrheit der Theologen dafür sei; aber auch noch gegen Ende des Jahrhunderts gab es Prediger, die den Ablass für Verstorbene als nützlos erklärten." *HDG*, IV, 3, p. 121. Cf. Paulus, III, pp. 374 ff., where he shows that it was the usual but not unanimous view of theologians and popes in the late Middle Ages that indulgences for the dead are efficacious only *per modum suffragii*, not *per modum auctoritatis*. In the Bulla "Exsurge Domine" of 1520 Leo named as one of the errors of Luther that he regarded indulgences for the dead as not necessary or useful. Denzinger, 762 (1473). Erasmus is correct that no council had made a definite statement on the question. Since the Council of Trent limited itself to the two dogmatic points that the Church has power to dispense indulgences and that their use is very salutary [Denzinger, 989 (1835)], this particular issue remains even yet a very open question, one which was not treated by Vatican II.

125. *Exomo.* (1524), LB, V, 167F.

126. In line with his hesitation in the problem of justification Erasmus fluctuates in the alternative to indulgences between the mercy of Christ and good deeds, although in the following passages the former is more prominent. To Paul Volz, 14 August 1518, Allen, III, 858, 405-408: "Veluti si quis admoneat tutius esse benefactis fidere quam pontificiis condonationibus, non utique damnat illius condonationes, sed praefert id quod ex Christi doctrina certius est." *Exomo.*, LB, V, 167E: "Ego ut nolim in totum damnare Pontificias relaxationes, ita tutius, arbitror, plenam delictorum remissionem a caritate et a Christi

misericordia sperare, quam a diplomatibus humanis." *Funus* (1526), LB, I, 816C; *Apol. adv. mon. Hisp.* (1528), LB, IX, 1090C; *De amab. Eccl. conc.* (1533), LB, V, 490B; *De praep. ad mort.* (1534), LB, V, 1316EF.

127. *Exomo.*, LB, V, 167F.

128. The basing of indulgences on the *thesaurus meritorum* was given authoritative, though not binding, expression in the Bull of Clement VI, "Unigenitus," 1343 [Denzinger, 550-552 (1025-1027)]. The opinions of Wyclif and Hus rejecting the power of indulgences were denied by the Council of Constance, 1415, 1418 [Denzinger, 622 (1192), 676 (1266)]. Sixtus IV (1479) rejected the same teaching by Peter of Osma [Denzinger, 729 (1416)]. Likewise, the power of the Church to grant indulgences on the basis of the treasure house of merits was defended against Luther in the decretal communicated to him by Cajetan in 1518 [Denzinger, 740a (1447, 1448)]. Also, in the bull "Exsurge Domine" of 1520, errors of Luther were repudiated on this subject [Denzinger, 757-762 (1467-1472)]. See Poschmann, *HDG*, IV, 3, p. 122. Erasmus does not refer to any of these ecclesiastical statements. He seems to recognize indulgences as a widely accepted institution with which one simply had to live, though he certainly hoped for its reform.

129. *Ratio* (1519), Holborn, 203, 6 ff., and LB, V, 89A.

130. LB, V, 1358EF.

131. Pt. 2, p. 112.

132. P. 606. This change took place gradually during the early Middle Ages, and is due largely to the fact that it was regarded as a supplementary part of the penance of the sick, which, except in case of extreme likelihood of death, was avoided by the faithful because of the severe penance enjoined on those who recovered from their illness as members of the *ordo paenitentium.* The receiving of unction was thus put off until the last moment. See Poschmann, *HDG*, IV, 3, p. 132. The *Decretum pro Armenis* states: "Hoc sacramentum nisi infirmo, de cuius morte timetur, dari non debet." Denzinger, 700 (1324).

133. P. 596. LB, VI, 1037C. On the varying interpretations of the scholastics on this point see Poschmann, *HDG*, IV, 3, p. 134. He points out that in the twelfth century the institution was almost universally ascribed to the Apostles. Alexander and Bonaventure (IV *Sent.* d 23 a l q l) were also of this opinion. Thomas, on the other hand, considered it probable that Christ instituted all the sacraments himself, although he promulgated only some himself while reserving others, such as confirmation and extreme unction, for the Apostles to promulgate. *Suppl.* q 29 a 3. Scotus, however, regarded all the sacraments not as probably but as certainly instituted by Christ. *Report.* IV d 23 n 9.

134. I therefore disagree with Tentler, who in discussing these same passages says: "Erasmus is suggesting here [that is, in the distinction between an implicit and explicit basis in the divine command]

that, in some sense, extreme unction is not necessary." That is a bit of eisegesis on the part of Tentler, which he himself seems to recognize when he follows with these remarks: "Nothing very conclusive can be drawn from these notes. He has not called the modern practice improper. But he says there is a clear difference." "The Problem of Anxiety," p. 137; "Forgiveness and Consolation," p. 126.

135. *Apol. ad concl. Iac. Stunicae* (1524), LB, IX, 389DE.

136. *Paraphr. in evang. Marci* (1523), LB, VII, 203D.

137. LB, X, 1562D.

138. LB, I, 684BC, tr. Thompson, *Colloquies*, p. 69. See his defense of this passage attacked by the Sorbonne in *Declar. ad cens.* (1532), LB, IX, 935F-936C.

139. LB, V, 414D.

140. LB, VII, 1140A-C. Under the influence of the text of James, the majority of the scholastics championed the deprecative formula, and the *Decretum pro Armenis* stated: "Per istam sanctam unctionem et suam piissimam misericordiam indulgeat tibi Dominus . . ." Denzinger, 700 (1325); cited by Poschmann, *HDG*, IV, 3, p. 135.

141. *De praep. ad mort.* (1534), LB, V, 1311A-C. Cf. *Symbolum* (1533), LB, V, 1176A: "His ceu donativis interim consolatur, animatque milites suos Iesu ducis effusa benignitas, donec consummato certamine provehantur ad coelestis vitae stipendium." See *Funus* (1526), where it is reported that Cornelius, the example of the proper Christian death, sought extreme unction along with the Eucharist just before he passed on. Having recently made confession, he did not confess again, because "Negabat enim quidquam scrupuli resedisse in animo." LB, I, 816A.

Whether Erasmus himself actually received the sacraments at death is not known. There is good attestation to his expressions of Christian and Catholic piety at death [not only "O Iesu, fili Dei, miserere mei, misericordias Domini et iudicium cantabo"—Allen, XI, 3134, 24-25; cited by H. de Vocht, "Le dernier 'amanuensis' d'Érasme," in *Revue d'histoire ecclésiastique*, 45 (1950), 174, n. 3; or "O Iesu, misericordia; Domine liberame; Domine fac finem; Domine miserere mei! et in Germanica lingua! Liever Got, hoc est Chare Deus"—Allen, I, III, 33-35; cited by de Vocht, p. 175, n. 1; but also "O Mater Dei memento mei," from Lambert Coomans, Erasmus' amanuensis, concerning the evidence for which, see de Vocht, pp. 180 ff.]. Cf., however, Vittorio de Caprariis, "Qualche Precisazione sulla Morte di Erasmo," *Rivista Storica Italiana*, 63 (1951), pp. 100-108, who is unduly skeptical of the testimony of Lambert Coomans. But there is no concrete evidence of Erasmus' having received the sacraments, in spite of R. G. Villoslada's contention that Erasmus' expressions of desire for the sacraments to be present at death, the fact that he practiced confession to his friend John of Breisgau during his last years in Freiburg, and the presence of Lambert Coomans, his amanuensis, a priest, at his side make it quite probable that Erasmus received the sacraments at death. "La muerte de Erasmo," pp. 402 ff. (I thank Mr. Ralph Lazzaro of Harvard Divinity School for assisting me in the translation of this article.)

H. de Vocht has shown that the weak link in the argument is the position of Erasmus' amanuensis, whom Villoslada supposes on slender evidence to have been a priest while in Erasmus' service. This scholar shows that when Lambert entered into Erasmus' service ". . . il ne connaissait que fort peu de latin, et n'était certainement pas prêtre" (p. 179).

Although it is dangerous to argue from silence, it seems likely that Erasmus did not receive the sacraments at the moment of death; otherwise there would probably be a report of it since there is such good attestation, however varied, to his last words. If he did not receive the sacraments, the answers to why he did not may be various. As Padberg states (p. 57, n. 72), it is quite possible that in Basel, a Protestant city, they could not be obtained, or it is possible that he considered the procuring of the sacraments so difficult that a *votum sacramenti* would suffice.

142. LB, VII, 203D and 1140AB.

143. LB, V, 1358EF:

"Unguinis extremi munus nos munit, et armat,
Migrantemque animam per summa pericula, tuto
Transmittit patriae, et superis commendat euntem."

144. *Symbolum* (1533), LB, V, 1176A. Increasingly after the tenth and eleventh centuries the greatest emphasis was placed upon the healing of the soul and its strengthening for the moment of death (at which time the sacrament of unction becomes the sacrament of extreme unction), but the healing of the body was not excluded. Poschmann, *HDG,* IV, 3, pp. 132, 135.

145. The problem has to do with what in line with James is remitted in this sacrament. Bonaventure (*Report.* IV d 23 q 1, 4) and, following him, Duns Scotus (IV *Sent.* d 23 a 1 q 1) think of venial sins, whereas Thomas thinks in terms of the "reliquiae peccati." *Suppl.* q 30 a 1, cited by Seeberg, *DG,* III, 553. Erasmus would undoubtedly have agreed with Benedict XIV, who regarded this as an idle question. Poschmann, *HDG,* IV, 3, p. 136.

CONCLUSION

1. LB, V, 31B; tr. F. L. Battles, *Library of Christian Classics,* XIV, ed. M. Spinka (Philadelphia, 1953), 336.

2. One must therefore disagree with those interpreters who overemphasize the spiritualism of Erasmus to the extent that they think the

sacraments have scarcely any role in his thought:

"L'esprit tend à se dégager de la matière; le rite n'est rien sans lui, mais lui peut exister sans le rite: tel est le point extrême ou me paraît aboutir la pensée d'Érasme." Pineau, *Érasme, sa pensée religieuse*, p. 161.

"C'est donc que l'humaniste ne reconnaissait aucune utilité au sacrement en soi du premier au septième ni aucune 'grâce' qu'il ne voyait plus même dans le baptême que promesse et dans les six autres que matière à vaine speculation métaphysique. . . . L'antisacramentarisme érasmien est donc, on le voit, radical et fondamental." Telle, p. 380.

"Dann waren die Sakramente in der Gefahr, spiritualisiert, moralisiert, rationalisiert-kurz, nicht verstanden zu werden. Das liesse sich an des Erasmus besonders anschaulich machen." W. Jetter, *Die Taufe beim jungen Luther* (Tübingen, 1954), p. 125.

Renaudet's repeated descriptions of Erasmus' religious thought as "la religion du pur esprit" seem to place him in the same camp. *Études érasmiennes*, p. 164; *Érasme, sa pensée religieuse*, pp. 9, 14, 20; *Érasme et l'Italie*, pp. 130, 134.

3. On the basis of an exclusively Thomistic point of view, Telle attacks Erasmus for failing to speak clearly about the efficacious causality of the sacraments, or of the sacraments as containing and mediating grace. But he would have to criticize the whole Franciscan tradition on the same basis. Telle, pp. 373 ff., 378 f. Notice the references to Thomas as the standard of judgment. *Ibid.*, p. 379, n. 35; p. 380, n. 37.

4. Pineau among others overstresses Erasmus' moralism when he says about baptism: "Si l'âme est pure, on peut être chrétien sans le baptême. Avec le baptême, si l'âme est mauvaise, on n'est pas chrétien. Le christianisme encore une fois, c'est l'honnêteté morale. Il ne dépend pas d'un rite, mais d'une transformation volontaire de l'âme." *Érasme, sa pensée religieuse*, p. 123.

5. While Lortz and Telle severely attack Erasmus for what they call respectively his spiritualism and antisacramentalism (Lortz, "Erasmus-kirchengeschichtlich," p. 304; Telle, pp. 263, 292, 379-380), another Roman Catholic scholar, Jacques Étienne, is more charitable in his judgment of what he calls the Erasmian spiritualism or personalism. Although he thinks Erasmus' lack of attention to the sacramental efficacy is a deficiency, he regards this deficiency as "bien plus l'exagération spiritualiste d'une heureuse réaction en faveur d'un christianisme authentique, que la prise de position à demi-hérétique d'un esprit insensible aux valeurs sacramentelles." *Spiritualisme érasmien et théologiens louvanistes* (Louvain, 1956), p. 16, n. 1. He is here critical of both Lortz and Telle, yet even he also somewhat exaggerates the so-called Erasmian spiritualism.

6. Gebhardt, who devotes less than ten pages to the sacraments in

his discussion of Erasmus' ecclesiology (pp. 302 ff.), does not note any qualifications of the Church's authority by Erasmus. For this author the humanist is thoroughly orthodox.

7. Telle, p. 71.

8. In his study of Erasmus' catechisms and their place in the medieval tradition, Padberg exaggerates the dependence of Erasmus on Thomas. Erasmus does briefly mention two works of Thomas in his *Symbolum* (LB, V, 1161F-1162A; cf. Padberg, *Erasmus als Katechet,* p. 125), presumably the *De articulis fidei et sacramentis* and the *Expositio super symbolo apostolorum scilicet credo in Deum,* cited by Padberg, p. 125, nn. 2 and 3, only the first of which Erasmus regards as genuine. However, Padberg fails sufficiently to demonstrate how Erasmus' thought in that work was materially shaped by Thomas, although he does show some formal dependence of Erasmus on these works. See pp. 125, 129 ff., 137, 140 f., 158.

Even more general is Bouyer's contention against Renaudet that there were connections between Erasmus and Thomism. He gives as the only basis for his position the work of Father Chenu [*Une école de théologie: le Saulchoir* (Paris, 1937)], who, according to Bouyer, ". . . a montré que thomistes et humanistes, au début de la renaissance, avaient fait un véritable front commun contre le nominalisme . . . " and the suggestion without proof that Erasmus' political thought was very close to that of Thomas. *Autour d'Érasme,* p. 134. He assumes that "il [Erasmus] ne vise pas la scolastique indistinctement et en général, mais très précisément les nominalistes . . ." (p. 143). Likewise does Kohls most recently attempt to show deep dependence of Erasmus upon Thomas, especially in his soteriology, but with little more success. See above our criticism of his interpretation of Erasmus' relation to Thomas on the question of grace and free will (p. 260, n. 30). All of these interpreters fail to recognize any positive relation of Erasmus to nominalism.

Auer is more correct than these scholars when he states, ". . . Thomas lag Erasmus wesensmässig so fern, dass er sich keine Mühe gab, ihn näher kennenzulernen." *Die vollkommene Frömmigkeit des Christen,* p. 166. That statement is somewhat of an exaggeration, since, as we have seen, Erasmus is acquainted with a large amount of Thomas' exegetical writings. However, although he may have studied to some extent the theological opus of Thomas, on the basis of our entire investigation of Erasmus' soteriology and sacramental theology, we must conclude that his thought was little shaped by what he read.

SELECTED BIBLIOGRAPHY

PRIMARY SOURCES
(in addition to works listed under "Abbreviations")

Erasmi opuscula. Edited by Wallace K. Ferguson. The Hague, 1933.
Inquisitio de fide. Edited by Craig R. Thompson. New Haven, 1950.
The Poems of Desiderius Erasmus. Introduced and edited by C. Reedijk. Leiden, 1956.
The Colloquies of Erasmus. Translated by Craig R. Thompson. Chicago, 1965.
The Enchiridion of Erasmus. Translated and edited by Raymond Himelick. Bloomington, Ind., 1963.
The Praise of Folly by Desiderius Erasmus. Translated by H. H. Hudson. Princeton, 1941.

Biel, Gabriel. *Gabrielis Biel Canonis misse expositio.* Edited by H. A. Oberman and W. J. Courtenay. Pars II. Wiesbaden, 1965.
Colet, John. *I. Coleti enarratio in primam epistolam S. Pauli ad Corinthios.* Translated and edited by J. H. Lupton. London, 1874.
————. *I. Coleti enarratio in epistolam S. Pauli ad Romanos.* Translated and edited by J. H. Lupton. London, 1873.
————. *I. Coleti opus de sacramentis ecclesiae.* Edited by J. H. Lupton. London, 1867.
————. *I. Coletus super opera Dionysii.* Translated and edited by J. H. Lupton. London, 1869.
Gerson, Jean Charlier de. *Opera omnia.* Edited by L. E. du Pin. 5 vols. Antwerp, 1706.
Jud, Leo. *Des hochgelerten Erasmi von Roterdam unnd Doctor Martin Luthers maynung vom Nachtmal unnsers herren Ihesu Christi neuwlich aussagangen auff den XVIII tag Aprellens.* N. p., 1526.
Oecolampadius, Ioannes. *De genuina verborum Domini 'Hoc est corpus meum' iuxta vetussimos authores expositione liber.* Strasbourg, 1525.
Pico della Mirandola, Giovanni Francesco. *De hominis dignitate.* Edited

under the title of *Dignita dell'uomo* by B. Cicognani. Florence, 1941.
Thomas à Kempis. *De imitatione Christi, Opera omnia,* ed. M. J. Pohl, Bd.
    II. Freiburg im Br., 1904.
Thomas Aquinas. *Summa theologiae.* Edited by Commissio Piana. 5 vols.
    Ottawa, 1953.
Zwingli, Ulrich. *Huldreich Zwinglis Sämtliche Werke.* Edited by Emil Egli
    et al. Vols. III and IV. Leipzig, 1914, 1927.

SECONDARY SOURCES

Aldridge, John W. *The Hermeneutic of Erasmus.* Richmond, 1966.
Anciaux, Paul. *La théologie du sacrement de pénitence au XIIe siècle.* Louvain,
    1949.
Andrén, Carl-Gustaf. "Die Konfirmationsfrage in der Reformations-
    zeit," in *Zur Geschichte und Ordnung der Konfirmation in den lutherischen
    Kirchen,* ed. Kurt Frör (Munich, 1962), pp. 36-58.
Auer, Alfons. *Die vollkommene Frömmigkeit des Christen.* Düsseldorf, 1954.
Bainton, Roland H. *Erasmus of Christendom.* New York, 1969.
Bouyer, Louis. *Autour d'Érasme.* Paris, 1955. And in translation, *Erasmus
    and His Times.* Translated by F. X. Murphy. Westminster, Md.,
    1959.
Beuscher, Gabriel. *The Eucharistic Teaching of William Ockham.* St. Bona-
    venture, N.Y., 1950.
Clark, Francis, S.J. *Eucharistic Sacrifice and the Reformation.* Westminster,
    Md., 1960.
Daniélou, Jean. *Origène.* Paris, 1948.
Dix, Gregory. *The Theology of Confirmation in Relation to Baptism.* London,
    1946.
Dolfen, Christian. *Die Stellung des Erasmus von Rotterdam zur Scholastischen
    Methode.* Osnabrück, 1936.
Dölger, F. J. *Sphragis: Eine altchristliche Taufbezeichnung in ihren Beziehun-
    gen zur profanen und religiösen Kultur des Altertums.* Paderborn, 1911.
Garin, Eugenio. *Italian Humanism.* Translated by Peter Munz. New
    York, 1965.
Gebhardt, Georg. *Die Stellung des Erasmus von Rotterdam zur Römischen
    Kirche.* Marburg an der Lahn, 1966.
Gewirth, Alan. *Marsilius of Padua.* 2 vols. New York, 1951-1956.
Ghellinck, J. de, *et al.,* eds. *Pour l'histoire du mot "sacramentum" I. les
    anténicéens.* Louvain, 1924.
Goerung, C. *La théologie d'après Érasme et Luther.* Paris, 1913.
Gögler, Rolf. *Zur Theologie des biblischen Wortes bei Origenes.* Düsseldorf,
    1963.
Hanson, R. P. C. *Allegory and Event.* London, 1959.
Heggelbacher, O. *Die christliche Taufe als Rechtsakt nach dem Zeugnis der*

frühen Christenheit. Freiburg, Switzerland, 1953.

Huizinga, Johan. *Erasmus of Rotterdam.* Translated by F. Hopman. London, 1952.

Humbertclaude, H. *Érasme et Luther, leur polémique sur le libre arbitre.* Paris, 1909.

Hyma, Albert. "Erasmus and the Sacrament of Matrimony," *ARG,* 48 (1957), 145-164.

Kohls, Ernst-Wilhelm. *Die Theologie des Erasmus.* 2 vols. Basel, 1966.

Köhler, Walther. *Zwingli und Luther: Der Streit über das Abendmahl nach seinen politischen und religiösen Beziehungen,* Vol. I. Vol. VI of *Quellen und Forschungen zur Reformationsgeschichte.* Leipzig, 1924.

Krodel, Gottfried. "Die Abendmahlslehre des Erasmus von Rotterdam und seine Stellung am Anfang des Abendmahlsstreites der Reformatoren." Unpublished doctoral dissertation, University of Erlangen, 1955.

Lampe, G. W. H. *The Seal of the Spirit.* London, 1951.

Lea, Henry Charles. *A History of Auricular Confession and Indulgences in the Latin Church.* 3 vols. Philadelphia, 1896.

Le Bras, Gabriel. "La doctrine du mariage chez les théologiens et les canonistes depuis l'an mille," in *DTC,* IX², 2123-2317.

Loofs, Friedrich. *Leitfaden zum Studium der Dogmengeschichte.* 6th ed. Edited by Kurt Aland. Tübingen, 1959.

Lortz, Joseph. "Erasmus-kirchengeschichtlich," in *Aus Theologie und Philosophie: Festschrift für F. Tillmann zu seinem 75. Geburtstag,* ed. Th. Steinbüchel and Th. Müncker (Düsseldorf, 1950), pp. 271-326.

Lubac, Henri de. *Exégèse Médiévale: Les quatre sens de l'Écriture.* 3 vols. Lyons, 1959-1964.

Lupton, J. H. *A Life of Dean Colet.* London, 1877.

Maurer, Wilhelm. *Gemeindezucht, Gemeindeamt, Konfirmation.* Kassel, 1940.

————. "Geschichte von Firmung und Konfirmation bis zum Ausgang der lutherischen Orthodoxie," in *Confirmatio, Forschungen zur Geschichte und Praxis der Konfirmation,* ed. Kurt Frör (Munich, 1959), pp. 9-38.

Mestwerdt, Paul. *Die Anfänge des Erasmus.* Leipzig, 1917.

Minges, Parthenius. *Die Gnadenlehre des Duns Scotus auf ihren angeblichen Pelagianismus und Semipelagianismus geprüft.* Münster i.w., 1906.

Morrall, John B. *Gerson and the Great Schism.* Manchester, 1960.

Neunheuser, Burkhard. *Taufe und Firmung.* Vol. IV, No. 2, in *HDG.* Freiburg im Br., 1956.

Oberman, Heiko A. *The Harvest of Medieval Theology.* Cambridge, Mass., 1963.

Oelrich, Karl Heinz. *Der späte Erasmus und die Reformation. Reformationsgeschichtliche Studien und Texte,* Heft 86. Münster i.w., 1961.

Padberg, Rudolf. *Erasmus als Katechet.* Freiburg im Br., 1956.

Pineau, J. B. *Érasme, sa pensée religieuse.* Paris, 1924.

Poschmann, Bernhard. *Die abendländische Kirchenbusse im Ausgang des christlichen Altertums.* Munich, 1928.

_____. *Die abendländische Kirchenbusse im frühen Mittelalter.* Breslau, 1930.

_____. *Der Ablass im Licht der Bussgeschichte.* Bonn, 1948.

_____. *Busse und Letze Ölung.* Vol. IV, No. 3, in *HDG.* Freiburg im Br., 1951.

Renaudet, Augustin. *Érasme et l'Italie.* Geneva, 1954.

_____. *Études érasmiennes (1521-1529).* Paris, 1939.

Seeberg, Reinhold. *Die Theologie des Johannes Duns Scotus: Eine dogmenge-schichtliche Untersuchung.* Leipzig, 1900.

Sigmund, Paul E. *Nicholas of Cusa and Medieval Political Thought.* Cambridge, Mass., 1963.

Smalley, Beryl. *The Study of the Bible in the Middle Ages.* 2nd ed. Oxford, 1952.

Smith, Preserved. *Erasmus.* New York, 1923.

Spitz, Lewis W. *The Religious Renaissance of the German Humanists.* Cambridge, Mass., 1963.

Spitzig, Joseph A. *Sacramental Penance in the Twelfth and Thirteenth Centuries.* Washington, D.C., 1947.

Spykman, Gordon J. *Attrition and Contrition at the Council of Trent.* Kampen, 1955.

Staehelin, Ernst. *Das theologische Lebenswerk des Johannes Oecolampadius.* Vol. XXI of *Quellen und Forschungen zur Reformationsgeschichte.* Leipzig, 1939.

Stone, Darwell. *A History of the Doctrine of the Eucharist.* 2 vols. London, 1909.

Telle, Émile V. *Érasme de Rotterdam et le septième sacrement.* Geneva, 1954.

Tentler, Thomas. "Forgiveness and Consolation in the Religious Thought of Erasmus," *Studies in the Renaissance,* 12 (1965), 110-133.

_____. "The Problem of Anxiety and Preparation for Death in Luther, Calvin, and Erasmus." Unpublished Ph.D. dissertation, Department of History, Harvard University, 1961.

Tierney, Brian. *Foundations of the Conciliar Theory.* Cambridge, England, 1955.

Vignaux, Paul. *Justification et prédestination au XIVᵉ siècle: Duns Scot, Pierre d'Auriole, Guillaume d'Occam, Grégoire de Rimini.* Paris, 1934.

_____. "Nominalisme," in *DTC,* XI, 717-784.

Watkins, O. D. *A History of Penance.* 2 vols. London, 1920.

Werner, Karl. *Die Scholastik des späteren Mittelalters: Die nachscotistische Scholastik.* Vol. II. New York, 1960. (Photo-reprint of Vienna edition, 1883.)

JOHN B. PAYNE is Associate Professor of History and Religious Studies at Bradley University, Peoria, Illinois. From 1960 to 1968 he taught at Randolph-Macon Woman's College, Lynchburg, Virginia. A graduate of Texas Christian University (A.B.) and Vanderbilt University (B.D.), he received his Ph.D. from Harvard University and has been a Fulbright Scholar at the University of Heidelberg. In 1969, under a Younger Scholar Fellowship of the National Endowment for the Humanities, he conducted research in Basel, Switzerland, on a critical edition of Erasmus' *Paraphrasis in epistolas Pauli.*

Dr. Payne's book *Erasmus: His Theology of the Sacraments* is the first to treat Erasmus' sacramental thought as a whole. It sets Erasmus' ideas on the sacraments within the framework of his total theology and of the late medieval period. The book deals with three major themes in Erasmus' sacramental understanding: the dialectical relationship between humanistic reason and the authority of the Church, the neo-Platonic contrast between flesh and spirit, and the remarkable influence of certain scholastics, especially the late medieval nominalists.

Comments Roland H. Bainton: "Dr. Payne has investigated Erasmus' sacramental theology with impartiality and scrupulous care. His study is of great historical and more than historical importance."